software project management

management

Fourth edition

software project management

Fourth edition

BOB HUGHES AND MIKE COTTERELL

The **McGraw·Hill** Companies

London   Boston   Burr Ridge, IL   Dubuque, IA   Madison, WI   New York   San Francisco
St. Louis   Bangkok   Bogotá   Caracas   Kuala Lumpur   Lisbon   Madrid   Mexico City
Milan   Montreal   New Delhi   Santiago   Seoul   Singapore   Sydney   Taipei   Toronto

Software Project Management
Fourth Edition
Bob Hughes and Mike Cotterell
ISBN-13 978-0-07-710989-9
ISBN-10 0077109899

Published by McGraw-Hill Education
Shoppenhangers Road
Maidenhead
Berkshire
SL6 2QL
Telephone: 44 (0) 1628 502 500
Fax: 44 (0) 1628 770 224
Website: www.mcgraw-hill.co.uk

British Library Cataloguing in Publication Data
A catalogue record for this book is available from the British Library

Library of Congress Cataloguing in Publication Data
The Library of Congress data for this book has been applied for from
the Library of Congress

Head of Development: Caroline Howell
Development Editor: Karen Mosman
Marketing Manager: Alice Duijser
Production Editor: James Bishop

Text Design by Fakenham Photosetting Limited
Cover design by ego creative limited
Printed and bound in Great Britain by Bell & Bain Ltd, Glasgow

ISBN-13 978-0-07-710989-9
ISBN-10 0077109899

Brief Table of Contents

Contents

Preface to the fourth edition

The risks of failure associated with development projects involving ICT (Information and Communication Technologies) are still of as much concern as they were ten years ago when the first edition of this book was published. The main concern of the book throughout its various editions has been to inculcate the fundamental practices of good project management needed by ICT practitioners as one of the foundations of their professional education. While it is hoped that current practitioners will find much that will be helpful, the main target audiences for the book are computing and information systems students on undergraduate and masters programmes.

The decision to write and adapt material for a new edition was triggered by developments in software project management which merited the expansion of some aspects of the book. Some of these developments are listed below.

- Advances in electronic communication have been exploited to support projects where the project team is geographically dispersed.

- Associated with the above, the practice of outsourcing software development to third world countries, particularly to India, has accelerated. It is significant that special Indian and Chinese editions of this book have appeared.

- A number of new and expanded international standards have appeared which address the assessment of the quality of both software products and the processes that create them. This needs to be seen in the context of the 'offshoring' because, where this happens, the quality of the software products being delivered will be a concern.

- The interest in agile methods has continued to grow, particularly extreme programming (XP). Once again this can be set in the context of the increasing move towards offshore development of software. Software developers in the West need to find ways of competing with low-cost developers and among these might be an increased responsiveness to client needs along with the improved speed of delivery that XP seems to offer.

In addition to responding to external developments, the old text was reviewed by a number of lecturers who had used the book on their courses. Wherever possible, their suggestions have been incorporated. One example is the material in Chapter 7 on Goldratt's critical chain management technique. In some cases we have been unable to incorporate ideas for additional topics as we have run out of both space and time, but hope to add the material to the supporting website.

Some topics that were previously covered in Appendices, such as the ISO/IEC 12207 standard and programme management, have now largely been made part of the main text. It was also felt that the material on the various project management qualifications and 'bodies of knowledge' (BOK) would be better placed on the supporting website.

During the course of preparing the new edition we have made use of materials produced by Abdullah Al Shehab and David I. Shepherd in the chapter on risk. David also offered some advice on the developments in earned value analysis. Our thanks go to them and to our colleagues at Brighton, especially Marian Eastwood and Joe Wilkinson for their advice and support. Particular thanks go to our reviewers for the time and trouble they have taken in providing us with valuable feedback.

The previous editions were dedicated to those former students of ours who are now grappling with problems of IT development in the 'real world' and we would like to repeat that dedication – there must be a lot more of them now.

Guided tour

Learning objectives

Each chapter opens with a set of learning objectives, summarizing what the reader should learn from each chapter.

Margin notes

New ideas, terms and references are placed in the margin where appropriate. Margin notes also indicate the links to ideas and concepts covered elsewhere in the textbook.

Figures and tables

Each chapter provides a number of clear figures to show the various models, project planning tools and charts.

Case Study examples

Brief case studies run throughout the chapters to illustrate the application of project management techniques.

Exercises

Brief exercises are dotted throughout the chapters, to allow students to practise the techniques and apply the methodology to real-world situations.

Chapter conclusions

This briefly reviews and reinforces the main topics covered in each chapter to ensure that students have acquired a solid understanding of the key topics.

Further exercises

These questions encourage you to review and apply the knowledge you have acquired from each chapter and to explore further some of the ideas in the chapter.

Appendices and solutions

The Appendices at the end of the book explain PRINCE2 and BS 6079:1996. Appendix C, Answer pointers, provides guide answers to the questions and exercises set in the book.

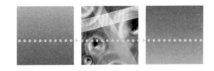

Technology to enhance learning and teaching

Online Resources

It is intended that the Online Learning Centre will contain updates of information related to software project management, which is likely to change over time. This will include references to useful resources and links.

Lecturers can find a number of useful resources to support their teaching of software project management at www.mcgraw-hill.co.uk/textbooks/hughes

Available for lecturers:

- PowerPoint slides
- Lecture tutorials
- Extra exercises and questions
- Artwork for the textbook

For lecturers: Primis Content Centre

If you need to supplement your course with additional cases or content, create a personalized e-Book for your students. Visit www.primiscontentcenter.com or e-mail primis_euro@mcgraw-hill.com for more information.

Study skills

We publish guides to help you study, research, pass exams and write essays, all the way through your university studies.

Visit **www.openup.co.uk/ss/** to see the full selection and get £2 discount by entering promotional code **study** when buying online!

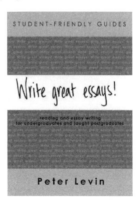

Computing skills

If you'd like to brush up on your computing skills, we have a range of titles covering MS Office applications such as Word, Excel, PowerPoint, Access and more.

Get a £2 discount off these titles by entering the promotional code **app** when ordering online at **www.mcgraw-hill.co.uk/app.**

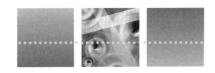

Acknowledgements

During the course of preparing the three previous editions since 1995, we have received assistance from many people. These people have included: Ken I'Anson, Chris Claire, David Howe, Martin Campbell Kelly, Barbara Kitchenham (for permission to use a project data set shown in Chapter 5), Paul Radford and Robyn Lawrie of Charismatek Software Metrics in Melbourne, David Garmus and David Herron (the last four, all for material in Chapter 10), David Purves, David Wynne, Dick Searles, John Pyman, Jim Watson, Mary Shepherd, Sunita Chulani, David Wilson, David Farthing, Charlie Svahnberg, Henk Koppelaar and Ian McChesney.

We would also like to thank the team at McGraw-Hill. In particular we would like to thank Karen Mosman who has been a real gem as our editor and has provided a stable and sympathetic point of contact in the dynamic and (for academics) sometimes confusing world of textbook publishing. However, we have not forgotten Dave Hatter who was our former editor at International Thomson Press and then at McGraw-Hill and we hope he is continuing to enjoy retirement in the groves and glades of Essex.

Our thanks also go to the following reviewers for their comments at various stages in the text's development:

Dave Farthing, University of Glamorgan, UK
Peter Lee, University of Newcastle-on-Tyne, UK
Robert Macredie, Brunel University, UK
Owen Johnson, University of Leeds, UK
Rory V. O'Connor, Dublin City University, Ireland
Andrew Rae, University of Paisley, UK
Torbjørn Strøm, Buskerud University College, Norway
A.S.M. Sajeev, University of New England, Armidale, Australia
Phil Thompson, Coventry University, UK

Introduction to software project management

Objectives

When you have completed this chapter you will be able to:

- define the scope of 'software project management';
- understand some problems and concerns of software project managers;
- define the usual stages of a software project;
- explain the main elements of the role of management;
- appreciate the need for careful planning, monitoring and control;
- identify the stakeholders of a project and their objectives;
- define the success criteria for a project.

1.1 Introduction

This textbook is about *'software* project management'. The main question that we attempt to answer in this first chapter is whether the management of *software* projects is really that different from that of other types of project. To answer this, we need to look at some key ideas about the planning, monitoring and control of software projects. We will see that all projects are about meeting objectives. Like any other project, a project to produce software is only worthwhile if it satisfies real needs and so we will examine how we can identify the stakeholders in a project and their objectives. Having identified those objectives, ensuring that they are met is the basis of successful project management. However, we cannot be sure that a project is going to meet its objectives unless there is accurate information, and how we obtain this will be explored.

1.2 Why is software project management important?

This book is written both for students of software engineering and computer science and also for those studying business information systems. More technically oriented students can sometimes be impatient at having to study something which is keeping them away from their code. So why is it important to become familiar with project management?

The information in this paragraph comes from a National Audit Office report, *Improving IT Procurement*, November 2004.

First of all there is the question of money. A lot of money is at stake with ICT projects. In the United Kingdom during the financial year 2002–2003, the central government spent more on contracts for ICT projects than on contracts related to roads (about £2.3 billion as opposed to £1.4 billion). The biggest departmental spender was the Department for Work and Pensions, who spent over £800 million on ICT. Mismanagement of ICT projects would mean that there is less money for good things like pensions.

Unfortunately, projects are not always successful. In a report published in 2003, the Standish Group in the United States analysed 13,522 projects and concluded that only a third of projects were successful; 82% of projects were late and 43% exceeded their budget.

The most commonly identified reason for these project shortcomings tends to be related to the management of projects. The National Audit Office in the UK, for example, among other factors causing project failure identified *'lack of skills and proven approach to project management and risk management'*.

1.3 What is a project?

Dictionary definitions of 'project' include:
'A specific plan or design'
'A planned undertaking'
'A large undertaking: e.g. a public works scheme',
Longman Concise English Dictionary, 1982.

The dictionary definitions put a clear emphasis on the project being a *planned* activity.

The definition of a project as being planned assumes that to a large extent we can determine how we are going to carry out a task before we start. There may be some projects of an exploratory nature where this might be quite difficult. Planning is in essence thinking carefully about something before you do it – and even in the case of uncertain projects this is worth doing as long as it is accepted that the resulting plans may be provisional and speculative. Other activities, relating for example to routine maintenance, might have been performed so many times that everyone involved knows exactly what needs to be done. In these cases, planning hardly seems necessary, although procedures might need to be documented to ensure consistency and to help newcomers to the job.

The types of activity that will benefit most from conventional project management are likely to lie between these two extremes – see Figure 1.1.

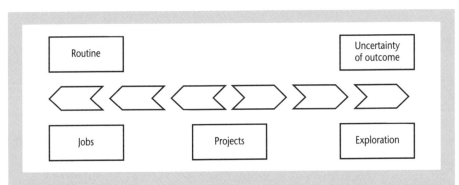

Figure 1.1 Activities most likely to benefit from project management

Programme management is often used to coordinate activities on concurrent jobs.

There is a hazy boundary between the non-routine project and the routine job. The first time you do a routine task it will be like a project. On the other hand, a project to develop a system similar to previous ones that you have developed will have a large element of the routine.

The characteristics which distinguish projects can be summarized as follows:

● non-routine tasks are involved;

● planning is required;

● specific objectives are to be met or a specified product is to be created;

● the project has a predetermined time span;

● work is carried out for someone other than yourself;

● work involves several specialisms;

● work is carried out in several phases;

● the resources that are available for use on the project are constrained;

● the project is large or complex.

The more any of these factors apply to a task, the more difficult that task will be. Project size is particularly important. A project that employs 20 project personnel is going to be trickier to manage than one with ten staff. The larger project is likely to be disproportionately more difficult – it could absorb more than twice the management effort needed for the smaller project because of the need for additional coordination. The examples and exercises used in this book usually relate to smaller projects. This is just to make them more manageable from a learning point of view: the techniques and issues discussed are of equal relevance to larger projects.

Exercise 1.1

Consider the following:

● producing an edition of a newspaper;

● putting a robot vehicle on Mars to search for signs of life;

● getting married;

● amending a financial computer system to deal with a common European currency;

● a research project into what makes a good human–computer interface;

● an investigation into the reason why a user has a problem with a computer system;

● a second-year programming assignment for a computing student;

● writing an operating system for a new computer;

● installing a new version of a word processing package in an organization.

Some would appear to merit the description 'project' more than others. Put them into an order that most closely matches your ideas of what constitutes a project. For each entry in the ordered list, describe the difference between it and the one above which makes it less worthy of the term 'project'.

There is no one correct answer to this exercise, but a possible solution to this and the other exercises you will come across may be found at the end of the book.

1.4   Software projects versus other types of project

Brooks, F. P. (1987). 'No silver bullet: essence and accidents of software engineering'. This essay has been included in *The Mythical Man-Month*, Anniversary Edition, Addison Wesley,1995.

Many of the techniques of general project management are applicable to software project management, but Fred Brooks pointed out that the products of software projects have certain characteristics which make them different.

Invisibility   When a physical artefact such as a bridge or road is being constructed the progress being made can actually be seen. With software, progress is not immediately visible. One way of perceiving software project management is as the process of making visible that which is invisible.

Complexity   Per dollar, pound or euro spent, software products contain more complexity than other engineered artefacts.

Conformity   The 'traditional' engineer is usually working with physical systems and physical materials like cement and steel. These physical systems can have some complexity, but are governed by physical laws that are consistent. Software developers have to conform to the requirements of human clients. It is not just that individuals can be inconsistent. Organizations, because of lapses in collective memory, in internal communication or in effective decision making, can exhibit remarkable 'organizational stupidity', which developers have to cater for.

Flexibility   The ease with which software can be changed is usually seen as one of its strengths. However, this means that where the software system interfaces with a physical or organizational system, it is expected that, where necessary, the software will change to accommodate the other components rather than vice versa. This means the software systems are likely to be subject to a high degree of change.

1.5   Contract management and technical project management

Many organizations contract out ICT development to outside specialist developers. In such cases, the client organization will often appoint a 'project manager' to supervise the contract. This project manager will be able to delegate many technically oriented decisions to the contractors. For instance, the project manager will not be concerned about estimating the effort needed to write individual software components as long as the overall project is fulfilled within budget and on time. On the supplier side, there will need to be project managers who are concerned with the more technical management issues. This book leans towards the concerns of these 'technical' project managers.

1.6   Activities covered by software project management

Chapter 4 on project analysis and technical planning looks at some alternative life cycles.

A software project is not only concerned with the actual writing of software. In fact, where a software application is bought in 'off the shelf', there may be no software writing as such. This is still fundamentally a software project because so many of the other elements associated with this type of project are present.

Usually there are three successive processes that bring a new system into being – see Figure 1.2.

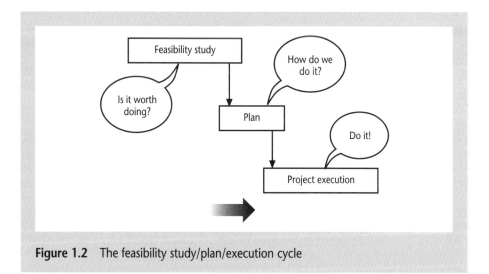

Figure 1.2 The feasibility study/plan/execution cycle

An outline of the content of a feasibility study is shown in Annex 1 to this chapter.

Chapter 3 explores some further aspects of programme management.

The PRINCE2 method, which is described in Appendix A, takes this planning by stages approach.

Annex 2 to this chapte, has an outline of the content of a plan

1. **The feasibility study** This investigates whether a prospective project is worth starting – that it has a valid *business case*. Information is gathered about the requirements of the proposed application. Requirements elicitation can, at least initially, be complex and difficult. The client and other stakeholders may be aware of the problems they wish to overcome and the aims they wish to pursue, but not be sure about the means of achievement. The probable developmental and operational costs, along with the value of the benefits of the new system, will also have to be estimated. With a large system, the feasibility study could be treated as a project in its own right – and have its own planning sub-phase. The study could be part of a strategic planning exercise examining and prioritizing a range of potential software developments. Sometimes an organization has a policy where a group of projects is planned as a *programme* of development.

2. **Planning** If the feasibility study produces results which indicate that the prospective project appears viable, then planning of the project can take place. However, for a large project, we would not do all our detailed planning right at the beginning. We would formulate an outline plan for the whole project and a detailed one for the first stage. More detailed planning of the later stages would be done as they approached. This is because we would have more detailed and accurate information upon which to base our plans nearer to the start of the later stages.

3. **Project execution** The project can now be executed. The execution of a project often contains *design* and *implementation* sub-phases. Students new to project planning often find it difficult to separate planning and design, and often the boundary between the two can be hazy. Essentially, design is thinking and making decisions about the precise form of the *products* that the project is to create. In the case of software, this could relate to the external appearance of the software, that is, the user interface, or the internal architecture. The plan lays down the *activities* that have to be carried out in order to create these products. Planning and design can be confused because at the most detailed level, planning decisions are influenced by design decisions. For example, if a software product is to have five major components, then it is likely that there will be five sets of activities that will create them.

Figure 1.3 The ISO 12207 software development life cycle

Figure 1.3 shows the typical sequence of software development activities recommended in the international standard ISO 12207. If readers look at the activities in the diagram they will see that some are concerned with the *system* while others relate to *software*. It is always the case that the development of software will be only one part of the whole project. Software could be developed, for example, for a project which will also require ICT infrastructure to be installed, user jobs to be designed and users trained in the use of the new software. The overall package is a system of which the software is one component.

Figure 1.3 suggests that these stages must be done strictly in sequence – we will see in Chapter 4 that other, iterative approaches can be adopted. However, the actual activities listed here would still be done.

● *Requirements analysis*   This starts with *requirements elicitation* which investigates what the potential users and their managers and employers require as features and qualities of the new system. These will relate to the system as a whole. A quality requirement might be, for instance, that the user should be able to complete a transaction within a certain time. In this case transaction time would be affected by the speed of human operation, as well as hardware and software performance. These 'customer-facing' requirements then have to be translated into technical requirements from which the developers of the new system can work.

- *Architecture design* This maps the requirements to the components of the system that is to be built. At the system level, decisions will need to be made about which processes in the new system will be carried out by the user and which can be computerized. This design of the *system architecture* thus forms an input to the development of the *software requirements*. A second architecture design process then takes place which maps the *software requirements* to *software components*.

- *Detailed design* Each software component is made up of a number of software units that can be separately coded and tested. The detailed design of these units is carried out separately.

- *Code and test* This could refer to writing code for each software unit in a procedural language such as C# or Java, or could refer to the use of an application-builder such as Microsoft Access. Initial testing to debug individual software units would be carried out at this stage.

- *Integration* The individual components are collected together and tested to see if they meet the overall requirements. Integration could be at the level of software where different software components are combined, or at the level of the system as a whole where the software and other components of the system such as the hardware platforms and networks and the user procedures are brought together.

- *Qualification testing* The system, including the software components, has to be tested carefully to ensure that all the requirements have been fulfilled.

- *Installation* This is the process of making the new system operational. It would include activities like setting up standing data (such as payroll details for employees if this were a payroll system). It would also include setting system parameters, installing the software onto the hardware platforms and user training.

- *Acceptance support* This is the resolving of problems with the newly installed system, including the correction of any errors that might have crept into the system, and any extensions and improvements that are required. It is possible to see software maintenance as a series of minor software projects. In many environments, most software development is in fact maintenance.

Exercise 1.2 Brightmouth College is a higher education institution which used to be managed by a local government authority but has now become autonomous. Its payroll is still administered by the local authority and pay slips and other output are produced in the local authority's computer centre. The authority now charges the college for this service. The college management are of the opinion that it would be cheaper to obtain an 'off-the-shelf' payroll package and do the payroll processing themselves.

What would be the main stages of the project to convert to independent payroll processing by the college? Bearing in mind that an off-the-shelf package is to be used, how would this project differ from one where the software was to be written from scratch?

1.7 Plans, methods and methodologies

A plan for an activity must be based on some idea of a *method* of work. To take a simple example, if you were asked to test some software, even though you do not know anything about the software to be tested, you could assume that you would need to:

- analyse the requirements for the software;
- devise and write test cases that will check that each requirement has been satisfied;
- create test scripts and expected results for each test case;
- compare the actual results and the expected results and identify discrepancies.

While a *method* relates to a type of activity in general, a *plan* takes that method (and perhaps others) and converts it to real activities, identifying for each activity:

- its start and end dates;
- who will carry it out;
- what tools and materials will be used.

'Materials' in this context could include information, for example a requirements document.

With complex procedures, several methods may be deployed, in sequence or in parallel. The output from one method might be the input to another. Groups of methods or techniques are often referred to as *methodologies*. Object-oriented design, for example, can be seen as a methodology made up of several component methods.

Exercise 1.3 This should ideally be done in groups of about four, but you can think about how you would go about this exercise on your own if needs be. You are probably in a building that has more than one storey. From the point of view of this exercise, the bigger the building the better.

In a group of four, work out how you would obtain an accurate estimate of the height of the building. (If you happen to be in a single-storey building, you can estimate the floor area instead!) Plan how you would carry out any actions needed to obtain your estimate. Spend twenty minutes on this – you must remain in the same room for this planning phase. Once planning is complete, implement your plan, timing how long it takes to produce your final figure.

If there is more than one group carrying out this exercise, after completion of the task you can compare answers and also the approach you used when coming up with your answer.

See Simon Bennett, Steve McRobb, and Ray Farmer, *Object Oriented Systems Analysis and Design using UML*, 3rd edition, McGraw-Hill, 2005.

1.8 Some ways of categorizing software projects

It is important to distinguish between the main types of software project because what is appropriate in one context may not be so in another. For example, some have suggested that the object-oriented approach, while useful in many contexts, might not be ideal for designing applications to be built around relational databases.

Information systems versus embedded systems

Embedded systems are also called real-time or industrial systems.

A traditional distinction has been between *information systems* and *embedded systems*. Very crudely, the difference is that in the former case the system interfaces with the organization, whereas in the latter case the system interfaces with a machine. A stock control system would be an information system that controls when the organization reorders stock. An embedded, or process control, system might control the air conditioning equipment in a building. Some systems may have elements of both so that the stock control system might also control an automated warehouse.

There are clearly some software products, such as computer games, that do not fall into either of these categories.

Exercise 1.4 Would an operating system on a computer be an information system or an embedded system?

Objectives versus products

Projects may be distinguished by whether their aim is to produce a *product* or to meet certain *objectives*.

A project might be to create a product, the details of which have been specified by the client. The client has the responsibility for justifying the product.

On the other hand, the project may be required to meet certain objectives. There could be several ways of achieving these objectives. A new information system might be implemented to improve some service to users inside or outside an organization. The level of service that is the target would be the subject of an agreement rather than the internal characteristics of a particular information system.

Service level agreements are becoming increasingly important as organizations contract out functions to external service suppliers.

Many software projects have two stages. The first stage is an objectives-driven project which results in a recommended course of action and may even specify a new software system to meet identified requirements. The next stage is a project actually to create the software product.

Exercise 1.5 Would the project to implement an independent payroll system at the Brightmouth College described in Exercise 1.2 above be an objectives-driven project or a product-driven project?

1.9 What is management?

It has been suggested that management involves the following activities:

- planning – deciding what is to be done;
- organizing – making arrangements;
- staffing – selecting the right people for the job etc.;
- directing – giving instructions;
- monitoring – checking on progress;
- controlling – taking action to remedy hold-ups;
- innovating – coming up with new solutions;
- representing – liaising with clients, users, developer, suppliers and other stakeholders.

Exercise 1.6   Paul Duggan is the manager of a software development section. On Tuesday at 10.00 a.m. he and his fellow section heads have a meeting with their group manager about the staffing requirements for the coming year. Paul has already drafted a document 'bidding' for staff. This is based on the work planned for his section for the next year. The document is discussed at the meeting. At 2.00 p.m. Paul has a meeting with his senior staff about an important project his section is undertaking. One of the programming staff has just had a road accident and will be in hospital for some time. It is decided that the project can be kept on schedule by transferring another team member from less urgent work to this project. A temporary replacement is to be brought in to do the less urgent work but this may take a week or so to arrange. Paul has to phone both the human resources manager about getting a replacement and the user for whom the less urgent work is being done, explaining why it is likely to be delayed.

Identify which of the eight management responsibilities listed above Paul was responding to at different points during his day.

1.10 Problems with software projects

One way of deciding what ought to be covered in 'software project management' is to consider what the problems are that it should address.

Traditionally, management has been seen as the preserve of a distinct class within the organization. As technology has made the tasks undertaken by an organization more sophisticated, many management tasks have become dispersed throughout the organization: there are management systems rather than managers. Nevertheless, the successful project will normally have one person who is charged with its success. Such people are focused on the overcoming of obstacles to success – they are primarily troubleshooters and their job is likely to be shaped by the problems that confront the project. A survey of managers some years ago identified the following commonly experienced problems:

● poor estimates and plans;
● lack of quality standards and measures;
● lack of guidance about making organizational decisions;
● lack of techniques to make progress visible;
● poor role definition – who does what?
● incorrect success criteria.

The above list looks at the project from the manager's point of view. What about the staff who make up the members of the project team? Below is a list of the problems identified by a number of Computing and Information Systems degree students who had just completed a year's industrial placement:

● inadequate specification of work;
● management ignorance of ICT;
● lack of knowledge of application area;
● lack of standards;
● lack of up-to-date documentation;
● preceding activities not completed on time – including late delivery of equipment;

- lack of communication between users and technicians;
- lack of communication leading to duplication of work;
- lack of commitment – especially when a project is tied to one person who then moves;
- narrow scope of technical expertise;
- changing statutory requirements;
- changing software environment;
- deadline pressure;
- lack of quality control;
- remote management;
- lack of training.

Many of the problems identified by the students stem from poor communications. A problem contributing to this is the wide range of ICT specialisms – an organization may be made up of lots of individuals each of whom is expert in one set of software techniques and tools but ignorant of those used by their colleagues. Communication problems are therefore bound to arise.

Stephen Flower's *Software Failure, Management Failure,* Wiley & Sons, 1996, is an interesting survey of failed computer projects.

What about the problems faced by the customers of the products of computer projects? Some reported problematic projects have swallowed up huge amounts of money:

- The United States Internal Revenue System abandoned a tax system modernization programme after having spent $4 billion.
- The state of California spent $1 billion on its non-functional welfare database system.

A debating point is whether it is better that a deficient system is never implemented, rather than being implemented and then causing problems. In the autumn of 2004 when this edition was being prepared, the following were in the US news:

- A system at Hewlett-Packard in California which was supposed to speed up order processing had problems which, it was reported, cut into corporate earnings in August 2004.
- The profits of Ross Stores Inc., in the United States, were reported to have been reduced by 40% because of software errors in a merchandise-tracking system.

Many of the stories about problem projects relate to public sector organizations. This may be misleading – private sector organizations tend to conceal their disasters and in any case many of the public projects are actually carried out by private sector contractors. Any lingering faith by users in the innate ability of ICT people to plan ahead properly will have been removed by the 'millennium bug', a purely self-inflicted ICT problem. On balance it might be a good idea not to survey users about their problems with ICT projects!

1.11 Setting objectives

Project objectives should be clearly defined.

To have a successful software project, the manager and the project team members must know what will constitute success. This will make them concentrate on what is essential to project success.

There may be several sets of users of a system and there may be several different groups of specialists involved its development. There is a need for well-defined objectives that are accepted by all these people. Where there is more than one user group, a *project authority* needs to be identified which has overall authority over what the project is to achieve.

This authority is often held by a *project steering committee* (or *project board* or *project management board*) which has overall responsibility for setting, monitoring and modifying objectives. The project manager still has responsibility for running the project on a day-to-day basis, but has to report to the steering committee at regular intervals. Only the steering committee can authorize changes to the project objectives and resources.

This committee is likely to contain user, development and management representatives.

Sub-objectives and goals

Defining sub-objectives requires assumptions about how the main objective is to be achieved.

Setting objectives can guide and motivate individuals and groups of staff. An effective objective for an individual must be something that is within the control of that individual. An objective might be that the software application to be produced must pay for itself by reducing staff costs over two years. As an overall business objective this might be reasonable. For software developers it would be unreasonable as, though they can control development costs, any reduction in operational staff costs depends not just on them but on the operational management after the application has 'gone live'. What would be appropriate would be to set a *goal* or sub-objective for the software developers to keep development costs within a certain budget.

Thus, objectives will need be broken down into goals or sub-objectives. Here we say that in order to achieve the objective we must achieve certain goals first. These goals are steps on the way to achieving an objective, just as goals scored in a football match are steps towards the objective of winning the match.

The mnemonic SMART is sometimes used to describe well-defined objectives:

● *Specific* Effective objectives are concrete and well defined. Vague aspirations such as *'to improve customer relations'* are unsatisfactory. Objectives should be defined in such a way that it is obvious to all whether the project has been successful or not.

This still leaves a problem about the level at which the target should be set, e.g. why, say, a 50% reduction in complaints and not 40% or 60%?

● *Measurable* Ideally there should be *measures of effectiveness* which tell us how successful the project has been. For example, 'to reduce customer complaints' would be more satisfactory as an objective than 'to improve customer relations'. The measure can, in some cases, be an answer to simple yes/no question, e.g. 'Did we install the new software by 1 June?'

● *Achievable* It must be within the power of the individual or group to achieve the objective.

● *Relevant* The objective must be relevant to the true purpose of the project.

● *Time constrained* There should be a defined point in time by which the objective should have been achieved.

Exercise 1.7 Bearing in mind the above discussion of objectives, comment on the appropriateness of the wording of each of the following 'objectives' for software developers:

(i) to implement the new application on time and within budget;

(ii) to implement the new software application with the fewest possible software errors that might lead to operational failures;

(iii)   to design a system that is user-friendly;

(iv)   to produce full documentation for the new system.

Measures of effectiveness

These concepts are explained more fully in Chapter 12 on software quality.

Measures of effectiveness provide practical methods of ascertaining whether an objective has been met. A measure of effectiveness will usually be related to the installed operational system. 'Mean time between failures' (mtbf) might, for example, be used to measure reliability. Such measures are *performance* measures and, as such, can only be taken once the system is operational. Project managers will want to get some idea of the likely performance of the completed system as it is being constructed. They will therefore be seeking *predictive* measures. For example, a large number of errors found during code inspections might indicate potential problems later with reliability.

Exercise 1.8   Identify the objectives and sub-objectives of the Brightmouth College payroll project. What measures of effectiveness could be used to check the success in achieving the objectives of the project?

1.12   Stakeholders

These are people who have a stake or interest in the project. It is important that they be identified as early as possible, because you need to set up adequate communication channels with them right from the start. The project leader also has to be aware that not everybody who is involved with a project has the same motivation and objectives. The end-users might, for instance, be concerned about the ease of use of the system while their managers might be interested in the staff savings the new system will allow.

Stakeholders might be internal to the project team, external to the project team but in the same organization, or totally external to the organization.

● *Internal to the project team*   This means that they will be under the direct managerial control of the project leader.

● *External to the project team but within the same organization*   For example, the project leader might need the assistance of the information management group in order to add some additional data types to a database or the assistance of the users to carry out systems testing. Here the commitment of the people involved has to be negotiated.

● *External to both the project team and the organization*   External stakeholders may be customers (or users) who will benefit from the system that the project implements or contractors who will carry out work for the project. One feature of the relationship with these people is that it is likely to be based on a legally binding contract.

B. W. Boehm and R. Ross, 'Theory W software project management: principles and examples', in B. W. Boehm (ed.) *Software Risk Management*, IEEE Computer Society Press, 1989.

Different types of stakeholder may have different objectives and one of the jobs of the successful project leader is to recognize these different interests and to be able to reconcile them. It should therefore come as no surprise that the project leader needs to be a good communicator and negotiator. Boehm and Ross proposed a 'Theory W' of software project management where the manager concentrates on creating situations where all parties involved in a project benefit from it and therefore have an interest in its success. (The 'W' stands for Everyone a Winner.)

Exercise 1.9 Identify the stakeholders in the Brightmouth College payroll project.

1.13 The business case

> The business case should be established at the time of the project's feasibility study.

Most projects need to have a justification or business case: the effort and expense of pushing the project through must be seen to be worthwhile in terms of the benefits that will eventually be felt. A cost–benefit analysis will often be part of the project's feasibility study. This will itemize and quantify the project's costs and benefits. The benefits will be affected by the completion date: the sooner the project is completed, the sooner the benefits can be experienced. The quantification of benefits will often require the formulation of a *business model* which explains how the new application can generate the claimed benefits.

A simple example of a business model is that a new web-based application might allow customers from all over the world to order a firm's products via the internet, increasing sales and thus increasing revenue and profits.

Any project plan must ensure that the business case is kept intact. For example:

- that development costs are not allowed to rise to a level which threatens to exceed the value of benefits;
- that the features of the system are not reduced to a level where the expected benefits cannot be realized;
- that the delivery date is not delayed so that there is an unacceptable loss benefits.

1.14 Requirement specification

Very often, especially in the case of product-driven projects, the objectives of the project are carefully defined in terms of functional requirements, quality requirements, and resource requirements.

- *Functional requirements* These define what the end-product of the project is to do. Systems analysis and design methods, such as SADT and Information Engineering, are designed primarily to provide functional requirements.

> These are sometimes called non-functional requirements.

- *Quality requirements* There will be other attributes of the application to be implemented that do not relate so much to what the system is to do but how it is to do it. These are still things that the user will be able to experience. They include, for example, response time, the ease of using the system and its reliability.

- *Resource requirements* A record of how much the organization is willing to spend on the system. There may be a trade-off between this and the time it takes to implement the system. In general it costs disproportionately more to implement a system by an earlier date than a later one. There may also be a trade-off between the functional and quality requirements and cost. We would all like exceptionally reliable and user-friendly systems which do exactly what we want but we may not be able to afford them.

All these requirements must be consistent with the business case.

1.15 Management control

Management, in general, can be seen as the process of setting objectives for a system and then monitoring the system to see what its true performance is. In Figure 1.4 the 'real world' is shown as being rather formless. Especially in the case of large undertakings, there will be a lot going on about which management should be aware.

Exercise 1.10

An ICT project is to replace locally held paper-based records with a centrally-organized database. Staff in a large number of offices that are geographically dispersed need training and then need to use the new ICT system to set up the backlog of manual records on the new database. The system cannot be properly operational until the last record has been transferred. The new system will only be successful if new transactions can be processed within certain time cycles.

Identify the data that you would collect to ensure that during execution of the project things were going to plan.

This will involve the local managers in *data collection*. Bare details, such as 'location X has processed 2000 documents', will not be very useful to higher management: *data processing* will be needed to transform this raw *data* into useful *information*. This might be in such forms as 'percentage of records processed', 'average documents processed per day per person' and 'estimated completion date'.

In our example, the project management might examine the 'estimated completion date' for completing data transfer for each branch. These can be checked against the overall target date for completion of this phase of the project. In effect they are comparing actual performance with one aspect of the overall project objectives. They might find that one or two branches will fail to complete the transfer of details in time. They would then need to consider what to do (this is represented in Figure 1.4 by the box *making decisions/plans*). One possibility would be to move staff temporarily from one branch to another. If this is done, there is always the danger that while the completion date for the one branch is pulled back to before the overall target date, the date for the branch from which staff are being moved is pushed forward beyond that date. The project manager would need to calculate carefully what the impact would be in moving staff from particular branches. This is *modelling* the consequences of a potential solution. Several different proposals could be modelled in this way before one was chosen for *implementation*.

Having implemented the decision, the situation needs to be kept under review by collecting and processing further progress details. For instance, the next time that progress is reported, a branch to which staff have been transferred could still be behind in transferring details. This might be because the reason why the branch has got behind in transferring details is because the manual records are incomplete and another department, for whom the project has a low priority, has to be

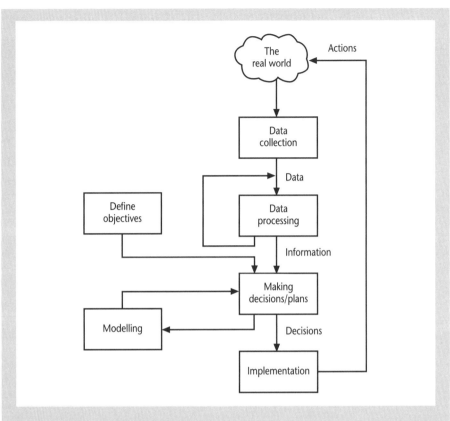

Figure 1.4   The project control cycle.

involved in providing the missing information. In this case, transferring extra staff to do data inputting will not have accelerated data transfer.

It can be seen that a project plan is dynamic and will need constant adjustment during the execution of the project.

1.16   Conclusion

This chapter has laid a foundation for the remainder of the book by defining what is meant by various terms such as 'software project' and 'management'. Among some of the more important points that have been made are the following:

● Projects are by definition non-routine and therefore more uncertain than normal undertakings.

● Software projects are similar to other projects but have some attributes that present particular difficulties, e.g. the relative invisibility of many of their products.

● A key factor in project success is having clear objectives. Different stakeholders in a project, however, are likely to have different objectives. This points to the need for a recognized overall project authority.

- For objectives to be effective there must be practical ways of testing that the objectives have been met.

- Where projects involve many different people, effective channels of information have to be established. Having objective measures of success helps unambiguous communication between the various parties to a project.

Annex 1 Contents list for a feasibility study

- Introduction: identifies what the document is
- Description of current situation
- Problem description
- Proposed development
  - business and financial aspects
  - technical aspects
  - organizational aspects
- Estimated costs
  - development costs
  - operational costs
- Envisaged benefits
- Recommendation

Annex 2 Contents list for a project plan

The detail that goes into these sections will be explained in later chapters. For example, Chapter 7 relates to risk while Chapter 12 explains aspects of the management of quality.

- Introduction
- Background: including reference to the business case
- Project objectives
- Constraints – these could be included with project objectives
- Methods
- Project products: both deliverable products that the client will receive and intermediate products
- Activities to be carried out
- Resources to be used
- Risks to the project
- Management of the project, including
  - organizational responsibilities
  - management of quality
  - configuration management

1.17 Further exercises

1. List the problems you experienced when you carried out a recent ICT-related assignment. Try to put these problems into some order of magnitude. For each problem consider whether there was some way in which the problem could have been reduced by better organization and planning by yourself.

2. Identify the main types of personnel employed in an information systems department. For each stage of a typical IS development project, list the types of personnel who are likely to be involved.

3. A public library is considering the implementation of a computer-based system to help administer book loans at libraries. Identify the stakeholders in such a project. What might be the objectives of such a project and how might the success of the project be measured in practical terms?

4. A software house has developed a customized order processing system for a client. You are an employee of the software house that has been asked to organize a training course for the end-users of the system. At present, a user handbook has been produced, but no specific training material. A plan is now needed for the project which will set up the delivery of the training courses. The project can be assumed to have been completed when the first training course starts. Among the things that will need to be considered are the following:

   ● training materials will need to be designed and created;
   ● a timetable will need to be drafted and agreed;
   ● date(s) for the course will need to be arranged;
   ● the people attending the course will need to be identified and notified;
   ● rooms and computer facilities for the course will need to be provided for.

   A. Identify the main stakeholders for this project.
   B. Draw up objectives for this project.
   C. For the objectives, identify the measures of effectiveness.
   D. For each objective, write down sub-objectives or goals and the stakeholders who will be responsible for their achievement.

5. A manager is in charge of a sub-project of a larger project. The sub-project requires the transfer of paper documents into a computer-based document retrieval system and their subsequent indexing so that they can be accessed via key-words. Optical character readers are to be used for the initial transfer but the text then needs to be clerically checked and corrected by staff. The project is currently scheduled to take twelve months using permanent staff. A small budget is available to hire temporary staff in the case of staff absences through holidays, sickness or temporary transfer to other, more urgent, jobs. Discuss the control system that will need to be in place to control that sub-project.

6. The idea behind a project is that students should be able to access details of available placements via an intranet. When there is a placement opportunity for which they wish to be considered, they would be able to apply for it electronically. This would cause a copy of their CV, which would also be held online, to be sent to the potential employer.

   Details of interviews and placement offers would all be sent by e-mail. While some human intervention would be needed, the process would be automated as far as possible.

You are required to produce a business case report for such an application, which justifies the potential development by showing that the value of its potential benefits outweigh its development and operational costs.

Create lists of the main benefits and costs for the project. You do not have to specify actual figures, just the headings under which they would appear.

CHAPTER 2

Step Wise: an overview of project planning

Objectives

When you have completed this chapter you will be able to:

- approach project planning in an organized step-by-step manner;
- see where the techniques described in other chapters fit into an overall planning approach;
- repeat the planning process in more detail for sets of activities within a project as the time comes to execute them.

2.1 Introduction to Step Wise project planning

This chapter describes a framework of basic steps in project planning upon which the following chapters build. Many different techniques can be used in project planning and this chapter gives an overview of the points at which these techniques can be applied during project planning. Chapter 4 will illustrate how different projects may need different technical approaches, but this framework should always apply to the planning process.

The framework described is called the Step Wise method to help to distinguish it from other methods such as PRINCE2. PRINCE2 is a set of project management standards that were originally sponsored by what was then the Central Computing and Telecommunications Agency (CCTA) for use on British government ICT projects. The standards are now also widely used on non-government projects in the United Kingdom. Step Wise should be compatible with PRINCE2. It should be noted, however, that Step Wise only covers the planning stages of a project and not monitoring and control.

In order to illustrate the Step Wise approach and how it might have to be adapted to deal with different circumstances, two parallel examples are used. Let us assume that there are two former Computing and Information Systems students who now have several years of software development experience under their belts.

Appendix A adds some further details about the PRINCE2 approach.

The CCTA has been renamed the Office of Government Commerce (OGC).

Brightmouth College Payroll

Brigette has been working for the Management Services department of a local authority when she sees an advertisement for the position of Information Systems Development Officer at Brightmouth College. She is attracted to the idea of being her own boss, working in a relatively small organization and helping them to set up appropriate information systems from scratch. She applies for the job and gets it. One of the first tasks that confronts her is the implementation of independent payroll processing. (This scenario has already been used as the basis of some examples in Chapter 1.)

International Office Equipment Group Maintenance Accounts

Amanda works for International Office Equipment (IOE), which manufactures and supplies various items of high-technology office equipment. An expanding area of their work is the maintenance of ICT equipment. They have now started to undertake maintenance of equipment for which they were not originally the suppliers. A computer-based batch processing system deals with invoicing on a job-by-job basis. An organization might have to call IOE out several times to deal with different bits of equipment and there is a need to be able to group the invoice details for work done into 'group accounts' for which monthly statements will be produced. Amanda has been given her first project management role, the task of implementing this extension to the invoicing system.

In Table 2.1 we outline the general approach that might be taken to planning these projects. Figure 2.1 provides an outline of the main planning activities. Steps 1 and 2 'Identify project scope and objectives' and 'Identify project infrastructure' could be tackled in parallel in some cases. Steps 5 and 6 will need to be repeated for each activity in the project.

A major principle of project planning is to plan in outline first and then in more detail as the time to carry out an activity approaches. Hence the lists of products and activities that are the result of Step 4 will be reviewed when the tasks connected with a particular phase of a project are considered in more detail. This will be followed by a more detailed iteration of Steps 5 to 8 for the phase under consideration.

Table 2.1 An outline of Step Wise planning activities

Step	Activities within step
0	Select project
1	Identify project scope and objectives
	1.1 Identify objectives and measures of effectiveness in meeting them
	1.2 Establish a project authority
	1.3 Identify stakeholders
	1.4 Modify objectives in the light of stakeholder analysis
	1.5 Establish methods of communications with all parties
2	Identify project infrastructure
	2.1 Establish relationship between project and strategic planning
	2.2 Identify installation standards and procedures
	2.3 Identify project team organization
3	Analyse project characteristics
	3.1 Distinguish the project as either objective- or product-driven
	3.2 Analyse other project characteristics
	3.3 Identify high-level project risks
	3.4 Take into account user requirements concerning implementation
	3.5 Select general life-cycle approach
	3.6 Review overall resource estimates
4	Identify project products and activities
	4.1 Identify and describe project products (including quality criteria)
	4.2 Document generic product flows
	4.3 Recognize product instances
	4.4 Produce ideal activity network
	4.5 Modify ideal to take into account need for stages and checkpoints
5	Estimate effort for each activity
	5.1 Carry out bottom-up estimates
	5.2 Revise plan to create controllable activities
6	Identify activity risks
	6.1 Identify and quantify activity-based risks
	6.2 Plan risk reduction and contingency measures where appropriate
	6.3 Adjust plans and estimates to take account of risks
7	Allocate resources
	7.1 Identify and allocate resources
	7.2 Revise plans and estimates to take account of resource constraints
8	Review/publicize plan
	8.1 Review quality aspects of project plan
	8.2 Document plans and obtain agreement
9/10	Execute plan/lower levels of planning
	This may require the reiteration of the planning process at a lower level

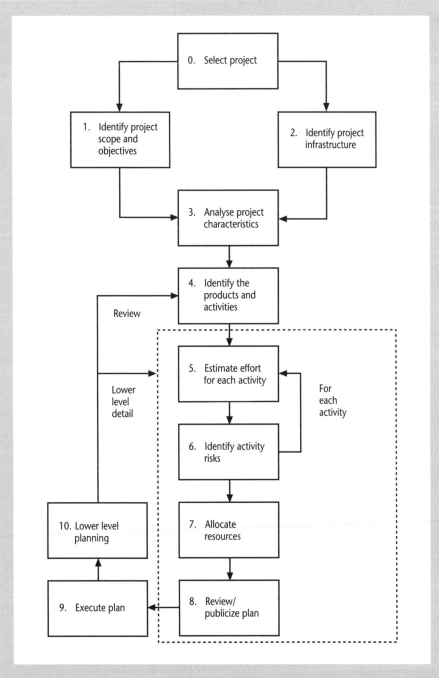

Figure 2.1 An overview of Step Wise

2.2   Step 0: Select project

Chapter 3 discusses
project evaluation in
more detail.

This is called Step 0 because in a way it is outside the main project planning process. Proposed projects do not appear out of thin air – some process must decide to initiate this project rather than some other. While a feasibility study might suggest that the project is worthwhile, it would still need to be established that it should have priority over other projects found to be worthwhile. This evaluation of the merits of projects could be part of strategic planning.

2.3   Step 1: Identify project scope and objectives

The activities in this step ensure that all the parties to the project agree on the objectives and are committed to the success of the project. A danger to be avoided is overlooking people who are affected by the project.

Step 1.1: Identify objectives and practical measures of the effectiveness in meeting those objectives

We discussed in Chapter 1 the need for agreed objectives for a project and ways of measuring the success in achieving those objectives.

CASE STUDY EXAMPLES

> **Project objectives**
>
> The project objectives for the Brightmouth College payroll project have already been discussed in Exercise 1.8.
>
> Amanda at IOE has the objectives clearly laid down for her in the recommendations of a feasibility study report which have been accepted by IOE management. The main objectives are to allow a detailed monthly statement to be sent to group account clients and to be able to reallocate the cash received to individual jobs when the client has paid on the monthly statement. Other objectives are laid down that refer to expected timescales and the resources that might be used.

Step 1.2: Establish a project authority

Throughout the text
we use capitalized
initial letters to
indicate a term that
has a precise meaning
in the PRINCE2
standards, e.g. Project
Board.

We have already noted in Chapter 1 that a single overall project authority needs to be established so that there is unity of purpose among all those concerned.

Step 1.3: Stakeholder analysis – identify all stakeholders in the project and their interests

Recall that this was the basis of a discussion in Chapter 1. Essentially all the parties who have an interest in the project need to be identified. In that chapter we listed as an example the stakeholders in the Brightmouth College payroll project.

Exercise 2.1

What important stakeholders outside the IOE organization might be considered in the case of the IOE maintenance group accounts system?

Case Study Examples: Project authorities

Amanda finds that her manager and the main user management have already set up a Project Board which will have overall direction of the project. She is a little concerned as the equipment maintenance staff are organized with different sections dealing with different types of equipment. This means that a customer could have work done by several different sections. Not all the sections are represented on the Project Board and Amanda is aware that there are some differences of opinion between some sections. It is left to the user representatives on the board to resolve those differences and to present an agreed policy to the systems developers.

Brigette finds that effectively she has two different clients for the payroll system: the finance and human resources departments. To help resolve conflicts, it is agreed that the managers of both departments should attend a monthly meeting with the vice-principal which Brigette has arranged in order to steer the project.

Step 1.4: Modify objectives in the light of stakeholder analysis

In order to gain the full cooperation of all concerned, it might be necessary to modify the project objectives. This could mean adding new features to the system which give a benefit to some stakeholders as a means of assuring their commitment to the project. This is potentially dangerous as the system size may be increased and the original objectives obscured. Because of these dangers, it is suggested that this process be done consciously and in a controlled manner.

Modified project objectives

The IOE maintenance staff are to be given the extra task of entering data about completed jobs. They do not benefit from this additional work. To give some benefit, the system is to be extended to reorder spare parts automatically when required.

At Brightmouth College, the human resources department has a lot of work preparing payroll details for finance. It would be tactful to agree to produce some management information reports for human resources from the payroll details held on the computer.

Step 1.5: Establish methods of communication with all parties

For internal staff this should be fairly straightforward, but a project leader implementing a payroll system would need to find a contact point with BACS (Bankers Automated Clearing Scheme) for instance.

2.4 Step 2: Identify project infrastructure

Projects are rarely carried out in a vacuum. There is usually some kind of existing infrastructure into which the project must fit. Where project managers are new to the organization, they must find out the precise nature of this infrastructure.

Step 2.1: Identify relationship between the project and strategic planning

Some of the issues of strategic planning are addressed in Chapter 3.

As well as identifying projects to be carried out, an organization needs to give priorities to the projects to be carried out. It also needs to establish the framework within which the proposed new systems are to fit. Hardware and software standards, for example, are needed so that various systems can communicate with each other. These strategic decisions must be documented in a strategic business plan or in an information technology plan that is developed from the business plan.

CASE STUDY EXAMPLES

> ### Role of existing strategic plans
>
> Amanda finds at IOE that there is a well-defined rolling strategic plan which has identified her group accounts subsystem as an important required development. Because it is an extension of an existing system, the hardware and software platforms upon which the application are to run are dictated.
>
> Brigette at Brightmouth College finds that there is an overall College strategic plan which describes new courses to be developed, and so on, and mentions in passing the need for 'appropriate administrative procedures' to be in place. There is a recommendation that independent payroll processing be undertaken in a short section in a consultant's report from an accountancy firm concerning the implications of financial autonomy. Although the college has quite a lot of ICT equipment for teaching purposes, there is no machine set aside for payroll processing and the intention is that the hardware to run the payroll will be acquired at the same time as the software.

Step 2.2: Identify installation standards and procedures

See discussion of the ISO/IEC 12207 standard in Chapter 10.

Any organization that develops software should define their development procedures. As a minimum, the normal stages in the software life cycle to be carried out should be documented along with the products created at each stage.

Change control and *configuration management* standards should be in place to ensure that changes to requirements are implemented in a safe and orderly way.

See Chapter 9 on monitoring and control.

The procedural standards may lay down the quality checks that need to be done at each point of the project life cycle or these may be documented in a separate *quality standards and procedures* manual.

The organization as part of its monitoring and control policy may have a *measurement programme* in place which dictates that certain statistics have to be collected at various stages of a project.

Finally the project manager should be aware of any *project planning and control standards*. These will relate to how the project is controlled: for example, the way that the hours spent by team members on individual tasks are recorded on timesheets.

Identifying standards

Amanda at IOE finds that there is a very weighty volume of development standards which, among other things, specifies that a specific structured systems analysis and design method be used. She finds that a separate document has been prepared which lays down quality procedures. This specifies when the reviews of work will be carried out and describes detailed procedures about how the reviews are to be done. Amanda also finds a set of project management guidelines modelled closely on PRINCE2.

Brigette finds no documents of the nature that Amanda found at IOE except for some handouts for students that have been produced by different lecturers at different times and which seem to contradict each other.

As a stop-gap measure, Brigette writes a brief document which states what the main stages of a 'project' (perhaps 'job for the user' would be a better term in this context) should be. This happens to be very similar to the list given in Chapter 1. She stresses that:

- no job of work to change a system or implement a new one is to be done without there being a detailed specification first;
- the users must record agreement to each specification in writing before the work is carried out.

She draws up a simple procedure for recording all changes to user requirements.

Brigette, of course, has no organizational quality procedures, but she dictates that each person in the group (including herself) has to get someone else to check through their work when they finish a major task and that, before any new or amended software is handed over to the users, someone other than the original producer should test it. She sets up a simple system to record errors found in system testing and their resolution. She also creates a log file of reported user problems with operational systems.

Brigette does not worry about timesheets but arranges an informal meeting with her colleagues each Monday morning to discuss how things are going and also arranges to see the vice-principal, who is her official boss, and the heads of the finance and personnel sections each month to review progress in general terms.

Step 2.3: Identify project team organization

Some of these issues will be discussed in Chapter 11 – Managing people and organizing teams.

Project leaders, especially in the case of large projects, might have some control over the way that their project team is to be organized. Often, though, the organizational structure will be dictated to them. For example, a high-level managerial decision might have been taken that software developers and business analysts will be in different groups, or that the development of business-to-customer web applications will be done within a separate group from that responsible for 'traditional' database applications.

    If the project leader does have some control over the project team organization then this would best be considered at a later stage (see Step 7: Allocate resources).

CASE STUDY EXAMPLES

> ### Project organization
>
> At IOE, there are groups of business analysts set up as teams which deal with individual user departments. Hence the users always know whom they should contact within the information systems department if they have a problem. Software developers, however, work in a 'pool' and are allocated to specific projects on an *ad hoc* basis.
>
> At Brightmouth College, a software developer has been seconded to Brigette from the technicians supporting the computing courses in the college. She is also allowed to recruit a trainee analyst/programmer. She is not unduly worried about the organizational structure needed.

2.5   Step 3: Analyse project characteristics

Chapter 4 elaborates on the process of analysing project characteristics.

The general purpose of this part of the planning operation is to ensure that the appropriate methods are used for the project.

Step 3.1: Distinguish the project as either objective- or product-driven

This has already been discussed in the first chapter. As development of a system advances it tends to become more product-driven, although the underlying objectives always remain and must be respected.

Step 3.2: Analyse other project characteristics (including quality-based ones)

For example, is an information system to be developed or a process control system, or will there be elements of both? Will the system be safety critical, where human life could be threatened by a malfunction?

Step 3.3: Identify high-level project risks

Consideration must be given to the risks that threaten the successful outcome of the project. Generally speaking, most risks can be attributed to the operational or development environment, the technical nature of the project or the type of product being created.

High-level risks

At IOE Amanda identifies the danger of there being resistance to the new system by maintenance engineers, especially as a new centralized group accounts office is to be set up. Amanda decides therefore that additional efforts are needed to consult all sections involved and that the new procedures should be introduced in small increments to accustom staff to them gradually.

Brigette at Brightmouth College considers the application area to be very well defined. There is a risk, however, that there may be no package on the market that caters for the way that things are done at the moment. Brigette, therefore, decides that an early task in the project is to obtain information about the features of the main payroll packages that are available.

Step 3.4: Take into account user requirements concerning implementation

The clients may have their own procedural requirements. For example, an organization might mandate the use of a particular development method.

Step 3.5: Select development methodology and life-cycle approach

Chapter 4 discusses life cycles in more detail.

The development methodology and project life cycle to be used for the project will be influenced by the issues raised above. The idea of a methodology, that is, the group of methods to be used in a project, was discussed in Chapter 1. For many software developers, the choice of methods will seem obvious: they will use the ones that they have always used in the past. In Chapter 4 we recommend caution in assuming that the current project is really similar to previous ones.

As well as the methods to be used, there are generic ways of structuring projects, such as the use of the Waterfall life cycle outlined in Chapter 4, that need to be considered. While the setting of objectives involves identifying the problems to be solved, this part of planning is working out the ways in which these problems are to be solved. For a project that is novel to the planner, some research into the methods typically used in the problem domain is worthwhile. For example, sometimes, as part of a project, a questionnaire survey has to be conducted. There are lots of books on the techniques used in such surveys and a wise move would be to look at one or two of them at the planning stage.

Step 3.6: Review overall resource estimates

Chapter 5 goes into more detail on this topic. Function points are an attempt to measure system size without using lines of code.

Once the major risks have been identified and the broad project approach has been decided upon, this would be a good point at which to re-estimate the effort and other resources required to implement the project. Where enough information is available a function point-based estimate might be appropriate.

2.6 Step 4: Identify project products and activities

The more detailed planning of the individual activities now takes place. The longer-term planning is broad and in outline, while the more immediate tasks are planned in some detail.

Step 4.1: Identify and describe project products (or deliverables)

Chapter 6 goes into this in more detail.

In general there can be no project products that do not have activities that create them. Wherever possible, we ought also to ensure the reverse: that there are no activities that do not produce a tangible product. Identifying all the things the project is to create helps us to ensure that all the activities we need to carry out are accounted for. Some of these products will be handed over to the client at the end of the project – these are *deliverables*. Other products might not be in the final configuration, but are needed as *intermediate* products used in the process of creating the deliverables.

These products will include a large number of *technical* products, including training material and operating instructions, but also products to do with the *management* and the *quality* of the project. Planning documents would, for example, be management products.

PRINCE2 suggests that the PBS be presented as a hierarchy diagram. In practice it may be more convenient to produce a structured list.

The products will form a hierarchy. The main products will have sets of component products which in turn may have sub-component products and so on. These relationships can be documented in a Product Breakdown Structure (PBS) – see Figure 2.2. In this example the products have been grouped into those relating to the system as a whole, and those related to individual modules. A third 'group', which happens to have only one product, is called 'management products' and consists of progress reports. The asterisk in the progress reports indicates that these will have new instances created repeatedly throughout the project.

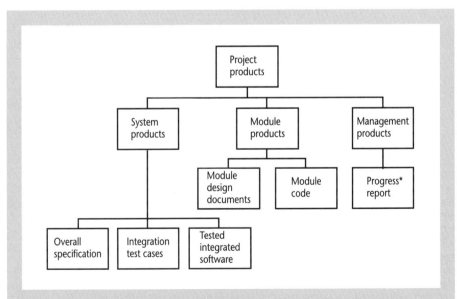

Figure 2.2 A fragment of a product breakdown structure for a system development task

Some products are created from scratch, for example new software components. A product could quite easily be a document, like a software design document. It might be a modified version of something that already exists, such as an amended piece of code. A product could even be a person, such as a 'trained user', a product of the process of training. Always remember that a product is the result of an activity. A common error is to identify as products things that are really activities, such as 'training', 'design' and 'testing'. Specifying 'documentation' as a product should also be avoided – by itself this term is just too vague.

This part of the planning process draws heavily on the standards laid down in PRINCE2. These specify that products at the bottom of the PBS should be documented by *Product Descriptions* which contain:

- the *name/identity* of the product;
- the *purpose* of the product;
- the *derivation* of the product (that is, the other products from which it is derived);
- the *composition* of the product;
- the *form* of the product;
- the relevant *standards*;
- the *quality* criteria that should apply to it.

CASE STUDY EXAMPLES

Product breakdown structures

At IOE, Amanda finds that there is a standard PBS that she can use as a checklist for her own project.

Brigette at Brightmouth College has no installation standard PBS, although she can, of course, refer to various books for standard checklists. She decides that one part of the PBS should contain the products needed to help select the appropriate hardware and software for the payroll application (Figure 2.3).

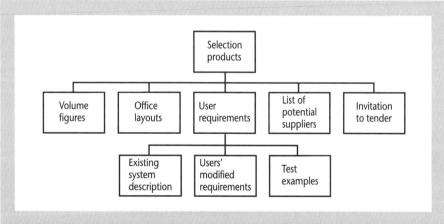

Figure 2.3 A product breakdown structure (PBS) for the products needed to produce an invitation to tender (ITT)

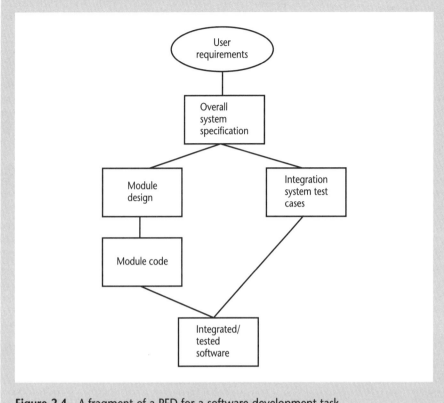

Figure 2.4   A fragment of a PFD for a software development task

The PFD effectively documents, in outline, the method (see Chapter 1) for the project.

Step 4.2: Document generic product flows

Some products will need one or more other products to exist first before they can be created. For example, a program design must be created before the program can be written and the program specification must exist before the design can be commenced. These relationships can be portrayed in a *Product Flow Diagram* (PFD). Figure 2.4 gives an example. Note that the 'flow' in the diagram is assumed to be from top to bottom and left to right. In the example in Figure 2.4, 'user requirements' is in an oval which means that it is used by the project but is not created by it. It is often convenient to identify an overall product at the bottom of the diagram, in this case 'integrated/tested software', into which all the other products feed.

CASE STUDY EXAMPLES

IOE has standard PFD

At IOE, Amanda has a standard installation PFD for software development projects. This is because a recognized software development method is used which lays down a sequence of documents that have to be produced. This sequence of products can be straightforwardly documented as a PFD.

Exercise 2.2 Draw up a possible Product Flow Diagram (PFD) based on the Product Breakdown Structure (PBS) shown in Figure 2.3. This identifies some of the products of the Brightmouth payroll project, particularly those generated when gathering information to be presented to potential suppliers of the hardware as part of an 'invitation to tender'. The volume figures are such things as the number of employees for whom records will have to be maintained.

This may be delayed to later in the project when more information is known.

Step 4.3: Recognize product instances

Where the same generic PFD fragment relates to more than one instance of a particular type of product, an attempt should be made to identify each of those instances. In the example in Figure 2.2, it could be that in fact there are just two component software modules in the software to be built.

Step 4.4: Produce ideal activity network

In order to generate one product from another there must be one or more activities which carry out the transformation. By identifying these activities we can create an activity network which shows the tasks that have to be carried out and the order in which they have to be executed.

CASE STUDY EXAMPLES

> **Activity network for IOE Maintenance Accounts**
>
> Part of the initial activity network developed from the PFD in Figure 2.4 for the software development task might look like Figure 2.5.

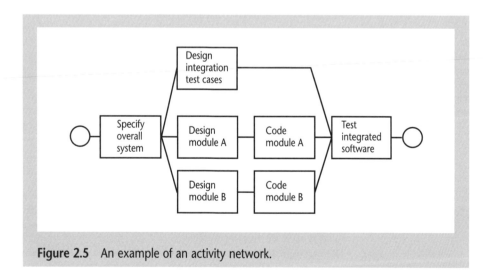

Figure 2.5 An example of an activity network.

Exercise 2.3 Draw up an Activity Network for the Product Flow Diagram that you created in Exercise 2.2 (or the PFD given in the solution if you prefer!).

The activity networks are 'ideal' in the sense that no account has been taken of resource constraints. For example, in Figure 2.5, it is assumed that resources are available for both the software modules to be developed in parallel. The rule is that activity networks are never amended to take account of resource constraints.

Step 4.5: Modify the ideal to take into account need for stages and checkpoints

The approach to sequencing activities described above encourages the formulation of a plan which will minimize the overall duration, or 'elapsed time', for the project. It assumes that an activity will start as soon as the preceding ones upon which it depends have been completed.

There might, however, be a need to modify this by dividing the project into stages and introducing checkpoint activities. These are activities which draw together the products of preceding activities to check that they are compatible. This could potentially delay work on some elements of the project – there has to be a trade-off between efficiency and quality.

The people to whom the project manager reports could decide to leave the routine monitoring of activities to the project manager. However, there could be some key activities, or *milestones*, which represent the completion of important stages of the project of which they would want to take particular note. Checkpoint activities are often useful milestones.

> Strictly, a milestone is a dummy activity with no duration that indicates the start or end of a group of activities. The milestone would therefore be *after* the checkpoint activity.

Exercise 2.4

In the example in Figure 2.5, it has been decided to check that the designs for modules A and B are to be checked for consistency by 'dry-running' them against the integration test cases before committing staff to software coding. Redraw the activity network to reflect this.

2.7 Step 5: Estimate effort for each activity

Step 5.1: Carry out bottom-up estimates

> Chapter 5 on software effort estimation deals with this topic in more detail.

Some top-down estimates of effort, cost and duration will already have been done (see Step 3.6).

At this point, estimates of the staff effort required, the probable elapsed time and the non-staff resources needed for each activity will need to be produced. The method of arriving at each of these estimates will vary depending on the type of activity.

The difference between *elapsed time* and *effort* should be noted. Effort is the amount of work that needs to be done. If a task requires three members of staff to work for two full days each, the effort expended is six days. Elapsed time is the time between the start and end of a task. In our example above, if the three members of staff start and finish at the same time then the elapsed time for the activity would be two days.

The individual activity estimates of effort should be summed to get an overall bottom-up estimate which can be reconciled with the previous top-down estimate.

The activities on the activity network can be annotated with their elapsed times so that the overall duration of the project can be calculated.

Step 5.2: Revise plan to create controllable activities

The estimates for individual activities could reveal that some are going to take quite a long time. Long activities make a project difficult to control. If an activity involving system testing is to take 12 weeks, it would be difficult after six weeks to judge accurately whether 50% of the work is completed. It would be better to break this down into a series of smaller subtasks.

IOE maintenance group accounts – breaking activities down into manageable tasks

At IOE, Amanda has to estimate the lines of code for each of the software modules. She looks at programs that have been coded for similar types of application at IOE in the past to get some idea of the size of the new modules. She then refers to some conversion tables that the information systems development department at IOE have produced which convert the lines of code into estimates of effort. Other tables allow her to allocate the estimated effort to the various stages of the project.

Although Brigette is aware that some additional programs might have to be written to deal with local requirements, the main software is to be obtained 'off the shelf' and so estimating based on lines of code would clearly be inappropriate. Instead, she looks at each individual task and allocates a time. She realizes that in many cases these represent 'targets' as she is uncertain at the moment how long these tasks will really take (see Step 6 below).

There might be a number of activities that are important, but individually take up very little time. For a training course, there might be a need to book rooms and equipment, notify those attending, register students on the training system, order refreshments, copy training materials and so on. In a situation like this it would be easier to bundle the activities into a portmanteau activity 'make training course arrangements' which could be supplemented with a checklist.

In general, try to make activities about the length of the reporting period used for monitoring and controlling the project. If you have a progress meeting every two weeks, then it would convenient to have activities of two weeks' duration on average, so that progress meetings would normally be made aware of completed tasks each time they are held.

2.8 Step 6: Identify activity risks

Step 6.1: Identify and quantify activity-based risks

Chapter 7 on risk touches on this topic in more detail.

Risks inherent in the overall nature of the project have already been considered in Step 3. We now want to look at each activity in turn and assess the risks to its successful outcome. Any plan is always based on certain assumptions. Say the design of a component is planned to take five days. This is based on the assumption that the client's requirement is clear and unambiguous. If it is not then additional effort to clarify the requirement would be needed. The possibility that an assumption upon which a plan is based is incorrect constitutes a risk. In this example, one way of expressing the uncertainty would be to express the estimate of effort as a range of values.

A project plan will be based on a huge number of assumptions, and so some way of picking out the risks that are most important is needed. The damage that each risk could cause and the likelihood of it occurring have to be gauged. This assessment can draw attention to the most serious risks. The usual effect if a problem materializes is to make the task longer or more costly.

Step 6.2: Plan risk reduction and contingency measures where appropriate

It may be possible to avoid or at least reduce some of the identified risks. On the other hand, *contingency plans* specify action that is to be taken if a risk materializes. For example, a contingency plan could be to use contract staff if a member of the project team is unavailable at a key time because of serious illness.

Step 6.3: Adjust overall plans and estimates to take account of risks

We may change our plans, perhaps by adding new activities which reduce risks. For example, a new programming language might mean we schedule training courses and time for the programmers to practise their new programming skills on some non-essential work.

CASE STUDY EXAMPLES

Identifying risks

As well as the new software modules that will have to be written, Amanda has identified several existing modules that will need to be amended. The ease with which the modules can be amended will depend upon the way that they were originally written. There is therefore a risk that they may take longer than expected to modify. Amanda takes no risk reduction measures as such but notes a pessimistic elapsed time for the amendment activity.

Brigette identifies as a risk the possible absence of key staff when investigating the user requirements, as this activity will take place over the holiday period. To reduce this risk, she adds a new activity, 'arrange user interviews', at the beginning of the project. This will give her advance notice of any likely problems of this nature.

2.9 Step 7: Allocate resources

Step 7.1: Identify and allocate resources

Chapter 8 on resource allocation covers this topic in more detail.

The type of staff needed for each activity is recorded. The staff available for the project are identified and are provisionally allocated to tasks.

Step 7.2: Revise plans and estimates to take into account resource constraints

Some staff may be needed for more than one task at the same time and, in this case, an order of priority is established. The decisions made here may have an effect on the overall duration of the project when some tasks are delayed while waiting for staff to become free.

	January	February	March	April	May
Specify overall system	[bar]	Jane			
Devise integration test cases		[bar]	Jane		
Design module A		[bar] Fred			
Code module A			[bar]	Fred	
Design module B		[bar]	Avril		
Code module B			[bar]	Avril	
Test integrated software				[bar]	Mo

Figure 2.6 Gantt chart showing when staff will be carrying out tasks

Gantt charts are named after Henry Gantt and 'Gantt' should therefore *not* be written in capital letters as if it stood for something!

Ensuring someone is available to start work on an activity as soon as the preceding activities have been completed might mean that they are idle while waiting for the job to start and are therefore used inefficiently.

The product of steps 7.1 and 7.2 would typically be a Gantt chart – see Figure 2.6. The Gantt chart gives a clear picture of when activities will actually take place and highlights which ones will be executed at the same time. Activity networks can be misleading in this respect

CASE STUDY EXAMPLES

Taking resource constraints into account

Amanda has now identified two new major software modules plus two existing software modules that will need extensive amendment. At IOE the specification of modules is carried out by the lead systems analyst for the project (who in this case is Amanda) assisted by junior analyst/designers. Four analyst/programmers are available to carry out the design, coding and unit testing of the individual modules. After careful consideration and discussion with her manager, Amanda decides to use only three analyst/programmers so as to minimize the risk of staff waiting between tasks. It is accepted that this decision, while reducing the cost of the project, will delay its end.

Brigette finds that she herself will have to carry out many important activities. She can reduce the workload on herself by delegating some work to her two colleagues, but she realizes that she will have to devote more time to specifying exactly what they will have to do and to checking their work. She adjusts her plan accordingly.

2.10   Step 8: Review/publicize plan

Step 8.1: Review quality aspects of the project plan

A danger when controlling any project is that an activity can reveal that an earlier activity was not properly completed and needs to be reworked. This, at a stroke, can transform a project that appears to be progressing satisfactorily into one that is badly out of control. It is important to know that when a task is reported as completed, it really is – hence the importance of quality reviews. Each task should have *quality criteria*. These are quality checks that have to be passed before the activity can be 'signed off' as completed.

CASE STUDY EXAMPLES

> **IOE existing quality standards**
>
> Amanda finds that at IOE, the Quality Standards and Procedures Manual lays down quality criteria for each type of task. For example, all module design documentation has to be reviewed by a group of colleagues before the coding of that module can commence.

Exercise 2.5   Brigette has no installation standards to help her apart from the minimal ones she has written herself. What quality checks might Brigette introduce to ensure that she has understood the users' requirements properly?

Step 8.2: Document plans and obtain agreement

It is important that the plans be carefully documented and that all the parties to the project understand and agree to the commitments required of them in the plan. This may sound obvious, but it is amazing how often this is not done.

Exercise 2.6   At the end of Chapter 1 the main sections of a project plan document were listed. Draw up a table showing which Step Wise activities provide material for which sections of the project plan.

2.11   Steps 9 and 10: Execute plan/lower levels of planning

Once the project is under way, plans will need to be drawn up in greater detail for each activity as it becomes due. Detailed planning of the later stages will need to be delayed because more information will be available nearer the start of the stage. Of course, it is necessary to make provisional plans for the more distant tasks, because thinking about what needs to be done can help unearth potential problems, but sight should not be lost of the fact that these plans are provisional.

Lower-level planning

While work is going on with the specification of the individual modules, Amanda has some time to start planning the integration tests in some detail. She finds that, in fact, integration testing of two of the four new or amended modules will be independent of the others. Testing of these two can start when they are ready without waiting for the remainder.

When Brigette comes to consider the activity 'draft invitation to tender', she has to familiarize herself with the detailed institutional rules and procedures that govern this process. She finds that in order to draft this document she will need to obtain some additional pieces of information from the users.

2.12 Conclusion

This chapter has presented a framework into which the techniques described in the other parts of the book should slot. It is suggested that any planning approach should have the following elements:

- the establishment of project objectives;

- the analysis of the characteristics of the project;

- the establishment of an infrastructure consisting of an appropriate organization and set of standards, methods and tools;

- the identification of the products of the project and the activities needed to generate those products;

- the allocation of resources to activities;

- the establishment of quality controls.

Project planning is an iterative process. As the time approaches for particular activities to be carried out they should be replanned in more detail.

2.13 Further exercises

1. List the products created by the Step Wise planning process.

2. What products must exist before the activity 'test program' can take place? What products does this activity create?

3. An employee of a training organization has the task of creating case study exercises and solutions for a training course which teaches a new systems analysis and design method. The person's work plan has a three-week task 'learn new method'. A colleague suggests that this is unsatisfactory as a task as there are no concrete deliverables or products from the activity. What can be done about this?

4. In order to carry out usability tests for a new word processing package, the software has to be written and debugged. User instructions have to be available describing

how the package is to be used. These have to be scrutinized in order to plan and design the tests. Subjects who will use the package in the tests will need to be selected. As part of this selection process, they will have to complete a questionnaire giving details of their past experience of, and training in, typing and using word processing packages. The subjects will carry out the required tasks using the word processing package. The tasks will be timed and any problems the subjects encounter with the package will be noted. After the test, the subjects will complete another questionnaire about what they felt about the package. All the data from the tests will be analysed and a report containing recommendations for changes to the package will be drawn up. Draw up a Product Breakdown Structure, a Product Flow Diagram and a preliminary activity network for the above.

5. Question 4 in the Further exercises for Chapter 1 refers to a scenario relating to a training exercise. Using that scenario, draw up a Product Breakdown Structure, a Product Flow Diagram and a preliminary activity network.

CHAPTER 3

Programme management and project evaluation

Objectives

When you have completed this chapter you will be able to:

- explain how individual projects can be grouped into programmes;
- explain how the implementation of programmes and projects can be managed so that the planned benefits are achieved;
- carry out an evaluation and selection of projects against strategic, technical and economic criteria;
- use a variety of cost–benefit evaluation techniques for choosing among competing project proposals;
- evaluate the risk involved in a project and select appropriate strategies for minimizing potential costs:

3.1 Introduction

In the Step Wise framework that was introduced in the last chapter, Step 0 was 'Select project'. It must be confessed that this is Step 0 rather than Step 1 because when the framework was originally drawn up, the process of deciding whether or not a project should be initiated was ignored. In one way this was justifiable as project teams are brought together after the decision to embark on the project has been made, and thus they are not a party to this decision. However, the success of a project, both technically and in business terms, is clearly built upon a sound initial evaluation of the technical, organizational and financial feasibility of the project.

As will be seen, in some cases managers will be able to justify a commitment to a single project as the financial benefits will clearly exceed the costs of the implementation and operation of the new application. In other cases, managers would not be able to approve a project on its own, but can see that it enables the fulfilment of strategic objectives when combined with the outcomes of other projects. For example, a project to establish an ICT infrastructure within an organization might not be able to deliver a direct financial benefit, but could provide a platform which allows subsequent projects to deliver benefits.

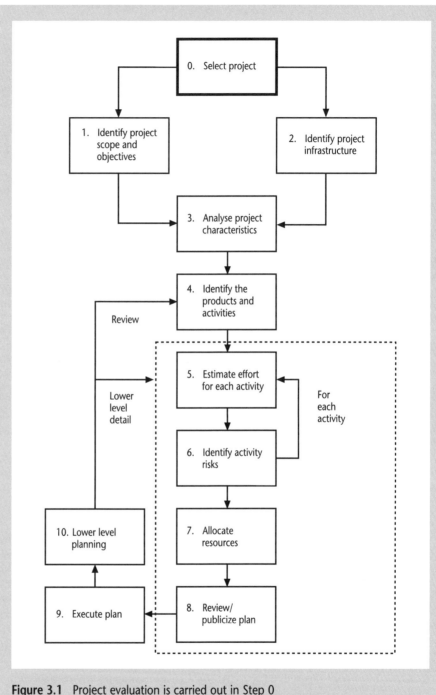

Figure 3.1 Project evaluation is carried out in Step 0

Another problem is that it might not be possible to measure the benefits of a project in simple financial terms. Creating systems, for example, which allow the more accurate recording of data concerning the medical condition of patients might contribute tangibly to the alleviation of pain and the preservation of life, but it would be difficult to put a money value on these benefits.

In this chapter we will first look at the way in which projects can be grouped into programmes. We will then go on to see how the benefits of projects and programmes can be identified and managed. Finally, some methods of evaluating the costs and benefits of individual projects will be explored.

Project evaluation is normally carried out in Step 0 of Step Wise (Figure 3.1).

The subsequent steps of Step Wise are then concerned with managing the development project that stems from this project selection.

3.2 Programme management

Ferns' paper appeared in the *International Journal of Project Management*, August, 1991.

D. C. Ferns defined a programme as *'a group of projects that are managed in a co-ordinated way to gain benefits that would not be possible were the projects to be managed independently'*.

Programmes can exist in different forms as can be seen below.

Strategic programmes

Several projects together can implement a single strategy. For example, the merging of two organizations could involve the creation of unified payroll and accounting applications, the physical reorganization of offices, training, new organizational procedures, re-creating a corporate image through advertising and so on. Each activity could be treated as a distinct project, but would be coordinated as a programme.

Business cycle programmes

The collection of projects that an organization undertakes within a particular planning cycle is sometimes referred to as a *portfolio*. Many organizations have a fixed budget for ICT development. Decisions have to be made about which projects to implement within that budget within the accounting period, which often coincides with the financial year. If expenditure on one project is delayed to a later year, then this could release resources for some other project. On the other hand, if a project absorbs more resources than expected, then this could be at the expense of other projects. Planners need to assess the comparative value and urgency of projects within a portfolio. This is straightforward if external circumstances – such as the adoption of the euro – dictate the priorities. However, balancing the relative needs of different groups of users can become very political.

Often the projects in the portfolio have to compete for a share of common pools of resources, such as teams of software developers. The allocation of available staff between projects poses particular problems, which will be discussed in the next section.

Infrastructure programmes

Some organizations have very integrated information systems. Other organizations can have various departments which have distinct, relatively self-contained, systems. In a local authority, one department might have responsibilities for the maintenance of highways, another for refuse collection, and another for education. These distinct activities will probably require distinct databases and information systems. However, other applications, such as those to do with accounting, cross over these boundaries. In such a situation, the central ICT function would have responsibility for setting up and maintaining the ICT infrastructure, including the networks, workstations and servers, upon which these distinct applications run. A uniform infrastructure would allow the sharing of applications between departments where that was desirable, and would make life easier for the central ICT function, as it would allow the bulk purchasing of equipment and the development of expertise for standard products. In these circumstances, a programme would refer to the activities of identifying a common ICT infrastructure and its implementation and maintenance.

Research and development programmes

Alan Webb, 'When project management doesn't work', *Project Management Today*, May, 2001.

Warren McFarlan's 'Portfolio approach to information systems', *Harvard Business Review* September/October, 1981, pp. 142–150 introduced the portfolio concept to information systems.

Truly innovative companies, especially those that are trying to develop new products for the market, are well aware that projects will vary in terms of their risk of failure and the potential returns that they might eventually reap. Some development projects will be relatively safe, and result in the final planned product, but that product might not be radically different from existing ones on the market. Other projects might be extremely risky, but the end result, if successful, could be a revolutionary technological breakthrough that meets some pressing but previously unsatisfied need.

An example of this is described by Alan Webb. In 1968, DuPont reviewed a range of long-term research projects that they were developing and tried to forecast which ones would create products that would be profitable in thirty years time. Thirty years later, it was possible to see how far they had been correct. A few had been very successful, but many had led to dead-ends. A company like Dupont needs to create and maintain a portfolio of projects which are a mixture of 'safe projects' with relatively low returns and some riskier projects that might fail, but if successful would generate handsome profits which will off-set the losses on the failures. Clearly, if a company gets this balance wrong it could get into serious difficulties.

The risks associated with an innovative project will fluctuate. Research work may lead to technological breakthroughs or to the discovery of insurmountable problems, so the portfolio of projects needs to be reviewed on a regular basis.

Innovative partnerships

Some technological developments, if handled properly, benefit whole industries. The development of the internet and the world wide web is an example. Often, technological products can only be exploited if they inter-operate with other products. The joke about the invention of the first telephone not being as important as the invention of the second comes to mind. Companies therefore often come together to work collaboratively on new technologies in a 'pre-competitive' phase. Separate projects in different organizations need to be coordinated and this might be done as a programme.

Table 3.1 Programme managers versus project managers

Programme manager	Project manager
Many simultaneous projects	One project at a time
Personal relationship with skilled resources	Impersonal relationship with resource type
Need to maximize utilization of resources	Need to minimize demand for resources
Projects tend to be similar	Projects tend to be dissimilar

3.3 Managing the allocation of resources within programmes

We are now going to examine in more detail programmes where resources have to be shared between concurrent projects. Typically, an ICT department has pools of particular types of expertise, such as software developers, database designers and network support staff, and these might be called upon to participate in a number of projects which can be going on at the same time.

In these circumstances, programme managers will have concerns about the optimal use of specialist staff. These concerns can be contrasted with those of project managers – see Table 3.1.

The project managers are said to have an 'impersonal relationship' with resource types because, essentially, they require, for example, a competent systems analyst and who fills that role does not matter. The programme manager has a number of individual systems analysts under his or her control whose deployment has to be planned.

We can see that when a project is planned, at the stage of allocating resources, programme management will be involved (Figure 3.2). Some activities in the project might have to be delayed until the requisite technical staff are freed from work on other projects. Where expensive technical staff are employed full-time, then you would want to avoid them having short periods of intense activity

The comparison is based on G. Reiss *Programme Management Demystified*, Chapman Hall, 1996.

Figure 3.2 Projects sharing resources

interspersed with long periods of idleness, during which they are still being paid. It is most economic when the demand for work is evenly spread from month to month.

As will be seen in Chapter 9 on monitoring and control, when a project is executed activities can take longer (or sometimes even less time) than planned. Delays can mean that specialist staff are prevented from moving on to their next project. Hence it can be seen that programme management needs to be concerned with the continual monitoring of the progress of projects and the use of resources.

3.4 Strategic programme management

A different form of programme management is where a portfolio of projects all contribute to a common objective. Take, for example, a business like Amanda's IOE which carries out maintenance work for clients. A customer's experience of the organization might be found to be very variable and inconsistent. The employee who records the customer's requirements is different from the people who actually carry out the work and different again from the clerk who deals with the accounts. Often a customer has to explain to one company employee a problem that has already been discussed at length with some other IOE employee. A business objective might be to present a consistent and uniform front to the client. This objective might require changes to a number of different systems which until now have been largely self-contained. The work to reorganize each individual area could be treated as a separate project, coordinated at a higher level as a programme.

Recall that OGC is the Office of Government Commerce which was formerly the Central Computing and Telecommunications Agency or CCTA.

These types of programme are most often needed by large organizations which have a large and complicated organizational structure. Government departments are typical examples and it is not surprising that the OGC, the United Kingdom government agency which was responsible (as the CCTA) for the introduction of PRINCE and PRINCE2 project management standards, has directed its attention to guidelines for effective programme management. The approach is based on the OGC guidelines.

3.5 Creating a programme

The programme mandate

The OGC envisages that the planning of a programme will be triggered by the creation of an agreed *programme mandate*. Ideally this should be a formal document describing:

● the new services or capabilities the programme should deliver;
● how the organization will be improved by use of the new services or capability;
● how the programme fits with corporate goals and any other initiatives.

At this point, a *programme director* ought to be appointed to provide initial leadership for the programme. To be successful, the programme needs a champion who is in a prominent position within the organization. This will signal the seriousness with which the organization takes the programme. The programme director is likely to come from the *sponsoring group* who have identified the need for a programme and have initiated its establishment.

The progamme brief

A *programme brief* is now produced which would be the equivalent of a feasibility study for the programme. It will have sections setting out:

- a preliminary *vision statement* which describes the new capacity that the organization seeks – it is described as 'preliminary' because this will later be elaborated;
- the *benefits* that the programme should create – including when they are likely to be generated and how they might be measured;
- risks and issues;
- estimated costs, timescales and effort.

The vision statement

The programme brief should have given the sponsoring group enough information to decide whether it is worth moving to a more detailed definition of the programme. This next stage will involve a lot of detailed planning work and would justify the setting up of a small team. At this point a *programme manager* who would have day-to-day responsibility for running the programme could well be appointed. The programme manager is likely to be someone with considerable project management experience.

This group can now take the vision statement outlined in the project brief and refine and expand it. It should describe in detail the new capability that the programme will give the organization. If estimates for costs, performance, and service levels cannot be provided, then there should at least be an indication of how they might be measured. For example, the headings under which costs will be incurred can be recorded. Similarly, for performance, one might be able to say that repeat business will be increased, even if the precise size of the increase cannot be provided.

The blueprint

The achievement of the improved capability described in the vision statement can only come about when changes have been made to the structure and operations of the organization. These are detailed in the *blueprint*. This should contain:

- business models outlining the new processes required;
- organizational structure – including the numbers of staff required in the new systems and the skills they will need;
- the information systems, equipment and other, non-staff, resources that will be needed;
- data and information requirements;
- costs, performance and service level requirements.

To return to the example of the organization which wants to present a consistent interface to its customers: while this aspiration might be stated in the vision statement, the way that it is to be achieved would have to be stated in the blueprint. This might, for example, suggest:

● the appointment of 'account managers' who could act as a point of contact for the client throughout their business transactions with the company;

● a common computer interface allowing the account manager to have access to all the information relating to a particular client or job, regardless of the computer system from which it originates.

The blueprint will need to be supported by *benefit profiles* which estimate when the expected benefits will start to be realized following the implementation of the enhanced capability. One principle underpinning programme management is that the programme should deliver tangible benefits. Because an organization is given the capability to do something, this does not guarantee that the capability will be used to obtain the benefits originally envisaged. For example, as a part of the programme above, the marketing department might be provided with a database of sales and demographic information which would allow them to target potential customers more accurately. This could be used to focus sales and promotions more effectively and improve the ratio of sales revenue to advertising costs. However, just because this database is made available does not mean that the marketing staff will necessarily make effective use of it. Evidence of the business benefits actually experienced needs to be collected. However, the timing of the benefits needs to be carefully considered. For instance, marketing campaigns that target particular customers might take some time to plan and organize. It follows that the benefits in increased sales and/or lower advertising costs could take some months to become apparent.

The management structure needed to drive this programme forward would also need to be planned and organized.

A preliminary list of the projects that the programme will need in order to achieve its objective will be created as the *programme portfolio*. This will contain an outline schedule to be presented to the sponsoring group with the preliminary estimated timescales for the projects.

Programmes will affect many different groups and individuals in an organization. A major risk is that some of those whose work will be affected by the programme or whose cooperation is needed will not be drawn into the programme effectively. A *stakeholder map* identifying the groups of people with an interest in the project and its outcomes and their particular interests could be drawn up. This can be used to write a *communications strategy* and *plan* showing how the appropriate information flows between stakeholders can be set up and maintained.

We noted back in Chapter 1 that with conventional project planning, it is not usually possible to plan all the phases of a project at the outset, as much of the information needed to produce the detailed plans will not be available until later in the project. It can easily be imagined that this is even more so with programmes. However, at the initial programme planning stage, a preliminary plan can be produced containing:

● the project portfolio;

● cost estimates for each project;

- the benefits expected (including the appropriate benefits profile);
- risks identified;
- the resources needed to manage, support and monitor the programme.

The gleaning of this information also allows a *financial plan* to be created. This allows higher management to put in place the budget arrangements to meet the expected costs at the times when they are due. The points in the programme when higher management have to review progress and authorize further expenditure will need to be identified.

3.6 Aids to programme management

Dependency diagrams

There will often be physical and technical dependencies between projects. For example, a project to relocate staff from one building to another might not be able to start until a project to construct a new building has been completed. Dependency diagrams, which are very similar to activity networks at project level, can be used to show these dependencies. Where projects run concurrently in a programme and pass products between one another, the dependency diagrams could become very quite complicated.

Earlier in this chapter we described an example of a programme that resulted from the need to merge two organizations. Figure 3.3 shows a dependency diagram for this programme, the constituent parts of which are explained below.

A. *Systems study/design* A project is carried out which examines the various existing IT applications in the two old organizations, analyses their functionality, and makes recommendations about how they are to be combined.

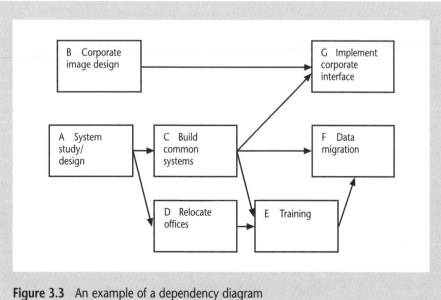

Figure 3.3 An example of a dependency diagram

B. *Corporate image design*   Independently of Project A, this project is designing the corporate image for the new organization. This would include design of the new logo to be put on company documents.

C. *Build common systems*   Once Project A has been completed, work can be triggered on the construction of the new common ICT applications.

There will be interdependencies between C and D that will need to be managed.

D. *Relocate offices*   This is the project that plans and carries out the physical collocation of the staff in the two former organizations. In this scenario, this has to wait until the completion of Project A because that project has examined how the two sets of applications for the previous organizations could be brought together, and this has repercussions on the departmental structure of the new merged organization.

E. *Training*   Once staff have been brought together, perhaps with some staff being made redundant, training in the use of the new systems can begin.

F. *Data migration*   When the new, joint, applications have been developed and staff have been trained in their use, data can be migrated from existing databases to the new consolidated database.

G. *Implement corporate interface*   Before the new applications can 'go live', the interfaces, including the documentation generated for external customers, must be modified to conform to the new company image.

Delivery planning

The creation of a delivery dependency diagram would typically be a precursor to more detailed programme planning. As part of this planning, *tranches* of projects could be defined. A tranche is a group of projects that will deliver their products as one step in the programme. The main criterion for grouping

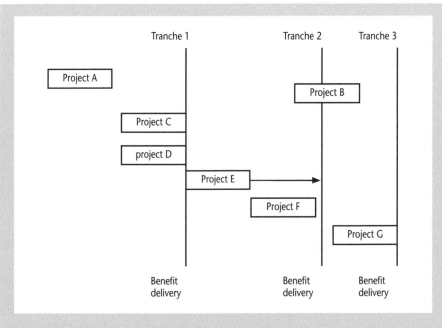

Figure 3.4   Delivering tranches of project deliverables

projects into tranches is that the deliverables of each of the projects combine to provide a coherent new capability or set of benefits for the client. An equally pressing consideration will be the need to avoid contention for scarce resources.

Figure 3.4 shows how the programme's portfolio of projects can be organized into tranches, each of which delivers some tangible benefits to the user.

At this point, the planning of individual projects can be considered. This could be initiated by the writing of *project briefs*, defining the scope and objectives of each project.

3.7 Benefits management

Thomas K. Landauer's *The Trouble with Computers: Usefulness, Usability and Productivity*, MIT Press, 1995, explores the issues of the 'productivity paradox' in IT.

We have already noted that providing an organization with a capability does not guarantee that the capability will be used to deliver the benefits originally envisaged. This is a very important point, because businesses have become aware of the lack of evidence of the some investments in ICT increasing the productivity of organizations. Even with *business process re-engineering* (BPR), the radical reorganization of businesses to deliver improvements in efficiency and effectiveness, there are many reported cases where the expected benefits have not materialized.

Benefits management is an attempt to remedy this. It encompasses the identification, optimization and tracking of the expected benefits from a business change in order to ensure that they are actually achieved.

To do this, you must:

● define the expected benefits from the programme;

● analyse the balance between costs and benefits;

● plan how the benefits will be achieved and measured;

● allocate responsibilities for the successful delivery of the benefits;

● monitor the realization of the benefits.

Benefits can be of many different types, including;

● *Mandatory compliance* Governmental or European legislation might make certain changes mandatory.

● *Quality of service* An insurance company, for example, might want to settle claims by customers more quickly.

● *Productivity* The same, or even more, work can be done at less cost in staff time.

Job enlargement and enrichment will be discussed in Chapter 11.

● *More motivated workforce* This might be because of an improved rewards system, or through job enlargement or job enrichment.

● *Internal management benefits* (for instance, better decision making) To take an insurance example, again, better analysis of insurance claims could pinpoint those categories of business which are most risky and allow an insurance company to adjust premiums to cover this.

● *Risk reduction* The insurance example might also be applicable here, but measures to protect an organization's networks and databases from intrusion and external malicious attack would be even more pertinent.

- *Economy* The reduction of costs, other than those related to staff – procurement policies might be put in place which encourage the consolidation of purchasing in order to take advantage of bulk-buying at discount.

- *Revenue enhancement/acceleration* The sooner bills reach customers, the sooner they can pay them.

- *Strategic fit* A change might not directly benefit a particular group within the organization but has to be made in order to obtain some strategic advantage for the organization as a whole.

A change could have more than one of these types of benefits. In fact, benefits are often inter-linked. An example of this is an insurance company which introduced a facility whereby when settling claims for damage to property, they directly arranged for contractors to carry out the remedial work. This improved quality of service for customers as it saved them the trouble of locating a reputable contractor, reduced costs to the insurance company because they could take advantage of the bulk purchase of services and improved staff morale because of the goodwill generated between the insurance company's front-line staff and the customer.

Quantifying benefits

Benefits can be:

- quantified and valued – that is, a direct financial benefit is experienced;
- quantified but not valued – for example, a decrease in the number of customer complaints;
- identified but not easily quantified – for example, public approval of the organization in the locality where it is based.

A particular activity might also have *disbenefits*. For example, increased sales might mean that more money has to be spent on expensive overtime working.

There can be controversy over a whether a business change will lead to the particular benefits claimed for it, for example that a new company logo will improve staff morale. Some key tests have been suggested in order to sound out whether a putative benefit is likely to be genuine:

- Can you explain in precise terms why this benefit should result from this business change?
- Can you identify the ways in which we will be able to see the consequences of this benefit?
- If the required outcomes do occur, can they be attributed directly to the change, or could other factors explain them?
- Is there any way in which the benefits can be measured?

We mentioned earlier the need for *benefit profiles* that estimate when and how benefits will be experienced. Specific staff have to be allocated responsibility for ensuring that the planned benefits actually materialize. These will often be *business change managers*.

Benefits cannot normally be monitored in a purely project environment because the project will almost certainly have been officially closed before the benefits start to filter through.

In our view, benefits management brings to the fore the powerful idea that developers and users are *jointly* responsible for ensuring the delivery of the benefits of projects.

3.8 Evaluation of individual projects

Having looked at how the benefits of a programme can be identified, we will now look more closely at how the feasibility of an individual project can be evaluated. Three major factors will need to be considered in the evaluation of potential projects: technical feasibility, the balance of costs and benefits, and finally the degree of risk associated with the project.

3.9 Technical assessment

Technical assessment of a proposed system consists of evaluating the required functionality against the hardware and software available. Organizational policy, aimed at the provision of a uniform and consistent hardware/software infrastructure, is likely to place limitations on the nature of technical solutions that might be considered. The constraints will, of course, influence the cost of the solution and this must be taken into account in the cost–benefit analysis.

3.10 Cost–benefit analysis

The most common way of carrying out an economic assessment of a proposed information system or software product, is by comparing the expected costs of development and operation of the system with the benefits of having it in place.

Assessment focuses on whether the estimated income and other benefits exceed the estimated costs. Additionally, it is usually necessary to ask whether the project under consideration is the best of a number of options. There might be more candidate projects than can be undertaken at any one time and, in any case, projects will need to be prioritized so that resources are allocated effectively.

Any project aiming at a return on investment must, as a minimum, provide a greater benefit than putting that investment in, say, a bank.

The standard way of evaluating the economic benefits of any project is cost–benefit analysis, comprising of two steps.

- *Identifying and estimating all of the costs and benefits of carrying out the project and operating the delivered application* These include the development costs, the operating costs and the benefits that are expected to accrue from the new system. Where the proposed system is replacing an existing one, these estimates should reflect the change in costs and benefits due to the new system. A new sales order processing system, for example, could not claim to benefit an organization by the total value of sales – only by the increase due to the use of the new system.

- *Expressing these costs and benefits in common units* We need to evaluate the net benefit, that is, the difference between the total benefit and the total cost of creating and operating the system. To do this, we must express each cost and each benefit in some common unit, that is, as money.

Many costs are easy to identify and measure in monetary terms.

Most direct costs are relatively easy to identify and quantify in approximate monetary terms. It is helpful to categorize costs according to where they originate in the life of the project.

- *Development costs* include the salaries and other employment costs of the staff involved in the development project and all associated costs.

- *Setup costs* include the costs of putting the system into place. These consist mainly of the costs of any new hardware and ancillary equipment but will also include costs of file conversion, recruitment and staff training.

- *Operational costs* consist of the costs of operating the system once it has been installed.

Benefits, on the other hand, are often quite difficult to quantify in monetary terms even once they have been identified. The different types of benefits have already been discussed in Section 3.7 in the context of benefits management. In cost–benefit analysis the focus has to be on the benefits that can be financially valued in some way.

Exercise 3.1   Brightmouth College are considering the replacement of the existing payroll service, operated by a third party, with a tailored, off-the-shelf computer-based system. List some of the costs they might consider under the headings of:

- Development costs

- Setup costs

- Operational costs

List some of the benefits under the headings:

- Quantified and valued benefits

- Quantified but not valued

- Identified but not easily valued

For each cost or benefit, explain how, in principle, it might be measured in monetary terms.

If a proposal shows an excess of benefits over costs then it is a candidate for further consideration. However, as we shall see later, it is not a sufficient justification for going ahead: we might not be able to afford the costs; there might be even better projects we could allocate our resources to instead; the project might be too risky.

3.11   Cash flow forecasting

As important as estimating the overall costs and benefits of a project is the forecasting of the cash flows that will take place and their timing. A cash flow forecast will indicate when expenditure and income will take place (Figure 3.5).

Figure 3.5 Typical product life cycle cash flow

Typically products generate a negative cash flow during their development followed by a positive cash flow over their operating life. There might be decommissioning costs at the end of a product's life.

We need to spend money, such as staff wages, during the development stages of a project. Such expenditure cannot be deferred until income is received (either from using the software if it is being developed for in-house use or from selling it). It is important that we know that we can fund the development expenditure either from the company's own resources or by borrowing from the bank. Thus some forecast is needed of when expenditure such as the payment of salaries and bank interest will take place and when any income is to be expected.

Accurate cash flow forecasting is not easy, as it is done early in the project's life cycle (at least before any significant expenditure is committed) and many items to be estimated (particularly the benefits of using software or decommissioning costs) might be some years in the future.

The difficulty and importance of cash flow forecasting is evidenced by the number of companies that suffer bankruptcy because, although they are developing profitable products or services, they cannot sustain an unplanned negative cash flow.

When estimating future cash flows, it is usual to ignore the effects of inflation. Forecasts of inflation rates tend to be uncertain. Moreover, if expenditure is increased due to inflation it is likely that income will increase proportionately. However, measures to deal with increases in costs where work is being done for an external customer must be in place – for example index linked prices where work involves use of raw materials.

Table 3.2 illustrates cash flow forecasts for four projects. In each case it is assumed that the cash flows take place at the end of each year. For short-term projects or where there are significant seasonal cash flow patterns, quarterly, or even monthly, cash flow forecasts could be appropriate.

3.12 Cost–benefit evaluation techniques

In the following sections we will take a brief look at some common methods for comparing projects on the basis of their cash flow forecasts.

Exercise 3.2

Consider the project cash flow estimates for four projects at IOE shown in Table 3.2. Negative values represent expenditure and positive values income.

Rank the four projects in order of financial desirability and make a note of your reasons for ranking them in that way before reading further.

Net profit

The net profit of a project is the difference between the total costs and the total income over the life of the project. Project 2 in Table 3.2 shows the greatest net

Cash flows take place at the end of each year. The year 0 figure represents the initial investment made at the start of the project.

Table 3.2 Four project cash flow projections – figures are end of year totals (£)

Year	Project 1	Project 2	Project 3	Project 4
0	−100,000	−1,000,000	−100,000	−120,000
1	10,000	200,000	30,000	30,000
2	10,000	200,000	30,000	30,000
3	10,000	200,000	30,000	30,000
4	20,000	200,000	30,000	30,000
5	100,000	300,000	30,000	75,000
Net profit	50,000	100,000	50,000	75,000

profit but this is at the expense of a large investment. Indeed, if we had £1m to invest, we might undertake all of the other three projects and obtain an even greater net profit. Note also, that all projects contain an element of risk and we might not be prepared to risk £1m. We shall look at the effects of risk and investment later in this chapter.

Moreover, the simple net profit takes no account of the timing of the cash flows. Projects 1 and 3 each have a net profit of £50,000 and therefore, according to this selection criterion, would be equally preferable. The bulk of the income occurs late in the life of project 1, whereas project 3 returns a steady income throughout its life. Having to wait for a return has the disadvantage that the investment must be funded for longer. Add to that the fact that, other things being equal, estimates in the more distant future are less reliable than short-term estimates and we can see that the two projects are not equally preferable.

Payback period

The *payback period* is the time taken to break even or pay back the initial investment. Normally, the project with the shortest payback period will be chosen on the basis that an organization will wish to minimize the time that a project is 'in debt'.

Exercise 3.3

Consider the four project cash flows given in Table 3.2 and calculate the payback period for each of them.

The advantage of the payback period is that it is simple to calculate and is not particularly sensitive to small forecasting errors. Its disadvantage as a selection technique is that it ignores the overall profitability of the project – in fact, it totally ignores any income (or expenditure) once the project has broken even. Thus the fact that projects 2 and 4 are, overall, more profitable than project 3 is ignored.

Return on investment

The *return on investment* (ROI), also known as the *accounting rate of return* (ARR), provides a way of comparing the net profitability to the investment required. There are some variations on the formula used to calculate the return on investment but a straightforward common version is:

$$ROI = \frac{average\ annual\ profit}{total\ investment} \times 100$$

Exercise 3.4

Calculating the ROI for project 1, the net profit is £50,000 and the total investment is £100,000. The return on investment is therefore calculated as

$$ROI = \frac{average\ annual\ profit}{total\ investment} \times 100$$

$$= \frac{50,000/5}{100,000} \times 100 = 10\%$$

Calculate the ROI for each of the other projects shown in Table 3.2 and decide which, on the basis of this criterion, is the most worthwhile.

The return on investment provides a simple, easy to calculate measure of return on capital. Unfortunately, it suffers from two severe disadvantages. Like the net profitability, it takes no account of the timing of the cash flows. More importantly, this rate of return bears no relationship to the interest rates offered or charged by banks (or any other normal interest rate) since it takes no account of the timing of the cash flows or of the compounding of interest. It is therefore, potentially, very misleading.

Net present value

Net present value (NPV) and internal rate of return (IRR) are collectively known as discounted cash flow (DCF) techniques.

The calculation of *net present value* is a project evaluation technique that takes into account the profitability of a project and the timing of the cash flows that are produced. This is based on the view that receiving £100 today is better than having to wait until next year to receive it, because the £100 next year is worth less than £100 now. We could, for example, invest the £100 in a bank today and have £100 plus the interest in a year's time. If we say that the *present value* of £100 in a year's time is £91, we mean that £100 in a year's time is the equivalent of £91 now.

The equivalence of £91 now and £100 in a year's time means we are discounting the future income by approximately 10% – that is, we would need an extra 10% to make it worthwhile waiting for a year. An alternative way of considering the equivalence of the two is to consider that, if we received £91 now and invested for a year at an annual interest rate of 10%, it would be worth £100 in a year's time. The annual rate by which we discount future earnings is known as the *discount rate* – 10% in the above example.

Note that this example uses approximate figures – when you have finished reading this section you should be able to calculate the exact figures yourself.

Similarly, £100 received in two years' time would have a present value of approximately £83 – in other words, £83 invested at an interest rate of 10% would yield approximately £100 in two years' time.

The present value of any future cash flow may be obtained by applying the following formula

$$Present\ value = \frac{value\ in\ year\ t}{(1+r)^t}$$

where r is the discount rate, expressed as a decimal value, and t is the number of years into the future that the cash flow occurs.

More extensive or detailed tables may be constructed using the formula

discount factor =

$$\frac{1}{(1+r)^t}$$

for various values of r (the discount rate) and t (the number of years from now).

Table 3.3 NPV discount factors

Year	Discount rate (%)					
	5	6	8	10	12	15
1	0.9524	0.9434	0.9259	0.9091	0.8929	0.8696
2	0.9070	0.8900	0.8573	0.8264	0.7972	0.7561
3	0.8638	0.8396	0.7938	0.7513	0.7118	0.6575
4	0.8227	0.7921	0.7350	0.6830	0.6355	0.5718
5	0.7835	0.7473	0.6806	0.6209	0.5674	0.4972
6	0.7462	0.7050	0.6302	0.5645	0.5066	0.4323
7	0.7107	0.6651	0.5835	0.5132	0.4523	0.3759
8	0.6768	0.6274	0.5403	0.4665	0.4039	0.3269
9	0.6446	0.5919	0.5002	0.4241	0.3606	0.2843
10	0.6139	0.5584	0.4632	0.3855	0.3220	0.2472
15	0.4810	0.4173	0.3152	0.2394	0.1827	0.1229
20	0.3769	0.3118	0.2145	0.1486	0.1037	0.0611
25	0.2953	0.2330	0.1460	0.0923	0.0588	0.0304

Alternatively, and rather more easily, the present value of a cash flow may be calculated by multiplying the cash flow by the appropriate discount factor. A small table of discount factors is given in Table 3.3.

The NPV for a project is obtained by discounting each cash flow (both negative and positive) and summing the discounted values. It is normally assumed that any initial investment takes place immediately (indicated as year 0) and is not discounted. Later cash flows are normally assumed to take place at the end of each year and are discounted by the appropriate amount.

Exercise 3.5

Assuming a 10% discount rate, the NPV for project 1 (Table 3.2) would be calculated as in Table 3.4. The net present value for project 1, using a 10% discount rate, is therefore £618. Using a 10% discount rate, calculate the net present values for projects 2, 3 and 4 and decide which, on the basis of this, is the most beneficial to pursue.

It is interesting to note that the net present values for projects 1 and 3 are significantly different – even though they both yield the same net profit and both have the same return on investment. The difference in NPV reflects the fact that, with project 1, we must wait longer for the bulk of the income.

Table 3.4 Applying the discount factors to project 1

Year	Project 1 cash flow (£)	Discount factor @ 10%	Discounted cash flow (£
0	−100,000	1.0000	−100,000
1	10,000	0.9091	9,091
2	10,000	0.8264	8,264
3	10,000	0.7513	7,513
4	20,000	0.6830	13,660
5	100,000	0.6209	62,090
Net Profit:	£50,000	NPV: £618	

Table 3.5 Three estimated project cash flows

Year	Project A (£)	Project B (£)	Project C (£)
0	− 8,000	− 8,000	−10,000
1	4,000	1,000	2,000
2	4,000	2,000	2,000
3	2,000	4,000	6,000
4	1,000	3,000	2,000
5	500	9,000	2,000
6	500	−6,000	2,000
Net Profit	4,000	5,000	6,000

The main difficulty with NPV for deciding between projects is selecting an appropriate discount rate. Some organizations have a standard rate but, where this is not the case, then the discount rate should be chosen to reflect available interest rates (borrowing costs where the project must be funded from loans) plus some premium to reflect the fact that software projects are inherently more risky than lending money to a bank. The exact discount rate is normally less important than ensuring that the same discount rate is used for all projects being compared. However, it is important to check that the ranking of projects is not sensitive to small changes in the discount rate – have a look at the following exercise.

Exercise 3.6

Calculate the net present value for each of the projects A, B and C shown in Table 3.5 using each of the discount rates 8%, 10% and 12%.

For each of the discount rates, decide which is the best project. What can you conclude from these results?

Alternatively, the discount rate can be thought of as a target rate of return. If, for example, we set a target rate of return of 15% we would reject any project that did not display a positive net present value using a 15% discount rate. Any project that displayed a positive NPV would be considered for selection – perhaps by using an additional set of criteria where candidate projects were competing for resources.

Internal rate of return

One disadvantage of NPV as a measure of profitability is that, although it may be used to compare projects, it might not be directly comparable with earnings from other investments or the costs of borrowing capital. Such costs are usually quoted as a percentage interest rate. The internal rate of return (IRR) attempts to provide a profitability measure as a percentage return that is directly comparable with interest rates. Thus, a project that showed an estimated IRR of 10% would be worthwhile if the capital could be borrowed for less than 10% or if the capital could not be invested elsewhere for a return greater than 10%.

The IRR is calculated as that percentage discount rate that would produce an NPV of zero. It is most easily calculated using a spreadsheet or other computer program that provides functions for calculating the IRR. Microsoft Excel, for example, provides IRR functions which, provided with an initial guess or seed value (which may be zero), will search for and return an IRR.

Manually, it must be calculated by trial-and-error or estimated using the technique illustrated in Figure 3.6.

The IRR may be estimated by plotting a series of guesses:
For a particular project, a discount rate of 8% gives a positive NPV of £7,898; a discount rate of 12% gives a negative NPV of −£5,829. The IRR is therefore somewhere between these two values. Plotting the two values on a chart and joining the points with a straight line suggests that the IRR is about 10.25%. The true IRR (calculated with a spreadsheet) is 10.167%.

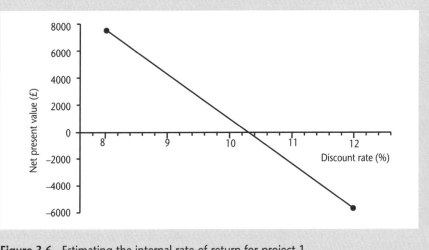

Figure 3.6   Estimating the internal rate of return for project 1

This technique consists of guessing two values (one either side of the true value) and using the resulting NPVs (one of which must be positive and the other negative) to estimate the correct value. Note that this technique will provide only an approximate value, but in many cases that can be sufficient to dismiss a project that has a small IRR or indicate that it is worth making a more precise evaluation.

The internal rate of return is a convenient and useful measure of the value of a project in that it is a single percentage figure that may be directly compared with rates of return on other projects or interest rates quoted elsewhere.

Table 3.6 illustrates the way in which a project with an IRR of 10% may be directly compared with other interest rates. The cash flow for the project is shown in column (a). Columns (b) to (e) show that if we were to invest £100,000 now at an annual interest rate of 10% in, say, a bank, we could withdraw the same amounts as we would earn from the project at the end of each year, column (e), and we would be left with a net balance of zero at the end. In other words, investing in a project that has an IRR of 10% can produce exactly the same cash flow as lending the money to a bank at a 10% interest rate. We can therefore reason that a project with an IRR greater than current interest rates will provide a

Table 3.6 A project cash flow treated as an investment at 10%

Year	(a) Project cash flow forecast (£)	(b) Capital at start of year (£)	(c) Interest during year (£)	(d) Capital at end of year (£)	(e) End of year withdrawal (£)
		Equivalent investment at 10%			
0	−100,000	—	—	—	—
1	10,000	100,000	10,000	110,000	10,000
2	10,000	100,000	10,000	110,000	10,000
3	10,000	100,000	10,000	110,000	10,000
4	20,000	100,000	10,000	110,000	20,000
5	99,000	90,000	9,000	99,000	99,000
6		0	0	0	0

£100,000 invested at 10% may be used to generate the cash flows shown. At the end of the 5-year period the capital and the interest payments will be entirely consumed leaving a net balance of zero.

better rate of return than lending the investment to a bank. We can also say that it will be worth borrowing to finance the project if it has an IRR greater than the interest rate charged on the loan.

One deficiency of the IRR is that it does not indicate the absolute size of the return. A project with an NPV of £100,000 and an IRR of 15% can be more attractive than one with an NPV of £10,000 and an IRR of 18% – the return on capital is lower but the net benefits greater.

An often quoted objection to the internal rate of return is that, under certain conditions, it is possible to find more than one rate that will produce a zero NPV. This is not a valid objection since, if there are multiple solutions, it is always appropriate to take the lowest value and ignore the others. Spreadsheets will normally always return the lowest value if provided with zero as a seed value.

NPV and IRR are not, however, a complete answer to economic project evaluation.

- A total evaluation must also take into account the problems of funding the cash flows – will we, for example, be able to repay the interest on any borrowed money and pay development staff salaries at the appropriate time?

- While a project's IRR might indicate a profitable project, future earnings from a project might be far less reliable than earnings from, say, investing with a bank. To take account of the risk inherent in investing in a project, we might require that a project earn a 'risk premium' (that is, it must earn, say, at least 15% more than current interest rates) or we might undertake a more detailed risk analysis as described in the following sections of this chapter.

- We must also consider any one project within the financial and economic framework of the organization as a whole – if we fund this one, will we also be able to fund other worthy projects?

3.13 Risk evaluation

Every project involves risk of some form. When assessing and planning a project, we are concerned with the risk that the project might not meet its objectives. In Chapter 7 we shall discuss ways of analysing and minimizing risk during the development of a software system. In this chapter, we are concerned with taking risk into account when deciding whether to proceed with a proposed project.

Risk identification and ranking

In any project evaluation we should attempt to identify the risks and quantify their potential effects. One common approach to risk analysis is to construct a project risk matrix utilizing a checklist of possible risks and to classify each risk according to its relative importance and likelihood. Note that the importance and likelihood need to be separately assessed – we might be less concerned with something that, although serious, is very unlikely to occur than with something less serious that is almost certain. Table 3.7 illustrates a basic project risk matrix listing some of the risks that might be considered for a project, with their importance and likelihood classified as high (H), medium (M), low (L) or exceedingly unlikely (—). So that projects may be compared the list of risks must be the same for each

Table 3.7 A fragment of a basic project risk matrix

Risk	Importance	Likelihood
Software never completed or delivered	H	—
Project cancelled after design stage	H	—
Software delivered late	M	M
Development budget exceeded $\leq$ 20%	L	M
Development budget exceeded > 20%	M	L
Maintenance costs higher than estimated	L	L
Response time targets not met	L	H

project being assessed. It is likely, in reality, that it would be somewhat longer than shown and more precisely defined.

The project risk matrix may be used as a way of evaluating projects (those with high risks being less favoured) or as a means of identifying and ranking the risks for a specific project. In Chapter 7 we shall consider a method for scoring the importance and likelihood of risks that may be used in conjunction with the project risk matrix to score and rank projects.

Risk and net present value

Where a project is relatively risky it is common practice to use a higher discount rate to calculate net present value. This risk premium, might, for example, be an additional 2% for a reasonably safe project or 5% for a fairly risky one. Projects may be categorized as high, medium or low risk using a scoring method and risk premiums designated for each category. The premiums, even if arbitrary, provide a consistent method of taking risk into account.

Cost–benefit analysis

A rather more sophisticated approach to the evaluation of risk is to consider each possible outcome and estimate the probability of its occurring and the corresponding value of the outcome. Rather than a single cash flow forecast for a project, we will then have a set of cash flow forecasts, each with an associated probability of occurring. The value of the project is then obtained by summing the cost or benefit for each possible outcome weighted by its corresponding probability. Exercise 3.7 illustrates how this may be done.

Exercise 3.7

BuyRight, a software house, is considering developing a payroll application for use in academic institutions and is currently engaged in a cost–benefit analysis. Study of the market has shown that, if they can target it efficiently and no competing products become available, they will obtain a high level of sales generating an annual income of £800,000. They estimate that there is a 1 in 10 chance of this happening. However, a competitor might launch a competing application before their own launch date and then sales might generate only £100,000 per year. They estimate that there is a 30% chance of this happening. The most likely outcome, they believe, is somewhere in between these two extremes – they will gain a market lead by launching before any competing product becomes available and achieve an annual income of £650,000. BuyRight have therefore calculated their expected sales income as in Table 3.8.

Table 3.8 BuyRight's income forecasts

Sales	Annual sales income (£)	Probability	Expected value (£)
	i	p	i × p
High	800,000	0.1	80,000
Medium	650,000	0.6	390,000
Low	100,000	0.3	30,000
Expected Income			500,000

Total development costs are estimated at £750,000 and sales are expected to be maintained at a reasonably constant level for at least four years. Annual costs of marketing and product maintenance are estimated at £200,000, irrespective of the market share gained. Would you advise them to go ahead with the project?

This approach is frequently used in the evaluation of large projects such as the building of new motorways, where variables such as future traffic volumes, and hence the total benefit of shorter journey times, are subject to uncertainty. The technique does, of course, rely on our being able to assign probabilities of occurrence to each scenario and, without extensive study, this can be difficult.

When used to evaluate a single major project, the cost–benefit approach, by 'averaging out' the negative and positive outcomes of the different scenarios, does not take account of the full force of damaging outcomes. Because of this, where overall profitability is the primary concern, it is often more appropriate for the evaluation of a portfolio of projects where more successful projects can offset the impact of less successful ones.

Risk profile analysis

An approach which attempts to overcome some of the objections to cost–benefit averaging is the construction of risk profiles using sensitivity analysis.

This involves varying each of the parameters that affect the project's cost or benefits to ascertain how sensitive the project's profitability is to each factor. We might, for example, vary one of our original estimates by plus or minus 5% and recalculate the expected costs and benefits for the project. By repeating this exercise for each of our estimates in turn we can evaluate the sensitivity of the project to each factor.

By studying the results of a sensitivity analysis we can identify those factors that are most important to the success of the project. We then need to decide whether we can exercise greater control over them or otherwise mitigate their effects. If neither is the case, then we must live with the risk or abandon the project.

For an explanation of the Monte Carlo technique see any textbook on operational research.

Sensitivity analysis demands that we vary each factor one at a time. It does not easily allow us to consider the effects of combinations of circumstances, neither does it evaluate the chances of a particular outcome occurring. In order to do this we need to use a more sophisticated tool such as Monte Carlo simulation. There are a number of risk analysis applications available (such as *@Risk* from Palisade) that use Monte Carlo simulation and produce risk profiles of the type shown in Figure 3.7.

All three projects have the same expected profitability. The profitability of project A is unlikely to depart greatly from its expected value (indicated by the vertical axis) compared to the likely variations for project B. Project A is therefore less risky than project B.

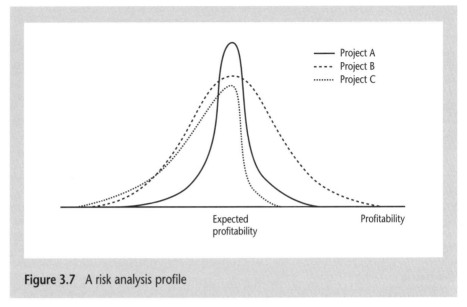

Figure 3.7 A risk analysis profile

Projects may be compared as in Figure 3.7, which compares three projects with the same expected profitability. Project A is unlikely to depart far from this expected value compared to project B, which exhibits a larger variance. Both of these have symmetric profiles, which contrast with project C. Project C has a skewed distribution, which indicates that although it is unlikely ever to be much more profitable than expected, it is quite likely to be far worse.

Using decision trees

The approaches to risk analysis discussed previously rather assume that we are passive bystanders allowing nature to take its own course – the best we can do is to reject over-risky projects or choose those with the best risk profile. There are many situations, however, where we can evaluate whether a risk is important and, if it is, indicate a suitable course of action.

Such decisions will limit or affect future options and, at any point, it is important to be able to assess how a decision will affect the future profitability of the project.

Prior to giving Amanda the job of extending their invoicing system, IOE must consider the alternative of completely replacing the existing system – which they will have to do at some point in the future. The decision largely rests upon the rate at which their equipment maintenance business expands – if their market share significantly increases (which they believe will happen if rumours of a competitor's imminent bankruptcy are fulfilled) the existing system might need to be replaced within two years. Not replacing the system in time could be an expensive option as it could lead to lost revenue if they cannot cope with the increase in invoicing demand. Replacing it immediately will, however, be expensive as it will mean deferring other projects that have already been scheduled.

They have calculated that extending the existing system will have an NPV of £75,000, although if the market expands significantly, this will be turned into a loss with an NPV of −£100,000 due to lost revenue. If the market does expand, replacing the system now has an NPV of £250,000 due to the benefits of being able

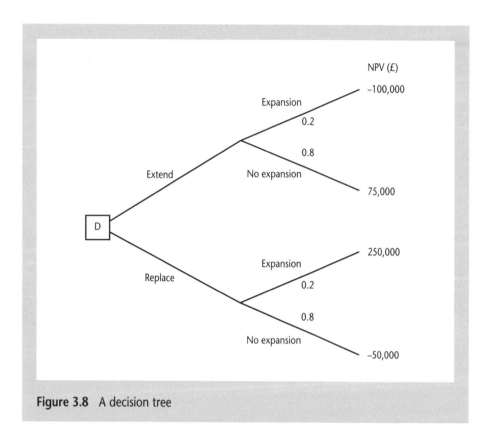

Figure 3.8 A decision tree

to handle increased sales and other benefits such as improved management information. If sales do not increase, however, the benefits will be severely reduced and
the project will suffer a loss with an NPV of −£50,000.

The company estimate the likelihood of the market increasing significantly at
20% – and, hence, the probability that it will not increase as 80%. This scenario
can be represented as a tree structure as shown in Figure 3.8.

The analysis of a decision tree consists of evaluating the expected benefit of
taking each path from a decision point (denoted by D in Figure 3.8). The expected
value of each path is the sum of the value of each possible outcome multiplied by
its probability of occurrence. The expected value of extending the system is therefore £40,000 (75,000 × 0.8 − 100,000 × 0.2) and the expected value of replacing
the system £10,000 (250,000 × 0.2 − 50,000 × 0.8). IOE should therefore choose
the option of extending the existing system.

This example illustrates the use of a decision tree to evaluate a simple decision
at the start of a project. One of the great advantages of using decision trees to
model and analyse problems is the ease with which they can be extended. Figure
3.9 illustrates an extended version of Amanda's decision tree, which includes the
possibility of a later decision should they decide to extend the system and then
find there is an early market expansion.

The net present values shown in italic are those identified in Amanda's original decision tree shown in Figure 3.8.

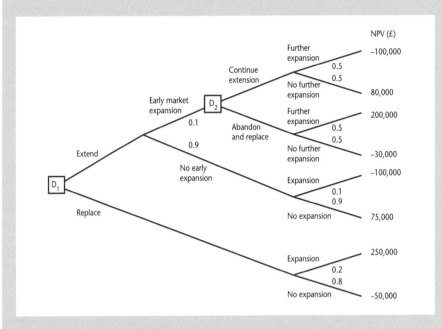

Figure 3.9 An extension to Amanda's decision tree

3.14 Conclusion

Some of the key points in this chapter are:

- projects must be evaluated on strategic, technical and economic grounds;

- many projects are not justifiable on their own, but are as part of a broader pro-gramme of projects that implement an organization's strategy;

- not all benefits can be precisely quantified in financial values;

- economic assessment involves the identification of all costs and income over the lifetime of the system, including its development and operation and checking that the total value of benefits exceeds total expenditure;

- money received in the future is worth less than the same amount of money in hand now, which may be invested to earn interest;

- the uncertainty surrounding estimates of future returns lowers their real value measured now;

- discounted cash flow techniques may be used to evaluate the present value of future cash flows taking account of interest rates and uncertainty;

- cost–benefit analysis techniques and decision trees provide tools for evaluating expected outcomes and choosing between alternative strategies.

3.15   Further exercises

1. Identify the major risks that could affect the success of the Brightmouth College payroll project and try to rank them in order of importance.

2. Working in a group of three or four, imagine that you are about to embark upon a programming assignment as part of the assessed work for your course. Draw up a list of the risks that might affect the assignment outcome. Individually classify the importance and likelihood of each of those risks as high, medium or low. When you have done this, compare your results and try to come up with an agreed project risk matrix.

3. Explain why discounted cash flow techniques provide better criteria for project selection than net profit or return on investment.

4. Consider the decision tree shown in Figure 3.9 and decide, given the additional possibilities, which option(s) IOE should choose.

CHAPTER 4

Selection of an appropriate project approach

Objectives

When you have completed this chapter you will be able to:

- take account of the characteristics of the system to be developed when planning a project;
- select an appropriate process model;
- make best use of the 'waterfall' process model where appropriate;
- reduce some risks by the creation of appropriate prototypes;
- reduce other risks by implementing of the project in increments;
- identify where unnecessary organizational obstacles can be removed by using 'agile' development methods.

4.1 Introduction

The development of software in-house usually means that:

- the developers and the users belong to the same organization;
- the application will slot into a portfolio of existing computer-based systems;
- the methodologies and technologies are largely dictated by organizational standards.

See Martyn Ould's *Managing Software Quality and Business Risk*, Wiley & Sons, 1999.

However, where successive development projects are carried out by a software supplier for a variety of external customers, the methodologies and technologies to be used need to be reviewed for each individual project. This decision-making process has been called 'technical planning' by some, although here we use the term 'project analysis'. Even where development is in-house, any characteristics of the new project requiring a different approach from previous projects need to be considered. It is this analysis that is the subject of this chapter.

The relevant part of the Step Wise approach is Step 3: *Analyse project characteristics*. The selection of a particular process model could add new products to the Project Breakdown Structure or new activities to the Activity Network. This will generate inputs for Step 4: Identify the products and activities of the project (see Figure 4.1).

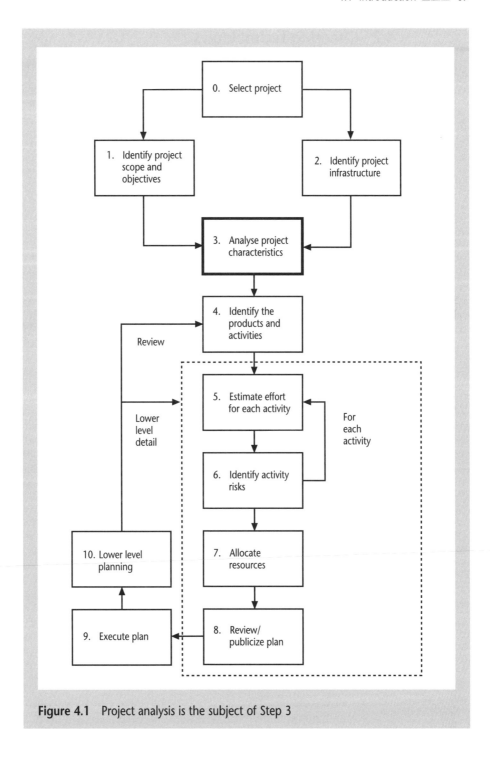

Figure 4.1   Project analysis is the subject of Step 3

In the remainder of this chapter we will look at how the characteristics of a project's environment and the application to be delivered influence the shape of the plan of a project. We will then look at some of the most common *process models*, namely the waterfall approach, prototyping and incremental delivery.

4.2 Choosing technologies

An outcome of project analysis will be the selection of the most appropriate methodologies and technologies. Methodologies include approaches like Unified Software Development Process (USDP), Structured Systems Analysis and Design Method (SSADM) and Human-Centred Design, while technologies might include appropriate application-building and automated testing environments.

As well as the products and activities, the chosen technology will affect:

- the training requirements for development staff;
- the types of staff to be recruited;
- the development environment – both hardware and software;
- system maintenance arrangements.

We are now going to describe some of the steps of project analysis.

Identify project as either objectives-driven or product-driven

In Chapter 1 we distinguished between *objectives-driven* and *product-driven* projects. Recall that with a product-driven project, the product to be created is defined before the start of the project. Often this type of project will have been preceded by an objectives-driven project which will have defined the general software solution that is to be implemented.

The project manager's ideal situation is to have well-defined objectives but as much freedom as possible about the way those objectives are to be satisfied. For example, the objective might be to pay staff in a start-up company reliably, accurately and with low administrative costs. Use of a particular packaged software solution does not have to be specified at the outset – but as we will see, there can be exceptions to this.

Sometimes the objectives of the project are uncertain or are the subject of disagreement. People might be experiencing problems but no one knows exactly how to solve these problems. ICT specialists might provide help with some problems but assistance from other specialisms might be needed with others. In these kinds of situation a *soft systems* approach might be considered.

> The soft systems approach is described in Checkland, P., and Scholes, J., *Soft Systems Methodology in Action*, John Wiley and Sons, 1999.

> We first introduced the difference between information systems and embedded systems in Chapter 1.

> Note that here we are talking about writing the software tool, not its use.

Analyse other project characteristics

The following questions can be usefully asked.

- *Is a data-oriented or process-oriented system to be implemented? Data-orientated* systems generally mean information systems that will have a substantial database. *Process-oriented* systems refer to embedded control systems. It is not uncommon to have systems with elements of both. Some writers suggest that the OO approach is more suitable for process-oriented systems where control is important than for systems dominated by a relational database.

- *Will the software that is to be produced be a general tool or application specific?* An example of a general tool would be a spreadsheet or a word processing package. An application-specific package could be, for example, an airline seat reservation system.

- *Are there specific tools available for implementing the particular type of application?* For example:

  - *does it involve concurrent processing?* – the use of techniques appropriate to the analysis and design of such systems would be considered;

  - *will the system to be created be knowledge-based?* – expert systems have rules which result in some 'expert advice' when applied to a problem, and specific methods and tools exist for developing such systems; or

  - *will the system to be produced make heavy use of computer graphics?*

- *Is the system to be created safety critical?* For instance, could a malfunction in the system endanger human life? If so, among other things, testing would become very important.

- *Is the system designed primarily to carry out predefined services or to be engaging and entertaining?* With software designed for entertainment, design and evaluation will need to be carried out differently from more conventional software products.

- *What is the nature of the hardware/software environment in which the system will operate?* The environment in which the final software will operate could be different from that in which it is to be developed. Embedded software might be developed on a large development machine which has lots of supporting software tools such as compilers, debuggers and static analysers, but then be downloaded to a small processor in the target configuration. A standalone desktop application needs a different approach to one for a mainframe or a client–server environment.

Exercise 4.1   How would you categorize each of the following systems according to the classification above?

(a) a payroll system;

(b) a system to control a bottling plant;

(c) a system which holds details of the plans of plant used by a water company to supply water to consumers;

(d) a software package to support project managers;

(e) a system used by lawyers to access case law relating to company taxation.

Identify high-level project risks

Chapter 3 has already touched on some aspects of risk which are developed further in Chapter 7.

At the beginning of a project, some managers might expect elaborate plans even though we are ignorant of many important factors affecting the project. For example, until we have analysed the users' requirements in detail we cannot estimate the effort needed to build a system to meet those requirements. The greater the uncertainties at the beginning, the greater the risk that the project will be unsuccessful. Once we recognize an area of uncertainty we can, however, take steps to reduce its uncertainty.

One suggestion is that uncertainty can be associated with the *products, processes,* or *resources* of a project.

- *Product uncertainty*   How well the requirements are understood? The users themselves could be uncertain about what a proposed information system is to do. The government, say, might introduce a new form of taxation but its detailed operation might not be known until case law has been built up. Some environments change so quickly that a seemingly precise and valid statement of requirements rapidly becomes out of date.

Extreme programming will be discussed in Section 4.13.

- *Process uncertainty* The project under consideration might be the first where an organization is using an approach like extreme programming (XP) or a new application-building tool. Any change in the way that the systems are developed introduces uncertainty.

- *Resource uncertainty* The main area of uncertainty here is likely to be the availability of staff of the right ability and experience. The larger the number of resources needed or the longer the duration of the project, the more inherently risky it will be.

Of course, some risk factors can increase both uncertainty and complexity.

Some factors – such as continually changing requirements – increase *uncertainty*, while others – for instance, software size – increase *complexity*. Different strategies are needed to deal with the two distinct types of risks.

Exercise 4.2

At IOE, Amanda has identified possible user resistance as a risk to the maintenance group accounts project. Would you classify this as a product, process or resource risk? It may be that it does not fit into any of these categories and some other is needed.

Brigette at Brightmouth College identified as a risk the possibility that no suitable payroll package would be available on the market. What other risks might be inherent in the Brightmouth College payroll project?

Take into account user requirements concerning implementation

We suggested earlier that staff planning a project should try to ensure that unnecessary constraints are not imposed on the way that a project's objectives are to be met. The example given was the specification of the exact payroll package to be deployed. Sometimes, such constraints are unavoidable, however. It might be that a company is a subsidiary of some larger group and the same package has to be used throughout the group to ensure compatibility.

Chapter 12 on software quality discusses BS EN ISO 9001.

A client organization often lays down standards that have to be adopted by any contractor providing software for them. Sometimes organizations specify that suppliers of software have BS EN ISO 9001:2000 or TickIT accreditation. This will affect the way projects are conducted.

Select general life-cycle approach

- *Control systems* A real-time system will need to be implemented using an appropriate methodology. Real-time systems that employ concurrent processing may have to use techniques such as Petri nets.

- *Information systems* Similarly, an information system will need a methodology, such as SSADM or Information Engineering, that matches that type of environment. SSADM would be especially appropriate where the project employs a large number of development staff whose work will need to be coordinated: the method lays down in detail the activities and products needed at each step. Team members would therefore know exactly what is expected.

- *General tools* Where the software is for the general market rather than application and user specific, then a methodology such as SSADM would have to be thought about with caution. The framers of this method make the assumption that identified users exist. Some parts in the method also assume an existing clerical system which can be analysed to yield the logical features of a new, computer-based, system.

- *Specialized techniques* For example, expert system shells and logic-based programming languages have been invented to expedite the development of *knowledge-based systems*. Similarly, a number of specialized techniques and standard components are available to assist in the development of *graphics-based systems*.

- *Hardware environment* The environment in which the system is to operate could put constraints on the way it is to be implemented. The need for a fast response time or restricted computer memory might mean that only low-level programming languages can be used.

- *Safety-critical systems* Where safety and reliability are essential, this might justify the additional expense of a formal specification using a notation such as Z or VDM. Extremely critical systems could justify the cost of having independent teams develop parallel systems with the same functionality. The operational systems can then run concurrently with continuous cross-checking. This is known as *n-version programming*.

- *Imprecise requirements* Uncertainties or a *novel hardware/software platform* mean that a prototyping approach should be considered. If the environment in which the system is to be implemented is a rapidly changing one, then serious consideration would need to be given to *incremental delivery*. If the users have *uncertain objectives* in connection with the project, then a *soft systems* approach might be desirable.

The implications of prototyping and the incremental approach are explored later in the chapter.

Exercise 4.3 What, in broad outline, would be the most suitable approach for each of the following?

(a) a system which calculates the amount of a drug that should be administered to a patient who has a particular complaint;

(b) a system to administer a student loans scheme;

(c) a system to control trains in the Channel Tunnel.

4.3 Technical plan contents list

Project analysis will produce practical requirements to be fed into the next stage of the planning process. These requirements might require additional project activities, the acquisition of items of software or hardware, or special staff training. As these would incur certain costs, they should be recorded formally.

A software supplier might produce a preliminary technical plan to help prepare a bid for a contract. Sometimes, the plan might actually be shown to the potential customer in order to explain the basis for the bid price and to impress the customer with the soundness of the intended approach.

The technical plan is likely to have the following contents.

1. *Introduction and summary of constraints:*

(a) character of the system to be developed;

(b) risks and uncertainties of the project;

(c) user requirements concerning implementation.

2. *Recommended approach:*

(a) selected methodology or process model;

(b) development methods;

(c) required software tools;

(d) target hardware/software environment.

3. *Development needs:*

(a) required development environment;

(b) required maintenance environment;

(c) required training.

4. *Implications:*

(a) project products and activities – this will have an effect on the schedule and staff-time;

(b) financial – this report will be used to produce costings.

The content of such a report could be incorporated into a general planning document which has the general format outlined in Annex 2 of Chapter 1. The *Recommended approach* could be absorbed into the *Methods* section of the project plan. *Development details* would be incorporated into the *Resources* section of the plan.

One outcome of project analysis could be the abandonment of the project if the costs of its implementation were now seen to exceed the expected benefits.

4.4   Choice of process models

The word 'process' is used to emphasize the idea of a system *in action*. In order to achieve an outcome, the system will have to execute one or more activities: this is its process. This idea can be applied to the development of computer-based systems where a number of interrelated activities have to be undertaken to create a final product. These activities can be organized in different ways and we can call these *process models*.

A major part of the planning will be choosing development methods and slotting them into an overall process model.

The planner needs to select methods and also specify how they are to be applied. With methods such as USDP or SSADM, there is a considerable degree of choice: not all parts of the method will be compulsory. Many student projects have the rather basic failing that at the planning stage they claim that, say, SSADM is to be used: in the event all that is produced are a few SSADM fragments such as a top-level data flow diagram and a preliminary logical data structure diagram. If this is all the particular project requires, it should be explicitly stated.

4.5   Structure versus speed of delivery

The principle behind structured methods is 'get it right first time'.

Although some 'object-oriented' specialists might object(!), we include the OO approach as a structured method – after all, we hope it is not unstructured. Structured methods are made up of sets of steps and rules which, when applied, generate system products such as use case diagrams. Each of these products is carefully documented. Such methods are often more time consuming than more intuitive approaches and this incurs additional cost. The pay-off, it is hoped, is a less error prone and more maintainable final system. This balance of costs and benefits is more likely to be justified on a large project involving many developers and users. This is not to say that smaller projects cannot justify the use of such methods.

It might be thought that users would generally welcome the more professional approach that structured methods imply. However, customers for software are concerned with getting working applications delivered quickly and at less cost and often see structured methods as unnecessarily bureaucratic and slow. One response to this has been *rapid application development* (RAD) which puts the emphasis on quickly producing prototypes of the software for users to evaluate.

Joint Application Development by Jane Wood and Denise Silver, Wiley and Sons, 1995, is a useful introduction to JAD.

The RAD approach does not preclude the use of some elements of structured methods such as the drafting of logical data structure diagrams but also adopts tactics such as *joint application development* (JAD) workshops. In these workshops, developers and users work together intensively for, say, three to five days and identify and agree fully documented system requirements. Often these workshops are conducted away from the normal business and development environments in *clean rooms*, special conference rooms free from outside interruption and suitably furnished with whiteboards and other aids to communication. Advocates of JAD believe these hot-house conditions can speed up communication and negotiation that might otherwise take several weeks or months.

Just because a project uses JAD does not mean that it is not structured. The definition of the scope of the project, the initial research involving the interviewing of key personnel and the creation of preliminary data and process models would need to planned and executed before the JAD sessions were organized. The results of JAD sessions could be implemented using quite conventional methods.

Another way of speeding up delivery is simply to deliver less. This can be done by breaking a large development into a series of small increments, each of which delivers a small amount of useful functionality quickly.

Two competing pressures can be seen. One is to get the job done as quickly and cheaply as possible, and the other is to make sure that the final product has a robust structure which will be able to meet evolving needs. We will return to some of these ideas in our later discussions on prototyping, the incremental approach and extreme programming.

4.6 The waterfall model

The first description of this approach is said to be that of H. D. Bennington in 'Production of Large Computer Programs' in 1956. This was reprinted in 1983 in *Annals of the History of Computing* 5(4).

This is the 'classical' model of system development that is also known as the *one-shot* or *once-through* model. As can be seen from the example in Figure 4.2, there is a sequence of activities working from top to bottom. The diagram shows some arrows pointing upwards and backwards. This indicates that a later stage may reveal the need for some extra work at an earlier stage, but this should definitely be the exception rather than the rule. After all, the flow of a waterfall should be downwards, with the possibility of just a little splashing back. The limited scope for iteration is in fact one of the strengths of this process model. With a large project you want to avoid reworking tasks previously thought to be completed. Having to reopen completed activities plays havoc with promised completion dates.

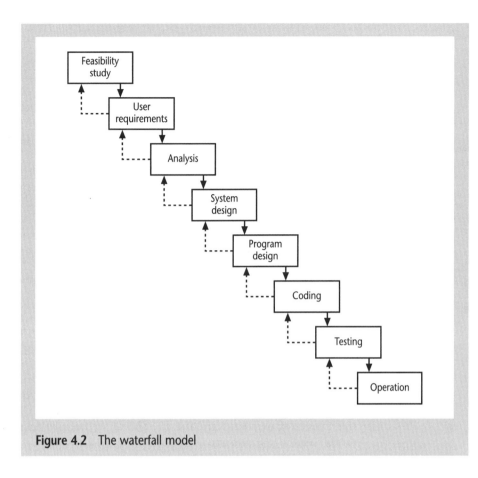

Figure 4.2 The waterfall model

Even though writers often advocate alternative models, there is nothing intrinsically wrong with the waterfall approach in the right place. It is the ideal for which the project manager strives. Where the requirements are well defined and the development methods are well understood, the waterfall approach allows project completion times to be forecast with some confidence, allowing the effective control of the project. However, where there is uncertainty about how a system is to be implemented, and unfortunately there very often is, a more flexible, iterative, approach might be required.

4.7 The V-process model

Figure 4.3 gives a diagrammatic representation of this model. This is an elaboration of the waterfall model and stresses the necessity for validation activities that match the activities that create the products of the project.

The V-process model can be seen as expanding the activity *testing* in the waterfall model. Each step has a matching validation process which can, where defects are found, cause a loop back to the corresponding development stage and a reworking of the following steps. Ideally this feeding back should only occur where a discrepancy has been found between what was specified by a particular activity and what was actually implemented in the next lower activity on the

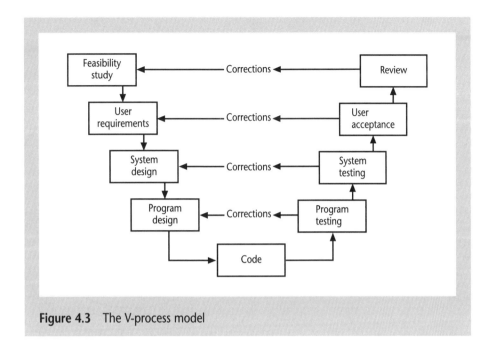

Figure 4.3 The V-process model

descent of the V loop. For example, the system designer might have written that a calculation be carried out in a certain way. A developer building code to meet this design might have misunderstood what was required. At system testing stage, the original designer would be responsible for checking that the software is doing what was specified and this would discover the coder's misreading of that document. Only corrections should be fed back, not any second thoughts of the system designer, otherwise the project would slip into 'evolutionary prototyping'.

Exercise 4.4 Figure 4.3 shows the V-process model. The review that is held after the system has been implemented is shown as possibly feeding corrections back to the feasibility study which may have been conducted months or years before. How would this work in practice?

4.8 The spiral model

The original ideas behind the spiral model can be found in B. W. Boehm's 1988 paper 'A spiral model of software development and enhancement' in *IEEE Computer* 21(5).

It could be argued that this is another way of looking at the waterfall model. In the waterfall model, it is possible to escape at the end of any activity in the sequence. A feasibility study might decide that the implementation of a proposed system would be beneficial. The management therefore authorize work on the detailed analysis of user requirements. Some analysis, for instance the interviewing of users, might already have taken place at the feasibility stage, but a more thorough investigation is now launched. This could reveal that the costs of implementing the system would be higher than projected benefits and lead to a decision to abandon the project.

A greater level of detail is considered at each stage of the project and a greater degree of confidence about the probability of success for the project should be justified. This can be portrayed as a loop or a spiral where the system to be

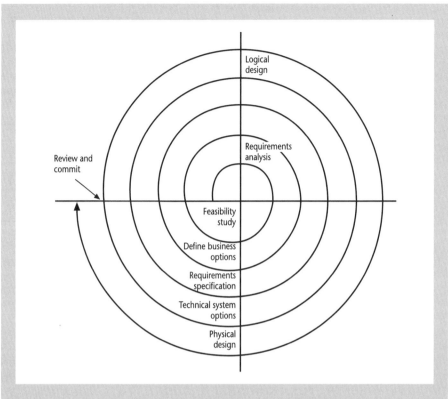

Figure 4.4 The application of the spiral model to SSADM version 4

implemented is considered in more detail in each sweep. Each sweep terminates with an evaluation before the next iteration is embarked upon. Figure 4.4 illustrates how SSADM can be interpreted in such a way.

4.9 Software prototyping

A prototype is a working model of one or more aspects of the projected system. It is constructed and tested quickly and inexpensively in order to test out assumptions.

Prototypes can be classified as throw-away or evolutionary.

● *Throw-away prototypes*   The prototype is used to test out some ideas and is then discarded when the true development of the operational system is commenced. The prototype could be developed using a different software or hardware environment. For example, a desktop application builder could be used to evolve an acceptable user interface. A procedural programming language could then be used for the final system where machine-efficiency was important.

● *Evolutionary prototypes*   The prototype is developed and modified until it is finally in a state where it can become the operational system. In this case the standards that are used to develop the software have to be carefully considered.

Some of the reasons that have been put forward for prototyping follow.

- *Learning by doing*   When we have just done something we can usually look back and see where we have made mistakes.

- *Improved communication*   Even if users read system specifications, they do not get a feel for how the system is likely to work in practice.

- *Improved user involvement*   The users can be more actively involved in design decisions about the new system.

- *Clarification of partially known requirements*   Where there is no existing system to mimic, users can often get a better idea of what might be useful to them by trying out prototypes.

The most important justification for a prototype is the need to reduce uncertainty by conducting an experiment.

- *Demonstration of the consistency and completeness of a specification*   Any mechanism that attempts to implement a specification on a computer is likely to uncover ambiguities and omissions. The humble spreadsheet can, for instance, check that calculations have been specified correctly.

- *Reduced need for documentation*   Because a working prototype can be examined there is less need for detailed documentation of requirements.

Some may argue, however, that this is a very dangerous suggestion.

- *Reduced maintenance costs*   If the user is unable to suggest modifications at the prototyping stage they are more likely to ask for changes to the operational system. This reduction of maintenance costs is the core of the financial case for prototypes.

- *Feature constraint*   If an application-building tool is used, then the prototype will tend to have features that are easily implemented by that tool. A paper-based design might suggest features that are expensive to implement.

- *Production of expected results*   The problem with creating test cases is generally not the creation of the test input but the accurate calculation of the expected results. A prototype can help here.

Software prototyping is not without its drawbacks and dangers, however.

- *Users can misunderstand the role of the prototype*   For example, they might expect the prototype to have as stringent input validation or as fast a response as the operational system, although this was not intended.

- *Lack of project standards possible*   Evolutionary prototyping could just be an excuse for a sloppy 'hack it out and see what happens' approach.

- *Lack of control*   It can be difficult to control the prototyping cycle if the driving force is the users' propensity to try out new things.

- *Additional expense*   Building and exercising a prototype will incur additional expenses. However, this should not be over-estimated as many analysis and design tasks have to be undertaken whatever the approach.

- *Machine efficiency*   A system built through prototyping, while sensitive to the users' needs, might not be as efficient in machine terms as one developed using more conventional methods.

- *Close proximity of developers*   Prototyping could mean that code developers have to be sited close to the users. One trend is for organizations in developed countries to transfer software development to developing countries with lower costs such as India. Prototyping might prevent this.

4.10   Other ways of categorizing prototypes

What is being learnt?

The most important reason for prototyping is a need to learn about an area of uncertainty. Thus it is essential to identify at the outset what is to be learnt from the prototype.

Computing students often realize that the software that they are to write as part of their final-year project could not safely be used by real users. They therefore call the software a 'prototype'. However, if it is a real prototype then they must:

- specify what they hope to learn from the prototype;
- plan how the prototype is to be evaluated;
- report on what has actually been learnt.

Prototypes can be used to find about new development techniques, by using them in a pilot project. Alternatively, the development methods might be well known, but the nature of the application uncertain.

Different projects will have uncertainties at different stages. Prototypes can therefore be used at different stages. A prototype might be used, for instance, at the requirements gathering stage to pin down requirements that seem blurred and shifting. A prototype might, on the other hand, be used at the design stage to test out the users' ability to navigate through a sequence of input screens.

To what extent is the prototyping to be done?

It would be unusual for the whole of the application to be prototyped. The prototyping usually simulates only some aspects of the target application. For example there might be:

- *Mock-ups*   As when copies of input screens are shown to the users on a terminal, but the screens cannot actually be used.
- *Simulated interaction*   For example, the user can type in a request to access a record and the system will show the details of a record, but the details shown are always the same and no access is made to a database.
- Partial working model:
  - *Vertical*   Some, but not all, features are prototyped fully.
  - *Horizontal*   All features are prototyped but not in detail – perhaps there is not full validation of input.

What is being prototyped?

- *The human–computer interface*   With business applications, processing requirements have usually been established at an early stage. Prototyping tends, therefore, to be confined to the nature of operator interaction. Here the physical vehicle for the prototype should be as similar as possible to the operational system.
- *The functionality of the system*   Here the precise way the system should function internally is not known. For example, a computer model of some real-world

phenomenon is being developed. The algorithms used might need to be repeatedly adjusted until they satisfactorily imitate real-world behaviour.

Exercise 4.5 At what stage of a system development project (for example, feasibility study, requirements analysis etc.) would a prototype be useful as a means of reducing the following uncertainties?

(a) There is a proposal that the senior managers of an insurance company have personal access to management information through an executive information system installed on personal computers located on their desks. Such a system would be costly to set up and there is some doubt about whether the managers would actually use the system.

(b) A computer system is to support sales office staff taking phone calls from members of the public enquiring about motor insurance and giving quotations over the phone.

(c) The insurance company is considering implementing the telephone sales system using the system development features supplied by Microsoft Access. They are not sure, at the moment, that it can provide the kind of interface that would be needed and are also concerned about the possible response times of a system developed using Microsoft Access.

Controlling changes during prototyping

A major problem with prototyping is controlling changes to the prototype following suggestions by the users. One approach has been to categorize changes as belonging to one of three types:

● *Cosmetic* (often about 35% of changes)

These are simple changes to the layout of the screens or reports. They are:

(a) implemented;

(b) recorded.

● *Local* (often about 60% of changes)

These change the way that a screen or report is processed but do not affect other parts of the system. They are:

(a) implemented;

Inspections are
discussed in
Chapter 12.

(b) recorded;

(c) backed-up so that they can be removed at a later stage if necessary;

(d) inspected retrospectively.

● *Global* (about 5% of changes)

These are changes that affect more than one part of the processing. All changes here have to be the subject of a design review before they can be implemented.

Figure 4.5 Intentional incremental delivery

4.11 Incremental delivery

Tom Gilb, whose
*Principles of Software
Engineering
Management* was
published by Addison-
Wesley in 1988, is a
prominent advocate of
this approach.

This approach breaks the application down into small components which are then implemented and delivered in sequence. Each component delivered must give some benefit to the user. Figure 4.5 gives a general idea of the approach.

Time-boxing is often associated with an incremental approach. Here the scope of deliverables for an increment is rigidly constrained by an agreed deadline. This deadline has to be met, even at the expense of dropping some of the planned functionality. Omitted features can be transferred to later increments.

Advantages of this approach

These are some of the justifications given for the approach.

- The feedback from early increments improves the later stages.
- The possibility of changes in requirements is reduced because of the shorter time span between the design of a component and its delivery.
- Users get benefits earlier than with a conventional approach.
- Early delivery of some useful components improves cash flow, because you get some return on investment early on.
- Smaller sub-projects are easier to control and manage.
- *Gold-plating*, that is, the requesting of features that are unnecessary and not in fact used, is less as users know that if a feature is not in the current increment then it can be included in the next.

- The project can be temporarily abandoned if more urgent work emerges.
- Job satisfaction is increased for developers who see their labours bearing fruit at regular, short, intervals.

Disadvantages

On the other hand, these disadvantages have been put forward.

- Later increments might require modifications to earlier increments. This is known as *software breakage*.
- Software developers may be more productive working on one large system than on a series of smaller ones.
- Grady Booch, an authority on OO, suggests that with what he calls 'requirements driven' projects (which equate to incremental delivery) *'Conceptual integrity sometimes suffers because there is little motivation to deal with scalability, extensibility, portability or reusability beyond what any vague requirements might imply.'* Booch also suggests there could be a tendency towards a large number of discrete functions with little common infrastructure.

This quotation is from Grady Booch's *Object Solutions: Managing the Object Oriented Project* Addison-Wesley, 1996.

The incremental delivery plan

The nature and order of each increment to be delivered to the users have to be planned at the outset.

This process is similar to strategic planning but at a more detailed level. Attention is given to increments of a user application rather than whole applications. The elements of the incremental plan are the *system objectives, incremental plan* and the *open technology plan*.

The process of planning the increments of a project as described by Gilb has similarities with strategic planning described in the previous chapter.

System objectives

Recall that earlier we suggested that project planners ideally want well-defined objectives, but as much freedom as possible about how these are to be met. These overall objectives can be expanded into more specific functional goals and quality goals.

Functional goals will include:

- objectives it is intended to achieve;
- jobs the system is to do;
- computer/non-computer functions to achieve them.

In addition, measurable quality characteristics should be defined, such as reliability, response and security. If this is done properly these over-arching quality requirements can go some way to meeting the concerns, expressed by Grady Booch, that these might get lost with the concentration on the requirements at increment level. It also reflects Tom Gilb's concern that system developers always keep sight of the objectives that they are trying to achieve on behalf of their clients. In the changing environment of an application individual requirements could change over the course of the project, but the objectives should not.

Chapter 12 discusses software quality characteristics.

Open technology plan

If the system is to be able to cope with new components being continually added then it needs to be extendible, portable and maintainable.

As a minimum this will require the use of:

- a standard high-level language;
- a standard operating system;
- small modules;
- variable parameters, for example items such as the names of an organization and its departments, charge rates and so on are held in a parameter file that can be amended without programmer intervention;
- a standard database management system.

These are all things that might be expected as a matter of course in a modern software development environment.

Although Gilb does not suggest this, following Booch's hints it would be desirable to draw up an initial logical data model or object model for the whole system. It is difficult to see how the next stage of planning the scope and order of each increment could be done without this foundation.

Incremental plan

Having defined the overall objectives and an open technology plan, the next stage is to plan the increments using the following guidelines:

A non-computer step could be something like a streamlined clerical procedure.

- Steps typically should consist of 1–5% of the total project!
- Non-computer steps should be included.
- An increment should, ideally, not exceed one month and should not, at worst, take more than three months.
- Each increment should deliver some benefit to the user.
- Some increments will be physically dependent on others.
- In other cases value-to-cost ratios may be used to decide priorities (see below).

A new system might be replacing an old computer system and the first increments could use parts of the old system. For example, the data for the database of the new system could initially be obtained from the old system's standing files.

A zero cost would mean the change can be implemented without software development – some costs might be incurred by users in changing procedures.

Which steps should be first? Some steps will be prerequisites because of physical dependencies but others can be in any order. Value-to-cost ratios (see Table 4.1) can be used to establish the order in which increments are to be developed. The customer is asked to rate the value of each increment with a score in the range 1–10. The developers also rate the cost of developing each of the increments with a score in the range 0–10. This might seem rather crude, but people are often unwilling to be more precise. Dividing the value rating by the cost rating generates a ratio which indicates the relative 'value for money' of each increment.

The value to cost ratio = V/C where V is a score 1–10 representing value to customer and C is a score 0–10 representing cost.

Table 4.1 Ranking by value to cost ratio

Step	Value	Cost	Ratio	Rank
Profit reports	9	1	9	(2nd)
Online data base	1	9	0·11	(6th)
Ad hoc enquiry	5	5	1	(4th)
Production sequence plans	2	8	0·25	(5th)
Purchasing profit factors	9	4	2·25	(3rd)
Clerical procedures	0	7	0	(7th)
Profit-based pay for managers	9	0	∞	(1st)

An incremental example

Tom Gilb describes a project where a software supplier negotiated a fixed-price contract with a three-month delivery time with the Swedish government to supply a system to support map-making. It later became apparent that the original estimate of effort upon which the bid was based was probably about half the real effort.

The project was replanned and divided into ten increments, each supplying something of use to the customer. The final increments were not available until three months after the contract's delivery date. The customer was not in fact unhappy about this as the most important parts of the application had actually been delivered early.

4.12 Dynamic Systems Development Method

A fuller explanation of DSDM can be found in Jennifer Stapleton's DSDM: A Framework for Business-centred Development, Addison-Wesley, 2002.

In the United Kingdom, SSADM (Structured Systems Analysis and Design Method) has until recently been a predominant methodology. In no small part, this has been because of sponsorship by the United Kingdom government. More recently, however, it has lost some favour, partly because it has been perceived as overly bureaucratic and prescriptive. In contrast, there has been an increased interest in the iterative and incremental approaches we have outlined above. As a consequence, a consortium has developed guidelines for the use of such techniques and has packaged the overall approach as the Dynamic Systems Development Method (DSDM). It is possible to attend courses on the method and to become an accredited DSDM practitioner.

Nine core DSDM principles have been enunciated:

1. Active user involvement is imperative.

2. DSDM teams must be empowered to make decisions.

3. Focus on frequent delivery of products.

4. Fitness for *business purpose* is the essential criterion for acceptance of deliverables.

5. Iterative and incremental delivery is necessary to converge on an accurate business solution.

6. All changes during development are reversible.

7. Requirements are base-lined at a *high level*.

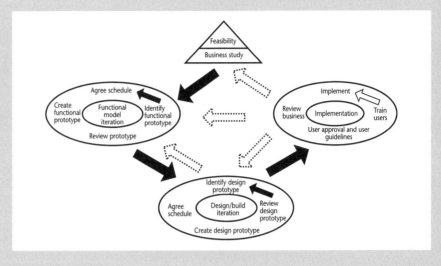

Figure 4.6   DSDM *process model*

JAD, Joint Application
Development,
was discussed in
Section 4.5.

8. Testing is integrated throughout the life cycle.

9. A collaborative and cooperative approach between all stakeholders is essential.

Figure 4.6 outlines the general approach. As with any other project, a feasibility study needs to be conducted before development starts. This will consider not just the business case for the project, but also its suitability for DSDM. A business requirement is then developed, probably using JAD. Prototypes might then be created which explore the functional requirements. These may be followed by further prototypes that establish the detailed design, particularly of the interfaces. Implementation of the components can then follow. The arrows between the various functions that are shown in Figure 4.6 illustrate how this order of activities is very flexible and iterative.

Time boxes were
discussed in the
previous section on
incremental delivery.

DSDM encourages the use of time boxes. It is suggested that these should typically be between two and six weeks in order to make participants focus on real needs. It will be recalled that in order to meet the deadline imposed by a time box, the implementation of less important features may be held over to later increments (or even dropped altogether). The relative importance of requirements can be categorized using the 'MoSCoW' classification:

● *Must have*: that is, essential features.

● *Should have*: these would probably be mandatory if you were using a conventional development approach – but the system can operate without them.

● *Could have*: these requirements can be delayed with some inconvenience.

● *Won't have*: these features are wanted, but their delay to a later increment is readily accepted.

The possibility of requirements being reallocated to different increments means that project plans will need to be constantly updated if the project is to be successfully controlled.

4.13 Extreme programming

See Kent Beck (with Cynthia Andreas), *Extreme Programming Explained: Embrace Change*, 2nd edition, Addison-Wesley, 2004.

The concept of extreme programming (XP) is particularly associated with Kent Beck and has its origins with the Chrysler C3 payroll project with which Beck was associated. XP is a further development of many of the RAD and DSDM principles that have been explored above. In some ways XP can be seen as 'super-programmers' describing their idea of coding heaven. XP belongs to a cluster of similar methodologies (including Jim Highsmith's Adaptive Software Development and Alistair Cockburn's Crystal Light methods) which have collectively been called *agile* methods.

Back in Chapter 1 it was noted that a common problem with software projects was communication. The larger the project the greater this problem becomes. Clearly larger projects mean that more people have to communicate, but, because these projects take longer to complete, information generated at the early stages of the project has to be recorded so that the later stages of the project can access it. It is easy for such information to be incomplete or simply out of date. One response to this has been to make communication more formal and structured. An alternative approach is to reduce the length of lines of communication and the time information has to be stored. Wherever possible, communication is made directly between the interested parties. Outcomes are immediately incorporated into the software and tested, allowing feedback on the implementation of agreed requirements to be produced quickly. Thus a representative of the users is actually a part of the team and can elucidate requirements on the spot. User requirements are documented on *cards* which contain 'stories' that describe the required features of the software. The developers and user representative then negotiate the order in which these features will be developed.

As with DSDM, XP advocates argue that applications should be written in increments of working software that should take a matter of weeks to complete. If anything, they seem to go further than DSDM and talk of increments ideally taking only one to three weeks. The customer for the software can at any stage suggest modifications to the functionality.

Within these increments, new features are integrated into the overall product at very frequent intervals and are immediately integration-tested. If any error is found in the new version of a software component, there is an immediate fallback to the previous version while the problems are resolved.

XP seems to argue against Booch's view that software development needs to be based on a careful preliminary design of a robust underlying structure. For a start, distinctions between designing the software structure and building the software are argued to be artificial. The principle adopted is that code should be developed simply to meet existing requirements and not possible future extensions to the application as future requirements tend to be uncertain. Clearly such an approach could lead to very unstructured code as an application develops in an ad hoc fashion. This is countered by the use of frequent redesigns of the code (or *refactoring*) to tidy up the code and the strict adherence to programming standards.

XP emphasizes the importance of testing. Test cases and expected results are devised before the design takes place. To do this, the developer and user must agree exactly what should happen given specific circumstances. As well as generating test cases, this helps to clarify the user's requirements. When the code is complete and tested, the test cases are merged with a consolidated set of test cases. After each new increment, this consolidated set of test cases is executed to ensure that the additions to functionality or the refactoring of old code has not introduced errors into what had previously worked correctly.

See Section 12.9 for more on reviews.

Perhaps the most radical principle of extreme programming is *pair programming*. Code is developed at the workstation by pairs of developers. One (the 'driver') actually types the code while the other (the 'navigator') watches, asks questions, and makes suggestions. From time to time the pair will change roles. In one way this is taking peer review of products a step further. Pair programming promotes the production of code that is well structured, easy to understand and relatively free of errors.

Helen Sharp of the Open University has studied XP in practice. One of her observations is that the social nature of the development process encourages a rhythm of group meetings, pair working and daily 'builds' when new code is integrated that helped to give the project momentum. Interestingly, this rhythm of activity and review acting as a heart-beat of the project has also been noted in a successful dispersed project.

4.14 Managing iterative processes

This discussion of agile methods might be confusing as it seems to turn many of our previous planning concepts on their head.

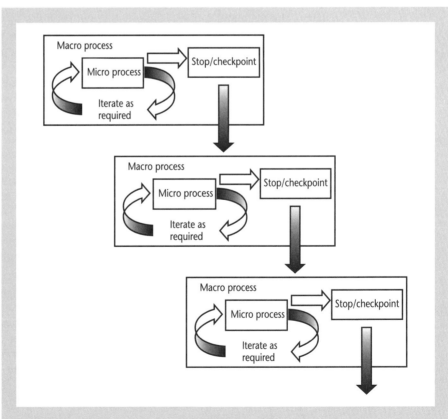

Figure 4.7 A macro process containing three iterative micro processes

Approaches like XP correctly emphasize the importance of communication and of removing artificial barriers to development productivity. XP to many might seem to be simply a 'licence to hack'. However, a more detailed examination of the techniques of XP shows that many (such as pair programming and installation standards) are conscious techniques to counter the excesses of hacking and to ensure good maintainable code is written.

Booch suggests that there are two levels of development: the macro process and the micro process. The macro process is closely related to the waterfall process model. At this level, a range of activities carried out by a variety of specialist groups has to be coordinated. We need to have some dates when we know that major activities will be finished so that we know when we will need to bring in staff to work on subsequent activities. Within this macro process there will be micro process activities which might involve iterative working. Systems testing has always been one. Figure 4.7. illustrates how a sequential macro process can be imposed on a number of iterative sub-processes. With iterative micro processes, the use of time boxes is needed to control at the macro level.

There are cases where the macro process itself can be iterative. It might be that a prototype for a complex technical system is produced in two or three successive versions, each taking several months to create and evaluate. In these circumstances, each iteration should be treated as a project in its own right.

4.15 Selecting the most appropriate process model

Construction of an application can be distinguished from its *installation*. It is possible to use different approaches for these two stages. For example, an application could be constructed using a waterfall or one-shot strategy but then be released to its users in increments. The only combinations of construction and installation strategies that are not feasible are the evolutionary installation with any other construction approach than evolutionary.

Where uncertainty is high then an evolutionary approach is to be favoured. An example of uncertainty would be where the users' requirements are not clearly defined. Where the requirements are relatively certain but there are many complexities, as with a large embedded system needing a large amount of code, then an incremental approach is favoured. Where deadlines are tight, then either an evolutionary or an incremental approach is favoured over a one-shot strategy, as both tactics should allow at least something to be delivered at the deadline, even if it is not all that was originally promised. Students about to plan final-year projects would do well to note this.

4.16 Conclusion

This chapter has stressed the need to examine each project carefully to see if it has characteristics which suggest a particular approach or process model. These characteristics might suggest the addition of specific activities to the project plan.

The classic waterfall process model, which attempts to minimize iteration, should lead to projects that are easy to control. Unfortunately, many projects do not lend themselves to this structure. Prototyping may be able to reduce project uncertainties by allowing knowledge to be bought through experimentation. The incremental approach encourages the execution of a series of small, manageable, 'mini-projects' but does have some costs.

4.17 Further exercises

1. A building society has a long history of implementing computer-based information systems to support the work of its branches. It uses a proprietary structured systems analysis and design method. It has been decided to create a computer model of the property market. This would attempt, for example, to calculate the effect of changes of interest rates on house values. There is some concern that the usual methodology used for IS development would not be appropriate for the new project.

   (a) Why might there be this concern and what alternative approaches should be considered?

   (b) Outline a plan for the development of the system which illustrates the application of your preferred methodology for this project.

2. A software package is to be designed and built to assist in software cost estimation. It will input certain parameters and produce initial cost estimates to be used at bidding time.

   (a) It has been suggested that a software prototype would be of value in these circumstances. Explain why this might be.

   (b) Discuss how such prototyping could be controlled to ensure that it is conducted in an orderly and effective way and within a specified time span.

3. An invoicing system is to have the following transactions: amend invoice, produce invoice, produce monthly statements, record cash payment, clear paid invoices from database, create customer records, delete customer.

   (a) What physical dependencies govern the order in which these transactions are implemented?

   (b) How could the system be broken down into increments which would be of some value to the users (hint – think about the problems of taking existing details onto a database when a system is first implemented).

4. In Section 4.10 the need was stressed of defining what is to be learnt from a prototype and the way that it will be evaluated to obtain the new knowledge. Outline the learning outcomes and evaluation for the following.

   (a) A final-year degree student is to build an application that will act as a 'suggestions box' in a factory. The application will allow employees to make suggestions about process improvements, and will track the subsequent progress of the suggestion as it is evaluated. The student wants to use a web-based front-end with a conventional database. The student has not previously developed any applications using this mix of technologies.

   (b) An engineering company has to maintain a large number of different types of document relating to current and previous projects. It has decided to evaluate the use of a computer-based document retrieval system and wishes to try it out on a trial basis.

   (c) A business which specializes in 'e-solutions', that is, the development of business applications that exploit the world wide web, has been approached by the computing school of a local university. The school is investigating setting up a special website for its former students. The website's core will be information about job and training opportunities and it is hoped that this will generate income through advertising. It is agreed that some kind of pilot to evaluate the scheme is needed.

5. In a college environment, an intranet for students that holds information about courses, such as lecture programmes, reading lists and assignment briefs, is often set

up. As a 'real' exercise, plan, organize and carry out a JAD session to design (or improve the design of) an intranet facilty.

This will require:

- preliminary interviews with representative key stakeholders (for example, staff who might be supplying information for the intranet);
- creation of documents for use in the JAD proceedings;
- recording of the JAD proceedings;
- creating a report which will present the findings of the JAD session.

Software effort estimation

5.1 Introduction

One definition of a successful project is that the system is delivered *'on time, within budget and with the required quality'* which implies that targets are set and the project manager then tries to meet those targets. This assumes that the targets are reasonable – no account is taken of the possibility of project managers achieving record levels of productivity from their teams, but still not meeting a deadline because of incorrect initial estimates. Realistic estimates are therefore crucial to the project manager.

In Chapter 1, the special characteristics of software identified by Brooks i.e. complexity, conformity, changeability and invisibility, were discussed.

What sorts of problems might a project leader such as Amanda, who is in charge of the IOE maintenance group accounts project, encounter when trying to do estimates? Estimating the effort required to implement software is notoriously difficult. Some of the difficulties of estimating are inherent in the very nature of software, especially its complexity and invisibility. In addition, the intensely human activities which make up system development cannot be treated in a purely mechanical way. Other difficulties include:

- *Novel applications of software* With traditional engineering projects, it is often the case that the system to be created is similar to one constructed previously but for a different customer or in a different location. The estimates for such a project can therefore be based on previous experience. With software, in most major projects the product will in some way be unique and will therefore be clouded with doubts and uncertainties.

- *Changing technology* For example, at IOE the original maintenance billing system might have been written in Cobol, while the new extension for group accounts that Amanda is directing might be developed using an application-building environment such as that provided by Oracle.

- *Lack of homogeneity of project experience* As we will see, effective estimating should be based on information about how past projects have performed. It is surprising how many organizations do not make this data available to staff. Amanda might also find that even where the previous project data is available, it may not be that useful.

The figures are taken from B. A. Kitchenham and N. R. Taylor, 'Software project development cost estimation' in *Journal of Systems and Software*, 1985 (5). The abbreviation SLOC stands for 'source lines of code'. SLOC is one way of indicating the size of a system.

Table 5.1 is a set of figures recorded for actual projects carried out by the same organization.

Table 5.1 Some project data – effort in work months (as percentage of total effort in brackets)

	Design		Coding		Testing		Total	
Project	wm	(%)	wm	(%)	wm	(%)	wm	SLOC
a	3·9	(23)	5·3	(32)	7·4	(44)	16·7	6050
b	2·7	(12)	13·4	(59)	6·5	(26)	22·6	8363
c	3·5	(11)	26·8	(83)	1·9	(6)	32·2	13334
d	0·8	(21)	2·4	(62)	0·7	(18)	3·9	5942
e	1·8	(10)	7·7	(44)	7·8	(45)	17·3	3315
f	19·0	(28)	29·7	(44)	19·0	(28)	67·7	38988
g	2·1	(21)	7·4	(74)	0·5	(5)	10·1	38614
h	1·3	(7)	12·7	(66)	5·3	(27)	19·3	12762
i	8·5	(14)	22·7	(38)	28·2	(47)	59·5	26500

Exercise 5.1

Calculate the productivity (i.e. SLOC per work month) of each of the projects in Table 5.1 and also for the organization as a whole. If the project leaders for projects a and d had correctly estimated the source number of lines of code (SLOC) and then used the average productivity of the organization to calculate the effort needed to complete the projects, how far out would their estimates have been from the actual effort?

It would be very difficult on the basis of this information to advise a project manager about what sort of productivity to expect, or about the probable distribution of effort between the phases of design, coding and testing that could be expected from a new project.

The ISO 12207 standard, touched upon in Chapter 1, is an attempt to address this problem by standardizing on some of the terms used.

There have been some attempts to set up industry-wide databases of past projects. However, this data seems to be of limited use to estimators as there are uncertainties in the way that various terms can be interpreted. For example, what exactly is meant by the term 'testing'? Does it cover the activities of the software developer when debugging code? Does 'design' include drawing up program structure diagrams or does this come under the heading of 'software development'?

- *Subjective nature of estimating* Some research shows that people tend to underestimate the difficulty of small tasks and over-estimate that of large ones. In the world of software development this is perhaps justifiable as large projects are usually disproportionately more complex and more difficult than smaller ones.

The possibility of the different groups with stakes in a project having different and possibly conflicting objectives was discussed in Chapter 1.

- *Political implications*   Different groups within an organization have different objectives. The IOE information systems development managers may, for example, want to see as many systems as possible implemented and will therefore put pressure on estimators to reduce cost estimates in order to encourage higher management to approve the project. As Amanda is responsible for the development of the maintenance group accounts subsystem, she may be concerned that the project does not exceed its budget and is not delivered late as this will reflect badly on herself. She might therefore try to increase the estimates in order to create a 'comfort zone'. To avoid these 'political' pressures, one suggestion is that all estimates be produced by a specialist estimating group, independent of both the users and the project team. Not all agree with this, as staff involved in a project are more likely to be committed to targets where they have participated in formulating them.

5.2   Where are estimates done?

Estimates are carried out at various stages of a software project. At each stage the reasons for the estimate and the methods used will vary.

Chapter 3 discusses strategic planning in some detail.

- *Strategic planning*   At this stage, the costs of computerizing potential applications and the benefits of doing so may need to be estimated to help decide what priority to give to each project. Such estimates may also influence the numbers of various types of development staff to be recruited by the organization.

- *Feasibility study*   This ascertains that the benefits of the potential system will justify the costs.

- *System specification*   Most system development methodologies usefully distinguish between the definition of the users' requirements and the design which documents how those requirements are to be fulfilled. The effort needed to implement different design proposals will need to be estimated. Estimates at the design stage will also confirm that the feasibility study is still valid, taking into account all that has been learnt during detailed requirements analysis.

The estimate at this stage cannot be based only on the user requirement: some kind of technical plan is also needed – see Chapter 4.

- *Evaluation of suppliers' proposals*   In the case of the IOE maintenance group accounts subsystem, for example, IOE might consider putting the actual system-building out to tender. Potential contractors considering a bid would need to scrutinize the system specification and produce estimates on which to base proposals. Amanda might still be required to carry out her own estimate to help judge the bids received. IOE may wish to question a proposal which seems too low: they might wonder, for example, whether the proposer had properly understood the requirements. If, on the other hand, the bids seem too high they might reconsider in-house development.

- *Project planning*   As the planning and implementation of the project progresses to greater levels of detail, more detailed estimates of smaller work components will be made. As well as confirming the earlier and more broad-brush estimates, these will help answer questions about, for example, when staff will have completed particular tasks and be available for new activities.

Two general points can be made here:

- as the project proceeds so the accuracy of the estimates should improve as knowledge about the nature of the project increases;
- a conventional wisdom is that at the beginning of the project the user requirement (that is, a logical model of the required system) is of paramount importance and that premature consideration of the physical implementation is to be avoided. In order to produce an estimate, however, the estimator will have to speculate about this physical implementation (for instance, about the number of software components to be written).

To set estimating into the context of the Step Wise framework (Figure 5.1) presented in Chapter 2, re-estimating could take place at almost any step, but specific provision is made for the production of a relatively high-level estimate at Step 3, 'Analyse project characteristics', and for each individual activity in Step 5. As Steps 5–8 are repeated at progressively lower levels, so estimates will be done at a finer degree of detail. As we will see later in this chapter, different methods of estimating are needed at these different planning steps.

5.3 Problems with over- and under-estimates

A project leader such as Amanda will need to be aware that the estimate itself, if known to the development team, will influence the time required to implement the system. An over-estimate may cause the project to take longer than it would otherwise. This can be explained by the application of two 'laws'.

Parkinson's law was originally expounded in C. Northcote Parkinson's tongue-in-cheek book *Parkinson's Law*, John Murray, 1957.
Brooks' law comes from *The Mythical Man-month* which has been referred to already.

- *Parkinson's Law* 'Work expands to fill the time available', that is, given an easy target staff will work less hard.
- *Brooks' Law* The effort required to implement a project will go up disproportionately with the number of staff assigned to the project. As the project team grows in size, so will the effort that has to go into management, coordination and communication. This has given rise, in extreme cases, to the notion of Brooks' Law: *'putting more people on a late job makes it later'*. If there is an over-estimate of the effort required then this could lead to more staff being allocated than are needed and managerial overheads being increased. This is more likely to be of significance with large projects.

See, for example, T. K. Hamid and S. E. Madnick, 'Impact of schedule estimation on software project behaviour' *IEEE Software*, July, 1986, 3(4), pp. 70–75.

Some have suggested that while the under-estimated project might not be completed on time or to cost, it might still be implemented in a shorter time than a project with a more generous estimate. There must, however, be limits to this phenomenon where all the slack in the project has been taken up.

The danger with the under-estimate is the effect on quality. Staff, particularly those with less experience, could respond to pressing deadlines by producing work which is substandard. Since we are into laws, this may be seen as a manifestation of Weinberg's zeroth law of reliability: *'if a system does not have to be reliable, it can meet any other objective'*. In other words, if there is no need for the program to actually work, you can meet any programming deadline that may be set! Substandard work might only become visible at the later, testing, phases of a project which are particularly difficult to control and where extensive rework can have catastrophic consequences for the project completion date.

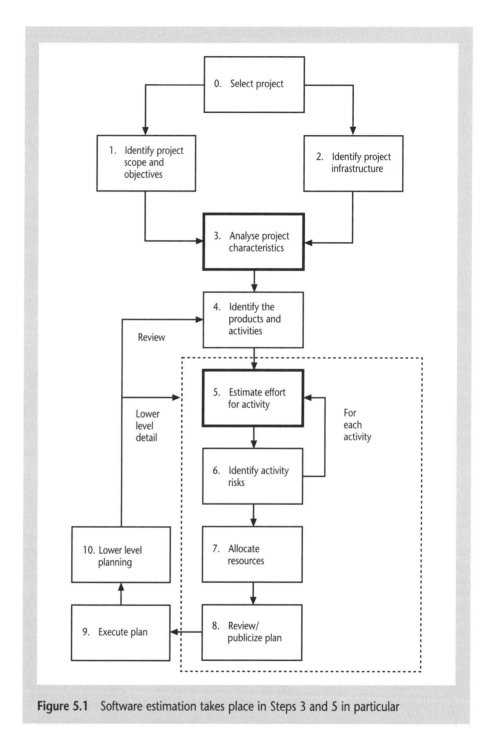

Figure 5.1 Software estimation takes place in Steps 3 and 5 in particular

Because of the possible effects on the behaviour of development staff, the size of estimates might be artificially reduced by their managers to increase pressure on staff. This will only work where staff are unaware that this has been done. Research has found that motivation and morale are enhanced where targets are achievable. If, over a period of time, staff become aware that the targets set are

Barry Boehm devised the COCOMO estimating models which are described later in this chapter.

unattainable and that projects are routinely not meeting their published targets then this will help to destroy motivation. Furthermore, people like to think of themselves as winners and there is a general tendency to put success down to our own efforts while failure is blamed on the organization.

In the end, an estimate is not really a prediction, it is a *management goal*. Barry Boehm has suggested that if a software development cost is within 20% of the estimated cost for the job then a good manager can turn it into a self-fulfilling prophecy. A project leader like Amanda will work hard to make the actual performance conform to the estimate.

5.4 The basis for software estimating

The need for historical data

Nearly all estimating methods need information about how projects have been implemented in the past. However, care needs to be taken in judging the applicability of data to the project under consideration because of possible differences in environmental factors such as the programming languages used, the software tools available, the standards enforced and the experience of the staff.

Measure of work

SLOC has already been used in Table 5.1.

It is normally not possible to calculate directly the actual cost or time required to implement a project. The time taken to write software may vary according to the competence or experience of the software developer, and a particular software developer might not yet have been allocated to the task. Implementation time might also vary because of environmental factors such as the software tools available. The usual practice is therefore to express the work content of the application to be implemented independently of effort using a measure such as source lines of code (SLOC). The reader may also come across the abbreviation KLOC which refers to thousands of lines of code.

R. E. Park has devised a standard for counting source statements that has been widely adopted – see *Software Size Measurement: A Framework for Counting Source Statements*, Software Engineering Institute, 1992.

As can be imagined, SLOC is a very imprecise measure. Does it include comment lines? Are data declarations to be included? Unfortunately, researchers have not been consistent on these points. The writers' view is that comment lines are excluded, but data declarations are included. Others may argue over this, but the main point is that consistency is essential.

Counting SLOC is difficult where application-building tools have been employed which often use tables or diagrams to record processing rules. Different measures of size are needed, such as function points, which are explained further on in this chapter.

Complexity

Differences in complexity may be one of the reasons for the inconsistencies in Table 5.1.

Two software components with the same KLOC will not necessarily take the same time to write, even if done by the same programmer in the same environment. One component might be more complex. Because of this, the effort estimate based on SLOC might have to be modified to take complexity into account. Attempts have been made to find objective measures of complexity, but often it will depend on the subjective judgement of the estimator.

5.5 Software effort estimation techniques

See B. W. Boehm, *Software Engineering Economics*, Prentice-Hall, 1981.

Barry Boehm, in his classic work on software effort models, identified the main ways of deriving estimates of software development effort as:

- *algorithmic models,* which use 'effort drivers' representing characteristics of the target system and the implementation environment to predict effort;
- *expert judgement,* where the advice of knowledgeable staff is solicited;
- *analogy,* where a similar, completed, project is identified and its actual effort is used as the basis of the estimate for the new project;
- *Parkinson,* which identifies the staff effort available to do a project and uses that as the 'estimate';
- *price to win,* where the 'estimate' is a figure that appears to be sufficiently low to win a contract;
- *top-down,* where an overall estimate is formulated for the whole project which is then broken down into the effort required for component tasks;
- *bottom-up,* where component tasks are identified and sized and these individual estimates are aggregated.

This is also the principle behind the concept of time boxing that was discussed in Chapter 4 in the context of DSDM.

Clearly, the 'Parkinson' method is not really an effort prediction method, but a method of setting the scope of a project. Similarly, 'price to win' is a way of identifying a price and not a prediction. On these grounds, Boehm rejects them as prediction techniques although they could have some value as management techniques. There is, for example, a perfectly acceptable engineering practice of '*design to cost*' which is one example of the broader approach of '*design by objectives*'.

We will now look at some of these techniques more closely. First we will examine the difference between top-down and bottom-up estimating.

Bottom-up estimating

Estimating methods can be generally divided into bottom-up and top-down approaches. With the bottom-up approach the estimator breaks the project into its component tasks and then estimates how much effort will be required to carry out each task. With a large project, the process of breaking down into tasks would be a repetitive one: each task would be analysed into its component sub-tasks and these in turn would be further analysed. It is suggested that this is repeated until you get to components that can be executed by a single person in about a week or two. The reader may wonder why this is not called a top-down approach: after all, you are starting from the top and working down. Although this top-down analysis is an essential precursor to bottom-up estimating, it is really a separate one – that of producing a Work Breakdown Schedule (WBS). The bottom-up part comes in adding up the calculated effort for each activity to get an overall estimate.

The bottom-up approach is most appropriate at the later, more detailed, stages of project planning. If this method is used early on in the project cycle then the estimator will have to make some assumptions about the characteristics of the final system, for example the number and size of software components. These will be working assumptions that imply no commitment when it comes to the actual design of the application.

Where a project is completely novel or there is no historical data available, the estimator would be forced to use the bottom-up approach.

Exercise 5.2   Brigette at Brightmouth College has been told that there is a requirement, now that the payroll system has been successfully installed, to create a subsystem that analyses the staffing costs for each course. Details of the pay that each member of staff receives may be obtained from the payroll standing data. The number of hours that each member of staff spends teaching on each course may be obtained from standing files in a computer-based timetabling system.

What tasks would have to be undertaken to implement this requirement? Try and identify tasks that would take one person about 1 or 2 weeks.

Which tasks are the ones whose durations are most difficult to estimate?

The top-down approach and parametric models

The top-down approach is normally associated with *parametric* (or *algorithmic*) *models*. These may be explained using the analogy of estimating the cost of rebuilding a house. This would be of practical concern to a house-owner who needs sufficient insurance cover to rebuild their property if destroyed. Unless the house-owner happens to be in the building trade it is unlikely that he or she would be able to work out how many bricklayer-hours, how many carpenter-hours, electrician-hours and so on would be required. Insurance companies, however, produce convenient tables where the house-owner can find an estimate of rebuilding costs based on such *parameters* as the number of storeys and the floor space that a house has. This is a simple parametric model.

The effort needed to implement a project will be related mainly to variables associated with characteristics of the final system. The form of the parametric model will normally be one or more formulae in the form:

$$effort = (system\ size) \times (productivity\ rate)$$

For example, system size might be in the form 'thousands of lines of code' (KLOC) and have the specific value of 3 KLOC while the productivity rate was 40 days per KLOC. These values will often be matters of judgement.

A model to forecast software development effort therefore has two key components. The first is a method of assessing the size of the software development task to be undertaken. The second assesses the rate of work at which the task can be done. For example, Amanda at IOE may estimate the first software module to be constructed is 2 KLOC. She may then judge that if Kate undertook the development of the code, with her expertise she could work at a rate of 40 days per KLOC per day and complete the work in 2×40 days, i.e. 80 days, while Ken, who is less experienced, would need 55 days per KLOC and take 2×55, i.e. 110 days to complete the task.

Some parametric models, such as that implied by function points, are focused on system or task size, while others, such are COCOMO, are more concerned with productivity factors.

Where applications are not built using procedural code, the size drivers might be different types of component. For example, where Microsoft Access is being used, an estimator might count tables, forms, queries, reports and so on.

Exercise 5.3 Students on a course are required to produce a written report on an ICT-related topic each semester. If you wanted to create a model to estimate how long it should take a student to complete such an assignment, what measure of work content would you use? Some reports might be more difficult to produce than others: what factors might affect the degree of difficulty?

At the earlier stages of a project, the top-down approach would tend to be used, while at later stages the bottom-up approach might be preferred.

Having calculated the overall effort required, the problem is then to allocate proportions of that effort to the various activities within that project.

The top-down and bottom-up approaches are not mutually exclusive. Project managers will probably try to get a number of different estimates from different people using different methods. Some parts of an overall estimate could be derived using a top-down approach while other parts could be calculated using a bottom-up method.

5.6 Expert judgement

See R. T. Hughes, 'Expert judgement as an estimating method', *Information and Software Technology*, 1996, 38(3), pp. 67–75.

This is asking for an estimate of task effort from someone who is knowledgeable about either the application or the development environment. This method is often used when estimating the effort needed to change an existing piece of software. The estimator would have to carry out some kind of impact analysis in order to judge the proportion of code that would be affected and from that derive an estimate. Someone already familiar with the software would be in the best position to do this.

Some have suggested that expert judgement is simply a matter of guessing, but our own research has shown that experts tend to use a combination of an informal analogy approach where similar projects from the past are identified (see below), supplemented by bottom-up estimating.

5.7 Estimating by analogy

The use of analogy is also called *case-based reasoning*. The estimator seeks out projects that have been completed (*source cases*) and that have similar characteristics to the new project (the *target case*). The effort that has been recorded for the matching source case can then be used as a base estimate for the target. The estimator should then identify any differences between the target and the source and make adjustments to the base estimate to produce an estimate of effort for the new project.

See M. Shepperd and C. Schofield, 'Estimating software project effort using analogies', in *IEEE Transactions in Software Engineering*, 1997, SE-23(11), pp. 736–743.

This can be a good approach where you have information about some previous projects but not enough to draw generalized conclusions about what might be useful drivers or typical productivity rates.

A problem is how you actually identify the similarities and differences between the different applications, especially where you have a large number of past projects upon which to draw. One attempt to automate this selection process is the ANGEL software tool. This identifies the source case that is nearest the target by measuring the Euclidean distance between cases. The Euclidean distance is calculated:

$$distance = square\text{-}root\ of\ ((\ target\_parameter_1 - source\_parameter_1)^2 +$$

$$\dots \quad (\ target\_parameter_n - source\_parameter_n)^2)$$

Example 5.1   Say that the cases are being matched on the basis of two parameters, the number of inputs to and the number of outputs from the application to be built. The new project is known to require 7 inputs and 15 outputs. One of the past cases, project A, has 8 inputs and 17 outputs. The Euclidean distance between the source and the target is therefore the square-root of $((7-8)^2+(17-15)^2)$, that is 2.24.

Exercise 5.4   Project B has 5 inputs and 10 outputs. What would be the Euclidean distance between this project and the target new project being considered above? Is project B a better analogy with the target than project A?

The above explanation is simply to give an idea of how Euclidean distance may be calculated. The ANGEL package uses rather more sophisticated algorithms based on this principle.

5.8 Albrecht function point analysis

See A. J. Albrecht and J. E. Gaffney Jr., 'Software function, source lines of code, and development effort prediction: a software science validation', in M. Shepperd (ed), *Software Engineering Metrics* (Vol. 1), McGraw-Hill, 1993.

This is a top-down method that was devised by Allan Albrecht when he worked for IBM. Albrecht was investigating programming productivity and needed some way to quantify the functional size of programs independently of the programming languages in which they had been coded. He developed the idea of function points (FPs).

The basis of function point analysis is that computer-based information systems comprise five major components, or '*external user types*' in Albrecht's terminology, that are of benefit to the users.

● *External input types* are input transactions which update internal computer files.

● *External output types* are transactions where data is output to the user. Typically these would be printed reports, as screen displays would tend to come under external inquiry types (see below).

● *Logical internal file types* are the standing files used by the system. The term 'file' does not sit easily with modern information systems. It refers to a group of data that is usually accessed together. It may be made up of one or more *record types*. For example, a purchase order file may be made up of a record type PURCHASE-ORDER plus a second which is repeated for each item ordered on the purchase order – PURCHASE-ORDER-ITEM. In structured systems analysis, a Logical Internal File would equate to a datastore, while record types would equate to relational tables or entity types.

Albrecht also dictates that outgoing external interface files should be double counted as logical internal file types as well.

● *External interface file types* allow for output and input that may pass to and from other computer applications. Examples of this would be the transmission of accounting data from an order processing system to the main ledger system or the production of a file of direct debit details on a magnetic or electronic medium to be passed to the Bankers Automated Clearing System (BACS). Files shared between applications would also be counted here.

● *External inquiry types* – note the US spelling of inquiry – are transactions initiated by the user which provide information but do not update the internal files. The user inputs some information that directs the system to the details required.

Table 5.2 Albrecht complexity multipliers

External user type	Multiplier		
	Low	Average	High
External input type	3	4	6
External output type	4	5	7
Logical internal file type	7	10	15
External interface file type	5	7	10
External inquiry type	3	4	6

The analyst has to identify each instance of each external user type in the projected system. Each component is then classified as having either high, average or low complexity. The counts of each external user type in each complexity band are multiplied by specified weights (see Table 5.2) to get FP scores which are summed to obtain an overall FP count which indicates the information processing size.

Exercise 5.5

The task for which Brigette has been made responsible in Exercise 5.2 needs a program which will extract yearly salaries from the payroll file, and hours taught on each course by each member of staff and the details of courses from two files maintained by the timetabling system. The program will produce a report showing for each course the hours taught by each member of staff and the cost of those hours.

Using the method described above, calculate the Albrecht function points for this subsystem assuming that the report is of high complexity, but that all the other elements are of average complexity.

The International FP User Group (IFPUG) have developed and published extensive rules governing FP counting. Hence Albrecht FPs are now often referred to as IFPUG FPs.

One problem with FPs as originally defined by Albrecht was that the question of whether the external user type was of high, low or average complexity was rather subjective. The International FP User Group (IFPUG) have now promulgated rules on how this is to be judged. For example, in the case of logical internal files and external interface files, the boundaries shown in Table 5.3 are used to decide the complexity level.

Example 5.2

A logical internal file might contain data about purchase orders. These purchase orders might be organized into two separate record types: the main PURCHASE-ORDER details, namely purchase order number, supplier reference and purchase order date and then details for each PURCHASE-ORDER-ITEM specified in the order, namely the product code, the unit price and number ordered. The number of record types for that file would therefore be 2 and the number of data types would be 6. According to Table 5.3, this file type would be rated as 'low'. This would mean that according to Table 5.2, the FP count would be 7 for this file.

Table 5.3 IFPUG file type complexity

Number of record types	Number of data types		
	<20	20–50	>50
1	Low	Low	Average
2 to 5	Low	Average	High
>5	Average	High	High

Table 5.4 IFPUG External input complexity

Number of file types accessed	Number of data types accessed		
	<5	5 to 15	>15
0 or 1	Low	Low	Average
2	Low	Average	High
>2	Average	High	High

Table 5.5 IFPUG External output complexity

Number of file types	Number of data types		
	<6	6–19	>19
0 or 1	Low	Low	Average
2 or 3	Low	Average	High
>3	Average	High	High

Tables 5.4 and 5.5 are used to scope external inputs and external outputs. Each external inquiry has to be counted as if it were both an external input and an external output and whichever score is higher is used.

Function point analysis now goes on to take into account the fact that the effort required to implement a computer-based information system will relate not just to the number and complexity of the features to be provided but also to the environment in which the system is to operate.

Fourteen factors have been identified which can influence the degree of difficulty associated with implementing a system. The list that Albrecht produced related particularly to the concerns of information system developers in the late 1970s and early 1980s. Some technology which was then new and relatively threatening is now well established.

The technical complexity adjustment (TCA) calculation has had many problems. Some have even found that it produces less accurate estimates than using the unadjusted function point count. Because of these difficulties, we are going to omit further discussion of the TCA.

Tables have been calculated to convert the FPs to lines of code for various languages. For example, it is suggested that 91 lines of Cobol are needed on average to implement an FP, while for C the figure is 128 and for Quick Basic it is 64. You can then use historical productivity data to convert the lines of code into an effort estimate.

Further details on TCA can be found in the Albrecht and Gaffney paper.

Some of these conversion factors do not seem to be very convincing (e.g. 6 SLOC per function point for spreadsheets).

Exercise 5.6

In the case of the subsystem described in Exercise 5.5 for which Brigette is responsible at Brightmouth HE College, how many lines of Cobol code should be needed to implement this subsystem, according to the standard conversion? Assuming a productivity rate of 50 lines of code a day, what would be the estimate of effort?

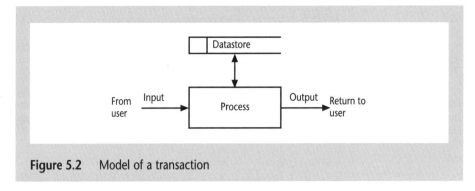

Figure 5.2   Model of a transaction

5.9   Function points Mark II

This method has came into the public domain with the publication of the book by Charles R. Symons, *Software Sizing and Estimating – Mark II FPA,* John Wiley and Sons, 1991.

The Mark II method was originally sponsored by what was then the CCTA (Central Computer and Telecommunications Agency, now the Office of Government Commerce or OGC) which lays down standards for UK government projects. At one time this Mark II approach seemed to be a good method to use with the structured systems analysis and design method, SSADM, but some drawbacks to this became apparent. The 'Mark II' label implies an improvement and replacement of the Albrecht method. The Albrecht (now IFPUG) method, however, has had many refinements made to it and FPA Mark II remains a minority method used mainly in the United Kingdom.

As with Albrecht, the information processing size is initially measured in unadjusted function points (UFPs) to which a technical complexity adjustment can then be applied (TCA). The assumption is that an information system comprises transactions which have the basic structure shown in Figure 5.2.

For each transaction the UFPs are calculated:

$$W_i \times (number\ of\ input\ data\ element\ types) +$$

$$W_e \times (number\ of\ entity\ types\ referenced) +$$

$$W_o \times (number\ of\ output\ data\ element\ types)$$

W_i, W_e and W_o are weightings that may be derived by asking developers what proportion of effort has been spent in previous projects developing those parts of the software that deal with processing inputs, accessing and modifying stored data and processing outputs. From this it should be possible to work out the average hours of work generated by instances of each type of element.

The averages are then normalized into ratios, or weightings, which add up to 2·5. If this way of getting hold of the weightings seems too time consuming then some industry averages are available which are currently 0·58 for W_i, 1·66 for W_e and 0·26 for W_o.

The only reason why 2·5 was adopted here was to produce FP counts similar to the Albrecht equivalents.

Example 5.3

A cash receipt transaction in the IOE maintenance accounts system accesses two entity types – INVOICE and CASH-RECEIPT.

The data elements that are input are:

Invoice number
Date received
Cash received

If an INVOICE record is not found for the invoice number then an error message is issued. If the invoice number is found then a CASH-RECEIPT record is created.

The error message constitutes the only output data element that the transaction has to cater for.

The unadjusted function points, using the industry average weightings, for this transaction would therefore be:

$$(0 \cdot 58 \times 3) + (1 \cdot 66 \times 2) + (0 \cdot 26 \times 1) = 5 \cdot 32$$

Exercise 5.7   The IOE maintenance group accounts subsystem for which Amanda is responsible will have a transaction which sets up details of new group account customers.

The operator will input:

Customer account number
Customer name
Address
Postcode
Customer type
Statement production date

All this information will be set up in a CUSTOMER record on the system's database. If a CUSTOMER account already exists for the account number that has been input, an error message will be displayed to the operator.

Calculate the number of unadjusted Mark II function points for this transaction, using the industry average weightings.

Mark II FPs follow the Albrecht method in recognizing that one system delivering the same functionality as another may be more difficult to implement (but also more valuable to the users) because of additional technical requirements. For example, the incorporation of additional security measures would increase the amount of effort to deliver the system. The original Albrecht FP method identified 14 technical complexity adjustment factors – Mark II FPs identify five more factors:

● interfaces to other applications;

● special security features;

● direct access for third parties;

● user training features;

● documentation requirements.

The identification of further factors to suit local circumstances is encouraged.

With both the Albrecht and Symons methods, FPs can be counted for previous projects where actual effort is known. If you have figures for the effort expended on past projects (in work-days for instance) and also the system sizes in FPs, you should be able to work out a productivity rate, as

$$productivity = size/effort$$

For new projects, the function points can be counted and then the effort can be projected using the productivity rate derived above:

$$effort = size/productivity$$

This simplified approach assumes rather unrealistically that the factors affecting productivity are the same for each project.

A more sophisticated way of doing this would be by using the statistical technique *least squares regression* to derive an equation in the form:

$$effort = constant_1 + (size \times constant_2)$$

Symons is very much against the idea of using function points to estimate SLOC rather than effort. One finding by Symons is that productivity, that is, the effort per function point to implement a system, is influenced by the size of the project. In general, larger projects, up to a certain point, are more productive because of economies of scale. However, beyond a certain size they tend to become less productive because of additional management overheads.

Some of the rules and weightings used in FP counting, especially in the case of the Albrecht flavour, are rather arbitrary and have been criticized by academic writers on this account. FPs, however, are often used in practice because of the lack of other methods of gauging the functional size of information systems.

5.10 COSMIC Full Function Points

To use the function point approach effectively an organization needs to have access to historical information about past projects, in particular the numbers of function points for each project and the actual effort that it needed. It might also want other information about the characteristics of the projects as different types of project could have different productivity rates. It takes time to build up such a database and changes in the way that function points have to be counted can mean that this data is made obsolete. Not unnaturally, this means that organizations – and consultants who might have built up their own databases – will be reluctant to accept new methods of counting function points, despite the flaws in the some of the existing methods.

COSMIC-FFP stands for Common Software Measurement Consortium – Full Function Points.

For example, some have suggested that approaches like that of IFPUG are suitable for information systems, but are not helpful when it comes to sizing real-time or embedded applications. A result of this perception has been the development of another version of function points – the COSMIC FFP method.

The full function point (FFP) method has its origins in the work of two interlinked research groups in Québec, Canada. At the start, the developers were at pains to stress that this method should be seen as simply an extension to the IFPUG method to allow real-time systems to be sized more accurately. The original work of FFPs has been taken forward by the formation of the Common Software Measurement Consortium (COSMIC) which has involved not just the original developers in Canada, but others from many parts of the world, including Charles Symons, the originator of Mark II function points. Interestingly, there has been next to no participation by anyone from the United States.

The argument is that existing function point methods make a fair job of assessing the work content of business-oriented information systems because in those systems, the size of the internal procedures mirrors the number of external features of various types. With a real-time, or embedded, system, its features might well be hidden because the software's user will probably not be a human but a hardware device or another software component.

COSMIC deals with this by requiring the analyst to break down the system architecture into a hierarchy of software *layers*. The software component to be sized can receive requests for services from layers above and can request services from those below it. At the same time there could be separate software components at the same level that engage in *peer-to-peer communication*. This helps to identify the boundary of the software component to be assessed and thus the points at which it receives inputs and transmits outputs. Inputs and outputs are aggregated into *data groups*, where each group brings together data items that relate to the same object of interest.

Data groups can be moved about in four ways:

- *entries* (E), which are effected by sub-processes that move the data group into the software component in question from a 'user' outside its boundary – this could be from another layer or another separate software component in the same layer via peer-to-peer communication;
- *exits* (X), which are effected by sub-processes that move the data group from the software component to a 'user' outside its boundary;
- *reads* (R), which are data movements that move data groups from persistent storage (such as a database) into the software component;
- *writes* (W), which are data movements that transfer data groups from the software component into persistent storage.

Exercise 5.8

A small computer system controls the entry of vehicles to a car park. Each time a vehicle pulls up before an entry barrier, a sensor notifies the computer system of the vehicle's presence. The system examines a count that it maintains of the number of vehicles that are currently in the car park. This count is kept on backing storage so that it will still be available if the system is temporarily shut down, for example because of a power cut. If the count does not exceed the maximum allowed then the barrier is lifted and the count is incremented. When a vehicle leaves the car park, a sensor detects the exit and reduces the count of vehicles.

There is a system administration system that can set the maximum number of cars allowed, and which can be used to adjust or replace the count of cars when the system is restarted.

Identify the entries, exits, reads and writes in this application.

The overall FFP count is derived by simply adding up the counts for each of the four types of data movement. The resulting units are *Cfsu* (COSMIC functional size units). The method does not take account of any processing of the data groups once they have been moved into the software component. The framers of the method do not recommend its use for systems involving complex mathematical algorithms, for example, but there is provision for the definition of local versions for specialized environments which could incorporate counts of other software features.

COSMIC FFPs have been incorporated into an ISO standard – ISO/IEC 19761:2003. Prior to this there have been attempts to produce a single ISO standard for 'functional size measurement' and there is an ISO document – ISO/IEC 14143–1:1998 – which lays down some general principles. ISO has decided, diplomatically, that it is unable to judge the relative merits of the four main methods in the field: IFPUG, Mark II, NESMA and COSMIC-FFP, and all four have been allowed to submit their methods as candidates to become ISO standards and then to 'let the market decide'.

The NESMA FP method has been developed by the Netherlands Software Measurement Association.

5.11 A procedural code-oriented approach

The previous approach would be useful at the design stage of a project and where a procedural programming language is not the primary vehicle for development. However, how could you estimate the effort to develop an individual software module using a procedural language? An approach might be based on the following steps.

(a) Envisage the number and type of software modules in the final system

'Software module' here implies a component that can be separately compiled and executed.

This is easiest where the system is of a conventional and well-understood nature. Most information systems are built from a small set of system operations, e.g. Insert, Amend, Update, Display, Delete, Print. The same principle should equally apply to embedded systems, albeit with a different set of primitive functions.

(b) Estimate the SLOC of each identified program

The estimator must have a particular implementation language in mind for this step.

One way to judge the number of instructions likely to be in a program is to draw up a program structure diagram and to visualize how many instructions would be needed to implement each identified procedure. The estimator may look at existing programs which have a similar functional description to assist in this process.

Function point analysis Mark II is also based on the idea that the number of data item types processed influences program size.

Where programs for an information system are similar (for instance, they are data validation programs) then the number of data item types processed by each program is likely to be the major influence on size.

(c) Estimate the work content taking into account complexity and technical difficulty

The practice is to multiply the SLOC estimate by a factor for complexity and technical difficulty. This factor will depend largely on the subjective judgement of the estimator. For example, the requirement to meet particular highly constrained performance targets can greatly increase programming effort.

See Chapter 4 for a discussion of prototypes.

A weighting may be given when there is uncertainty, for example about a new technique used in particular module, but this should not be excessive. Where there is a large amount of uncertainty then specific measures should be taken to reduce this, e.g. by the use of exploratory prototypes.

(d) Calculate the work-days effort

Historical data can be used to provide ratios to convert weighted SLOC to effort. These conversion factors are often based on the productivity of a 'standard programmer' of about 15–18 months of experience. In installations where the rate of turnover is lower and the average programmer experience is higher, this may be reflected in the conversion rate employed.

Note that the steps above can be used to derive an estimate of lines of code that can be used as an input to one of the COCOMO models which are about to be described.

Exercise 5.9 Draw up an outline program structure diagram for a program to do the processing described in Exercise 5.7 which sets up CUSTOMER records. For each box on your diagram estimate the number of lines of code needed to implement the routine in a programming language that you are familiar with, such as Java.

5.12 COCOMO: a parametric model

Because there is now a newer COCOMO II, the older version is now referred to as COCOMO81.

Boehm's COCOMO (COnstructive COst MOdel) is often referred to in the literature on software project management, particularly in connection with software estimating. The term COCOMO really refers to a group of models.

Boehm originally based his models in the late 1970s on a study of 63 projects. Of these only seven were business systems and so the models could be used with applications other than information systems. The basic model was built around the equation

$$(effort) = c(size)^k$$

where *effort* was measured in *pm* or the number of 'person-months' consisting of units of 152 working hours, *size* was measured in *kdsi*, thousands of delivered source code instructions, and *c* and *k* were constants.

The first step was to derive an estimate of the system size in terms of *kdsi*. The constants, *c* and *k* (see Table 5.6), depended on whether the system could be classified, in Boehm's terms, as 'organic', 'semi-detached' or 'embedded'. These related to the technical nature of the system and the development environment.

Generally, information systems were regarded as organic while real-time systems were embedded.

- *Organic mode*   This would typically be the case when relatively small teams developed software in a highly familiar in-house environment and when the system being developed was small and the interface requirements were flexible.

- *Embedded mode*   This meant the product being developed had to operate within very tight constraints and changes to the system were very costly.

- *Semi-detached mode*   This combined elements of the organic and the embedded modes or had characteristics which came between the two.

The exponent value *k*, when it is greater than 1, means that larger projects are seen as requiring disproportionately more effort than smaller ones. This reflected Boehm's finding that larger projects tended to be less productive than smaller ones because they needed more effort for management and coordination.

Exercise 5.10 Apply the basic COCOMO model to the lines of code figures in Table 5.1 to generate estimated work-months of effort, assuming an organic mode. Compare the calculated figures with the actuals.

Table 5.6 COCOMO constants

System type	c	k
Organic	2·4	1·05
Semi-detached	3·0	1·12
Embedded	3·6	1·20

As well as the
intermediate model, a
further, detailed,
COCOMO model
attempts to allocate
effort to individual
project phases.

Boehm in fact found this, by itself, to be a poor predictor of the effort required and so went on to develop the intermediate version of COCOMO which took into account 15 cost drivers. In the intermediate model, a nominal effort estimate (pm_{nom}) is derived in a similar way as for the basic model.

The nominal estimate is then adjusted by a development effort multiplier *(dem)*:

$$(pm_{est}) = (pm_{nom}) \times (dem)$$

where *dem* is calculated by taking into account multipliers based on the effort drivers in Table 5.7.

These multipliers take into account such influences on productivity as Boehm's finding that having a programming team fully conversant with the programming language to be used could reduce the effort required to implement the project by up to 20% compared to a team with a very low or initially non-existent familiarity with the programming language. In fact, the biggest influence on productivity, according to Boehm, relates to the capabilities of the implementation team.

As an example of the approach, an organization may decide to use the following multipliers for assessing the effect of analyst capability (ACAP).

Very low	1.46
Low	1.19
Nominal	1.00
High	0.8
Very High	0.71

If the analysts involved in a project, taken as a whole, generally possess above-average talent and productivity then the estimator might rate the ACAP as high and use a multiplier of 0.8, effectively reducing the nominal estimate by 20%.

Table 5.7 COCOMO81 intermediate cost drivers

Driver type	Code	Cost driver
Product attributes	RELY	Required software reliability
	DATA	Database size
	CPLX	Product complexity
Computer attributes	TIME	Execution time constraints
	STOR	Main storage constraints
	VIRT	Virtual machine volatility – degree to which the operating system changes
	TURN	Computer turnaround time
Personnel attributes	ACAP	Analyst capability
	AEXP	Application experience
	PCAP	Programmer capability
	VEXP	Virtual machine (i.e. operating system) experience
	LEXP	Programming language experience
Project attributes	MODP	Use of modern programming practices
	TOOL	Use of software tools
	SCED	Required development schedule

The overall *dem* is calculated by multiplying the multipliers selected for each cost driver in Table 5.7 to create a single combined multiplier.

Exercise 5.11

At IOE, most of the systems that are developed are technically similar so that the product, computer and project attributes, as listed in Table 5.7, do not change from one project to another and are given a unit multiplier of 1.0. Only personnel attributes differ and the following table is used by the organization to take this into account.

Attribute	Very low	Low	Nominal	High	Very high
ACAP	1.46	1.19	1.00	0.86	0.71
AEXP	1.29	1.13	1.00	0.91	0.82
PCAP	1.42	1.17	1.00	0.86	0.70
VEXP	1.21	1.10	1.00	0.90	
LEXP	1.14	1.07	1.00	0.95	

On the new IOE group maintenance accounts project, the analyst is regarded as being of exceptionally high quality. The software developers are of high quality but have little experience of the particular application area and are going to use a programming language that is new to them. They are, however, familiar with the operating system environment and thus can be rated as high on VEXP.

What would be the *dem* for this project? If the nominal estimate for this project was 4 staff-months, what would be the final estimate?

The detailed COCOMO II Model Definition Manual has been published by the Center for Software Engineering, University of Southern California.

A new family of models, COCOMO II, has been refined by Barry Boehm and his co-workers. This approach uses various multipliers and exponents the values of which have been set initially by experts. However, a database containing the performance details of executed projects is being built up and periodically analysed so that the expert judgements can be progressively replaced by values derived from actual projects. The new models take into account that there is now a wider range of process models in common use for software development projects than in the late 1970s and early 1980s. As we noted earlier, estimates are required at different stages in the system life cycle and COCOMO II has been designed to accommodate this by having models for three different stages.

Application composition Here the external features of the system that the users will experience are designed. Prototyping will typically be employed to do this. With small applications that can be built using high-productivity application-building tools, development can stop at this point.

Early design Here the fundamental software structures are designed. With larger, more demanding systems, where, for example, there will be large volumes of transactions and performance is important, careful attention will need to be paid to the architecture to be adopted.

See R. D. Banker, R. Kauffman and R. Kumar, 'An empirical test of object-based output measurement metrics' *Journal of MIS*, 8(3), 1992.

Post architecture Here the software structures undergo final construction, modification and tuning to create a system that will perform as required.

To estimate the effort for *application composition,* the counting of *object points* is recommended by the developers of COCOMO II. This follows the function point approach of counting externally apparent features of the software. It differs by focusing on the physical features of the application, such as screens and reports, rather than 'logical' ones like entity types. This is seen as being more useful whether requirements are being elicited via prototypes.

At the *early design* stage, FPs are recommended as the way of gauging a basic system size. An FP count may be converted to a LOC equivalent by multiplying the FPs by a factor for the programming language that is to be used.

The following model can then be used to calculate an estimate of person-months.

$$pm = A(size)^{(sf)} \times (em_1) \times (em_2) \times \ldots (em_n)$$

where *pm* is the effort in 'person-months', *A* is a constant (which was, in 1998, 2.45), *size* is measured in *kdsi* (which may have been derived from an FP count as explained above), and *sf* is exponent scale factor.

The scale factor is derived thus:

$$sf = 1.01 + 0.01 \times \Sigma \; (exponent \; driver \; ratings).$$

Exercise 5.12 What is the maximum value that the scale factor (*sf*) can have given that there are five exponent drivers and the maximum rating for an individual driver is five and the minimum is zero?

The qualities that govern exponent drivers used to calculate the scale factor are listed below. Note that the less each quality is applicable, the bigger the value given to the exponent driver. The fact that these factors are used to calculate an exponent implies that the lack of these qualities will increase the effort required disproportionately more on larger projects.

● *Precedentedness* This quality refers to the degree to which there are precedents, that is, similar cases in the past, for the project that is being planned. The greater the novelty of the new system, the more uncertainty there is and the higher the value given to the exponent driver.

● *Development flexibility* This is the degree to which the requirements can be met in a number of different ways. The less flexibility there is, the higher the value of the exponent driver.

● *Architecture/risk resolution* This relates to the degree of uncertainty there is about the requirements. If they are not firmly fixed and are liable to change then this would lead to a high value being given to this exponent driver.

● *Team cohesion* This reflects the degree to which there is a large dispersed team (perhaps in several countries) as opposed to there being a small tightly knit team.

● *Process maturity* The chapter on software quality explains the process maturity model. The more structured and organized the way the software is produced, the lower the uncertainty and the lower the rating will be for this exponent driver.

Exercise 5.13 A new project has 'average' novelty for the software supplier that is going to execute it and is thus given a 3 rating on this account for precedentedness. Development flexibility is high to the extent that this generates a zero rating, but requirements may change radically and so the risk resolution exponent is rated at 4. The team is very cohesive and this generates a rating of 1, but the software house as a whole tends to be very informal in its standards and procedures and the process maturity driver has therefore been given a value of 4.

What would be the scale factor (*sf*) that would be applicable in this case?

In the COCOMO II model the *effort multipliers* (*em*) are similar in nature to the development effort multipliers (*dem*) used in the original COCOMO. There are seven of these multipliers that are relevant to early design and sixteen that can be used at the post architecture stage. Table 5.8 lists the effort multipliers for early design and Table 5.9 for post architecture. As with COCOMO81, each of these multipliers may, for a particular application, be given a rating of very low, low, nominal, high or very high. Each rating for each effort multiplier has a value associated with it. A value greater than 1 means that development effort is increased, while a value less than one causes effort to be decreased. The nominal rating means that the multiplier has no effect on the estimate, i.e. it is 1. The intention is that the ratings that these and other values use in COCOMO II will be modified and refined over time as details of actual projects are added to the database.

Table 5.8 COCOMO II Early design effort multipliers

Code	Effort modifier
RCPX	Product reliability and complexity
RUSE	Required reusability
PDIF	Platform difficulty
PERS	Personnel capability
PREX	Personnel experience
FCIL	Facilities available
SCED	Schedule pressure

Table 5.9 COCOMO II Post architecture effort multipliers

Modifier type	Code	Effort modifier
Product attributes	RELY	Required software reliability
	DATA	Database size
	DOCU	Documentation match to life-cycle needs
	CPLX	Product complexity
	REUSE	Required reusability
Platform attributes	TIME	Execution time constraint
	STOR	Main storage constraint
	PVOL	Platform volatility
Personnel attributes	ACAP	Analyst capabilities
	AEXP	Application experience
	PCAP	Programmer capabilities
	PEXP	Platform experience
	LEXP	Programming language experience
	PCON	Personnel continuity
Project attributes	TOOL	Use of software tools
	SITE	Multisite development
	SCED	Schedule pressure

5.13 Conclusion

To summarize some key points:

● estimates are really management targets;

● collect as much information about previous projects as possible;

● use more than one method of estimating;

● top-down approaches will be used at the earlier stages of project planning while bottom-up approaches will be more prominent later on;

● be careful about using other people's historical productivity data as a basis for your estimates, especially if it comes from a different environment (this includes COCOMO!);

● seek a range of opinions;

● document your method of doing estimates and record all your assumptions.

5.14 Further exercises

1. Identify the factors affecting the size of the task and work rates for the following activities:
   ● installing computer workstations in a new office;
   ● transporting assembled personal computers from the factory where they were assembled to warehouses distributed in different parts of the country;
   ● typing in and checking the correctness of data that is populating a new database;
   ● system testing a newly written software application.

2. If you were asked as an expert to provide an estimate of the effort needed to make certain changes to an existing piece of software, what information would you like to have to hand to assist you in making that estimate?

3. A small application maintains a telephone directory. The database for the application contains the following data types:
   ● Staff reference
   ● Surname
   ● Forenames
   ● Title
   ● Department code
   ● Room number
   ● Telephone extension
   ● E-mail address
   ● Fax number

   Transactions are needed which:
   (i)   set up new entries;
   (ii) amend existing entries;
   (iii) delete entries;
   (iv) allow enquirers to list online the details for a particular member of staff;
   (v)   produce a complete listing of the telephone directory entries in alphabetical order.

(a) Use this scenario to produce an estimated Mark II FP count. List all the assumptions you will need to make.

(b) Another requirement could be to produce the listing in (v) in departmental order. In your view, should this increase FP count and if so by how much?

4. The following details are held about a previously developed software modules.

Module	Inputs	Entity types accessed	Outputs	Days
a	1	2	10	2.60
b	10	2	1	3.90
c	5	1	1	1.83
d	2	3	11	3.50
e	1	3	20	4.30

A new module has 7 inputs, one entity type access and 7 outputs. Which of the modules a to e is the closest analogy in terms of Euclidean distance?

5. Using the data in exercise 4 above, calculate the Symons Mark II FPs for each module. Using the results, calculate the effort needed for the new module described in further exercise 4. How does this estimate compare to the one based on analogy?

6. Given the project data below:

Project	Inputs	Outputs	Entity accesses	System users	Programming language	Developer days
1	210	420	40	10	x	30
2	469	1406	125	20	x	85
3	513	1283	76	18	y	108
4	660	2310	88	200	y	161
5	183	367	35	10	z	22
6	244	975	65	25	z	42
7	1600	3200	237	25	y	308
8	582	874	111	5	z	62
X	180	350	40	20	y	
Y	484	1190	69	35	y	

(a) What items are size drivers?
(b) What items are productivity drivers?
(c) What are the productivity rates for programming languages x, y and z?
(d) What would be the estimated effort for projects X and Y using a Mark II function point count?
(e) What would be the estimated effort for X and Y using an approximate analogy approach?
(f) What would have been the best estimating method if the actual effort for X turns out to be 30 days and for Y turns out to be 120 days? Can you suggest why the results are as they are and how they might be improved.

7. A report in a college timetabling system produces a report showing the students who should be attending each timetabled teaching activity. Four files are accessed: the STAFF file, the STUDENT file, the STUDENT-OPTION file and the TEACHING-ACTIVITY file. The report contains the following information:

Teaching activity reference
Topic name
Staff forenames
Staff surname
Title
Semester (1 or 2)
Day of week
Time
Duration
Location
For each student:
  student forename
  student surnames

Calculate both the IFPUG and Mark II FPs that this transaction would generate. Can you identify the factors that would tend to make the two methods generate divergent counts?

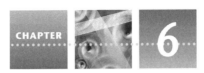

Activity planning

6.1 Introduction

In earlier chapters we looked at methods for forecasting the effort required for a project – both for the project as a whole and for individual activities. A detailed plan for the project, however, must also include a schedule indicating the start and completion times for each activity. This will enable us to:

- ensure that the appropriate resources will be available precisely when required;
- avoid different activities competing for the same resources at the same time;
- produce a detailed schedule showing which staff carry out each activity;
- produce a detailed plan against which actual achievement may be measured;
- produce a timed cash flow forecast;
- replan the project during its life to correct drift from the target.

To be effective, a plan must be stated as a set of targets, the achievement or non-achievement of which can be unambiguously measured. The activity plan does this by providing a target start and completion date for each activity (or a window within which each activity may be carried out). The starts and completions of activities must be clearly visible and this is one of the reasons why it is advisable to ensure that each and every project activity produces some tangible product or 'deliverable'. Monitoring the project's progress is then, at least in part, a case of ensuring that the products of each activity are delivered on time.

As a project progresses it is unlikely that everything will go according to plan. Much of the job of project management concerns recognizing when something has gone wrong, identifying its causes and revising the plan to mitigate its effects. The activity plan should provide a means of evaluating the consequences of not meeting any of the activity target dates and guidance as to how the plan might

Project monitoring is discussed in more detail in Chapter 9.

117

most effectively be modified to bring the project back to target. We shall see that the activity plan may well also offer guidance as to which components of a project should be most closely monitored.

6.2   The objectives of activity planning

In addition to providing project and resource schedules, activity planning aims to achieve a number of other objectives which may be summarized as follows.

- *Feasibility assessment*   Is the project possible within required timescales and resource constraints? It is not until we have constructed a detailed plan that we can forecast a completion date with any reasonable knowledge of its achievability. The fact that a project may have been estimated as requiring two work-years effort might not mean that it would be feasible to complete it within, say, three months were eight people to work on it – that will depend upon the availability of staff and the degree to which activities may be undertaken in parallel.

- *Resource allocation*   What are the most effective ways of allocating resources to the project. When should the resources be available? The project plan allows us to investigate the relationship between timescales and resource availability (in general, allocating additional resources to a project shortens its duration) and the efficacy of additional spending on resource procurement.

- *Detailed costing*   How much will the project cost and when is that expenditure likely to take place? After producing an activity plan and allocating specific resources, we can obtain more detailed estimates of costs and their timing.

Chapter 11 discusses motivation in more detail.

- *Motivation*   Providing targets and being seen to monitor achievement against targets is an effective way of motivating staff, particularly where they have been involved in setting those targets in the first place.

This coordination will normally form part of Programme Management.

- *Co-ordination*   When do the staff in different departments need to be available to work on a particular project and when do staff need to be transferred between projects? The project plan, particularly with large projects involving more than a single project team, provides an effective vehicle for communication and coordination among teams. In situations where staff may need to be transferred between project teams (or work concurrently on more than one project), a set of integrated project schedules should ensure that such staff are available when required and do not suffer periods of enforced idleness.

In Chapter 2 we saw that Amanda's wish to check that four module specifications were correct, while increasing the likely quality of the product, created a constraint that could potentially delay the next stage of the project.

Activity planning and scheduling techniques place an emphasis on completing the project in a minimum time at an acceptable cost or, alternatively, meeting a set target date at minimum cost. These are not, in themselves, concerned with meeting quality targets, which generally impose constraints on the scheduling process.

One effective way of shortening project durations is to carry out activities in parallel. Clearly we cannot undertake all the activities at the same time – some require the completion of others before they can start and there are likely to be resource constraints limiting how much may be done simultaneously. Activity scheduling will, however, give us an indication of the cost of these constraints in terms of lengthening timescales and provide us with an indication of how timescales may be shortened by relaxing those constraints. It is up to us, if we try relaxing precedence constraints by, for example, allowing a program coding task to commence before the design has been completed, to ensure that we are clear about the potential effects on product quality.

6.3 When to plan

Planning is an ongoing process of refinement, each iteration becoming more detailed and more accurate than the last. Over successive iterations, the emphasis and purpose of planning will shift.

During the feasibility study and project start-up, the main purpose of planning will be to estimate timescales and the risks of not achieving target completion dates or keeping within budget. As the project proceeds beyond the feasibility study, the emphasis will be placed upon the production of activity plans for ensuring resource availability and cash flow control.

Throughout the project, until the final deliverable has reached the customer, monitoring and replanning must continue to correct any drift that might prevent meeting time or cost targets.

6.4 Project schedules

On a large project, detailed plans for the later stages will be delayed until information about the work required has emerged from the earlier stages.

Before work commences on a project or, possibly, a stage of a larger project, the project plan must be developed to the level of showing dates when each activity should start and finish and when and how much of each resource will be required. Once the plan has been refined to this level of detail we call it a project schedule. Creating a project schedule comprises four main stages.

The first step in producing the plan is to decide what activities need to be carried out and in what order they are to be done. From this we can construct an ideal activity plan – that is, a plan of when each activity would ideally be undertaken were resources not a constraint. It is the creation of the ideal activity plan that we shall discuss in this chapter. This activity plan is generated by Steps 4 and 5 of Step Wise (Figure 6.1).

The ideal activity plan will then be the subject of an activity risk analysis, aimed at identifying potential problems. This might suggest alterations to the ideal activity plan and will almost certainly have implications for resource allocation. Activity risk analysis is the subject of Chapter 7.

The third step is resource allocation. The expected availability of resources might place constraints on when certain activities can be carried out, and our ideal plan might need to be adapted to take account of this. Resource allocation is covered in Chapter 8.

The final step is *schedule production*. Once resources have been allocated to each activity, we will be in a position to draw up and publish a project schedule, which indicates planned start and completion dates and a resource requirements statement for each activity. Chapter 9 discusses how this is done and the role of the schedule in managing a project.

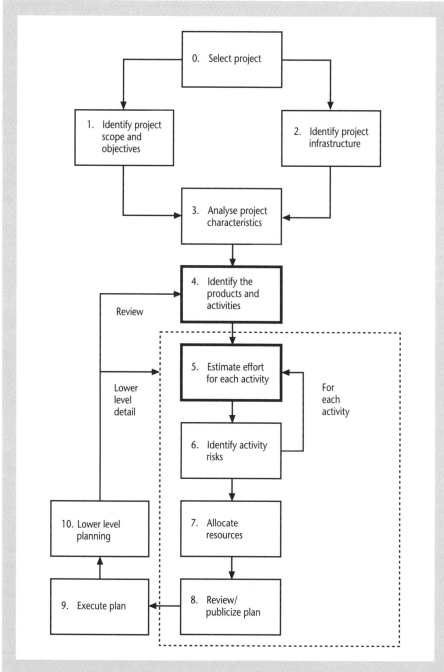

Figure 6.1   Activity planning is carried out in Steps 4 and 5

6.5 Projects and activities

Defining activities

Before we try to identify the activities that make up a project it is worth reviewing what we mean by a project and its activities and adding some assumptions that will be relevant when we start to produce an activity plan.

Activities must be defined so that they meet these criteria. Any activity that does not meet these criteria must be redefined.

● A project is composed of a number of interrelated activities.

● A project may start when at least one of its activities is ready to start.

● A project will be completed when all of the activities it encompasses have been completed.

● If an activity must have a clearly defined start and a clearly defined end-point, normally marked by the production of a tangible deliverable.

● An activity requires a resource (as most do) then that resource requirement must be forecastable and is assumed to be required at a constant level throughout the duration of the activity.

● The duration of an activity must be forecastable – assuming normal circumstances, and the reasonable availability of resources.

● Some activities might require that others are completed before they can begin (these are known as precedence requirements).

Identifying activities

Essentially there are three approaches to identifying the activities or tasks that make up a project – we shall call them the *activity-based approach, the product-based approach* and the *hybrid approach.*

The activity-based approach

The activity-based approach consists of creating a list of all the activities that the project is thought to involve. This might involve a brainstorming session involving the whole project team or it might stem from an analysis of similar past projects. When listing activities, particularly for a large project, it might be helpful to subdivide the project into the main life-style stages and consider each of these separately.

Rather than doing this in an ad hoc manner, with the obvious risks of omitting or double-counting tasks, a much favoured way of generating a task list is to create a *Work Breakdown Structure* (WBS). This involves identifying the main (or high-level) tasks required to complete a project and then breaking each of these down into a set of lower-level tasks. Figure 6.2 shows a fragment of a WBS where the design task has been broken down into three tasks and one of these has been further decomposed into two tasks.

WBSs are advocated by BS 6079, which is discussed in Appendix B.

Activities are added to a branch in the structure if they directly contribute to the task immediately above – if they do not contribute to the parent task, then they should not be added to that branch. The tasks at each level in any branch should include everything that is required to complete the task at the higher level – if they are not a comprehensive definition of the parent task, then something is missing.

When preparing a WBS, consideration must be given to the final level of detail

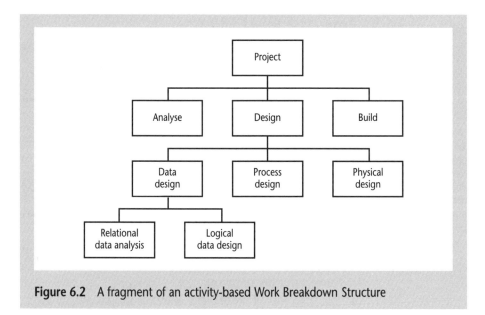

Figure 6.2 A fragment of an activity-based Work Breakdown Structure

or depth of the structure. Too great a depth will result in a large number of small tasks that will be difficult to manage, whereas a too shallow structure will provide insufficient detail for project control. Each branch should, however, be broken down at least to a level where each leaf may be assigned to an individual or responsible section within the organization.

A complete task catalogue will normally include task definitions along with task input and output products and other task-related information.

Advantages claimed for the WBS approach include the belief that it is much more likely to result in a task catalogue that is complete and is composed of non-overlapping activities. Note that it is only the leaves of the structure that comprise the list of activities in the project – higher-level nodes merely represent collections of activities.

The WBS also represents a structure that may be refined as the project proceeds. In the early part of a project we might use a relatively high-level or shallow WBS, which can be developed as information becomes available, typically during the project's analysis and specification phases.

Once the project's activities have been identified (whether or not by using a WBS), they need to be sequenced in the sense of deciding which activities need to be completed before others can start.

The product-based approach

The product-based approach, used in PRINCE2 and Step Wise, has already been described in Chapter 2. It consists of producing a Product Breakdown Structure and a Product Flow Diagram. The PFD indicates, for each product, which other products are required as inputs. The PFD can therefore be easily transformed into an ordered list of activities by identifying the transformations that turn some products into others. Proponents of this approach claim that it is less likely that a product will be left out of a PBS than that an activity might be omitted from an unstructured activity list.

This approach is particularly appropriate if using a methodology such as SSADM, which clearly specifies, for each step or task, each of the products

Most good texts on SSADM will explain the tailoring of the generic PBSs and Activity Networks. The illustrations here are taken from M. Goodland and C. Slater, *SSADM Version 4: A Practical Approach*, McGraw-Hill, 1995.

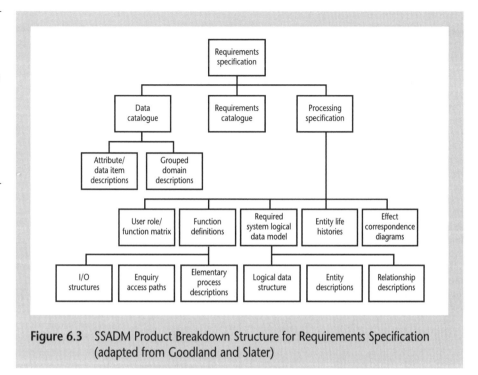

Figure 6.3 SSADM Product Breakdown Structure for Requirements Specification (adapted from Goodland and Slater)

required and the activities required to produce it. The SSADM Reference Manual provides a set of generic PBSs for each stage in SSADM (such as that shown in Figure 6.3), which can be used as a basis for generating a project-specific PBS.

The SSADM Reference Manual also supplies generic activity networks and, using the project-specific PBS and derived PFD, these may be used as a basis for developing a project-specific activity network. Figure 6.4 illustrates an activity network for the activities required to create the products in Figure 6.3.

The activity numbers in Figure 6.4 are the step numbers used by SSADM version 4.

Notice how the development of a PFD leads directly to an activity network that indicates the sequencing of activities – in Figure 6.4, activity 340 (Enhance required data model) requires products from activity 330 and activity 360 needs products from both activities 330 and 340.

The hybrid approach

BS 6079 states that WBSs may be product-based, cost-centre-based, task-based or function-based but states that product-based WBSs are preferred.

The WBS illustrated in Figure 6.2 is based entirely on a structuring of activities. Alternatively, and perhaps more commonly, a WBS may be based upon the project's products as illustrated in Figure 6.5, which is in turn based on a simple list of final deliverables and, for each deliverable, a set of activities required to produce that product. Figure 6.5 illustrates a flat WBS and it is likely that, in a project of any size, it would be beneficial to introduce additional levels – structuring both products and activities. The degree to which the structuring is product-based or activity-based might be influenced by the nature of the project and the particular development method adopted. As with a purely activity-based WBS, having identified the activities we are then left with the task of sequencing them.

Not all of the products in this activity structuring will be final products. Some will be further refined in subsequent steps. The current version of the SSADM reference manual provides generic PBSs and generic activity networks but not generic PFDs. Stress is placed on the fact that these are generic structures and it is important that project-specific versions are created. A project-specific PFD would be produced as part of this process.

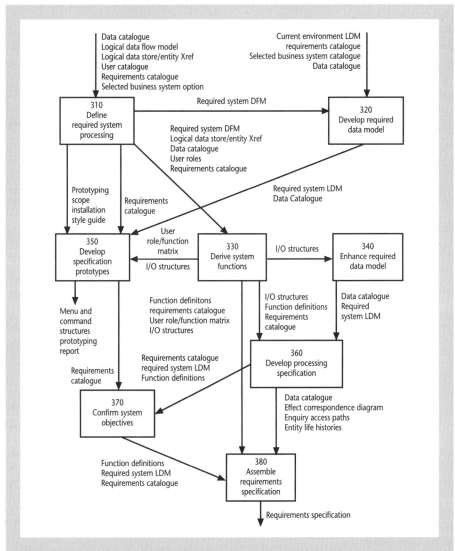

Figure 6.4 A structuring of activities for the SSADM Requirements Specification stage (from Goodland and Slater)

A framework dictating the number of levels and the nature of each level in the structure may be imposed on a WBS. For example, in their MITP methodology, IBM recommend that the following five levels should be used in a WBS:

● *Level 1: Project.*

● *Level 2: Deliverables* such as software, manuals and training courses.

● *Level 3: Components* which are the key work items needed to produce deliverables, such as the modules and tests required to produce the system software.

● *Level 4: Work-packages* which are major work items, or collections of related tasks, required to produce a component.

● *Level 5: Tasks* which are tasks that will normally be the responsibility of a single person.

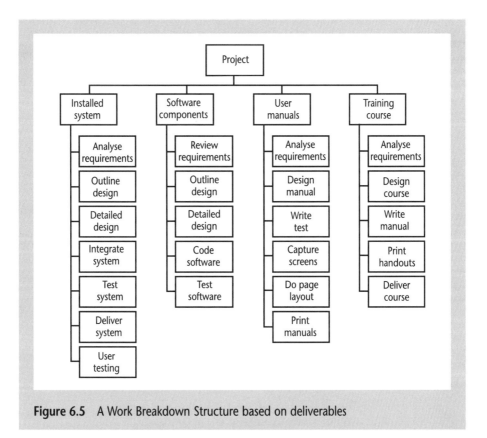

Figure 6.5 A Work Breakdown Structure based on deliverables

6.6 Sequencing and scheduling activities

Throughout a project, we will require a schedule that clearly indicates when each of the project's activities is planned to occur and what resources it will need. We shall be considering scheduling in more detail in Chapter 8, but let us consider in outline how we might present a schedule for a small project. One way of presenting such a plan is to use a bar chart as shown in Figure 6.6.

The chart shown has been drawn up taking account of the nature of the development process (that is, certain tasks must be completed before others may start) and the resources that are available (for example, activity C follows activity B because Andy cannot work on both tasks at the same time). In drawing up the chart, we have therefore done two things – we have sequenced the tasks (that is, identified the dependencies among activities dictated by the development process) and scheduled them (that is, specified when they should take place). The scheduling has had to take account of the availability of staff and the ways in which the activities have been allocated to them. The schedule might look quite different were there a different number of staff or were we to allocate the activities differently.

In the case of small projects, this combined sequencing–scheduling approach might be quite suitable, particularly where we wish to allocate individuals to particular tasks at an early planning stage. However, on larger projects it is better to separate out these two activities: to sequence the tasks according to their logical

The bar chart does not show why certain decisions have been made. It is not clear, for example, why activity H is not scheduled to start until week 9. It could be that it cannot start until activity F has been completed or it might be because Charlie is going to be on holiday during week 8.

Separating the logical sequencing from the scheduling may be likened to the principle in systems analysis of separating the logical system from its physical implementation.

Weeks Task : Person	1	2	3	4	5	6	7	8	9	10	11	12	13
A : Andy	■												
B : Andy		■											
C : Andy			■										
D : Andy				■									
E : Bill				■	■								
F : Bill								■	■				
G : Charlie						■	■	■					
H : Charlie									■				
I : Dave										■	■	■	

Activity key	A : Overall design	F : Code module 3
	B : Specify module 1	G : Code module 2
	C : Specify module 2	H : Integration testing
	D : Specify module 3	I : Sytem tesing
	E : Code module 1	

Figure 6.6   A project plan as a bar chart

relationships and then to schedule them taking into account resources and other factors.

Approaches to scheduling that achieve this separation between the logical and the physical use networks to model the project and it is these approaches that we will consider in subsequent sections of this chapter.

6.7   Network planning models

CPM was developed by the DuPont Chemical Company who published the method in 1958, claiming that it had saved them $1 million in its first year of use.

These project scheduling techniques model the project's activities and their relationships as a network. In the network, time flows from left to right. These techniques were originally developed in the 1950s – the two best known being CPM (Critical Path Method) and PERT (Program Evaluation Review Technique).

Both of these techniques used an *activity-on-arrow* approach to visualizing the project as a network where activities are drawn as arrows joining circles, or nodes, which represent the possible start and/or completion of an activity or set of activities. More recently a variation on these techniques, called *precedence networks*, has become popular. This method uses *activity-on-node* networks where activities are represented as nodes and the links between nodes represent precedence (or sequencing) requirements. This latter approach avoids some of the problems inherent in the activity-on-arrow representation and provides more scope for easily representing certain situations. It is this method that is adopted in the majority of computer applications currently available. These three methods are very similar and it must be admitted that many people use the same name (particularly CPM) indiscriminately to refer to any or all of the methods.

In the following sections of this chapter, we will look at the critical path method applied to precedence (activity-on-node) networks followed by a brief introduction to activity-on-arrow networks – a discussion of PERT will be reserved for Chapter 7 when we look at risk analysis.

**CASE STUDY
EXAMPLES**

In Chapter 2 we saw how Amanda identified that two new software components would need to be developed and a further two components would need to be written. Figure 6.7 shows the fragment of a network that she has developed as an activity-on-node network. Figure 6.8 shows how this network would look represented as an activity-on-arrow network. Study each of the networks briefly to verify that they are, indeed, merely different graphical representations of the same thing.

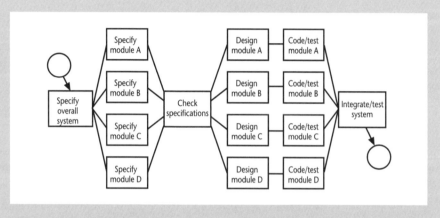

Figure 6.7 The IOE maintenance group accounts project activity network fragment with a checkpoint activity added

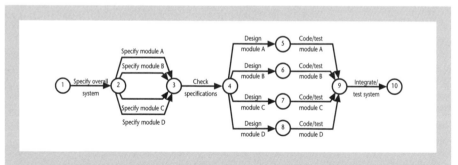

Figure 6.8 The IOE maintenance group accounts project activity network fragment represented as a CPM network

6.8 Formulating a network model

The first stage in creating a network model is to represent the activities and their interrelationships as a graph. In activity-on-node we do this by representing activities as links (arrowed lines) in the graph – the nodes (circles) representing the events of activities starting and finishing.

Constructing precedence networks

Before we look at how networks are used, it is worth spending a few moments considering some rules for their construction.

A project network should have only one start node   Although it is logically possible to draw a network with more than one starting node, it is undesirable to do so as it is a potential source of confusion. In such cases (for example, where more than one activity can start immediately the project starts) it is normal to invent a 'start' activity which has zero duration but may have an actual start date.

A project network should have only one end node   The end node designates the completion of the project and a project may only finish once! Although it is possible to draw a network with more than one end node it will almost certainly lead to confusion if this is done. Where the completion of a project depends upon more than one 'final' activity it is normal to invent a 'finish' activity.

A node has duration   A node represents an activity and, in general, activities take time to execute. Notice, however, that the network in Figure 6.7 does not contain any reference to durations. This network drawing merely represents the logic of the project – the rules governing the order in which activities are to be carried out.

Links normally have no duration   Links represent the relationships between activities. In Figure 6.9 installation cannot start until program testing is complete. Program testing cannot start until both coding and data take-on have been completed.

Later we will look at the possibility of 'lag' between activities.

Precedents are the immediate preceding activities   In Figure 6.9, the activity 'Program test' cannot start until both 'Code' and 'Data take-on' have been completed and activity 'Install' cannot start until 'Program test' has finished. 'Code' and 'Data take-on' can therefore be said to be precedents of 'Program test', and 'Program test' is a precedent of 'Install'. Note that we do not speak of 'Code' and 'Data take-on' as precedents of 'Install' – that relationship is implicit in the previous statement.

Time moves from left to right   If at all possible, networks are drawn so that time moves from left to right. It is rare that this convention needs to be flouted but some people add arrows to the lines to give a stronger visual indication of the time flow of the project.

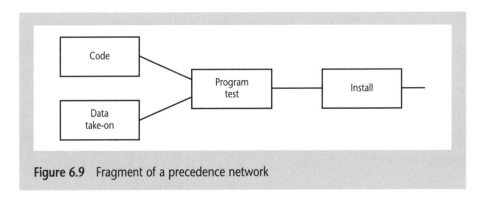

Figure 6.9 Fragment of a precedence network

Figure 6.10 A loop represents an impossible sequence

A network may not contain loops   Figure 6.10 demonstrates a loop in a network. A loop is an error in that it represents a situation that cannot occur in practice. While loops, in the sense of iteration, may occur in practice, they cannot be directly represented in a project network. Note that the logic of Figure 6.10 suggests that program testing cannot start until the errors have been corrected.

If we know the number of times we expect to repeat a set of activities, a test–diagnose–correct sequence, for example, then we can draw that set of activities as a straight sequence, repeating it the appropriate number of times. If we do not know how many times a sequence is going to be repeated then we cannot calculate the duration of the project unless we adopt an alternative strategy such as redefining the complete sequence as a single activity and estimating how long it will take to complete it.

Although it is easy to see the loop in this simple network fragment, very large networks can easily contain complex loops which are difficult to spot when they are initially constructed. Fortunately, all network planning applications will detect loops and generate error messages when they are found.

A network should not contain dangles   A dangling activity such as 'Write user manual' in Figure 6.11 should not exist as it is likely to lead to errors in subsequent analysis. Indeed, in many cases dangling activities indicate errors in logic when activities are added as an afterthought. If, in Figure 6.11, we mean to indicate that the project is complete once the software has been installed *and* the user manual written then we should redraw the network with a final completion activity – which, at least in this case, is probably a more accurate

Figure 6.11   A dangle

Figure 6.12 Resolving the dangle

representation of what should happen. The redrawn network is shown in Figure 6.12.

Representing lagged activities

We might come across situations where we wished to undertake two activities in parallel so long as there is a lag between the two. We might wish to document amendments to a program as it was being tested – particularly if evaluating a prototype. In such a case we could designate an activity 'test and document amendments'. This would, however, make it impossible to show that amendment recording could start, say, one day after testing had begun and finish a little after the completion of testing.

Where activities can occur in parallel with a time lag between them we represent the lag with a duration on the linking arrow as shown in Figure 6.13. This indicates that documenting amendments can start one day after the start of prototype testing and will be completed two days after prototype testing is completed.

Hammock activities

Hammock activities are activities which, in themselves, have zero duration but are assumed to start at the same time as the first 'hammocked' activity and to end at the same time as the last one. They are normally used for representing overhead

Documenting amendments may take place alongside prototype testing so long as it starts at least one day later and finishes two days later.

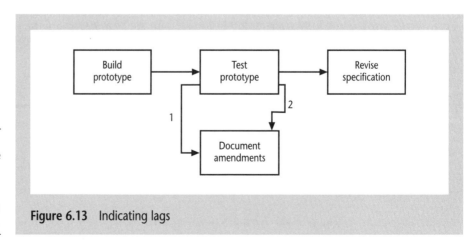

Figure 6.13 Indicating lags

costs or other resources that will be incurred or used at a constant rate over the duration of a set of activities.

Labelling conventions

Activity label	Duration
Earliest start	Activity description	Earliest finish
Latest start	Latest finish
Activity span	Float

There are a number of differing conventions that have been adopted for entering information on an activity-on-node network. One of the more common conventions for labelling nodes, and the one adopted here, is shown on the left.

The activity label is usually a code developed to uniquely identify the activity and may incorporate a project code (for example, InvExt/P/3 to designate one of the programming activities for IOE's invoice extension project). The activity description will normally be a brief activity name such as 'Test take-on module'. The other items in our activity node will be explained as we discuss the analysis of a project network.

6.9 Adding the time dimension

Having created the logical network model indicating what needs to be done and the interrelationships between those activities, we are now ready to start thinking about when each activity should be undertaken.

The critical path approach is concerned with two primary objectives: planning the project in such a way that it is completed as quickly as possible; and identifying those activities where a delay in their execution is likely to affect the overall end date of the project or later activities' start dates.

The method requires that for each activity we have an estimate of its duration. The network is then analysed by carrying out a *forward pass*, to calculate the earliest dates at which activities may commence and the project be completed, and a *backward pass*, to calculate the latest start dates for activities and the *critical path*.

In practice we would use a software application to carry out these calculations for anything but the smallest of projects. It is important, though, that we understand how the calculations are carried out in order to interpret the results correctly and understand the limitations of the method.

The description and example that follow use the small example project outlined in Table 6.1 – a project composed of eight activities whose durations have been estimated as shown in the table.

Table 6.1 An example project specification with estimated activity durations and precedence requirements

Activity		Duration (weeks)	Precedents
A	Hardware selection	6	
B	Software design	4	
C	Install hardware	3	A
D	Code & test software	4	B
E	File take-on	3	B
F	Write user manuals	10	
G	User training	3	E, F
H	Install & test system	2	C, D

Figure 6.14 illustrates
the network for the
project specified in
Table 6.1.

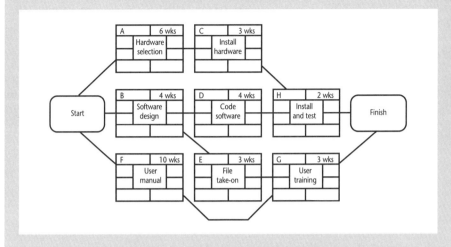

Figure 6.14 The precedence network for the example project

Exercise 6.1 Draw an activity network using precedence network conventions for the project specified in Table 6.1. When you have completed it, compare your result with that shown
in Figure 6.14.

6.10 The forward pass

The forward pass is carried out to calculate the earliest dates on which each
activity may be started and completed.

During the forward
pass, earliest dates are
recorded as they are
calculated.

Where an actual start date is known, the calculations may be carried out using
actual dates. Alternatively we can use day or week numbers and that is the
approach we shall adopt here. By convention, dates indicate the end of a period
and the project is therefore shown as starting at the end of week zero (or the
beginning of week 1).

The forward pass and the calculation of earliest start dates is calculated
according to the following reasoning.

● Activities A, B and F may start immediately, so the earliest date for their start is
zero.

● Activity A will take 6 weeks, so the earliest it can finish is week 6.

● Activity B will take 4 weeks, so the earliest it can finish is week 4.

● Activity F will take 10 weeks, so the earliest it can finish is week 10.

● Activity C can start as soon as A has finished so its earliest start date is week 6.
It will take 3 weeks so the earliest it can finish is week 9.

● Activities D and E can start as soon as B is complete so the earliest they can each
start is week 4. Activity D, which will take 4 weeks, can therefore finish by
week 8 and activity E, which will take 3 weeks, can therefore finish by week 7.

● Activity G cannot start until both E and F have been completed. It cannot

The forward pass rule: the earliest start date for an activity is the earliest finish date for the preceding activity. Where there is more than one immediately preceding activity we take the *latest* of the *earliest finish dates* for those activities.

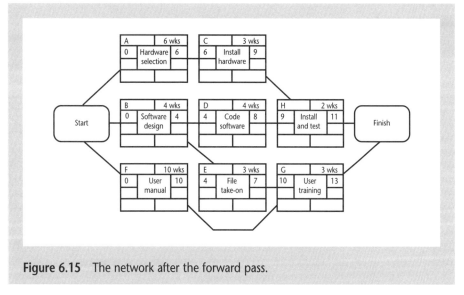

Figure 6.15 The network after the forward pass.

therefore start until week 10 – the later of weeks 7 (for activity E) and 10 (for activity F). It takes 3 weeks and finishes in week 13.

- Similarly, Activity H cannot start until week 9 – the later of the two earliest finished dates for the preceding activities C and D.

- The project will be complete when both activities H and G have been completed. Thus the earliest project completion date will be the later of weeks 11 and 13 – that is, week 13.

The results of the forward pass are shown in Figure 6.15.

6.11 The backward pass

The second stage in the analysis of a critical path network is to carry out a backward pass to calculate the latest date at which each activity may be started and finished without delaying the end date of the project. In calculating the latest dates, we assume that the latest finish date for the project is the same as the earliest finish date – that is, we wish to complete the project as early as possible.

Figure 6.16 illustrates our network after carrying out the backward pass.

The latest activity dates are calculated as follows.

- The latest completion date for activities G and H is assumed to be week 13.

- Activity H must therefore start at week 11 at the latest (13−2) and the latest start date for activity G is week 10 (13−3).

- The latest completion date for activities C and D is the latest date at which activity H must start – that is, week 11. They therefore have latest start dates of week 8 (11−3) and week 7 (11−4) respectively.

- Activities E and F must be completed by week 10 so their earliest start dates are weeks 7 (10−3) and 0 (10−10) respectively.

- Activity B must be completed by week 7 (the latest start date for both activities D and E) so its latest start is week 3 (7−4).

The backward pass rule:
the latest finish date for an activity is the latest start date for all the activities that may commence immediately that activity is complete. Where more than one activity can commence we take the earliest of the latest start dates for those activities.

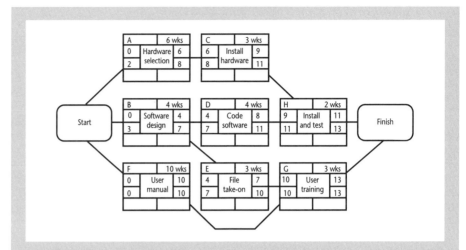

Figure 6.16   The network after the backward pass

- Activity A must be completed by week 8 (the latest start date for activity C) so its latest start is week 2 (8−6).

- The latest start date for the project start is the earliest of the latest start dates for activities A, B and F. This is week zero. This is, of course, not very surprising since it tells us that if the project does not start on time it won't finish on time.

6.12   Identifying the critical path

There will be at least one path through the network (that is, one set of successive activities) that defines the duration of the project. This is known as the *critical path*. Any delay to any activity on this critical path will delay the completion of the project.

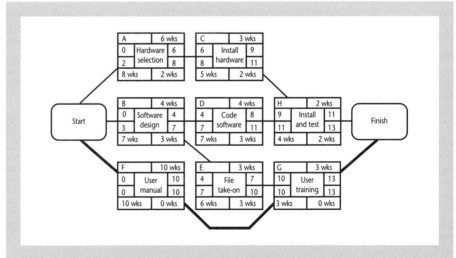

The critical path is the longest path through the network.

Figure 6.17   The critical path

This float is also known as total float to distinguish it from other forms of float – see Section 6.13.

The difference between an activity's earliest start date and its latest start date (or, equally, the difference between its earliest and latest finish dates) is known as the activity's *float* – it is a measure of how much the start or completion of an activity may be delayed without affecting the end date of the project. Any activity with a float of zero is critical in the sense that any delay in carrying out the activity will delay the completion date of the project as a whole. There will always be at least one path through the network joining those critical activities – this path is known as the critical path and is shown bold in Figure 6.17.

The significance of the critical path is two-fold.

- In managing the project, we must pay particular attention to monitoring activities on the critical path so that the effects of any delay or resource unavailability are detected and corrected at the earliest opportunity.

- In planning the project, it is the critical path that we must shorten if we are to reduce the overall duration of the project.

Figure 6.17 also shows the *activity span*. This is the difference between the earliest start date and the latest finish date and is a measure of the maximum time allowable for the activity. However, it is subject to the same conditions of interpretation as activity float, which is discussed in the next section.

Exercise 6.2 Refer back to Amanda's CPM network illustrated in Figure 6.7.

Using the activity durations given in Table 6.2, calculate the earliest completion date for the project and identify the critical path on your network.

6.13 Activity float

Total float may only be used once.

Although the total float is shown for each activity, it really 'belongs' to a path through the network. Activities A and C in Figure 6.16 each have 2 weeks' total float. If, however, activity A uses up its float (that is, it is not completed until week 8) then activity B will have zero float (it will have become critical). In such circumstances it may be misleading and detrimental to the project's success to publicize total float!

There are a number of other measures of activity float, including the following:

- *Free float:* the time by which an activity may be delayed without affecting any subsequent activity. It is calculated as the difference between the earliest

Table 6.2 Estimated activity durations for Amanda's network

Activity	Estimated duration (days)	Activity	Estimated duration (days)
Specify overall system	34	Design module C	4
Specify module A	20	Design module D	4
Specify module B	15	Code/test module A	30
Specify module C	25	Code/test module B	28
Specify module D	15	Code/test module C	15
Check specification	2	Code/test module D	25
Design module A	7	System integration	6
Design module B	6		

completion date for the activity and the earliest start date of the succeeding activity. This might be considered a more satisfactory measure of float for publicizing to the staff involved in undertaking the activities.

- *Interfering float:* the difference between total float and free float. This is quite commonly used, particularly in association with the free float. Once the free float has been used (or if it is zero), the interfering float tells us by how much the activity may be delayed without delaying the project end date – even though it will delay the start of subsequent activities.

Exercise 6.3   Calculate the free float and interfering float for each of the activities shown in the activity network (Figure 6.17).

6.14   Shortening the project duration

If we wish to shorten the overall duration of a project we would normally consider attempting to reduce activity durations. In many cases this can be done by applying more resources to the task – working overtime or procuring additional staff, for example. The critical path indicates where we must look to save time – if we are trying to bring forward the end date of the project, there is clearly no point in attempting to shorten non-critical activities. Referring to Figure 6.17, it can be seen that we could complete the project in week 12 by reducing the duration of activity F by one week (to 9 weeks).

Exercise 6.4   Referring to Figure 6.17, suppose that the duration for activity F is shortened to 8 weeks. Calculate the end date for the project.

What would the end date for the project be if activity F were shortened to 7 weeks? Why?

As we reduce activity times along the critical path we must continually check for any new critical path emerging and redirect our attention where necessary.

There will come a point when we can no longer safely, or cost-effectively, reduce critical activity durations in an attempt to bring forward the project end date. Further savings, if needed, must be sought in a consideration of our work methods and by questioning the logical sequencing of activities. Generally, time savings are to be found by increasing the amount of parallelism in the network and the removal of bottlenecks (subject always, of course, to resource and quality constraints).

6.15   Identifying critical activities

For a more in-depth discussion of the role of the critical path in project monitoring, see Chapter 9.

The critical path identifies those activities which are critical to the end date of the project; however, activities that are not on the critical path may become critical. As the project proceeds, activities will invariably use up some of their float and this will require a periodic recalculation of the network. As soon as the activities along a particular path use up their total float then that path will become a critical path and a number of hitherto non-critical activities will suddenly become critical.

It is therefore common practice to identify *near-critical* paths – those whose lengths are within, say, 10–20% of the duration of the critical path or those with a total float of less than, say, 10% of the project's uncompleted duration.

The importance of identifying critical and near-critical activities is that it is they that are most likely to be the cause of delays in completing the project. We shall see, in the next three chapters, that identifying these activities is an important step in risk analysis, resource allocation and project monitoring.

6.16 Activity-on-arrow networks

The developers of the CPM and PERT methods both originally used activity-on-arrow networks. Although now less common than activity-on-node networks, they are still used and introduce an additional useful concept – that of events. We will therefore take a brief look at how they are drawn and analysed using the same project example shown in Table 6.1.

In activity-on-arrow networks activities are represented by links (or arrows) and the nodes represent events of activities (or groups of activities) starting or finishing. Figure 6.18 illustrates our previous example drawn as an activity-on-arrow network.

Activity-on-arrow network rules and conventions

A project network may have only one start node   This is a requirement of activity-on-arrow networks rather than merely desirable as is the case with activity-on-node networks.

A project network may have only one end node   Again, this is a requirement for activity-on-arrow networks.

A link has duration   A link represents an activity and, in general, activities take time to execute. Notice, however, that the network in Figure 6.18 does not contain any reference to durations. The links are not drawn in any way to rep-

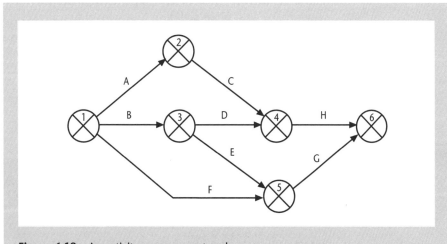

Figure 6.18   An activity-on-arrow network

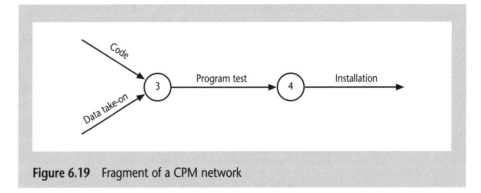

Figure 6.19 Fragment of a CPM network

resent the activity durations. The network drawing merely represents the logic of the project – the rules governing the order in which activities are to be carried out.

Nodes have no duration Nodes are events and, as such, are instantaneous points in time. The source node is the event of the project becoming ready to start and the sink node is the event of the project becoming completed. Intermediate nodes represent two simultaneous events – the event of all activities leading in to a node having been completed and the event of all activities leading out of that node being in a position to be started.

In Figure 6.19 node 3 is the event that both 'coding' and 'data take-on' have been completed and activity 'program test' is free to start. 'Installation' may be started only when event 4 has been achieved, that is, as soon as 'program test' has been completed.

Time moves from left to right As with activity-on-node networks, activity-on-arrow networks are drawn, if at all possible, so that time moves from left to right.

Nodes are numbered sequentially There are no precise rules about node numbering but nodes should be numbered so that head nodes (those at the 'arrow' end of an activity) always have a higher number than tail events (those at the 'non-arrow' end of an activity). This convention makes it easy to spot loops.

A network may not contain loops Figure 6.20 demonstrates a loop in an activity-on-arrow network. As discussed in the context of precedence networks, loops

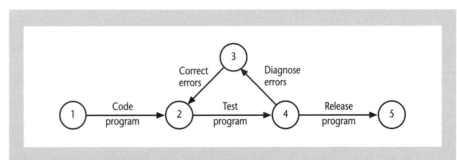

Figure 6.20 A loop represents an impossible sequence

Dangles are not allowed in activity-on-arrow networks.

Figure 6.21 A dangle

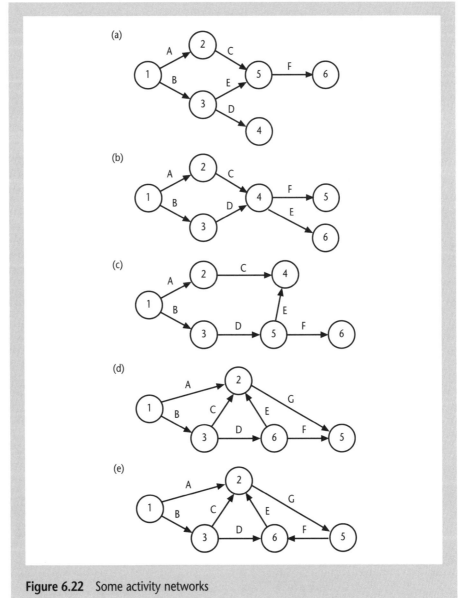

Figure 6.22 Some activity networks

are either an error of logic or a situation that must be resolved by itemizing iterations of activity groups.

A network may not contain dangles   A dangling activity such as 'Write user manual' in Figure 6.21, cannot exist, as it would suggest there are two completion points for the project. If, in Figure 6.21 node 5 represents the true project completion point and there are no activities dependent on activity 'Write user manual', then the network should be redrawn so that activity 'Write user manual' starts at node 2 and terminates at node 5 – in practice, we would need to insert a dummy activity between nodes 3 and 5. In other words, all events, except the first and the last, must have at least one activity entering them and at least one activity leaving them and all activities must start and end with an event.

Exercise 6.5   Take a look at the networks in Figure 6.22. State what is wrong with each of them and, where possible, redraw them correctly.

Using dummy activities

When two paths within a network have a common event although they are, in other respects, independent, a logical error such as that illustrated in Figure 6.23 might occur.

Suppose that, in a particular project, it is necessary to specify a certain piece of hardware before placing an order for it and before coding the software. Before coding the software it is also necessary to specify the appropriate data structures, although clearly we do not need to wait for this to be done before the hardware is ordered.

Figure 6.23 is an attempt to model the situation described above, although it is incorrect in that it requires both hardware specification and data structure design to be completed before either an order may be placed or software coding may commence.

We can resolve this problem by separating the two (more or less) independent paths and introducing a dummy activity to link the completion of 'specify hardware' to the start of the activity 'code software'. This effectively breaks the link between data structure design and placing the order and is shown in Figure 6.24.

Dummy activities, shown as dotted lines on the network diagram, have a zero duration and use no resources. They are often used to aid in the layout of network

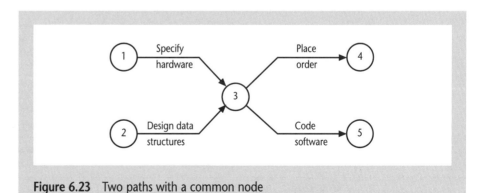

Figure 6.23   Two paths with a common node

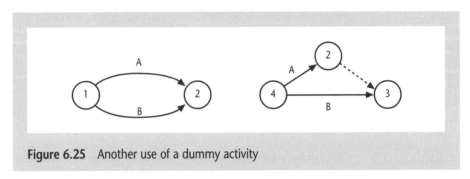

Figure 6.24   Two paths linked by a dummy activity

Figure 6.25   Another use of a dummy activity

drawings as in Figure 6.25. The use of a dummy activity where two activities share the same start and end nodes makes it easier to distinguish the activity end-points.

These are problems that do not occur with activity-on-node networks.

Exercise 6.6   Take another look at Brigette's college payroll activity network fragment, which you developed in Exercise 2.3 (or take a look at the model answer in Figure C.3). Redraw this as an activity-on-arrow network.

Representing lagged activities

Activity-on-arrow networks are less elegant when it comes to representing lagged parallel activities. We need to represent these with pairs of dummy activities as shown in Figure 6.26. Where the activities are lagged because a stage in one

Where parallel activities have a time lag we may show this as a 'ladder' of activities: documentation may proceed alongside prototype testing so long as it starts at least a day later and will finish two days after the completion of prototype testing.

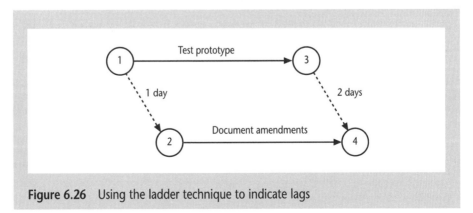

Figure 6.26   Using the ladder technique to indicate lags

activity must be completed before the other may proceed, it is likely to be better to show each stage as a separate activity.

Activity labelling

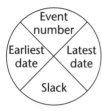

There are a number of differing conventions that have been adopted for entering information on an activity-on-arrow network. Typically the diagram is used to record information about the events rather than the activities – activity-based information (other than labels or descriptions) is generally held on a separate activity table.

One of the more common conventions for labelling nodes, and the one adopted here, is to divide the node circle into quadrants and use those quadrants to show the event number, the latest and earliest dates by which the event should occur, and the event slack (which will be explained later).

Network analysis

Analysis proceeds in the same way as with activity-on-node networks although the discussion places emphasis on the events rather than activity start and completion times.

During the forward pass, earliest dates are recorded as they are calculated. For events, they are recorded on the network diagram and for activities they are recorded on the activity table.

The forward pass   The forward pass is carried out to calculate the earliest date on which each event may be achieved and the earliest dates on which each activity may be started and completed. The earliest date for an event is the earliest date by which all activities upon which it depends can be completed. Using Figure 6.18 and Table 6.1, the calculation proceeds according to the following reasoning.

- Activities A, B and F may start immediately, so the earliest date for event 1 is zero and the earliest start date for these three activities is also zero.

- Activity A will take 6 weeks, so the earliest it can finish is week 6 (recorded in the activity table). Therefore the earliest we can achieve event 2 is week 6.

- Activity B will take 4 weeks, so the earliest it can finish and the earliest we can achieve event 3 is week 4.

- Activity F will take 10 weeks, so the earliest it can finish is week 10 – we cannot, however, tell whether or not this is also the earliest date that we can achieve event 5 since we have not, as yet, calculated when activity E will finish.

- Activity E can start as early as week 4 (the earliest date for event 3) and, since it is forecasted to take 3 weeks, will be completed, at the earliest, at the end of week 7.

- Event 5 may be achieved when both E and F have been completed, that is, week 10 (the later of 7 and 10).

- Similarly, we can reason that event 4 will have an earliest date of week 9. This is the later of the earliest finish for activity D (week 8) and the earliest finish for activity C (week 9).

- The earliest date for the completion of the project, event 6, is therefore the end of week 13 – the later of 11 (the earliest finish for H) and 13 (the earliest finish for G).

The results of the forward pass are shown in Figure 6.27 and Table 6.3.

The forward pass rule: the earliest date for an event is the earliest finish date for all the activities terminating at that event. Where more than one activity terminates at a common event we take the latest of the earliest finish dates for those activities.

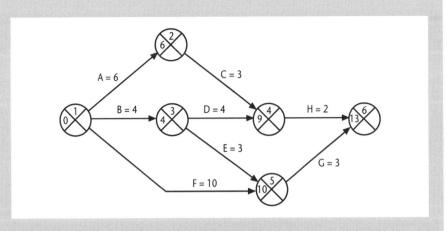

Figure 6.27   A CPM network after the forward pass.

Table 6.3 The activity table after the forward pass

Activity	Duration (weeks)	Earliest start date	Latest start date	Earliest finish fate	Latest finish date	Total float
A	6	0		6		
B	4	0		4		
C	3	6		9		
D	4	4		8		
E	3	4		7		
F	10	0		10		
G	3	10		13		
H	2	9		11		

The backward pass   The second stage is to carry out a backward pass to calculate the latest date at which each event may be achieved, and each activity started and finished, without delaying the end date of the project. The latest date for an event

The backward pass rule: the latest date for an event is the latest start date for all the activities that may commence from that event. Where more than one activity commences at a common event we take the earliest of the latest start dates for those activities.

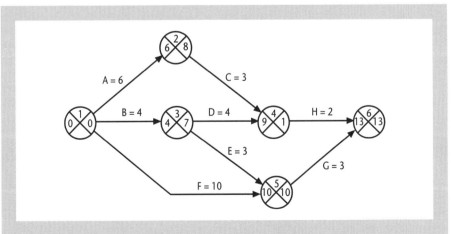

Figure 6.28   The CPM network after the backward pass

Table 6.4 The activity table following the backward pass

Activity	Duration (weeks)	Earliest start date	Latest start date	Earliest finish fate	Latest finish date	Total float
A	6	0	2	6	8	
B	4	0	3	4	7	
C	3	6	8	9	11	
D	4	4	7	8	11	
E	3	4	7	7	10	
F	10	0	0	10	10	
G	3	10	10	13	13	
H	2	9	11	11	13	

is the latest date by which all immediately following activities must be started for the project to be completed on time. As with activity-on-node networks, we assume that the latest finish date for the project is the same as the earliest finish date – that is, we wish to complete the project as early as possible.

Figure 6.28 illustrates our network and Table 6.4 the activity table after carrying out the backward pass – as with the forward pass, event dates are recorded on the diagram and activity dates on the activity table.

Identifying the critical path   The critical path is identified in a way similar to that used in activity-on-node networks. We do, however, use a different concept, that of *slack*, in identifying the path. Slack is the difference between the earliest date and the latest date for an event – it is a measure of how late an event may be without affecting the end date of the project. The critical path is the path joining all nodes with a zero slack (Figure 6.29).

The critical path is the longest path through the network.

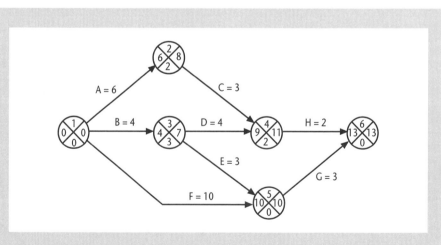

Figure 6.29   The critical path

6.17 Conclusion

In this chapter, we have discussed the use of the critical path method and precedence networks to obtain an ideal activity plan. This plan tells us the order in which we should execute activities and the earliest and latest we can start and finish them.

These techniques help us to identify which activities are critical to meeting a target completion date.

In order to manage the project we need to turn the activity plan into a schedule that will specify precisely when each activity is scheduled to start and finish. Before we can do this, we must consider what resources will be required and whether or not they will be available at appropriate times. As we shall see, the allocation of resources to an activity may be affected by how we view the importance of the task and the risks associated with it. In the next two chapters we look at these aspects of project planning before we consider how we might publish a schedule for the project.

6.18 Further exercises

1. Draw an activity network using either activity-on-node or activity-on-arrow network conventions for each of the following projects:

   ● getting married;
   ● choosing and purchasing a desktop computer;
   ● organizing and carrying out a survey of users' opinions of an information system.

2. If you have access to a project planning application, use it to produce a project plan for the IOE maintenance group accounts project. Base your plan on that used for Exercise 6.2 and verify that your application reports the same information as you calculated manually when you did the exercise.

3. Based on your answer to Exercise 6.2, discuss what options Amanda might consider if she found it necessary to complete the project earlier than day 104.

CHAPTER 7

Risk management

Objectives

When you have completed this chapter you will be able to:

- identify the factors putting a project at risk;
- categorize and prioritize actions for risk elimination or containment;
- quantify the likely effects of risk on project timescales.

7.1 Introduction

In Chapter 6 we saw how, at IOE, Amanda planned the way that the software needed for the new group maintenance accounts application was to be produced. This planning included estimating how long each task in the plan would take – see Figure 6.8 and Table 6.2. However, suppose that when the project actually starts, Amanda recalls that she based her plan on the assumption that she would have four experienced programmers available for the coding of modules A, B, C and D. This seemed reasonable at the time the plan was created as the development team allocated to do the work had such staff. However, two of the developers then left for better-paid jobs, and so far only one replacement has been recruited, who happens to be a trainee.

In the case of Brigette and the Brightmouth payroll implementation project, imagine that a payroll package has been carefully selected and purchased. However, a new requirement emerges that the details stored on the payroll database should be accessible by a new application that calculates the staff costs for each course delivered by the college. Unfortunately, the purchased payroll application does not allow external applications to access the payroll database.

In some work environments 'problems' in this context are referred to as 'issues'.

Both Amanda and Brigette will have to deal with these *problems* as part of the monitoring and control process outlined in Chapter 9. In this chapter we are going to consider whether the two project leaders could have foreseen that these problems were likely to occur and have made plans to deal with them. In other words, could these problems have been identified as *risks* at the planning stage?

7.2 Risk

PM-BOK stands for Project Management Body of Knowledge, a project management standard published by the Project Management Institute in the USA.

PM-BOK defines risk as *'an uncertain event or condition that, if it occurs, has a positive or negative effect on a project's objectives'*. PRINCE2, the UK government-sponsored project management standard, defines risk as *'the chance of exposure to the adverse consequences of future events'*. The difference between the two definitions is that the first includes situations where a future uncertainty actually turns out to work in our favour and presents us with an opportunity. We will return to this point later in the chapter.

People may use different terms, but the key elements of a risk follow.

- *It relates to the future* Risk planning involves speculating about future events. The future is inherently uncertain. Some things which seem obvious when a particular project is over, for example that the costs were under-estimated or that a new technology was overly difficult to use, might not have been so obvious during planning.

The ISPL risk model (formerly Euromethod) refers to hazards as 'situational factors').

- *It involves **cause** and **effect*** For example, a 'cost over-run' might be identified as a risk, but the simple description of 'cost over-run' gives the consequence of some adverse event, but does not say what caused it. Was it, for example, an inaccurate estimate of effort, the use of untrained staff, or a poor specification? A good definition of a specific risk identifies a situation (or *hazard*), such as 'inexperienced staff', and a particular type of negative outcome, such as 'lower productivity'.

Exercise 7.1 Match the following causes – a to d – to their possible effects – i to iv. The relationships are not necessarily one-to-one. Explain the reasons for each match.

Causes

(a) staff inexperience;

(b) lack of top management commitment;

(c) new technology;

(d) users uncertain of their requirements.

Effects

(i) testing takes longer than planned;

(ii) planned effort and time for activities exceeded;

(iii) project scope increases;

(iv) time delays in getting changes to plans agreed.

It is difficult to draw a boundary between risk management and normal, day-to-day software project management. For example, when we were selecting the best general approach to a project – as described in Chapter 4 – one of the considerations was the possible consequences of future adverse events. As will be seen in Chapter 12, most of the techniques used to assure the quality of software, such as reviews and testing, are designed to reduce the risk of faults in the final deliverable of a project. Risk management is not a self-contained topic within project management. However, the distinctive feature of risk management is consideration of the uncertainty that remains after a plan has been formulated and accepted. Every plan must be based on assumptions and risk management tries to plan for and control the situations where those assumptions turn out to be incorrect.

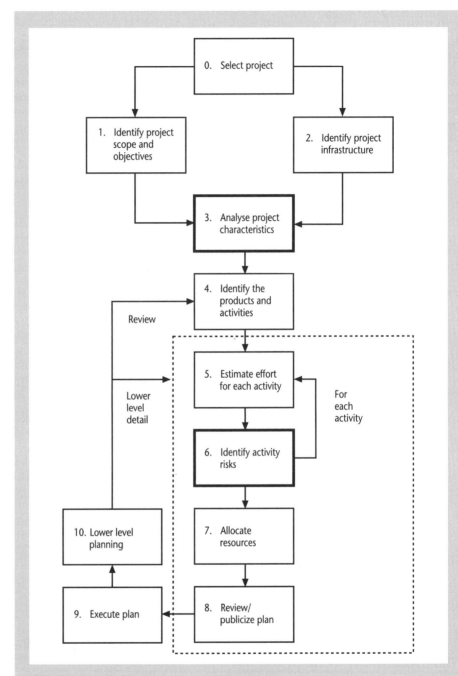

Figure 7.1   Risk planning is carried out primarily in Steps 3 and 6

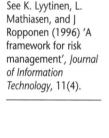

7.3 Categories of risk

The project manager in charge of the implementation of an ICT system is normally given the objective of installing the required application by a specified deadline and within an agreed budget. Other objectives might be set, especially with regard to the quality requirements of the application to be delivered. *Project risks* are those that could prevent the achievement of the objectives given to the project manager and the project team.

The client organization that needed the application would have their own reasons for initiating the project. They might, in the case of an e-commerce application, hope the delivered system would generate more sales. It might happen that some external factors, such as an economic downturn or the import of cheaper alternative products, could prevent these business objectives from being achieved. Dealing with these *business risks* is likely to be outside the direct responsibilities of the application implementation team. However, the failure to meet any project objective could have a negative impact on the business case for the project. For example, an increase in development cost might mean that the income (or savings) generated by the delivered application no longer represents a good return on the increased investment.

See K. Lyytinen, L. Mathiasen, and J Ropponen (1996) 'A framework for risk management', *Journal of Information Technology*, 11(4).

Risks have been categorized in other ways. Kalle Lyytinen and his colleagues, for instance, have proposed a *sociotechnical model* of risk, a diagrammatic representation of which appears in Figure 7.2.

The box labeled *'Actors'* refers to all the people involved in the development of the application in question. These include the various development specialists, the different user groups, and managers with differing responsibilities. A typical risk in this area is that high staff turnover leads to information of value to the project being lost. For example, if a software developer builds a software component and then leaves before it has been fully tested, the team member taking over that component might find that their lack of familiarity with the software makes diagnosis and correction of faults difficult.

In Figure 7.2, the box labeled *'Technology'* encompasses both the technology used to implement the application and that embedded in the delivered products.

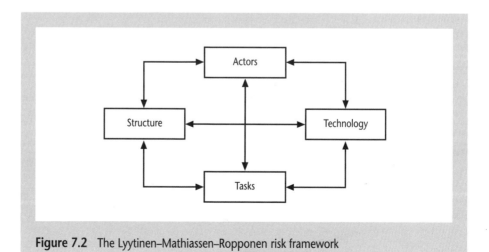

Figure 7.2 The Lyytinen–Mathiassen–Ropponen risk framework

Risks here could relate to the appropriateness of the technologies and to possible faults within them, especially if they are novel.

'*Structure*' in Figure 7.2 describes the management structures and systems, including those affecting planning and control. For example, the implementation will need the users to carry out some tasks, but the responsibility for managing the users' contribution to the project might not have been clearly allocated.

'*Tasks*', in the same diagram, relates to the work to be carried out. For instance, the complexity of the work might lead to delays because of the additional time required to coordinate and integrate the large number of different elements.

In Figure 7.2 each box is linked to all the remaining boxes. Risks often arise from the relationships among the groups of factors – for example between technology and people. If a development technology is novel then the developers might not be experienced in its use and therefore need extra time. The products might also initially be more fault prone. In many cases, the novelty of the new technology is really a characteristic of the developers: once they are used to the technology, it can no longer be called 'novel'. If the technology is then used in a new environment, with new developers unfamiliar with it, the technology would suddenly re-acquire its 'novelty'.

Exercise 7.2	In the cases of the Brightmouth payroll implementation project and the IOE group accounts development project, identify one risk for each of the four categories in Figure 7.2.

The ISPL model (which has repackaged what was formerly called Euromethod) identifies the two *domains* containing *situational factors* which are likely to lead to particular types of adverse consequences – see Table 7.1

The classes of situational factors in the project domain are similar to those identified by Lyytinen *et al.* above. The ISPL model subdivides the individual factors within each domain/class into those that relate to *complexity*, where the tasks are made difficult by the size of the problems to be dealt with, and *uncertainty*, where certain key knowledge is missing or unstable.

ISPL stands for 'Information Services Procurement Library' and was set up by the European Union SPRITE-S2 programme – see the url *projekte.fast.de/ Euromethod*

Table 7.1 ISPL situational factors

Domain	Class	Description
Target	Information system	The characteristics of the information system – these are independent of the technologies that might be used
	Computer system	The characteristics of the part of the information system that has been computerized
Project	Project	The types of task to be undertaken
	Structure	The communication systems, management structures, work flows etc
	Actors	The people involved in the project
	Technology	The methods, techniques and tools to be used

For each class within each domain, specific factors have been identified in the ISPL model. Within the information systems domain, heterogeneity in the actors (for example, having many different types of user), the size of the distribution (that is, the geographical area within which the new application is to be deployed) and the complexity of the information involved (which might be reflected in the number of entity types in the underlying logical data structure) suggest complexity that could lead to problems. On the other hand, a lack of stability in the environment (for example, when changes of government lead to changes in requirements) and the use of unstructured and informal types of information in the current clerical systems could warn of adverse consequences stemming from a lack of certainty about requirements.

7.4 A framework for dealing with risk

Planning for risk includes these steps:

(i)   risk identification;

(ii)   risk analysis and prioritization;

(iii) risk planning;

(iv) risk monitoring.

Steps (i) to (iii) above will probably be repeated. When the major risks that could prevent a project from being successful have been identified, plans can be made to reduce or remove the threat of those risks. The risks should then be reassessed to make sure that the original risks have been reduced sufficiently and that new risks have not been inadvertently introduced. Say that a risk is identified that staff inexperience with a new technology could lead to delays in software development. To reduce this risk, consultants expert in the new technology might be introduced. However, the use of consultants might introduce new risks, for example that knowledge about the new technology is not transferred to the permanent staff, which makes software maintenance problematic when the consultants leave. Having identified this new risk, further risk reduction activities can be planned.

7.5 Risk identification

The two main approaches to the identification of risks are the use of *checklists* and *brainstorming*.

Checklists are simply lists of the risks that have been found to occur regularly in software development projects. Two checklists – that of Lyytinen and his colleagues and the ISPL/Euromethod model – have already been mentioned, but others exist, including a specialized list of software development risks by Barry Boehm – a modified version of which appears in Table 7.2. Ideally a group of representative project stakeholders should go through a checklist deciding which risks might apply to their project. In many cases the creators of the checklist have also suggested potential countermeasures for each risk.

Project managers might use the checklist on their own. The part of Amanda's IOE group accounts project that deals solely with software development might be regarded as fairly straightforward. She might decide to check a standard list of

This top ten list of software risks is based on one presented by Barry Boehm in his *Tutorial on Software Risk Management*, IEE Computer Society, 1989.

Table 7.2 Software project risks and strategies for risk reduction

Risk	Risk reduction techniques
Personnel shortfalls	Staffing with top talent; job matching; teambuilding; training and career development; early scheduling of key personnel
Unrealistic time and cost estimates	Multiple estimation techniques; design to cost; incremental development; recording and analysis of past projects; standardization of methods
Developing the wrong software functions	Improved software evaluation; formal specification methods; user surveys; prototyping; early user manuals
Developing the wrong user interface	Prototyping; task analysis; user involvement
Gold plating	Requirements scrubbing; prototyping; cost–benefit analysis; design to cost
Late changes to requirements	Stringent change control procedures; high change threshold; incremental development (deferring changes)
Shortfalls in externally supplied components	Benchmarking; inspections; formal specifications; contractual agreements; quality assurance procedures and certification
Shortfalls in externally performed tasks	Quality assurance procedures; competitive design or prototyping; contract incentives
Real-time performance shortfalls	Simulation; benchmarking; prototyping; tuning; technical analysis
Development technically too difficult	Technical analysis; cost–benefit analysis; prototyping; staff training and development

The 'lessons learnt' report differs from a 'post implementation review' (PIR). It is written on project completion and focuses on project issues. A PIR, produced when the application has been operational for some time, focuses on business benefits.

possible project risks against her perceptions of the project. If she identifies some areas of uncertainty, she can select some countermeasures to cope with them. She circulates her findings to some of her colleagues for comment.

Project management methodologies, such PRINCE2, often recommend that on completion of a project a review identifies any problems during the project and the steps that were (or should have been) taken to resolve or avoid them. These problems could in some cases be added to an organizational risk checklist for use with new projects.

Brainstorming

Representatives of the main stakeholders can be brought together, ideally, once some kind of preliminary plan has been drafted. They then identify, using their individual knowledge of different parts of the project, the particular problems that might occur. Brainstorming can also be used to identify possible solutions to the problems that emerge. One useful outcome of such an approach is that the collaborative approach may generate a sense of ownership in the project. A process that is beneficial explicitly asks stakeholders about their anxieties and then explores ways of reducing those concerns.

Brainstorming might be used with Brigette's Brightmouth payroll implementation project as she realizes that there are some aspects of college administration of which she is unaware. She therefore suggests to the main stakeholders in the project, which include staff from the finance office and the personnel office, that they have a meeting where the risks facing the project are discussed. She decides not to use the term 'brainstorming' as she thinks it might discourage some people from participating.

'Brainstorming' is also mentioned in Chapter 12 in connection with quality circles.

Causal mapping

Causal mapping has been particularly associated with Colin Eden and his colleagues – see, for example, 'The analysis of cause maps', Journal of Management Studies, 29, 309–24 (1992).

One way of identifying possible threats to the success of a project and the measures that might eliminate or reduce them is the use of causal mapping. Causal maps and diagrams represent the chains of causes and effects that will influence the outcomes in a particular area of activity. Figure 7.3 shows an example of such a map. The nodes in the diagram represent various factors or *concept variables* that people see as being important. It should be noted that these are *not* activities. They are generally characteristics of the environment or the project approach. Examples of these factors could be 'high staff turnover', 'uncertain user requirements', 'developer experience'. Where possible, positive and negative aspects of the concept variable are provided, for example 'stable . . . unstable requirements'. The arrows between the nodes show how the different factors influence one another. The influence could be positive where a high value in one factor tends to lead to a high value in another. For example you would expect that having experienced development staff would tend to lead to higher software development

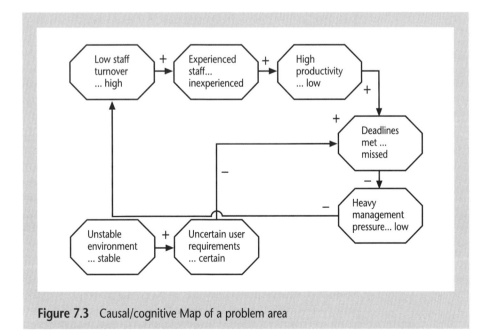

Figure 7.3 Causal/cognitive Map of a problem area

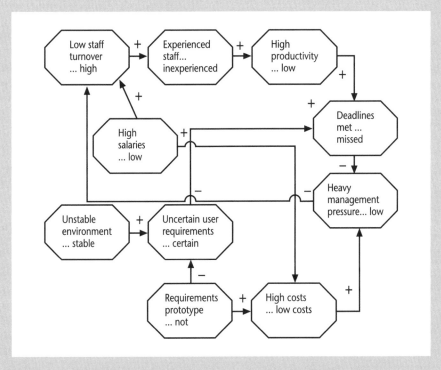

Figure 7.4 A causal/cognitive map of a problem area with proposed solutions

productivity. The influence could, on the other hand, be negative, for example where staff turnover is high one would expect staff experience to be low. This is normally shown on the map by a minus sign next to an arrow: this indicates that the head of the first concept variable is linked with the tail of the second.

The situation in Figure 7.3 illustrates two things in particular. The first is a *vicious circle* where delays in meeting deadlines lead to increased management pressure. This in turn causes staff turnover to increase which leads to further delays in meeting deadlines. The second is the destabilizing effect on the project of *uncontrolled external influences*, such as an unstable environment leading to continual changes to requirements.

Figure 7.4 shows a situation where two different policies have been introduced to reduce the likelihood of the undesirable outcomes to the project that are suggested by the map in Figure 7.3. One is an increase in the salaries for development staff which, it is hoped, will encourage staff to stay with the organization. The other is the use of prototypes to reduce the uncertainty that surrounds the precise requirements of the users. Although increased salaries might decrease staff turnover, they will also have a possible detrimental effect on the overall cost of the project. Similarly, prototypes might decrease user uncertainty about their requirements, which might prevent extra costs in the longer term brought about by the implementation of requested changes. However, the creation of a prototype would itself have a cost. Where factors have both positive and negative effects, this indicates that a degree of uncertainty remains in the project. When future trends are being considered it should be noted that a causal map reflects people's perceptions, not necessarily the actual situation – hence the diagram is often referred to as a *cognitive map*.

Exercise 7.3   Discuss why the measures taken to remedy the situation in Figure 7.3 might not be successful.

7.6   Risk assessment

A common problem with risk identification, particularly for the more anxious, is that a list of risks is potentially endless. Some way is therefore needed of distinguishing the more damaging and likely risks. This can be done by estimating the *risk exposure* for each risk using the formula:

$$risk\ exposure = (potential\ damage) \times (probability\ of\ occurrence)$$

Using the most rigorous – but not necessarily the most practical – approach, the potential damage would be assessed as a money value. Say all the software being developed for an application was stored on a computer that could be destroyed by a flood. It might be estimated that if a flood occurred a new computer configuration could be installed and the software developed again from scratch for £500,000. It might also be estimated that where the computer is located there is a 1 in 100 chance of flooding actually happening, that is a probability of 0.01.

The risk exposure in this case would be:

$$£500,000 \times 0.01 = £5,000$$

A crude way of understanding this value is as the minimum amount of money an insurance company would require by way of a premium if you could insure against this loss. If 100 companies, all in the same position, each contributed £5,000 to a fund then, when the 1 in 100 chance of the flood actually occurred, there would be enough money in the fund to cover the cost of recovery.

Exercise 7.4   What conditions would have to exist for the risk pooling arrangement described above to work?

One limitation with the calculation of risk exposure above is that it assumes that the amount of damage sustained will always be the same. However, it is usually the case that there could be varying amounts of damage. In the flooding example, the rework required if development had only just started would be a lot less than after several months of effort.

With some risks, it is possible for there to be not only damage but also gains. The testing of a software component might have been scheduled to take five days, but only needs three days in reality. A team leader might therefore feel justified in producing a probability chart like the one in Figure 7.5.

We noted in Chapter 5 on software estimation that the Parkinson's Law principle means that tasks will tend to finish at the target time, even if they could have been completed earlier. In Section 7.12 we explore how this might be better controlled.

Our clients would very likely object if we presented our estimates of completion times in the form shown in Figure 7.5. We would almost certainly have to pick one of the days as the target. This target could be 'aggressive', for instance five

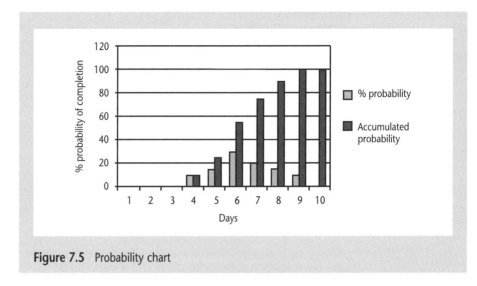

Figure 7.5 Probability chart

days in the above scenario, but with a fair chance that it might be missed – in fact, a 75% chance of failure according to the chart. A safer estimate by far would be eight days which, according to the chart, would have a probability of failure of only 10%. This point, too, will be returned to later on in this chapter.

A final point to note is that in Figure 7.5 the 'loss' is effectively being measured in days, rather than a money value. With project planning, days, or some other unit of personal effort, is often used as a *surrogate* for a financial loss.

Most managers resist producing very precise estimates of loss or of the probability of something occurring. One reason for this reluctance is that such figures are guesses in most cases. Barry Boehm has suggested that, because of this, both the risk losses and the probabilities be assessed using relative scales in the range 0 to 10. The two figures could then be multiplied together to get a notional risk exposure. Table 7.4 provides an example, based on Amanda's IOE group accounts project, of where this has been done. This value could be used to prioritize the importance of risks, even though more sophisticated risk calculations could not be carried out.

Table 7.4 Part of Amanda's risk exposure assessment

Ref	Hazard	Likelihood	Impact	Risk exposure
R1	Changes to requirements specification during coding	8	8	64
R2	Specification takes longer than expected	3	7	21
R3	Significant staff sickness affecting critical path activities	5	7	35
R4	Significant staff sickness affecting non-critical activities	10	3	30
R5	Module coding takes longer than expected	4	5	20
R6	Module testing demonstrates errors or deficiencies in design	4	8	32

Table 7.5 Qualitative descriptors of risk probability and associated range values

Probability level	Range
High	Greater than 50% chance of happening
Significant	30–50% chance of happening
Moderate	10–29% chance of happening
Low	Less than 10% chance of happening

Table 7.6 Qualitative descriptors of impact on cost and associated range values

Impact level	Range
High	More than 30% above budgeted expenditure
Significant	20 to 29% above budgeted expenditure
Moderate	10 to 19% above budgeted expenditure
Low	Within 10% of budgeted expenditure.

Boehm suggests that planners focus attention on the ten risks with the highest risk exposure scores. For smaller projects – including the final-year projects of computing students – the focus could be on a smaller number of risks.

Even using indicative numbers in the range 0 to 10, as opposed to using precise money values and probabilities, is not completely satisfactory. The values are likely to be subjective, and different analysts will pick different numbers for the same risk. Another approach is to use qualitative descriptions of the possible impact and the likelihood of each risk – see Tables 7.5 and 7.6 for examples. Consistency between assessors is facilitated by associating each qualitative description with a range of values.

In Table 7.6, the potential amount of damage has been categorized in terms of its impact on *project costs*. Similar tables could be produced to show the impact of risks on *project duration* or on the *quality of the project deliverables*.

To some extent, the project manager, in conjunction with the project sponsor, can choose whether the damage inflicted by a risk affects cost, duration or the quality of deliverables. In Amanda's list of risks in Table 7.4, R5 refers to the coding of modules taking longer than planned. This would have an impact on both the duration of the project and the costs, as more staff time would be needed. A response might be adding software developers and splitting the remaining development work between them. This will increase costs, but could save the planned completion date. Another option is to save both duration and staff costs by reducing software testing before the software is released. This is likely to be at the price of decreased quality in the project deliverable.

Where the potential damage and likelihood of a risk are defined by qualitative descriptors, the risk exposure cannot be calculated by multiplying the two factors together. In this case, the risk exposure is indicated by the position of the risk in a matrix – see Figure 7.6. These matrices have variously been called *probability impact grids* or *summary risk profiles*.

In Figure 7.6 some of the cells in the top right of the matrix have been zoned off by a ***tolerance line***. Risks that appear within this zone have a degree of seriousness that merits particular attention.

See P. Goodwin and G.Wright *Decision Analysis for Management Judgement*, Wiley, 2004, for further discussion of this issue.

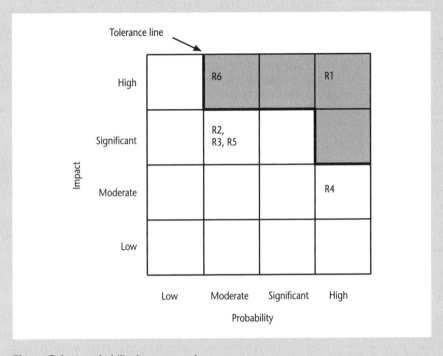

Figure 7.6 A probability impact matrix

The term *risk proximity* is used to describe this attribute of risk.

Chapter 5 stressed the need for frequent reassessment of effort and duration estimates during a project. This applies to risk exposure as well, as some risks apply only at certain stages. A risk might be that key users are unavailable when needed to supply details of their requirements. As requirements are gathered, so this risk will diminish until it is no longer significant. In general, the element of uncertainty will lessen as a project progresses and more is learnt by the developers about user requirements and any new technology. This would be reflected in lower risk probabilities. On the other hand, the potential damage will tend to increase as the amount invested in the project grows. If you type a substantial report using a word processor and neglect to take back-ups, as each day adds more text to the report, it also adds to the number of days needed to re-key the report in the event of file loss.

7.7 Risk planning

Having identified the major risks and allocated priorities, the task is to decide how to deal with them. The choices discussed will be:

● risk acceptance;
● risk avoidance;
● risk reduction and mitigation;
● risk transfer;

Risk acceptance

This is the do-nothing option. We will already, in the risk prioritization process, have decided to ignore some risks in order to concentrate on the more likely or damaging. We could decide that the damage inflicted by some risks would be less than the costs of action that might reduce the probability of a risk happening.

Risk avoidance

Some activities may be so prone to accident that it is best to avoid them altogether. If you are worried about crocodiles then don't go into the water. For example, given all the problems with developing software solutions from scratch, managers might decide to retain existing clerical methods, or to buy an off-the-shelf solution.

Risk reduction

Here we decide to go ahead with a course of action despite the risks, but take precautions that reduce the probability of the risk.

This chapter started with a scenario where two of the staff scheduled to work on Amanda's development project at IOE departed for other jobs. If this has been identified as a risk, steps might have been taken to reduce possible departures of staff. For instance, the developers might have been promised generous bonuses to be paid on successful completion of the project.

It must be appreciated that each risk reduction action is likely to involve some cost. This is discussed in the next section.

Recall that Brigette had a problem at Brightmouth College: after the purchase of the payroll package, a requirement for the payroll database to be accessed by another application was identified. Unfortunately, the application that had been bought did not allow such access. An alternative scenario might have been that Brigette identified this as a possible risk early on in the project. She might have come across Richard Fairley's four COTS (commercial off-the-shelf) software acquisition risks – see Table 7.7 – where one risk is difficulty in integrating the data formats and communication protocols of different applications. Brigette might have specified that the selected package must use a widely accepted data management system like Oracle that allows easier integration.

Risk mitigation can sometimes be distinguished from risk reduction. *Risk reduction* attempts to reduce the likelihood of the risk occurring. *Risk mitigation* is action

---

Table 7.7 *Fairley's four commercial off-the-shelf (COTS) software acquisition risks*

Integration	Difficulties in integrating the data formats and communication protocols of different applications.
Upgrading	When the supplier upgrades the package, the package might no longer meet the users' precise requirements. Sticking with the old version could mean losing the supplier's support for the package.
No source code	If you want to enhance the system, you might not be able to do so as you do not have access to the source code.
Supplier failures or buyouts	The supplier of the application might go out of business or be bought out by a rival supplier.

taken to ensure the impact of the risk is lessened when it occurs. For example, taking regular back-ups of data storage would reduce the impact of data corruption but not its likelihood. Mitigation is closely associated with contingency planning which is discussed presently.

Risk transfer

Risk transfer is what effectively happens when you buy insurance.

In this case the risk is transferred to another person or organization. With software projects, an example of this would be where a software development task is outsourced to an outside agency for a fixed fee. You might expect the supplier to quote a higher figure to cover the risk that the project takes longer than the 'average' expected time. On the other hand, a well-established external organization might have productivity advantages as its developers are experienced in the type of development to be carried out. The need to compete with other software development specialists would also tend to drive prices down.

7.8 Risk management

Contingency

Risk reduction activities would appear to have only a small impact on reducing the probability of some risks, for example staff absence through illness. While some employers encourage their employees to adopt a healthy lifestyle, it remains likely that some project team members will at some point be brought down by minor illnesses like flu. These kinds of risk need a *contingency plan*. This is a planned action to be carried out if the particular risk materializes. If a team member involved in urgent work were ill then the project manager might draft in another member of staff to cover that work.

The preventative measures that were discussed under the 'Risk reduction' heading above will usually incur some cost regardless of the risk materializing or not. The cost of a contingency measure will only be incurred if the risk actually materializes. However, there may be some things that have to be done in order for the contingency action to be feasible. An obvious example is that back-ups of a database have to be taken if the contingency action when the database is corrupted is to restore it from back-ups.

Exercise 7.5   In the case above where staff could be absent through illness, what pre-conditions could facilitate contingency actions such as getting other team members to cover on urgent tasks? What factors would you consider in deciding whether these preparatory measures would be worthwhile?

Deciding on the risk actions

Five generic responses to a risk have been discussed above. For each actual risk, however, specific actions have to be planned. In many cases experts have produced lists recommending practical steps to cope with the likelihood of particular risks; see, for example, Boehm's 'top ten' software engineering risks in Table 7.2. The ISPL model also does this, and much of its advice is similar to Boehm's. The ISPL model differentiates between risks caused by *uncertainty* and those caused by *complexity*. Uncertainty is where key information is missing. A client's requirements might not be well defined, or untried technology is to be deployed. The ISPL model recommends some kind of prototyping approach to buy knowledge in these cases. Complexity, on the other hand, could be caused by very detailed and constrained user requirements or by the complexity of the environment in which the application is to be embedded. Here the ISPL model recommends an incremental, divide-and-rule, approach.

Whatever the countermeasures that are considered, they must be cost-effective. On those occasions where a risk exposure value can be calculated as a financial value using the (*value of damage*) $\times$ (*probability of occurrence*) formula – recall

RISK RECORD						
Risk id		Risk title				
Owner		Date raised		Status		
Risk description						
Impact description						
Recommended risk mitigation						
Probability/impact values						
		Probability	Impact			
			Cost	Duration	Quality	
Pre-mitigation						
Post-mitigation						
Incident/action history						
Date	Incident/action		Actor	Outcome/comment		

Figure 7.7 Risk register page

Section 7.6 – the cost-effectiveness of a risk reduction action can be assessed by calculating the *risk reduction leverage (RRL)*.

$$Risk\ reduction\ leverage = (RE_{before} - RE_{after})/(cost\ of\ risk\ reduction)$$

RE_{before} is the risk exposure, as explained in Section 7.6, before risk reduction actions have been taken. RE_{after} is the risk exposure after taking the risk reduction action. An RRL above 1.00 indicates that the reduction in risk exposure achieved by a measure is greater than its cost. To take a rather unrealistic example, it might cost £200,000 to replace a hardware configuration used to develop a software application. There is a 1% chance of a fire (because of the particular location of the installation, say). The risk exposure would be 1% of £200,000, that is £2000. Installing fire alarms at a cost of £500 would reduce the chance of fire to 0.5%. The new risk exposure would be £1000, a reduction of £1000 on the previous exposure. The RRL would be (2000−1000)/500, that is 2.0, and the action would therefore be deemed worthwhile.

Earlier in this chapter, we likened risk exposure to the amount you might pay to an insurance company to cover a risk. To continue the analogy, an insurance company in the above example might be willing to drop the premium you pay to have cover against fire from £2000 to £1000 if you installed fire alarms. As the fire alarms would cost you only £500 and save £1000, the cost would clearly be worthwhile.

Creating and maintaining the risk register

When the project planners have picked out and examined what appear to be the most threatening risks to the project, they need to record their findings in a *risk register*. The typical content of such a register is shown in Figure 7.7. After work starts on the project more risks will emerge and be added to the register. At regular intervals, probably as part of the project control life cycle described in Chapter 9, the risk register should be reviewed and amended. Many risks threaten just one or two activities, and when the project staff have completed these the risk can then be 'closed' as no longer relevant. In any case, as noted earlier, the probability and impact of a risk are likely to change during the course of the project.

7.9 Evaluating risks to the schedule

In Section 7.6 we showed a probability chart – Figure 7.5. This illustrated the point that a forecast of the time needed to do a job is most realistically presented as a graph of likelihood of a range of figures with the most likely duration as the peak and the chances of the job taking longer or shorter shown as curves sloping down on either side of the peak. Thus we can show that a job might take five days but that there is a small chance it might need four or six days, and a smaller chance of three or seven days and so on. If a task in a project takes longer than planned, we might hope that some other task might take less and thus compensate for this delay. In the following sections we will examine PERT, a technique which takes account of the uncertainties in the durations of activities within a project. We will also touch upon Monte Carlo simulation, which is a more powerful and flexible tool that tackles the same problem.

A drawback to the application of methods like PERT is that in practice there is a tendency for developers to work to the schedule even if a task could be completed more quickly. Even if tasks are completed earlier than planned, project managers are not always quick to exploit the opportunities to start subsequent activities earlier than scheduled. Critical chain management will be explored as a way of tackling this problem.

7.10 Applying the PERT technique

Using PERT to evaluate the effects of uncertainty

PERT was developed to take account of the uncertainty surrounding estimates of task durations. It was developed in an environment of expensive, high-risk and state-of-the-art projects – not that dissimilar to many of today's large software projects.

PERT (program evaluation and review technique) was published in the same year as CPM. Developed for the Fleet Ballistic Missiles Program it is said to have saved considerable time in development of the Polaris missile.

The method is very similar to the CPM technique (indeed many practitioners use the terms PERT and CPM interchangeably) but, instead of using a single estimate for the duration of each task, PERT requires three estimates.

- *Most likely time:* the time we would expect the task to take under normal circumstances. We shall denote this by the letter m.

- *Optimistic time:* the shortest time in which we could expect to complete the activity, barring outright miracles. We shall use the letter a to denote this.

- *Pessimistic time:* the worst possible time allowing for all reasonable eventualities but excluding 'acts of God and warfare' (as they say in most insurance exclusion clauses). We shall denote this by b.

PERT then combines these three estimates to form a single expected duration, t_e, using the formula

$$t_e = \frac{a + 4m + b}{6}$$

Exercise 7.6

Table 7.8 provides additional activity duration estimates for the network shown in Figure 6.29. There are new estimates for a and b and the original activity duration estimates have been used as the most likely times, m. Calculate the expected duration, t_e, for each activity.

Using expected durations

The expected durations are used to carry out a forward pass through a network, using the same method as the CPM technique. In this case, however, the calculated event dates are not the earliest possible dates but the dates by which we expect to achieve those events.

Exercise 7.7

Before reading further, use your calculated expected activity durations to carry out a forward pass through the network (Figure 6.29) and verify that the project duration is 13.5 weeks. What does an expected duration of 13.5 weeks mean in terms of the completion date for the project?

Table 7.8 PERT activity time estimates

| Activity | Activity durations (weeks) | | |
	Optimistic (a)	Most likely (m)	Pessimistic (b)
A	5	6	8
B	3	4	5
C	2	3	3
D	3.5	4	5
E	1	3	4
F	8	10	15
G	2	3	4
H	2	2	2.5

The PERT network illustrated in Figure 7.8 indicates that we expect the project to take 13.5 weeks. In Figure 7.8 we have used an activity-on-arrow network as this form of presentation makes it easier to separate visually the estimated activity data (expected durations and, later, their standard deviations) from the calculated data (expected completion dates and target completion dates). The method can, of course, be equally well supported by activity-on-node diagrams.

Unlike the CPM approach, the PERT method does not indicate the earliest date by which we could complete the project but the expected (or most likely) date. An advantage of this approach is that it places an emphasis on the uncertainty of the real world. Rather than being tempted to say *'the completion date for the project is . . .'* we are led to say *'we expect to complete the project by . . .'.*

It also focuses attention on the uncertainty of the estimation of activity durations. Requesting three estimates for each activity emphasizes the fact that we are not certain what will happen – we are forced to take into account the fact that estimates are approximate.

Even number	Target date
Expected date	Standard deviation

The PERT event labelling convention adopted here indicates event number and its target date along with the calculated values for expected time and standard deviation.

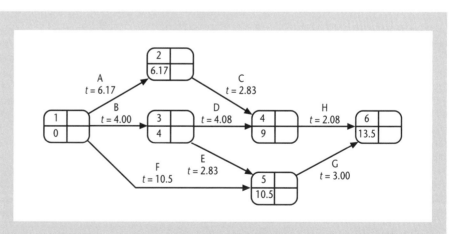

Figure 7.8 The PERT network after the forward pass

This standard deviation formula is based on the rationale that there are approximately six standard deviations between the extreme tails of many statistical distributions.

Activity standard deviations

A quantitative measure of the degree of uncertainty of an activity duration estimate may be obtained by calculating the standard deviation s of an activity time, using the formula

$$s = \frac{b - a}{6}$$

The activity standard deviation is proportional to the difference between the optimistic and pessimistic estimates, and can be used as a ranking measure of the degree of uncertainty or risk for each activity. The activity expected durations and standard deviations for our sample project are shown in Table 7.9.

Table 7.9 Expected times and standard deviations

Activity	Activity durations (weeks)			Expected (te)	Standard deviation (s)
	Optimistic (a)	Most likely (m)	Pessimistic (b)		
A	5	6	8	6.17	0.50
B	3	4	5	4.00	0.33
C	2	3	3	2.83	0.17
D	3.5	4	5	4.08	0.25
E	1	3	4	2.83	0.50
F	8	10	15	10.50	1.17
G	2	3	4	3.00	0.33
H	2	2	2.5	2.08	0.08

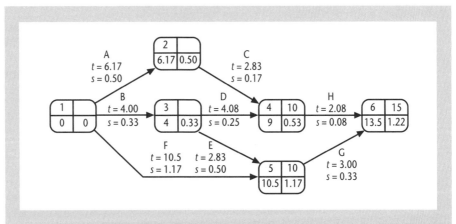

Figure 7.9 The PERT network with three target dates and calculated event standard deviations

The likelihood of meeting targets

The main advantage of the PERT technique is that it provides a method for estimating the probability of meeting or missing target dates. There might be only a single target date – the project completion – but we might wish to set additional intermediate targets.

Suppose that we must complete the project within 15 weeks at the outside. We expect it will take 13.5 weeks but it could take more or, perhaps, less. In addition, suppose that activity C must be completed by week 10, as it is to be carried out by a member of staff who is scheduled to be working on another project, and that event 5 represents the delivery of intermediate products to the customer, which must take place by week 10. These three target dates are shown on the PERT network in Figure 7.9.

The PERT technique uses the following three-step method for calculating the probability of meeting or missing a target date:

● calculate the standard deviation of each project event;

● calculate the z value for each event that has a target date;

● convert z values to a probabilities.

The square of the standard deviation is known as the variance. Standard deviations may not be added together but variances may.

Calculating the standard deviation of each project event

Standard deviations for the project events can be calculated by carrying out a forward pass using the activity standard deviations in a manner similar to that used with expected durations. There is, however, one small difference – to add two standard deviations we must add their squares and then find the square root of the sum. Exercise 7.8 illustrates the technique.

Exercise 7.8 The standard deviation for event 3 depends solely on that of activity B. The standard deviation for event 3 is therefore 0.33.

For event 5 there are two possible paths, B + E or F. The total standard deviation for path B + E is $\sqrt{(0.33^2 + 0.50^2)} = 0.6$ and that for path F is 1.17; the standard deviation for event 5 is therefore the greater of the two, 1.17.

Verify that the standard deviations for each of the other events in the project are as shown in Figure 7.9.

Calculating the z values

The z value is calculated for each node that has a target date. It is equivalent to the number of standard deviations between the node's expected and target dates. It is calculated using the formula

$$z = \frac{T - t_e}{s}$$

where t_e is the expected date and T the target date.

Exercise 7.9 The z value for event 4 is $(10 - 9.00)/0.53 = 1.8867$.

Calculate the z values for the other events with target dates in the network shown in Figure 7.9.

This graph is the equivalent of tables of z values, also known as standard normal deviates, which may be found in most statistics textbooks.

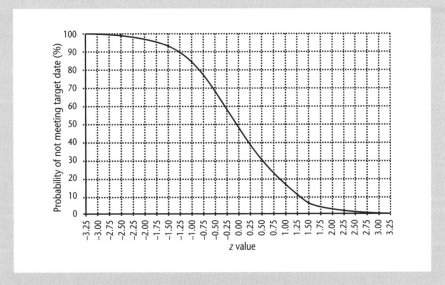

Figure 7.10 The probablility of obtaining a value within z standard deviations of the mean for a normal distribution

Converting z values to probabilities

A z value may be converted to the probability of not meeting the target date by using the graph in Figure 7.10.

Exercise 7.10 The z value for the project completion (event 6) is 1.23. Using Figure 7.10 we can see that this equates to a probability of approximately 11%, that is, there is an 11% risk of not meeting the target date of the end of week 15.

Find the probabilities of not achieving events 4 or 5 by their target dates of the end of week 10.

What is the likelihood of completing the project by week 14?

The advantages of PERT

We have seen that by requesting multivalued activity duration estimates and calculating expected dates, PERT focuses attention on the uncertainty of forecasting. We can use the technique to calculate the standard deviation for each task and use this to rank them according to their degree of risk. Using this ranking, we can see, for example, that activity F is the one regarding which we have greatest uncertainty, whereas activity C should, in principle, give us relatively little cause for concern.

If we use the expected times and standard deviations for forward passes through the network we can, for any event or activity completion, estimate the probability of meeting any set target. In particular, by setting target dates along the critical path, we can focus on those activities posing the greatest risk to the project's schedule.

Figure 7.11 Risk profile for an activity generated using Monte Carlo simulation

7.11 Monte Carlo simulation

Monte Carlo
simulation was also
discussed in Section
3.13 in the context of
project evaluation.

As an alternative to the PERT technique, and to provide a greater degree of flexibility in specifying likely activity durations, we can use Monte Carlo simulation techniques to evaluate the risks of not achieving deadlines. The basis of this technique involves calculating activity completion times for a project network a large number of times, each time selecting estimated activity times randomly from a set of estimates for each activity. The results can then be tabulated, summarized or displayed as a graph such as that shown in Figure 7.11.

Activity duration estimates can be specified in a variety of forms, depending upon the information available. If, for example, we have historic data available about the durations of similar activities, we might be able to specify durations as a probability distribution. With less information available we should, at least, be able to provide three time estimates as used by PERT.

The calculation required for this is clearly extensive as we may have to carry out the forward pass through the network many hundreds of times before obtaining a representative selection of possible completion times. Fortunately, there are a number of packages available for carrying out Monte Carlo simulation. Some will exchange data with project-scheduling applications and some interface to standard spreadsheet software. The majority of these packages will apply Monte Carlo risk analysis to cost and resource as well as duration estimates.

7.12 Critical chain concepts

This chapter has stressed the idea that the forecast for the duration of an activity cannot in reality be a single number, but must be a range of durations that can be displayed on a graph such as Figure 7.5. However, we would want to pick one value in that range which would be the target.

The duration chosen as the target might be the one that seems to be the most likely. In the discussion above on the PERT risk technique this was one of the three numbers specified for each activity. When the project is actually being executed, the project manager will be forced to focus on the activities where the actual durations exceed the target. Activities which are actually completed before the target date are likely to be overlooked. These early completions, properly handled, could put some time in hand that might still allow the project to meet its target completion date if the later activities are delayed.

Michiel van Genuchten 'Why is software late? An empirical study of reasons for delay in software development', *IEEE Transactions in Software Engineering,* 17(6), 582–590.

Figure 7.12 shows the findings of Michiel van Genuchten, a researcher who analysed the reasons for delays in the completion of software development tasks. This bar chart shows that about 30% of activities were finished on time, while 9% were a week early and 17% were a week late. The big jump of 21 percentage points between being a week early and being on time is compatible with the 'Parkinson's Law' principle that *'work expands to fill the time available'*. This tendency should not be blamed on inherent laziness. Van Genuchten found that the most common reason for delay was the time that had to be spent on non-project work. It seems that developers used spare time provided by generous estimates to get on with other urgent work.

Figure 7.12 Percentage of activities early of late (after Genuchen, 1991)

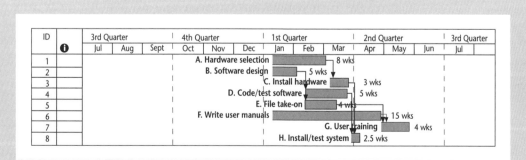

Figure 7.13 Gantt chart – 'traditional' planning approach

ID	ⓘ	3rd Quarter			4th Quarter			1st Quarter			2nd Quarter			3rd Quarter	
		Jul	Aug	Sept	Oct	Nov	Dec	Jan	Feb	Mar	Apr	May	Jun	Jul	
1						A. Hardware selection			6 wks						
2						B. Software design		4 wks							
3						C. Install hardware		3 wks							
4						D. Code/test software		4 wks							
5						E. File take-on	3 wks								
6						F. Write user manuals		10 wks							
7						G. User training	3 wks								
8						H. Install/test system	2 wks								

Figure 7.14 Gantt chart – plan using 'expected times' and starting all activities as late as possible

One approach which attempts to solve some of these problems is the application of the *critical chain* concept originally developed by Eliyahu Goldratt. In order to demonstrate the principles of this approach, the example shown in Figure 7.9 will be reworked as a Gantt chart. Figure 7.13 shows what the Gantt chart for this project might look like if a 'traditional approach' were adopted and the pessimistic durations were used to supply 'comfort times' for each activity.

The general steps in the Critical Chain approach are as follows.

● The target date given to the developer is one where it is estimated that there is a 50% chance of success – this approximates to the expected time identified in the PERT risk method.

● Working backwards from the target completion date, each activity is scheduled to start as late as possible. Among other things, this should reduce the chance of staff being pulled off the project on to other work. It also makes every activity 'critical'. If it is late the whole project is late.

In the example shown in Figure 7.14, all the most likely durations have been used and every activity is scheduled to start as late as possible as long as the project is completed by 1 March.

● To cope with activity overruns, a *project buffer* is inserted at the end of the project before the target completion date. This buffer is the equivalent of 50% of the length of the 'comfort zone' that has been removed from the *critical chain*. The critical chain is the longest chain of activities in the project, taking account of both task and resource dependencies. This is different from the *critical path* as the latter only takes account of task dependencies. A *resource dependency* is where one activity has to wait for a resource (usually a person) which is being used by another activity to become available. If an activity is late it will push the project completion date further into the project buffer.

● Buffers are also inserted into the project schedule where a subsidiary chain of activities feeds into the critical chain. These *feeding buffers* could be set at 50% of the length of the 'comfort zone' removed from the subsidiary or *feeding chain*.

The 'comfort zone' is the difference between the pessimistic and the most likely durations.

Figure 7.15 shows the results of this process. The critical chain in this example happens to be the same as the critical path, that is activities F and G which have

Figure 7.15 Gantt chart – feeding buffers added

comfort zones of 5 and 1 weeks respectively, making a total of 6 weeks. The project buffer is therefore 3 weeks.

Subsidiary chains feed into the critical chain where activity H links into the project buffer and where activity E links into G which is part of the critical chain. For the first buffer the duration would be 50% of the saved comfort zone of A, C and H, that is $(2 + 0 + 0.5)/2 = 1.25$ weeks. In the second case it would be 50% of the comfort zones of activities B and E, that is 1 week.

When the project is executed, the following principles are followed:

- No chain of tasks should be started earlier than scheduled, but once it has been started it should be finished as soon as possible – this invokes the *relay race principle*, where developers should be ready to start their tasks as soon as the previous, dependent, tasks are completed.

- Buffers are divided into three zones: green, amber and red, each of an even (33%) size:

  - *green*, where no action is required if the project completion date creeps into this zone;

  - *amber*, where an action plan is formulated if the project completion dates moves into this zone;

  - *red*, where the action plan above is executed if the project penetrates this zone.

7.13   Conclusion

In this chapter, we have seen how to identify and manage the risks that might affect the success of a project. Risk management is concerned with assessing and prioritizing risks and drawing up plans for addressing those risks before they become problems.

This chapter has also described techniques for estimating the effect of risk on the project's activity network and schedule.

Many of the risks affecting software projects can be reduced by allocating more experienced staff to those activities that are affected. In the next chapter we consider the allocation of staff to activities in more detail.

7.14   Further exercises

1. Fiona is a final-year computing undergraduate student who in her third year undertook a placement with the ICT department of an insurance company as a support analyst and then a network manager. The placement year was very busy and rewarding as the company saw ICT as providing business advantage in a what was a very dynamic and aggressively competitive sector. The project that Fiona proposes to do in her final year will use the insurance company as a client. The proposed project involves gathering requirements for an application that records details of change requests for operational systems made by users and then tracks the subsequent progress of the change. Having gathered the requirements she is to design the application, then build and implement it.

   Identify possible risks in the proposed project of which Fiona should take account.

2. Mo is a systems analyst who is gathering requirements for an application which will record details of the training undertaken by fire fighters in the client fire brigade. Details of the training units successfully completed by fire fighters are to be input to the application by trainers who are themselves senior and active fire-fighters. Mo needs to interview a trainer to obtain his/her requirements. Because of the senior fire fighters' other duties the interview has to be arranged two weeks in advance. There is then a 20% chance of the fire fighter being unable to attend the interview because of an emergency call-out. Each week that the project is delayed costs the fire brigade approximately £1000.

   (a) Provide an estimate of the risk exposure (as a financial value) for the risk that the senior fire fighter might not be able to attend at the times needed.

   (b) Suggest possible risk mitigation actions.

3. In Exercise 7.2 you were asked to identify risks under the four headings of Actors, Technology, Structure and Tasks for the IOE maintenance group accounts and the Brightmouth College payroll scenarios. Now identify risks for each scenario that relate to pairs of domains, for example Actors–Technology, Actors–Tasks and so on.

4. The Wet Holiday Company specializes in the provision of holidays which involve water sports of various types. There are three major divisions with the following lines of business:
   ● boat holidays on canals;

- villa holidays in various parts of the Mediterranean which involve sailing in some way;
- canoeing holidays in France.

Wet Holiday feel that they are particularly appealing to a young active market and that having the facility for customers to book via the web is essential. They call in ICT consultants to advise them on their IT strategy. The consultants advise them that before they can have a web presence, they need to have a conventional ICT-based booking system to support their telesales operation first. Because of the specialized nature of their business, an off-the-shelf application would not be suitable and they would need to have a specially written software application, based on a client–server architecture. The top priority needs to be given to a system to support villa holiday bookings because this has the largest number of customers and generates the most revenue.

Wet Holiday have some in-house IT development staff, but these are inexperienced in client–server technology. To meet this short-fall, contractors are employed.

It turns out that development takes much longer than planned. Much of this delay occurs at acceptance testing when the users find many errors and performance shortcomings, which require extensive rework. Part of the problem relates to getting the best performance out of the new architecture; this has a particular impact on response times which are initially unacceptable to staff who are dealing with customers over the phone. The contractors are not closely monitored and some of the code that they produce is found to have many careless mistakes and to be poorly structured and documented. This makes it difficult to make changes to the software after the contractors have left on the expiry of their contracts.

The villa booking system can only be implemented at the beginning of a holiday season and the deadline for the beginning of the 2002 to 2003 season is missed, leading to a 12-month delay in the implementation. The delay in implementation seems to encourage the users to ask for further modifications to the original requirements, which adds even more to development costs.

The delays in implementing this application mean that the other scheduled IT development, for other lines of business have to be put back. Managers of customer-facing business functions at Wet Holiday are suggesting that the whole IT function should be completely outsourced.

(a) Draw up a causal map which analyses the reasons for the problems faced by Wet Holiday.

(b) Use the causal map to identify interventions which could have prevented the problems arising.

5. In this chapter the application of risk management to software development projects has been strongly advocated. In practice, however, managers are often reluctant to apply the techniques. What do you think might be the reasons for this?

Resource allocation

Objectives

When you have completed this chapter you will be able to:

- identify the resources required for a project;
- make the demand for resources more even throughout the life of a project;
- produce a work plan and resource schedule.

8.1 Introduction

In Chapter 6, we saw how to use activity network analysis techniques to plan *when* activities should take place. This was calculated as a time span during which an activity should take place – bounded by the earliest start and latest finish dates. In Chapter 7 we used the PERT technique to forecast a range of expected dates by which activities would be completed. In both cases these plans took no account of the availability of resources.

In this chapter we shall see how to match the activity plan to available resources and, where necessary, assess the efficacy of changing the plan to fit the resources. Figure 8.1 shows where resource allocation is applied in Step Wise.

In general, the allocation of resources to activities will lead us to review and modify the ideal activity plan. It may cause us to revise stage or project completion dates. In any event, it is likely to lead to a narrowing of the time spans within which activities may be scheduled.

The final result of resource allocation will normally be a number of schedules, including:

These schedules will provide the basis for the day-to-day control and management of the project. These are described in Chapter 9.

- *activity schedule* indicating the planned start and completion dates for each activity;
- *resource schedule* showing the dates on which each resource will be required and the level of that requirement;
- *cost schedule* showing the planned cumulative expenditure incurred by the use of resources over time.

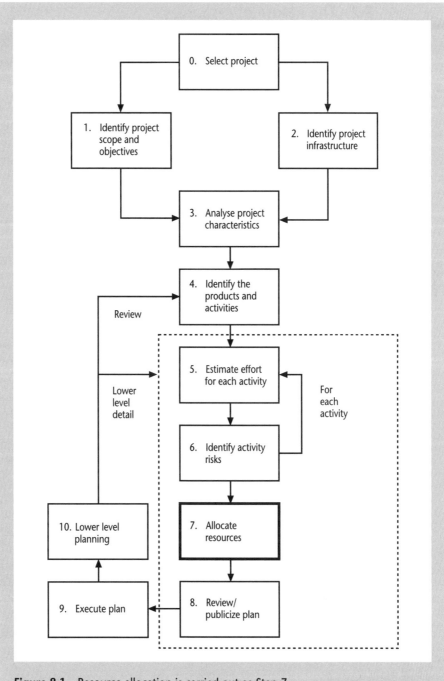

Figure 8.1 Resource allocation is carried out as Step 7

8.2   The nature of resources

A resource is any item or person required for the execution of the project. This covers many things – from paper clips to key personnel – and it is unlikely that we would wish to itemize every resource required, let alone draw up a schedule for their use! Stationery and other standard office supplies, for example, need not normally be the concern of the project manager – ensuring there is always an adequate supply is the role of the office manager. The project manager must concentrate on those resources where there is a possibility that, without planning, they might not be sufficiently available when required.

Some resources, such as a project manager, will be required for the duration of the project whereas others, such as a specific software developer, might be required for a single activity. The former, while vital to the success of the project, does not require the same level of scheduling as the latter. Individual programmers, for example, might be committed to working on a number of projects and it will be important to book their time well in advance.

In general, resources will fall into one of seven categories.

- *Labour*   The main items in this category will be members of the development project team such as the project manager, systems analysts and software developers. Equally important will be the quality assurance team and other support staff and any employees of the client organization who might be required to undertake or participate in specific activities.

- *Equipment*   Obvious items will include workstations and other computing and office equipment. We must not forget that staff also need basic equipment such as desks and chairs.

- *Materials*   Materials are items that are consumed, rather than equipment that is used. They are of little consequence in most software projects but can be important for some – software that is to be widely distributed might, for example, require supplies of disks to be specially obtained.

- *Space*   For projects that are undertaken with existing staff, space is normally readily available. If any additional staff (recruited or contracted) should be needed then office space will need to be found.

- *Services*   Some projects will require procurement of specialist services – development of a wide area distributed system, for example, requires scheduling of telecommunications services.

- *Time*   Time is the resource that is being offset against the other primary resources – project timescales can sometimes be reduced by increasing other resources and will almost certainly be extended if they are unexpectedly reduced.

The cost of money as a resource is a factor taken into account in DCF evaluation.

- *Money*   Money is a secondary resource – it is used to buy other resources and will be consumed as other resources are used. It is similar to other resources in that it is available at a cost – in this case interest charges.

8.3 Identifying resource requirements

The first step in producing a resource allocation plan is to list the resources that will be required along with the expected level of demand. This will normally be done by considering each activity in turn and identifying the resources required. It is likely, however, that there will also be resources required that are not activity specific but are part of the project's infrastructure (such as the project manager) or required to support other resources (office space, for example, might be required to house contract software developers).

CASE STUDY EXAMPLES

Amanda has produced a precedence network for the IOE project (Figure 8.2) and used this as a basis for a resource requirements list, part of which is shown in Table 8.1. Notice that, at this stage, she has not allocated individuals to tasks but has decided on the type of staff that will be required. The activity durations assume that they will be carried out by 'standard' analysts or software developers.

Figure 8.2 The IOE precedence network

Table 8.1 Part of Amanda's resource requirements list

Stage	Activity	Resource	Days	Quantity	Notes
ALL		Project manager	104 F/T		
1	All	Workstation		34	Check software availability
	IoE/P/1	Senior analyst	34 F/T		
2	All	Workstation	—	3	One per person would be ideal
	IoE/P/2	Analyst/designer	20 F/T		
	IoE/P/3	Analyst/designer	15 F/T		
	IoE/P/4	Analyst/designer	25 F/T		
	IoE/P/5	Analyst/designer	15 F/T		Could use analyst/programmer
3	All	Workstation		2	
	IoE/P/6	Senior analyst*	2 F/T		
4	All	Workstation	—	3	As stage 2
	IoE/P/7	Analyst/designer	7 F/T		
	IoE/P/8	Analyst/designer	6 F/T		
	IoE/P/9	Analyst/designer	4 F/T		
	IoE/P/10	Analyst/designer	4 F/T		
5	All	Workstation	—	4	One per programmer
	All	Office space	—		If contract programmers used
	IoE/P/11	Programmer	30 F/T		
	IoE/P/12	Programmer	28 F/T		
	IoE/P/13	Programmer	15 F/T		
	IoE/P/14	Programmer	25 F/T		
6	All	Full machine access	—		Approx. 16 hours for full system test
	IoE/P/15	Analyst/designer	6 F/T		

* In reality, this would normally be done by a review involving all the analysts working on stage 2.

At this stage, it is necessary that the resource requirements list be as comprehensive as possible – it is better that something is included that may later be deleted as unnecessary than to omit something essential. Amanda has therefore included additional office space as a possible requirement, should contract software development staff be recruited.

8.4 Scheduling resources

Note that in section 7.12 an argument for starting activities as late as possible was presented! The resource allocation process is similar regardless of the policy adopted in this respect.

Having produced the resource requirements list, the next stage is to map this on to the activity plan to assess the distribution of resources required over the duration of the project. This is best done by representing the activity plan as a bar chart and using this to produce a resource histogram for each resource.

Figure 8.3 illustrates Amanda's activity plan as a bar chart and a resource histogram for analyst/designers. Each activity has been scheduled to start at its earliest start date – a sensible initial strategy, since we would, other things being equal, wish to save any float to allow for contingencies. Earliest start date scheduling, as is the case with Amanda's project, frequently creates resource histograms that start with a peak and then tail off.

Changing the level of resources on a project over time, particularly personnel, generally adds to the cost of a project. Recruiting staff has costs and, even where

White rectangles indicate when an activity is scheduled and shaded rectangles the total float.

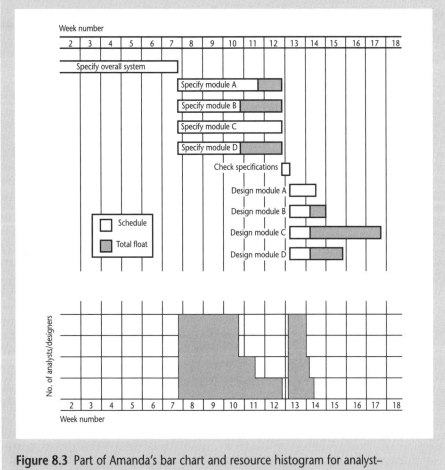

Figure 8.3 Part of Amanda's bar chart and resource histogram for analyst–designers.

staff are transferred internally, time will be needed for familiarization with the new project environment.

The resource histogram in Figure 8.3 poses particular problems in that it calls for two analyst/designers to be idle for twelve days, one for seven days and one for two days between the specification and design stage. It is unlikely that IOE would have another project requiring their skills for exactly those periods of time and this raises the question as to whether this idle time should be charged to Amanda's project. The ideal resource histogram will be smooth with, perhaps, an initial build-up and a staged run-down.

An additional problem with an uneven resource histogram is that it is more likely to call for levels of resource beyond those available. Figure 8.4 illustrates how, by adjusting the start date of some activities and splitting others, a resource histogram can, subject to constraints such as precedence requirements, be smoothed to contain resource demand at available levels. The different letters represent staff working on a series of module testing tasks, that is, one person working on task A, two on tasks B and C etc.

Some project planning applications will carry out resource smoothing automatically, although they are unlikely to take into account all the factors that could be used by a project manager. The majority of project planning software applications will produce resource histograms based on earliest activity start dates.

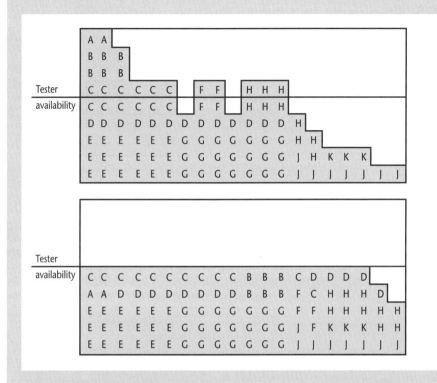

Figure 8.4 A resource histogram showing demand for staff before and after smoothing

In Figure 8.4, the original histogram was created by scheduling the activities at their earliest start dates. The resource histogram shows the typical peaked shape caused by earliest start date scheduling and calls for a total of nine staff where only five are available for the project.

By delaying the start of some of the activities, it has been possible to smooth the histogram and reduce the maximum level of demand for the resource. Notice that some activities, such as C and D, have been split. Where non-critical activities can be split they can provide a useful way of filling troughs in the demand for a resource, but in software projects it is difficult to split tasks without increasing the time they take.

Some of the activities call for more than one unit of the resource at a time – activity F, for example, requires two programmers, each working for two weeks. It might be possible to reschedule this activity to use one programmer over four weeks, although that has not been considered in this case.

Exercise 8.1 Amanda has already decided to use only three analyst/designers on the project in order to reduce costs. Her current resource histogram, however, calls for four during both stage 2 and stage 4. Suggest what she might do to smooth the histogram and reduce the number of analyst/designers required to three.

In practice, resources have to be allocated to a project on an activity-by-activity basis and finding the 'best' allocation can be time consuming and difficult. As soon as a member of the project team is allocated to an activity, that activity acquires a scheduled start and finish date and the team member becomes unavailable for other activities for that period. Thus, allocating a resource to one activity limits the flexibility for resource allocation and scheduling of other activities.

It is therefore helpful to prioritize activities so that resources can be allocated to competing activities in some rational order. The priority must always be to allocate resources to critical path activities and then to those activities that are most likely to affect others. In that way, lower priority activities are made to fit around the more critical, already scheduled activities.

Of the various ways of prioritizing activities, two are described below.

- *Total float priority*   Activities are ordered according to their total float, those with the smallest total float having the highest priority. In the simplest application of this method, activities are allocated resources in ascending order of total float. However, as scheduling proceeds, activities will be delayed (if resources are not available at their earliest start dates) and total floats will be reduced. It is therefore desirable to recalculate floats (and hence reorder the list) each time an activity is delayed.

P. J. Burman, *Precedence Networks for Planning and Control*, McGraw-Hill, 1972.

- *Ordered list priority*   With this method, activities that can proceed at the same time are ordered according to a set of simple criteria. An example of this is Burman's priority list, which takes into account activity duration as well as total float:

  1. shortest critical activity;

  2. critical activities;

  3. shortest non-critical activity;

  4. non-critical activity with least float;

  5. non-critical activities.

Unfortunately, resource smoothing, or even containment of resource demand to available levels, is not always possible within planned timescales – deferring activities to smooth out resource peaks often puts back project completion. Where that is the case, we need to consider ways of increasing the available resource levels or altering working methods.

Exercise 8.2

Amanda finds that, with only three analyst/designers, the specification of module D (see Figure 8.3) will have to be deferred until after the specification of module B and this will add five days to the overall project duration (making 109 in total). She had hoped to have the project completed within 100 days and this is a further disappointment. She therefore decides to have another look at her activity plan.

You will remember that early on she decided that she should check all of the specifications together (activity IoE/P/6) before allowing design to start. It is now apparent that this is causing a significant bottleneck and delaying module D will only exacerbate the problem. She therefore decides on a compromise – she will check the specifications for modules A, B and D together but will then go ahead with their design without waiting for the module C specification. This will be checked against the others when it is complete.

She redraws her precedence network to reflect this, inserting the new activity of checking the module C specification against the others (activity IoE/P/6a). This is shown in Figure 8.5. Draw a new resource histogram to reflect this change.

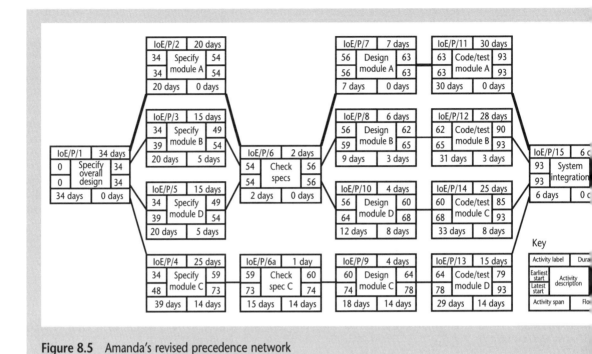

Figure 8.5   Amanda's revised precedence network

8.5   Creating critical paths

Scheduling resources can create new critical paths. Delaying the start of an activity because of lack of resources will cause that activity to become critical if this uses up its float. Furthermore, a delay in completing one activity can delay the availability of a resource required for a later activity. If the later one is already critical then the earlier one might now have been made critical by linking their resources.

Amanda's revised schedule, which still calls for four analyst/designers but only for a single day, is illustrated in the solution to Exercise 8.2 (check it in the back of the book if you have not done so already). Notice that in rescheduling some of the activities she has introduced additional critical activities. Delaying the specification of module C has used up all of its float – and that of the subsequent activities along that path! Amanda now has two critical paths – the one shown on the precedence network and the new one.

In a large project, resource-linked criticalities can be quite complex – a hint of the potential problems may be appreciated by looking at the next exercise.

Exercise 8.3   Amanda decides to delay the specification of module C for a further day to ensure that only three analyst–designers will be required. The relevant part of her revised bar chart and resource histogram are shown in Figure 8.6.

Which activities will now be critical?

Figure 8.6 Amanda's project scheduled to require three analyst/designers

8.6 Counting the cost

The discussion so far has concentrated on trying to complete the project by the earliest completion date with the minimum number of staff. We have seen that doing this places constraints on when activities can be carried out and increases the risk of not meeting target dates.

Alternatively, Amanda could have considered using additional staff or lengthening the overall duration of the project. The additional costs of employing extra staff would need to be compared to the costs of delayed delivery and the increased risk of not meeting the scheduled date. The relationship between these factors is discussed later in this chapter.

8.7 Being specific

Allocating resources and smoothing resource histograms is relatively straightforward where all resources of a given type can be considered more or less equivalent. When allocating labourers to activities in a large building project we need not distinguish among individuals – there are likely to be many labourers and they may be treated as equals so far as skills and productivity are concerned.

This is seldom the case with software projects. We saw in Chapter 5 that, because of the nature of software development, skill and experience play a significant part in determining the time taken and, potentially, the quality of the final product. With the exception of extremely large projects, it makes sense to allocate individual members of staff to activities as early as possible, as this can lead us to revise our estimate of their duration.

In allocating individuals to tasks, a number of factors need to be taken into account.

- *Availability* We need to know whether a particular individual will be available when required. Reference to the departmental work plan determines this but the wise project manager will always investigate the risks that might be involved – earlier projects might, for example, overrun and affect the availability of an individual.

- *Criticality* Allocation of more experienced personnel to activities on the critical path often helps in shortening project durations or at least reduces the risk of overrun.

Reappraisal of the critical path and PERT or Monte Carlo risk analysis might need to be carried out in parallel with staff allocation.

- *Risk* We saw how to undertake activity risk assessment in the previous chapter. Identifying those activities posing the greatest risk, and knowing the factors influencing them, helps to allocate staff. Allocating the most experienced staff to the highest-risk activities is likely to have the greatest effect in reducing overall project uncertainties. More experienced staff are, however, usually more expensive.

- *Training* It will benefit the organization if positive steps are taken to allocate junior staff to appropriate non-critical activities where there will be sufficient slack for them to train and develop skills. There can even be direct benefits to the particular project since some costs may be allocated to the training budget.

- *Team building* The selection of individuals must also take account of the final shape of the project team and the way they will work together. This and additional aspects of personnel management are discussed in Chapter 11.

Exercise 8.4

Amanda has decided that, where possible, whoever writes the specification for a module should also produce the design, as she believes this will improve the commitment and motivation of the three analyst/designers, Belinda, Tom and Daisy.

She has decided that she will use Tom, a trainee analyst/designer, for the specification and design of module D as both of these activities have a large float compared to their activity span ($^5/_{21}$ and $^5/_{13}$ of their span respectively). Since the specification and design of module C are on the critical path, she decides to allocate both of these tasks to Belinda, a particularly experienced and capable member of staff.

Having made these decisions, she has almost no flexibility in how she assigns the other specification and design activities. Work out from the activity bar chart produced as part of the solution to Exercise 8.2 (shown in Figure 8.6) whom she assigns to which of the remaining specification and design activities.

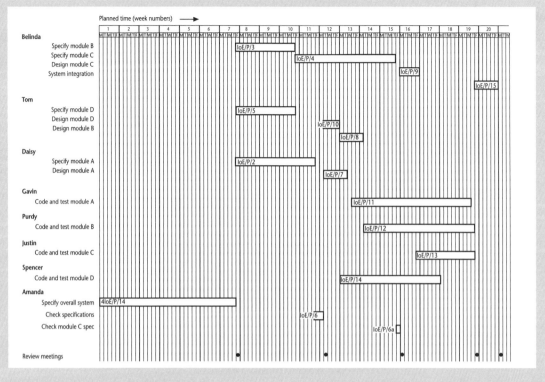

Figure 8.7 Amanda's work schedule

8.8 Publishing the resource schedule

In allocating and scheduling resources we have used the activity plan (a precedence network in the case of the examples in this chapter), activity bar charts and resource histograms. Although good as planning tools, they are not the best way of publishing and communicating project schedules. For this we need some form of work plan. Work plans are commonly published either as lists or charts such as that illustrated in Figure 8.7. In this case Amanda has chosen not to include activity floats (which could be indicated by shaded bars) as she fears that one or two members of the team might work with less urgency if they are aware that their activities are not critical.

Notice that, somewhat unusually, it is assumed there are no public holidays or other non-productive periods during the 100 days of the project and that none of the team has holidays for the periods they are shown as working.

Amanda has also made no explicit allowance for staff taking sick leave.

Amanda now transfers some of the information from the work schedule to her precedence network. In particular, she amends the earliest start dates for activities and any other constraints (such as revised latest finish dates where resources need to be made available) that have been introduced. A copy of her revised precedence network is shown in Figure 8.8 – notice that she has highlighted all critical activities and paths.

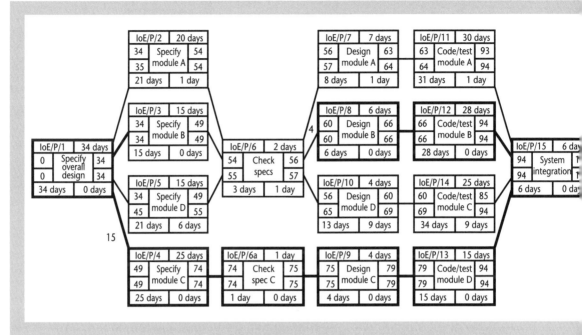

Figure 8.8   Amanda's revised precedence network showing scheduled start and completion dates

8.9   Cost schedules

It is now time to produce a detailed cost schedule showing weekly or monthly costs over the life of the project. This will provide a more detailed and accurate estimate of costs and will serve as a plan against which project progress can be monitored.

Calculating cost is straightforward where the organization has standard cost figures for staff and other resources. Where this is not the case, then the project manager will have to calculate the costs.

In general, costs are categorized as follows.

- *Staff costs*   These will include staff salaries as well as the other direct costs of employment such as the employer's contribution to social security funds, pension scheme contributions, holiday pay and sickness benefit. These are commonly charged to projects at hourly rates based on weekly work records completed by staff. Note that contract staff are usually charged by the week or month – even when they are idle.

- *Overheads*   Overheads represent expenditure that an organization incurs, which cannot be directly related to individual projects or jobs, including space rental, interest charges and the costs of service departments (such as human resources). Overhead costs can be recovered by making a fixed charge on development departments (in which case they usually appear as a weekly or monthly charge for a project), or by an additional percentage charge on direct staff employment costs. These additional charges or oncosts can easily equal or exceed the direct employment costs.

Table 8.2 Staff costs (including oncosts) for Amanda's project team

Staff member	Daily cost (£)
Amanda	300
Belinda	250
Tom	175
Daisy	225
Gavin	150
Purdy	150
Justin	150
Spencer	150

- *Usage charges* In some organizations, projects are charged directly for use of resources such as computer time (rather than their cost being recovered as an overhead). This will normally be on an 'as used' basis.

Exercise 8.5   Amanda finds that IOE recovers some overheads as oncosts on direct staff costs although others are recovered by charging a fixed £200 per day against projects. Staff costs (including overheads) are as shown in Table 8.2. Amanda has been working as project leader on the project for its duration. She also estimates that, in total, she will have spent an additional 10 days planning the project and carrying out the post-project review.

Calculate the total cost for Amanda's project on this basis. How is the expenditure spread over the life of the project?

Figure 8.9 shows the weekly costs over the 20 weeks that Amanda expects the project to take. This is a typical cost profile – building up slowly to a peak and then tailing off quite rapidly at the end of the project. Figure 8.10 illustrates the cumulative cost of the project and it is generally this that would be used for cost control purposes.

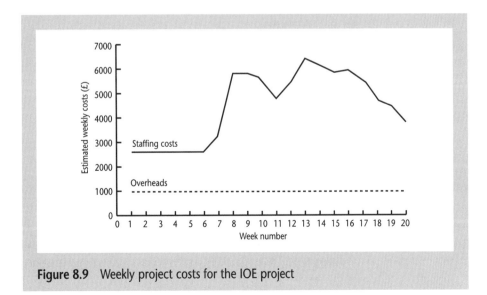

Figure 8.9   Weekly project costs for the IOE project

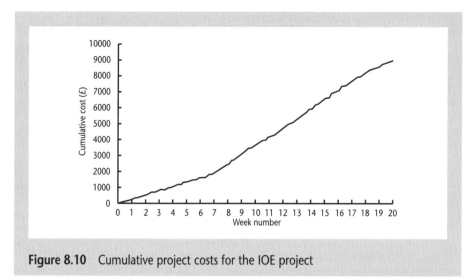

Figure 8.10 Cumulative project costs for the IOE project

8.10 The scheduling sequence

Going from an ideal activity plan to a costed schedule can be represented as a sequence of steps, rather like the classic waterfall life-cycle model. In the ideal world, we would start with the activity plan and use this as the basis for our risk assessment. The activity plan and risk assessment would provide the basis for our resource allocation and schedule from which we would produce cost schedules.

In practice, as we have seen by looking at Amanda's project, successful resource allocation often necessitates revisions to the activity plan, which, in turn, will affect our risk assessment. Similarly, the cost schedule might indicate the need or desirability to reallocate resources or revise activity plans – particularly where that schedule indicates a higher overall project cost than originally anticipated.

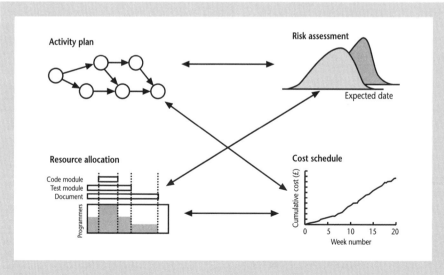

Figure 8.11 Successful project scheduling is not a simple sequence

The interplay between the plans and schedules is complex – any change to any one will affect each of the others. Some factors can be directly compared in terms of money – the cost of hiring additional staff can be balanced against the costs of delaying the project's end date. Some factors, however, are difficult to express in money terms (the cost of an increased risk, for example) and will include an element of subjectivity.

While good project planning software will assist greatly in demonstrating the consequences of change and keeping the planning synchronized, successful project scheduling is largely dependent upon the skill and experience of the project manager in juggling the many factors involved (Figure 8.11).

8.11 Conclusion

In this chapter we have discussed the problems of allocating resources to project activities and the conversion of an activity plan to a work schedule. In particular, we have seen the importance of the following:

- identifying all the resources needed;

- arranging activity starts to minimize variations in resource levels over the duration of the project;

- allocating resources to competing activities in a rational order of priority;

- taking care in allocating the right staff to critical activities.

8.12 Further exercises

1. Burman's priority ordering for allocating resources to activities takes into account the activity duration as well as its total float. Why do you think this is advantageous?

2. If you have access to project planning software, use it to produce an activity plan for Amanda's project and include the staff resource requirements for each activity. Explore the facilities of your software and answer the following questions.
   - Can you set up resource types and ask the application to allocate individuals to tasks?
   - Will your software allow you to specify productivity factors for individual members of staff so that the duration of an activity depends upon who is carrying it out?
   - Will your software carry out resource smoothing or provide a minimum cost solution?
   - Can you replicate Amanda's resource schedule (see Figure 8.7) – or produce a better one?

3. On a large project it is often be the responsibility of a team leader to allocate tasks to individuals. Why might it be unsatisfactory to leave such allocations entirely to the discretion of the team leader?

4. In scheduling her project, Amanda ignored the risks of absence due to staff sickness. What might she have done to estimate the likelihood of this occurring and how might she have taken account of the risk when scheduling the project?

Monitoring and control

When you have completed this chapter you will be able to:

- monitor the progress of projects;
- assess the risk of slippage;
- visualize and assess the state of a project;
- revise targets to correct or counteract drift;
- control changes to a project's requirements.

9.1 Introduction

Once work schedules have been published and the project is under way, attention must be focused on ensuring progress. This requires monitoring of what is happening, comparison of actual achievement against the schedule and, where necessary, revision of plans and schedules to bring the project as far as possible back on target.

In earlier chapters we have stressed the importance of producing plans that can be monitored – for example, ensuring that activities have clearly defined and visible completion points. We will discuss how information about project progress is gathered and what actions must be taken to ensure a project meets its targets.

The final part of this chapter discusses how we can deal with changes that are imposed from outside – namely, changes in requirements.

9.2 Creating the framework

Exercising control over a project and ensuring that targets are met is a matter of regular monitoring, finding out what is happening, and comparing it with current targets. If there is a mismatch between the planned outcomes and the actual ones then either replanning is needed to bring the project back on target or the target will have to be revised. Figure 9.1 illustrates a model of the project control cycle and shows how, once the initial project plan has been published, project control is a continual process of monitoring progress against that plan and, where necessary, revising the plan to take account of deviations. It also illustrates the important

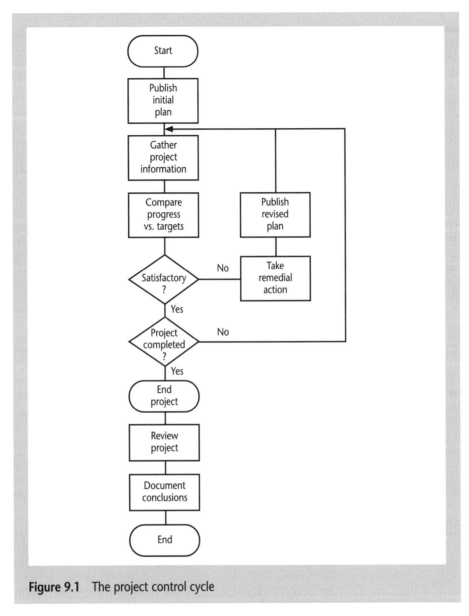

Figure 9.1 The project control cycle

steps that must be taken after completion of the project so that the experience gained in any one project can feed into the planning stages of future projects, thus allowing us to learn from past mistakes.

See Chapter 12 for a discussion of software quality.

In practice we are normally concerned with departures from the plan in four dimensions – delays in meeting target dates, shortfalls in quality, inadequate functionality, and costs going over target. In this chapter we are mainly concerned with the first and last of these.

Responsibility

The overall responsibility for ensuring satisfactory progress on a project is often the role of the *project steering committee* or *Project Board*. Day-to-day responsibility will

In a PRINCE2 environment, there is a Project Assurance function reporting to the Project Board and independent of the Project Manager.

Figure 9.2   Project reporting structures

rest with the project manager and, in all but the smallest of projects, aspects of this can be delegated to team leaders.

Figure 9.2 illustrates the typical reporting structure found with medium and large projects. With small projects (employing around half a dozen or fewer staff) individual team members usually report directly to the project manager, but in most cases team leaders will collate reports on their section's progress and forward summaries to the project manager. These, in turn, will be incorporated into project-level reports for the steering committee and, via them or directly, progress reports for the client.

The concept of a reporting hierarchy was introduced in Chapter 1.

Reporting may be oral or written, formal or informal, or regular or *ad hoc* and some examples of each type are given in Table 9.1. While any effective team leader or project manager will be in touch with team members and available to discuss problems, any such informal reporting of project progress must be complemented by formal reporting procedures – and it is those we are concerned with in this chapter.

Table 9.1   Categories of reporting

Report type	Examples	Comment
Oral formal regular	Weekly or monthly progress meetings	While reports may be oral, formal written minutes should be kept
Oral formal *ad hoc*	End-of-stage review meetings	While largely oral, likely to receive and generate written reports
Written formal regular	Job sheets, progress reports	Normally weekly using forms
Written formal *ad hoc*	Exception reports, change reports	
Oral informal *ad hoc*	Canteen discussion, social interaction	Often provides early warning; must be backed up by formal reporting

Assessing progress

Progress assessment will normally be made on the basis of information collected and collated at regular intervals or when specific events occur. Wherever possible, this information will be objective and tangible – whether or not a particular report has been delivered, for example. However, such end-of-activity deliverables might not occur sufficiently frequently throughout the life of the project. Here progress assessment will have to rely on the judgement of the team members who are carrying out the project activities.

Setting checkpoints

The PRINCE2 standard described in Appendix A has its own terminology.

It is essential to set a series of checkpoints in the initial activity plan. Checkpoints may be:

- regular (monthly, for example);
- tied to specific events such as the production of a report or other deliverable.

Taking snapshots

Short, Monday-morning team progress meetings are a common way of motivating staff to meet short-term targets.

The frequency with which a manager needs to receive information about progress will depend upon the size and degree of risk of the project or that part of the project under their control. Team leaders, for example, need to assess progress daily (particularly when employing inexperienced staff) whereas project managers may find weekly or monthly reporting appropriate. In general, the higher the level, the less frequent and less detailed the reporting needs to be.

There are, however, strong arguments in favour of formal weekly collection of information from staff carrying out activities. Collecting data at the end of each week ensures that information is provided while memories are still relatively fresh and provides a mechanism for individuals to review and reflect upon their progress during the past few days.

Major, or project-level, progress reviews will generally take place at particular points during the life of a project – commonly known as *review points* or *control points*. PRINCE2, for example, designates a series of checkpoints where the status of work in a project or for a team is reviewed. At the end of each project Stage, PRINCE2 provides for an End Stage Assessment where an assessment of the project and consideration of its future are undertaken.

9.3 Collecting the data

As a rule, managers will try to break down long activities into more controllable tasks of one or two weeks' duration. However, it will still be necessary to gather information about partially completed activities and, in particular, forecasts of how much work is left to be completed. It can be difficult to make such forecasts accurately.

Exercise 9.1
A software developer working on Amanda's project has written the first 250 lines of a Java program that is estimated to require 500 lines of code. Explain why it would be unreasonable to assume that the programming task is 50% complete.

How might you make a reasonable estimate of how near completion it might be?

Weekly timesheets are a valuable source of information about resources used. They are often used to provide information about what has been achieved. However, requesting partial completion estimates where they cannot be obtained from objective measures encourages the 99% complete syndrome – tasks are reported as on time until 99% complete, and then stay at 99% complete until finished.

Time Sheet

Staff _____John Smith_____   Week ending _____30/3/07_____

Rechargeable hours

Project	Activity code	Description	Hours this week	% complete	Scheduled completion	Estimated completion
P21	A243	Code mod A3	12	30	24/4/07	24/4/07
P34	B771	Document take-on	20	90	6/4/07	4/4/07

Total recharged hours	32

Non-rechargeable hours

Code	Description	Hours this week	Comment and authorization
Z99	Day in lieu	8	Authorized by RB

Total non-rechargeable hours	8

Figure 9.3 A weekly timesheet and progress review form

Where there is a series of products, partial completion of activities is easier to estimate. Counting the number of record specifications or screen layouts produced, for example, can provide a reasonable measure of progress.

In some cases, intermediate products can be used as in-activity milestones. The first successful compilation of a program, for example, might be considered a milestone even though it is not the final product of the activity code and test.

Partial completion reporting

Many organizations use standard accounting systems with weekly timesheets to charge staff time to individual jobs. The staff time booked to a project indicates the work carried out and the charges to the project. It does not, however, tell the project manager what has been produced or whether tasks are on schedule.

It is therefore common to adapt or enhance existing accounting data collection systems to meet the needs of project control. Weekly timesheets, for example, are frequently adapted by breaking jobs down to activity level and requiring information about work done in addition to time spent. Figure 9.3 shows a typical example of such a report form, in this case requesting information about likely slippage of completion dates as well as estimates of completeness.

Asking for estimated completion times can be criticized on the grounds that frequent invitations to reconsider completion dates deflects attention away from the importance of the originally scheduled targets and can generate an ethos that it is acceptable for completion dates to slip.

Risk reporting

One popular way of overcoming the objections to partial completion reporting is to avoid asking for estimated completion dates, but to ask instead for the team members' estimates of the likelihood of meeting the planned target date.

One way of doing this is the traffic-light method. This consists of the following steps:

There are a number of variations on the traffic-light technique. The version described here is in use in IBM and is described in Down, Coleman and Absolon, *Risk Management for Software Projects*, McGraw-Hill, 1994.

- identify the key (first level) elements for assessment in a piece of work;
- break these key elements into constituent elements (second level);
- assess each of the second-level elements on the scale *green* for 'on target', *amber* for 'not on target but recoverable', and *red* for 'not on target and recoverable only with difficulty';
- review all the second-level assessments to arrive at first-level assessments;
- review first- and second-level assessments to produce an overall assessment.

For example, Amanda decides to use a version of the traffic-light method for reviewing activities on the IOE project. She breaks each activity into a number of component parts (deciding, in this case, that a further breakdown is unnecessary) and gets the team members to complete a return at the end of each week. Figure 9.4 illustrates Justin's completed assessment at the end of week 16.

Traffic-light assessment highlights only risk of non-achievement; it is not an attempt to estimate work done or to quantify expected delays.

Following completion of assessment forms for all activities, the project manager uses these as a basis for evaluating the overall status of the project. Any critical activity classified as amber or red will require further consideration and often leads

Note that this form refers only to uncompleted activities. Justin would still need to report activity completions and the time spent on activities.

Activity Assessment Sheet

Staff ____Justin____

Ref: IoE/P/13   Activity: Code and test module C

Week number	13	14	15	16	17	18	
Activity summary	G	A	A	R			
Component							Comments
Screen handling procedures	G	A	A	G			
File update procedures	G	G	R	A			
Housekeeping procedures	G	G	G	A			
Compilation	G	G	G	R			
Test data runs	G	G	G	A			
Program documentation	G	G	A	R			

Figure 9.4 A traffic-light assessment of IoE/P/13

to a revision of the project schedule. Non-critical activities are likely to be considered as a problem if they are classified as red, especially if all their float is likely to be consumed.

9.4 Visualizing progress

Having collected data about project progress, a manager needs some way of presenting that data to greatest effect. In this section, we look at some methods of presenting a picture of the project and its future. Some of these methods (such as Gantt charts) provide a static picture, a single snapshot, whereas others (such as timeline charts) try to show how the project has progressed and changed through time.

The Gantt chart

One of the simplest and oldest techniques for tracking project progress is the Gantt chart. This is essentially an activity bar chart indicating scheduled activity dates and durations frequently augmented with activity floats. Reported progress is recorded on the chart (normally by shading activity bars) and a 'today cursor' provides an immediate visual indication of which activities are ahead or behind schedule. Figure 9.5 shows part of Amanda's Gantt chart as at the end of Tuesday of week 17. 'Code & test module D' has been completed ahead of schedule and 'Code & test module A' appears also to be ahead of schedule. The coding and testing of the other two modules are behind schedule.

Henry Gantt (1861–1919) was an industrial engineer interested in the efficient organization of work.

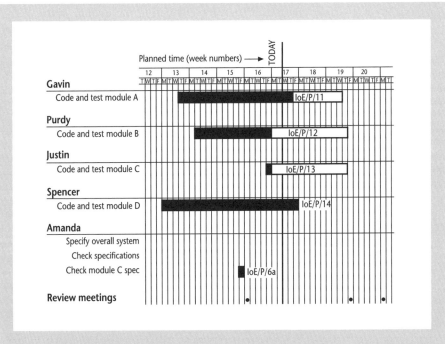

Figure 9.5 Part of Amanda's Gantt chart with the 'today cursor' in week 17

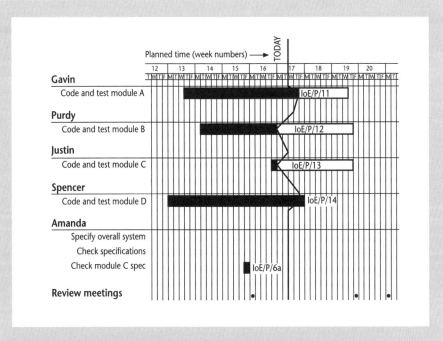

Figure 9.6 The slip chart emphasizes the relative position of each activity

The slip chart

A slip chart (Figure 9.6) is a very similar alternative favoured by some project managers who believe it provides a more striking visual indication of those activities that are not progressing to schedule – the more the slip line bends, the greater the variation from the plan. Additional slip lines are added at intervals and, as they build up, the project manager will gain an idea as to whether the project is improving (subsequent slip lines bend less) or not. A very jagged slip line indicates a need for rescheduling.

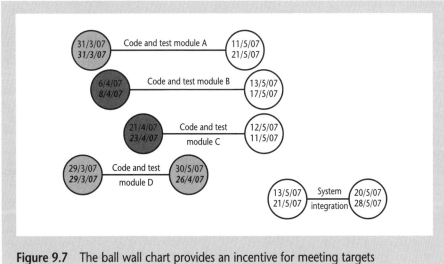

Figure 9.7 The ball wall chart provides an incentive for meeting targets

Ball charts

A somewhat more striking way of showing whether or not targets have been met is to use a ball chart as in Figure 9.7. In this version of the ball chart, the circles indicate start and completion points for activities. The circles initially contain the original scheduled dates. Whenever revisions are produced, these are added as second dates in the appropriate circle until an activity is actually started or completed, when the relevant date replaces the revised estimate (in bold italic in Figure 9.7). Circles will therefore contain only two dates, the original and most recent target dates, or the original and actual dates.

David Youll in *Making Software Development Visible*, John Wiley & Sons, 1990, describes a version of the ball chart using three sets of dates and part-coloured balls.

Where the actual start or finish date for an activity is later than the target date, the circle is coloured red (dark grey in Figure 9.7) – where an actual date is on time or earlier than the target then the circle is coloured green (light grey in Figure 9.7).

Such charts are frequently placed in a prominent position and the colour-coded balls provide a constant reminder to the project team. Where more than one team is working in close proximity, such a highly visible record of achievement can encourage competitiveness between teams.

Another advantage of ball charts over Gantt and slip charts is that they are relatively easy to keep up to date – only the dates and possibly colours need to be changed, whereas the others need to be redrawn each time target dates are revised.

The timeline

One disadvantage of the charts described so far is that they do not show clearly the slippage of the project completion date through the life of the project. Knowing the current state of a project helps in revising plans to bring it back on target, but analysing and understanding trends helps to avoid slippage in future projects.

The timeline chart is a method of recording and displaying the way in which targets have changed throughout the duration of the project.

Figure 9.8 shows a timeline chart for Brigette's project at the end of the sixth week. Planned time is plotted along the horizontal axis and elapsed time down the vertical axis. The lines meandering down the chart represent scheduled activity completion dates – at the start of the project 'analyse existing system' is scheduled to be completed by the Tuesday of week 3, 'obtain user requirements' by Thursday of week 5, 'issue tender', the final activity, by Tuesday of week 9, and so on.

At the end of the first week Brigette reviews these target dates and leaves them as they are – lines are therefore drawn vertically downwards from the target dates to the end of week one on the actual time axis.

At the end of week 2, Brigette decides that 'obtain user requirements' will not be completed until Tuesday of week 6 – she therefore extends that activity line diagonally to reflect this. The other activity completion targets are also delayed correspondingly.

By the Tuesday of week 3, 'analyse existing system' is completed and Brigette puts a blob on the diagonal timeline to indicate that this has happened. At the end of week 3 she decides to keep to the existing targets.

At the end of week 4 she adds another three days to 'draft tender' and 'issue tender'.

Brigette's timeline chart contains only the critical activities for her project; ● indicates actual completion of an activity.

For the sake of clarity, the number of activities on a timeline chart must be limited. Using colour helps to distinguish activities, particularly where lines cross.

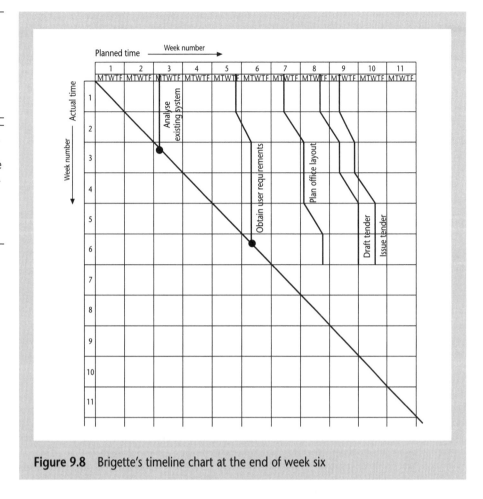

Figure 9.8 Brigette's timeline chart at the end of week six

Note that, by the end of week 6, two activities have been completed and three are still unfinished. Up to this point she has revised target dates on three occasions and the project as a whole is running seven days late.

Exercise 9.2

By the end of week 8 Brigette has completed planning the office layout but finds that drafting the tender is going to take one week longer that originally anticipated.

What will Brigette's timeline chart look like at the end of week 8?

If the rest of the project goes according to plan, what will Brigette's timeline chart look like when the project is completed?

The timeline chart is useful both during the execution of a project and as part of the post-implementation review. Analysis of the timeline chart, and the reasons for the changes, can indicate failures in the estimation process or other errors that might, with that knowledge, be avoided in future.

Project costs may be monitored by a company's accounting system. By themselves, they provide little information about project status.

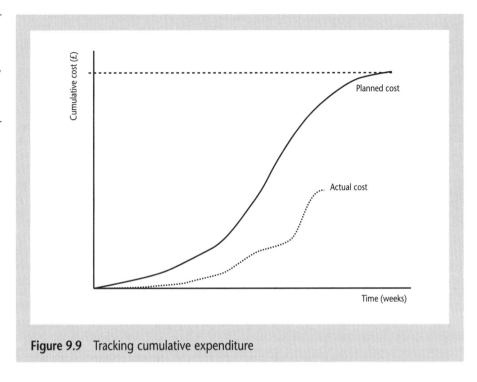

Figure 9.9 Tracking cumulative expenditure

9.5 Cost monitoring

Expenditure monitoring is an important component of project control. Not only in itself, but also because it provides an indication of the effort that has gone into (or at least been charged to) a project. A project might be on time but only because more money has been spent on activities than originally budgeted. A cumulative expenditure chart such as that shown in Figure 9.9 provides a simple method of comparing actual and planned expenditure. By itself it is not particularly meaningful – Figure 9.9 could, for example, illustrate a project that is running late or one that is on time but has shown substantial costs savings! We need to take account of the current status of the project activities before attempting to interpret the meaning of recorded expenditure.

Cost charts become much more useful if we add projected future costs calculated by adding the estimated costs of uncompleted work to the costs already incurred. Where a computer-based planning tool is used, revision of cost schedules is generally provided automatically once actual expenditure has been recorded. Figure 9.10 illustrates the additional information available once the revised cost schedule is included – in this case it is apparent that the project is behind schedule and over budget.

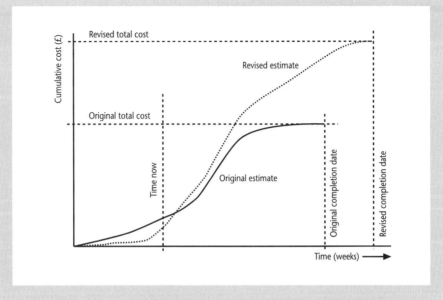

Project costs augmented by project monitoring can be used to generate forecasts of future costs.

Figure 9.10 The cumulative expenditure chart can also show revised estimates of cost and completion date

9.6 Earned value analysis

Earned value analysis, also known as budgeted cost of work performed, is recommended by a number of agencies including the US and Australian departments of defence. It is also recommended in BS 6079.

Earned value analysis has gained in popularity in recent years and may be seen as a refinement of the cost monitoring discussed in the previous section. Earned value analysis is based on assigning a 'value' to each task or work package (as identified in the WBS) based on the original expenditure forecasts. The assigned value is the original budgeted cost for the item and is known as the *planned value* (PV) or *budgeted cost of work scheduled* (BCWS). A task that has not started is assigned the value zero and when it has been completed, it, and hence the project, is credited with the value of the task. The total value credited to a project at any point is known as the *earned value* (EV) or budgeted cost of work performed (BCWP) and this can be represented as a value or as a percentage of the PV.

Where tasks have been started but are not yet complete, some consistent method of assigning an earned value must be applied. Common methods in software projects are:

- *the 0/100 technique:* where a task is assigned a value of zero until such time that it is completed when it is given a value of 100% of the budgeted value;

- *the 50/50 technique:* where a task is assigned a value of 50% of its value as soon as it is started and then given a value of 100% once it is complete;

- *the milestone technique:* where a task is given a value based on the achievement of milestones that have been assigned values as part of the original budget plan.

Of these, we prefer the 0/100 technique. The 50/50 technique can give a false sense of security by over-valuing the reporting of activity starts. The mile-

Table 9.2 Amanda's baseline budget calculation

Task	Budgeted workdays	Scheduled completion	Cumulative workdays	% cumulative earned value
Specify overall system	34	34	34	14.35
Specify module B	15	49 ⎫	64	27.00
Specify module D	15	49 ⎭		
Specify module A	20	54	84	35.44
Check specifications	2	56	86	36.28
Design module D	4	60	90	37.97
Design module A	7	63	97	40.93
Design module B	6	66	103	43.46
Specify module C	25	74	128	54.01
Check module C spec	1	75	129	54.43
Design module C	4	79	133	56.12
Code & test module D	25	85	158	66.67
Code & test module A	30	93	188	79.32
Code & test module B	28	94 ⎫	231	97.47
Code & test module C	15	94 ⎭		
System integration	6	100	237	100.00

stone technique might be appropriate for activities with a long duration estimate but, in such cases, it is better to break that activity into a number of smaller ones.

The baseline budget

The first stage in setting up an earned value analysis is to create the *baseline budget*. The baseline budget is based on the project plan and shows the forecast growth in earned value through time. Earned value may be measured in monetary values but, in the case of staff-intensive projects such as software development, it is common to measure earned value in person-hours or workdays. Amanda's baseline budget, based on the schedule shown in Figure 8.7, is shown in Table 9.2 and diagrammatically in Figure 9.11. Notice that she has based her baseline budget on workdays and is using the 0/100 technique for crediting earned value to the project.

Amanda's project is not expected to be credited with any earned value until day 34, when the activity 'specify overall system' is to be completed. This activity was forecast to consume 34 person-days and it will therefore be credited with 34 person-days of earned value when it has been completed. The other steps in the baseline budget chart coincide with the scheduled completion dates of other activities.

Monitoring earned value

Having created the baseline budget, the next task is to monitor earned value as the project progresses. This is done by monitoring the completion of tasks (or activity starts and milestone achievements in the case of the other crediting techniques).

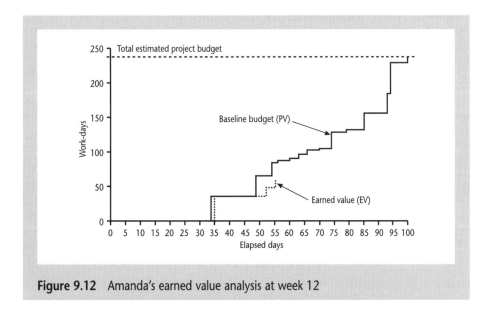

Figure 9.11 Amanda's baseline budget

Exercise 9.3 Figure 9.12 shows Amanda's earned value analysis at the start of week 12 of the project. The earned value (EV) is clearly lagging behind the baseline budget, indicating that the project is behind schedule.

By studying Figure 9.12, can you tell exactly what has gone wrong with her project and what the consequences might be?

As well as recording EV, the actual cost of each task can be collected as *actual cost* (AC). This is also known as the *actual cost of work performed* (ACWP). This is shown in Figure 9.13, which, in this case, records the values as percentages of the total budgeted cost.

Figure 9.12 Amanda's earned value analysis at week 12

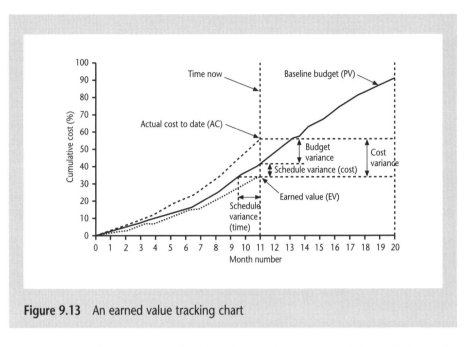

Figure 9.13 An earned value tracking chart

Figure 9.13 also illustrates the following performance statistics, which can be shown directly or derived from the earned value chart.

Schedule variance (SV)

The schedule variance is measured in cost terms as $EV - PV$ and indicates the degree to which the value of completed work differs from that planned. Figure 9.13 also indicates the schedule variance in time, which indicates the degree to which the project is behind schedule. A negative SV means the project is behind schedule.

Cost variance (CV)

This is calculated as $EV - AC$ and indicates the difference between the budgeted cost and the actual cost of completed work. It is also an indicator of the accuracy of the original cost estimates. A negative CV means the project is over cost.

Performance ratios

Two ratios are commonly tracked: the *cost performance index* (CPI = EV/AC) and the *schedule performance index* (SPI = EV/PV). They can be thought of as a 'value-for-money' indices. A value greater than one indicates that work is being completed better than planned, whereas a value of less than one means that work is costing more than and/or proceeding more slowly than planned.

CPI can be used to produce a revised cost estimate for the project (or estimate at completion – EAC). EAC is calculated as BAC/CPI where BAC (budget at completion) is the current projected budget for the project.

In the same way that the expenditure analysis in Figure 9.9 was augmented to show revised expenditure forecasts, we can augment the simple earned value tracking chart with forecasts as illustrated in Figure 9.14.

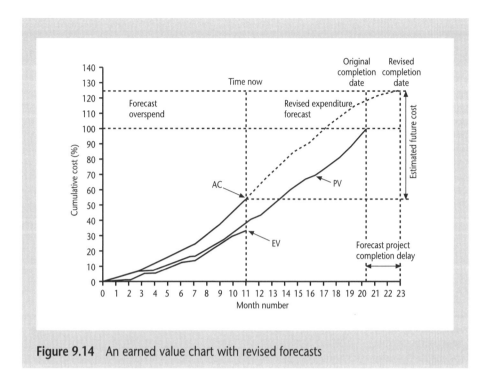

Figure 9.14 An earned value chart with revised forecasts

Earned value analysis has not yet gained universal acceptance for use with software development projects, perhaps largely because of the attitude that, whereas a half-built house has a value reflected by the labour and materials that have been used, a half-completed software project has virtually no value at all. This is to misunderstand the purpose of earned value analysis, which, as we have seen, is a method for tracking what has been achieved on a project – measured in terms of the budgeted costs of completed tasks or products.

9.7 Prioritizing monitoring

So far we have assumed that all aspects of a project will receive equal treatment in terms of the degree of monitoring applied. We must not forget, however, that monitoring takes time and uses resources that might sometimes be put to better use!

In this section we list the priorities we might apply in deciding levels of monitoring.

- *Critical path activities* Any delay in an activity on the critical path will cause a delay in the completion date for the project. Critical path activities are therefore likely to have a very high priority for close monitoring.

Free float is the amount of time an activity may be delayed without affecting any subsequent activity.

- *Activities with no free float* A delay in any activity with no free float will delay at least some subsequent activities even though, if the delay is less than the total float, it might not delay the project completion date. These subsequent delays can have serious effects on our resource schedule as a delay in a subsequent activity could mean that the resources for that activity will become unavailable before that activity is completed because they are committed elsewhere.

- *Activities with less than a specified float* If any activity has very little float it might use up this float before the regular activity monitoring brings the problem to the project manager's attention. It is common practice to monitor closely those activities with less than, say, one week free float.

PERT and the significance of activity duration variance was described in Chapter 7.

- *High risk activities* A set of high-risk activities should have been identified as part of the initial risk profiling exercise. If we are using the PERT three-estimate approach we will designate as high risk those activities that have a high estimated duration variance. These activities will be given close attention because they are most likely to overrun or overspend.

- *Activities using critical resources* Activities can be critical because they are very expensive (as in the case of specialized contract programmers). Staff or other resources might be available only for a limited period, especially if they are controlled outside the project team. In any event, an activity that demands a critical resource requires a high level of monitoring.

9.8 Getting the project back to target

A contingency plan should, of course, already exist as a result of the risk analysis methods described in Chapter 7.

Almost any project will, at one time or another, be subject to delays and unexpected events. One of the tasks of the project manager is to recognize when this is happening (or, if possible, about to happen) and, with the minimum delay and disruption to the project team, attempt to mitigate the effects of the problem. In most cases, the project manager tries to ensure that the scheduled project end date remains unaffected. This can be done by shortening remaining activity durations or shortening the overall duration of the remaining project in the ways described in the next section.

The schedule is not sacrosanct – it is a plan that should be adhered to so long as it is relevant and cost-effective.

It should be remembered, however, that this might not always be the most appropriate response to disruptions to a plan. There is little point in spending considerable sums in overtime payments in order to speed up a project if the customer is not overly concerned with the delivery date and there is no other valuable work for the team members once this project is completed.

There are two main strategies to consider when drawing up plans to bring a project back on target – shortening the critical path or altering the activity precedence requirements.

Shorten the critical path

The overall duration of a project is determined by the current critical path, so speeding up non-critical path activities will not bring forward a project completion date.

Exhorting staff to 'work harder' might have some effect, although frequently a more positive form of action is required, such as increasing the resources available for some critical activity. Fact-finding, for example, might be speeded up by allocating an additional analyst to interviewing users. It is unlikely, however, that the coding of a small module would be shortened by allocating an additional programmer – indeed, it might be counterproductive because of the additional time needed organizing and allocating tasks and communicating.

Resource levels can be increased by making them available for longer. Thus, staff might be asked to work overtime for the duration of an activity and computing resources might be made available at times (such as evenings and week-ends) when they might otherwise be inaccessible.

Time/cost trade-off:
there is a general rule
that timescales can be
shortened by buying
more (or more
expensive) resources;
sometimes this is true.

Where these do not provide a sufficient solution, the project manager might consider allocating more efficient resources to activities on the critical path or swapping resources between critical and non-critical activities. This will be particularly appropriate with staff – an experienced programmer should be significantly more productive than a more junior member of the team.

By such means we can attempt to shorten the timescale for critical activities until such time as either we have brought the project back to schedule or further efforts prove unproductive or not cost-effective. Remember, however, that short-ening a critical path often causes some other path, or paths, to become critical (see Section 6.14).

Reconsider the precedence requirements

If attempting to shorten critical activities proves insufficient, the next step is to consider the constraints by which some activities have to be deferred pending completion of others. The original project network would most probably have been drawn up assuming 'ideal' conditions and 'normal' working practices. It might be that, to avoid the project delivering late, it is now worth questioning whether as yet unstarted activities really do have to await the completion of others. It might, in a particular organization, be 'normal' to complete system testing before commencing user training. In order to avoid late completion of a project it might, however, be considered acceptable to alter 'normal' practice and start training earlier.

One way to overcome precedence constraints is to subdivide an activity into a component that can start immediately and one that is still constrained as before. For example, a user handbook can be drawn up in a draft form from the system specification and then be revised later to take account of subsequent changes.

If we do decide to alter the precedence requirements in such a way, it is clearly important to be aware that quality might be compromised and to make a considered decision to compromise quality where needed. It is equally important to assess the degree to which changes in work practices increase risk. It is poss-ible, for example, to start coding a module before its design has been completed. It would normally, however, be considered foolhardy to do so since, as well as compromising quality, it would increase the risk of having to redo some of the coding once the final design had been completed and thus delay the project even further.

9.9 Change control

So far in this chapter, we have assumed that the nature of the tasks to be carried out has not changed. A project leader like Amanda or Brigette might find, however, that requirements are modified because of changing circumstances or because the users get a clearer idea of what is really needed. The payroll system that Brigette is implementing might, for instance, need to be adjusted if the staffing structure at the college is reorganized.

Other, internal, changes will crop up. Amanda might find that there are inconsistencies in the program specifications that become apparent only when the programs are coded, and these would result in amendments to the specifications.

Careful control of these changes is needed because an alteration in one document often implies changes to other documents and the system products based on that document. The Product Flow Diagrams that have been explained in Chapter 2 indicate relationships between the products of a project where this is the case.

<table>
<tr><td>Exercise 9.4</td><td>A change in a program specification will normally be carried through into changes to the program design and then changed code. What other products might need to be modified?</td></tr>
</table>

Configuration librarian's role

BS EN ISO 9001:1994 (formerly BS 5750) requires that a formal change control procedure be in place.

Control of changes and documentation ought to be the responsibility of someone who may variously be named the Configuration Librarian, the Configuration Manager or Project Librarian. Among this person's duties would be:

● the identification of all items that are subject to change control;

● the establishment and maintenance of a central repository of the master copies of all project documentation and software products;

● the setting up and running of a formal set of procedures to deal with changes;

● the maintenance of records of who has access to which library items and the status of each library item (e.g. whether under development, under test or released).

It will be recalled that it was suggested that the setting up of change control procedures might be one of the first things the Brigette would want to do at Brightmouth College.

Change control procedures

A simple change control procedure for operational systems might have the following steps:

1. One or more users might perceive a need for a modification to a system and ask for a change request to be passed to the development staff.

2. The user management consider the change request and, if they approve it, pass it to the development management.

3. The development management delegate a member of staff to look at the request and to report on the practicality and cost of carrying out the change. They would, as part of this, assess the products that would be affected by the change.

4. The development management report back to the user management on the findings and the user management decide whether, in view of the cost quoted, they wish to go ahead.

5. One or more developers are authorized to take copies of the master products that are to be modified.

6. The copies are modified. In the case of software components this would involve modifying the code and recompiling and testing it.

7. When the development of new versions of the product has been completed the user management will be notified and copies of the software will be released for user acceptance testing.

8. When the user is satisfied that the products are adequate they will authorize their operational release. The master copies of configuration items will be replaced.

Exercise 9.5 The above steps relate to changes to operational systems. How could they be modified to deal with systems under development?

Changes in scope of a system

This is sometimes called scope creep.

A common occurrence with IS development projects is for the size of the system gradually to increase. One cause of this is changes to requirements that are requested by users.

Exercise 9.6 Think of other reasons why there is a tendency for scope creep.

The scope of a project needs to be carefully monitored and controlled. One way is to re-estimate the system size in terms of SLOC or function points at key milestones.

9.10 Conclusion

In this chapter we have discussed the requirements for the continual monitoring of projects and the need for making progress visible. Among the important points to emerge were:

● planning is pointless unless the execution of the plan is monitored;

● activities that are too long need to be subdivided to make them more controllable;

● ideally, progress should be measured through the delivery of project products;

● progress needs to be shown in a visually striking way, such as through ball charts, in order to communicate information effectively;

● costs need to be monitored as well as elapsed time;

● delayed projects can often be brought back on track by shortening activity times on the critical path or by relaxing some of the precedence constraints.

9.11 Further exercises

1. Take a look at Amanda's project schedule shown in Figure 8.7. Identify those activities scheduled to last more than three weeks and describe how she might monitor progress on each of them on a fortnightly or weekly basis.

2. Amanda's Gantt chart at the end of week 17 (Figure 9.5) indicates that two activities are running late. What effect might this have on the rest of the project? How might Amanda mitigate the effects of this delay?

3. Table 9.2 illustrates Amanda's earned value calculations based on workdays. Revise the table using monetary values based on the cost figures that you used in Exercise 8.5. Think carefully about how to handle the costs of Amanda as project manager and the recovered overheads and justify your decisions about how you treat them.

4. If you have access to project planning software, investigate the extent to which it offers support for earned value analysis. If it does not do so directly, investigate ways in which it would help you to generate a baseline budget (PV) and track the earned value (EV).

5. Describe a set of change control procedures that would be appropriate for Brigette to implement at Brightmouth College.

Managing contracts

Objectives

When you have completed this chapter you will be able to:

- follow the stages needed to acquire software from an external supplier;
- distinguish between the different types of contract;
- outline the contents of a contract for goods and services;
- plan the evaluation of a proposal or product;
- administer a contract from its signing until the final acceptance of project completion.

10.1 Introduction

In the Brightmouth College scenario, the management of the college have made a decision to obtain their software from an external supplier. Given the range of payroll software on the market and their own limited capability for developing new and reliable software, this would seem sensible. Meanwhile at IOE, Amanda has, at least in theory, a team of software developers available who are employees of IOE. However, the demand for software design and construction effort fluctuates, rising when a new project is initiated and trailing off as it is completed. In-house developers could thus have periods of intense pressure interspersed by periods of relative quiet. The IOE management might therefore decide that it would be more cost-effective to employ outside software developers to carry out the new development while a reduced group of in-house software development staff occupied itself in maintaining and giving support to the users of existing systems.

It is not unusual for a major organization to spend 6 to 12 months and 40% of the total acquisition and implementation budget on package evaluation with major customer service and support applications (Demian Martinez, Decision Drivers Inc., *Computing*, 23 July, 1998).

The buying in of both goods and services, rather than 'doing it yourself', is attractive when is money is available but other, less flexible, types of resource, especially staff time, are in short supply. However, where an organization adopts this policy there are hazards arising from the considerable staff time and attention still needed to manage a contracted-out project successfully. Although the motivation for contracting out may have been to reduce management effort, it is essential that customer organizations such as Brightmouth College and IOE find time to make clear their exact requirements at the beginning of the planned work, and also to ensure that the goods and services that result are in fact what are actually required.

Also, potential suppliers are more likely to be flexible and accommodating before any contract has been signed than they will be afterwards – especially if the contract is for a fixed price. Thus, as much forethought and planning is needed with an acquisition project as with an internal development project.

In the remainder of this chapter, we will first provide an overview of the interlocking acquisition and supply processes based on the ISO 12207 international standard. The different types of contract that can be used will then be explored. We will then follow through, in a little more depth, the general steps that ought to be followed when placing a contract. The issues that ought to be considered when drafting a contract are then examined. We conclude by describing some of the things that may need to be done while the contract is actually being executed.

Note that the bargaining position of the customer will stronger if their business is going to be valuable. If you are buying a cut-price computer game from a local store, you are unlikely to be able to negotiate variations on the supplier's standard contract of sale. (Indeed, because of the inequality of the parties in such circumstances, such sales are subject to special consumer protection laws.) Potential suppliers will weigh up carefully the time and money they are willing to spend responding to a customer's initial request as there is no guarantee of their obtaining the final contract.

> It was, for example, reported that two consortia led by Sema and EDS, respectively, had spent £4 million over 2 years bidding for a UK government project to renew the ICT infrastructure in the prison service – the final job was estimated as being worth £350 million (*Computing*, 13 August, 1998).

10.2   The ISO 12207 approach to the acquisition and supply of software

The ISO 12207 standard identifies five major processes relating to software.

- acquisition;
- supply;
- operation;
- maintenance;
- development.

Clearly, maintenance and operation are processes that really belong to the post-implementation phase of a conventional development project. A justification for the inclusion of these post-implementation activities is that sometimes a customer will contract a supplier both to develop a system and operate it on their behalf. Similarly, a software supplier could be responsible contractually both for the construction of a software-based system and its maintenance after installation. Our attention here is given primarily to the acquisition and supply processes.

The acquisition process is the set of procedures that a customer for software (or 'acquirer' in ISO 12207 terminology) should follow in order to obtain that software from an external source. The supply process is the opposite side to the acquisition process and is the set of procedures that the supplier should adopt in order to satisfy the acquirer's needs. The supplier may use an existing piece of software or may develop new software. In the latter case they would need to invoke the development process.

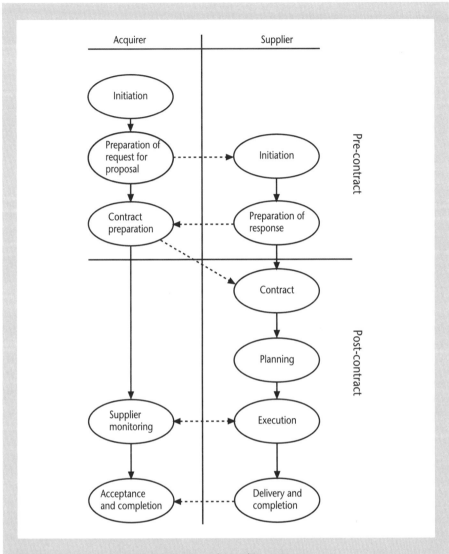

Figure 10.1 ISO 12207 Acquisition and supply processes

Initiation

Figure 10.1 portrays the main activities that comprise the acquisition process. The *initiation* activity starts with the acquirer describing the 'concept' that the acquirer wishes to make real, or the need which they wish to satisfy. The requirements of the system that it is felt would fulfil that need should then be defined by the acquirer organization. Often, an external expert could be employed for this purpose, but the responsibility for the accuracy of these requirements would remain with the acquirer.

ISO 12207 distinguishes between *system requirements* and *software requirements*. System requirements are broader and relate not just to the software but to the platforms upon which it would run and to changes in the organizational environment needed for the successful operation of the new system. In the case of the

Table 10.1 Topics in a request for proposal document

Request for proposal – contents
- System requirements
- Scope statement
- Instructions for bidders
- List of software products
- Control of subcontracts
- Technical constraints
    (e.g. the target environment)

Brightmouth College payroll application, for example, the college would need to acquire equipment upon which to run the payroll and to find and train staff to look after the system. Software requirements, on the other hand, relate to the distinctly software components within the delivered system and will have to be extracted from the broader system requirements. Once this has been done, a decision needs to be taken about the best way to acquire the software, for example whether to make or buy.

Having made this decision, the acquirer is now in a position to prepare the acquisition plan, detailing the steps needed to take to acquire the software. The precise scope of the work to be undertaken externally needs to be decided. For example, would maintenance and support for the new software be dealt with in-house or by the supplier? Other questions relate to potential risks and the criteria for final system acceptance, including methods by which compliance with requirements is to be evaluated.

Request for proposal

Another name for 'request for proposal' is 'invitation to tender'.

The groundwork has now been laid for the production of the request for proposal (RFP) document. This should include sections on the topics listed in Table 10.1.

ISO 12207 makes provision for the tailoring of the standard set of activities expected of the supplier to suit the particular situation. Some activities could be deleted, while the contract for a particular project could add activities if these are needed.

Contract preparation and update

Before you can have a contract, you must have a supplier with whom to have the contract. With this in mind, the criteria for selecting the supplier and the method of judging the degree of compliance by potential suppliers with the criteria have to be set down. Based on these, the preferred supplier is now selected. The form of the contract between the supplier and acquirer can now be negotiated and agreed. This may involve some agreed adjustments to the processes that ISO 12207 assumes would be executed during the project.

Monitor supplier

This will be done using joint reviews, audit, verification and validation.

Accept completed contract

When the supplier finally delivers the product, the acquirer will conduct acceptance tests and if the specified acceptance criteria are satisfied, the completed software can be signed off as completed.

10.3 The supply process

This process mirrors the acquisition process, but documents the activities that a supplier would need to undertake in response to the request of a supplier. Figure 10.1 outlines the main activities involved. There may be occasions where the sequence of activities is not that shown and yet other occasions when some of the activities will have to iterated a number of times.

Initiation

The process is started when a potential supplier receives a request for a proposal from an acquirer and the supplier decides to bid for the work.

Preparation of a response

The supplier, after consulting people with various types of expert knowledge, now prepares a response. This should include any proposals about how ISO 12207 is to be tailored for the project in view.

Contract

If all goes well, the supplier's proposal makes the right impression and leads to acceptance by the acquirer. The details of the contract are then negotiated and signed.

Planning

Recall that RFP stands for 'request for proposal'. This is the ISO 12207 term for what others often call an 'invitation to tender' (ITT).

The supplier can now draw up a detailed plan of how the work is to be done. The starting point for this will be the requirements as laid down in the RFP. You would normally expect this to include the life-cycle approach to be applied by the supplier as this will to some extent dictate the points at which consultation between supplier and acquirer is to take place during the development process. Recall that the acquirer may have considered, as part of the acquisition process, the options of make versus buy and also whether to use in-house or external sources. ISO 12207 now makes provision for the supplier to make a similar choice, and having done this, to develop a plan accordingly.

Execution and control

The plan can now be executed. If the contract is for the development of software, then at this point the development process is invoked. Depending on whether the contract is for systems development, operation or maintenance, the ISO 12207 processes stipulated in each case should be undertaken.

During execution of the plan, the standard expects the supplier to monitor and control progress and product quality, and to have a mechanism for identifying and recording the problems that occur and to have a mechanism for their analysis and resolution. The supplier will also be responsible for passing on requirements that accurately reflect those of the acquirer to any subcontractors and for ensuring the compliance of subcontractors with those requirements. The supplier also needs to cooperate fully with any independent verification and validation processes that were laid down in the contract.

Review and evaluation

The provisions here are mainly to ensure that the supplier allows the acquirer access to the information needed to review the progress of the project, although the precise extent to which the acquirer has a reviewing role and access to supplier documentation is to be specified in the contract.

Delivery and completion

Attention may have to be given in any management plans to the way in which this is to be done and to how any required post-delivery support is to be provided.

10.4 Types of contract

The external resources required could be in the form of *services*. A simple example of this could be using temporary staff on short-term contracts to carry out some project tasks. At Brightmouth College, Brigette could use temporary staff to input the personnel details needed to set up the payroll standing data for the new system. At IOE, meanwhile, it might be decided to carry out application building in-house but to augment the permanent staff with contract developers. A more far-reaching use of external services would be for the contractor not only to supply the new system but to also operate it on the customer's behalf. For example, Brightmouth College might abandon the idea of buying a package and instead get a payroll services agency to carry out all the payroll work.

On the other hand, the contract could be placed for the supply of a *completed software package*. This could be:

- a *bespoke* system, that is, a system that is created from scratch specifically for one customer;
- an *off-the-shelf* package which you buy 'as is' – this is sometimes referred to as *shrink-wrapped* software;

David's *Introduction to Computer Law*, Longman, 5th edition, 2004 is highly recommended as a guide to the legal aspects of IT contracts.

- *customized off-the-shelf* (COTS) software – this is a basic core system which is modified to meet the needs of a particular client.

Where equipment is purchased then, in English law, this is normally a contract for the supply of *goods*. In the case of the supply of software this may be regarded as supplying a service (i.e. to write the software) or the granting of a *licence* (i.e. permission) to use the software which remains in the ownership of the supplier. These distinctions will have legal implications.

Exercise 10.1   Which of the three system options (i.e. bespoke, off-the-shelf or COTS) might Amanda consider with regard to the IOE maintenance group accounts system? What factors would she need to take into account?

The section on ways of assessing supplier payments draws heavily on material from Paul Radford and Robyn Lawrie of Charismatek Software Metrics, Melbourne, Australia.

Another way of classifying contracts is by the way that the payment to suppliers is calculated. We will look at:

- fixed price contracts;
- time and materials contracts;
- fixed price per delivered unit contracts.

Fixed price contracts

As the name implies, in this situation a price is fixed when the contract is signed. The customer knows that, if there are no changes in the contract terms, this is the price they will have to pay on the completion of the work. In order for this to be effective, the customer's requirement has to be known and fixed at the outset. In other words, when the contract is to construct a software system, the detailed requirements analysis must already have been carried out. Once the development is under way the customer organization will not normally be able to change their requirements without renegotiating the price of the contract.

The advantages of this method are seen as being:

- *Known customer expenditure*   If the requirements have been defined adequately and there are few subsequent changes, then the customer will have a known outlay.
- *Supplier motivation*   The supplier has a motivation to manage the delivery of the system in a cost-effective manner.

The disadvantages include:

The cost could still be lower than in-house development because the supplier may be able to exploit economies of scale and also expertise acquired doing similar jobs in the past.

- *Higher prices to allow for contingency*   The supplier absorbs the risk for any errors in the original estimate of product size. To reduce the impact of this risk, the supplier will add a margin when calculating the price to be quoted in a tender.
- *Difficulties in modifying requirements*   The need to change the scope of the requirements may become apparent as the system is developed – this may cause friction between the supplier and customer.
- *Upward pressure on the cost of changes*   When competing against other potential suppliers, the supplier will try to quote as low a price as possible. Once the contract is signed, if further requirements are put forward, the supplier is in a strong position to demand a high price for these changes.
- *Threat to system quality*   The need to meet a fixed price could mean that the quality of the software suffers.

Time and materials contracts

With this type of contract, the customer is charged at a fixed rate per unit of effort, for example per staff-hour. At the start of the project, the supplier may provide an estimate of the overall cost based on their current understanding of the customer's requirements, but this is not the basis for the final payment.

The advantages of this approach are said to be:

- *Ease of changing requirements* Changes to requirements are dealt with easily. Where a project has a research orientation and the direction of the project may change as options are explored, then this may be an appropriate method of calculating payment.

- *Lack of price pressure* The lack of price pressure may allow better quality software to be produced.

The disadvantages of this approach are:

- *Customer liability* The customer absorbs all the risks associated with poorly defined or changing requirements.

- *Lack of incentives for supplier* The supplier has no incentive to work in a cost-effective manner or to control the scope of the system to be delivered.

Because the supplier appears to be given a blank cheque, this approach does not normally find favour with customers. However, the employment of contract development staff may in effect involve this type of contract.

Fixed price per unit delivered contracts

Function point counting was discussed in Chapter 5.

This is often associated with function point (FP) counting. The size of the system to be delivered is calculated or estimated at the outset of the project. The size of the system to be delivered may be estimated in lines of code, but FPs can be more easily and reliably derived from requirements documents. A price per unit is also quoted. The final price is then the unit price multiplied by the number of units. Table 10.2 shows a typical schedule of prices.

The company in question was RDI Technologies in the USA. These figures are now several years old.

The company who produced this table in fact charge a higher fee per FP for larger systems. For example, a system to be implemented contains 2,600 FPs. The overall charge would be 2,000 × $967, plus 500 × $1,1019, plus 100 × $1,058.

One problem already noted is that the scope of the system to be delivered can grow during development. The software supplier might first carry out the system design. A charge could then be made for design work based on the figures in the 'Function design cost per FP' column. This, if the designed system was counted at 1,000 FPs, would be 1000 × $242 i.e. $242,000. If the design was implemented, and the actual software constructed and delivered, then the additional 1000 × $725 would be charged i.e. $725,000. If the scope of the system grows because the

This table comes from David Garmus and David Herron, *Measuring the software process*, Prentice Hall, 1996.

Table 10.2 A schedule of charges per function point

Function point count	Function design cost per FP	Implementation cost per FP	Total cost per FP
Up to 2,000	$242	$725	$967
2,001–2,500	$255	$764	$1,019
2,501–3,000	$265	$793	$1,058
3,001–3,500	$274	$820	$1,094
3,501–4,000	$284	$850	$1,134

users find new requirements, these new requirements would be charged at the combined rate for design and implementation, e.g. if new requirements amounting to 100 extra FPs were found, then the charge for this extra work would be 967×100 i.e. $96,700.

Exercise 10.2   A system to be designed and implemented is counted as comprising 3,200 FPs. What would be the total charge according to the schedule in Table 10.2?

The advantages of this approach are:

- *Customer understanding*   The customer can see how the price is calculated and how it will vary with changed requirements.
- *Comparability*   Pricing schedules can be compared.
- *Emerging functionality*   The supplier does not bear the risk of increasing functionality.
- *Supplier efficiency*   The supplier still has an incentive to deliver the required functionality in a cost-effective manner (unlike with time and materials contracts).
- *Life-cycle range*   The requirements do not have to be definitively specified at the outset. Thus the development contract can cover both the analysis and design stages of the project.

The disadvantages of this approach are:

The impact of late changes will be further discussed in Chapter 12 on software quality.

- *Difficulties with software size measurement*   Lines of code can easily be inflated by adopting a verbose coding style. With FPs, there may be disagreements about what the FP count should really be: in some cases, FP counting rules may be seen as unfairly favouring either the supplier or customer. Users, in particular, will almost certainly not be familiar with the concept of FPs and special training may be needed for them. The solution to these problems may be to employ an independent FP counter.
- *Changing requirements*   Some requested changes may affect existing transactions drastically but not add to the overall FP count. A decision has to be taken about how to deal with these changes. A change made late in the development cycle will almost certainly require more effort to implement than one made earlier.

To reduce the last difficulty, one suggestion from Australia has been to vary the charge depending on the point at which they have been requested – see Table 10.3.

The table comes from the draft *Acquisition of Customised Software Policy* document, published by the Department of State Development, Victoria, 1996.

Table 10.3 Examples of additional charges for changed functionality

	Pre-acceptance testing handover	Post-acceptance testing handover
Additional FPs	100%	100%
Changed FPs	130%	150%
Deleted FPs	25%	50%

Exercise 10.3

A contract stipulates that a computer application is to be designed, constructed and delivered at a cost of $600 per FP. After acceptance testing, the customer asks for changes to some of the functions in the system amounting to 500 FPs and some new functions which amount to 200 additional FPs. Using Table 10.3, calculate the additional charge.

In addition to the three payment methods above, there are other options and permutations of options. For instance, the implementation of an agreed specification could be at a fixed price, with provision for any additions or changes to the requirements to be charged for on a per FP basis. Another example could be where the contractor may have to buy in large amounts of equipment, the price of which may fluctuate through no fault of the contractor. In this case it is possible to negotiate a contract where the final price contains a fixed portion for labour plus an amount that depends on the actual cost of a particular component used.

Exercise 10.4

It is easy to see why passing on fluctuations in equipment costs may be advantageous to the contractor. However, is there any advantage to the customer in such an arrangement?

An underlying problem with software can once again be seen when the questions of contractual obligations and payment are considered – namely its relative invisibility and flexibility. Thus system size and consequently development effort tend to be very difficult to judge. If contractors are realistically to quote firm prices for work then the tasks they are asked to undertake must be carefully constrained. For example, it would be unrealistic for a contractor to be asked to quote a single price for all the stages of a development project: how can they estimate the construction effort needed when the requirements are not yet established? For this reason it may be necessary to negotiate a series of contracts, each covering a different part of the system development life cycle.

Another way of categorizing contracts, at least initially, is according to the approach that is used in contractor selection, namely

This categorization is based on European Union regulations.

- open
- restricted
- negotiated.

Open tendering process

Recall that invitation to tender (ITT) and request for proposal (RFP) are interchangeable terms.

In this case, any supplier can bid to supply the goods and services. Furthermore, all bids that are compliant with the original conditions laid down in the *invitation to tender* must be considered and evaluated in the same way. With a major project with many bids this evaluation process can be time consuming and expensive.

In recent years there has been a global movement towards removing artificial barriers that hamper businesses in one country supplying goods and services in another. Examples of this are the drives by bodies such as the World Trade Organisation (WTO) and the European Community to ensure that national governments and public bodies do not unfairly favour fellow nationals when granting contracts. Among the agreements overseen by the WTO is one on government procurement. One element of this is the laying down of rules about how tendering processes should be carried out. In certain circumstances, these may demand that an open tendering process be adopted.

Restricted tendering process

In this case, there are bids only from suppliers who have been invited by the customer. Unlike the open tendering process, the customer may at any point reduce the number of potential suppliers being considered. This is usually the best approach to adopt. However, it is not without risk: where the resulting contract is at a fixed price, the customer assumes responsibility for the correctness and completeness of the requirements specified to the prospective suppliers. Defects in this requirements documentation may allow a successful bidder to subsequently claim for additional payments.

Negotiated procedure

There may, however, be some good reasons why the restricted tendering process may not be the most suitable in some particular sets of circumstances. Say, for example, that there is a fire that destroys part of an office, including ICT equipment. The key concern here may be to get replacement equipment up and running as quickly as possible and there may simply not be the time to embark on a lengthy tendering process. Another situation might be where a new software application had been successfully built and implemented by an outsider, but the customer realizes that they would like to have some extensions to the system. As the original supplier has staff who have complete familiarity with the existing system, it may once again be inconvenient to approach other potential suppliers via a full tendering process. In these cases, an approach to a single supplier may be justified. However, it takes little imagination to realize that approaching a single supplier could open the customer up to charges of favouritism and should only be done where there is a clear justification.

10.5 Stages in contract placement

In Section 10.2 we presented an outline, based on the ISO 12207 standard, of a typical acquisition process. We are now going to discuss in more depth the individual steps involved in awarding a contract.

Requirements analysis

This discussion assumes that a feasibility study has already provisionally identified the need for the intended software.

Before potential suppliers can be approached, you need to have a clear set of requirements. Two points need to be emphasized here. The first is that it is easy for this step to be skimped where the user management have many day-to-day pressures and not much time to think about future developments. In this situation, it can be useful to bring in an external consultant to draw up a requirements document. Even here, users and their managers need to look carefully at the resulting requirements document to ensure that it accurately reflects their needs. As David Bainbridge has pointed out: 'the *lack of, or defects in, the specification are probably the heart of most disputes resulting from the acquisition of computer equipment and software*'.

Table 10.4 Main sections in a requirements document

1 Introduction
2 A description of any existing systems and the current environment
3 The customer's future strategy or plans
4 System requirements
  – mandatory
  – desirable
5 Deadlines
6 Additional information required from potential suppliers

The requirements document might typically have sections with the headings shown in Table 10.4.

The requirements define carefully the *functions* that need to be carried out by the new application and all the necessary *inputs* and *outputs* for these functions. The requirements should also state any *standards* with which there should be compliance, and the existing systems with which the new system needs to be compatible. As well as these functional requirements, there will also need to be operational and quality requirements concerning such matters as the required response times, reliability, usability and maintainability of the new system.

In general, the requirements document should state *needs* as accurately as possible and should avoid technical specifications of possible solutions. The onus should be placed on the potential suppliers to identify the technical solutions that they believe will meet the customer's stated needs. After all, they are the technical experts who should have access to the most up-to-date information about current technology.

Each requirement needs to be identified as being either *mandatory* or *desirable*.

- *Mandatory* If a proposal does not meet this requirement then the proposal is to be immediately rejected. No further evaluation would be required.

- *Desirable* A proposal may be deficient in this respect, but other features of the proposal could compensate for this.

For example, in the case of the Brightmouth College payroll package acquisition project, Brigette might identify a mandatory requirement that any new system should be able to carry out all the processes previously carried out by the old system. However, a desirable feature might be that the new payroll package should be able to produce accounting details of staff costs in an electronic format that can be read directly by the college's accounting computer system.

Among the other details that should be included in the requirements document issued to potential suppliers would be requests for information needed to help judge the standing of the organization itself. This could include financial reports, references from past customers and the CVs of key development staff.

Evaluation plan

Having drawn up a list of requirements, we now need to draw up a plan of how the proposals which are submitted are to be evaluated. The situation will be slightly different if the contract is for a system that is to be specially written as

---

This requirements document is sometimes called an operational requirement or OR.

Chapter 12 on software quality discusses how aspects of quality can be measured.

One suggestion is that the weighting between product criteria and supplier criteria when selecting software ought to be 50:50 (Demian Martinez, Decision Drivers Inc., Computing, 23 July, 1998).

opposed to an off-the-shelf package. In the latter case, it is the system itself that is being evaluated while in the former situation it is a proposal for a system.

First, ways of checking that all the mandatory requirements have been met need to be identified. The next consideration is how the desirable requirements can be evaluated. The problem here is weighing the value of one quality against another. The ISO 9126 standard, which is discussed in Chapter 12 on software quality, may be used to decide that one system has more of some quality than another, but if there is a difference in price between the two, we need to be able to estimate if the increase in quality is worth the additional price. Hence 'value for money' is often the key criterion. For example, a financial value could be placed on the existence of the accounting link file in the case above. If we were to cost clerical effort at £20 an hour and we knew that four hours of clerical effort a month went into inputting staffing costs into the accounting computer system, then we could conclude that over a four-year period (£20 an hour × 4 hours a month × 48 months), or £3,840, would be saved. If system A has this feature and costs £1,000 more than system B which does not, then this would seem to give system A an advantage. If, however, system A cost £5,000 more than B then the picture would be different.

It needs to be stressed that the costs to be taken into account are those for the whole of the lifetime of the proposed system, not just the costs of acquiring the system. Also, where the relationship with the supplier is likely to be ongoing, the supplier organization needs to be assessed as well as its products.

Exercise 10.5

One desirable feature sought in the Brightmouth College payroll is the ability to raise staff automatically to the next point in their salary scale at the beginning of each payroll year. At present, the new scale points have to be input clerically and then be checked carefully. This takes about 20 hours of staff effort each year, which can be costed at £20 an hour. System X has this feature, but system Y does not. System X also has a feature which can automatically produce bar charts showing payroll expenditure per department. Such a report currently has to be produced twice a year by hand and on each occasion takes about 12 hours' effort to complete. With system Y, changes to department names can be carried out without any coding effort whereas in the case of system X, the supplier would charge a minimum of £300 to do this. The college authorities estimate that there is 50% chance that this could occur during the expected four-year lifetime of the system. System X costs £500 more than system Y. On the basis of this information, which system appears to give better value for money?

Invitation to tender

Having produced the requirements and the evaluation plan, it is now possible to issue the invitation to tender to prospective suppliers. Essentially, this will be the requirement document with a supporting letter which will have additional information about how responses to the invitation are to be lodged. A deadline will be specified and it is hoped that by then a number of proposals with price quotations will have been received.

In English law, for a contract to exist there must be an offer on one side which must be accepted by the other side. The invitation to tender is not an offer itself but an invitation for prospective suppliers to make an offer.

Certain new problems might now emerge. The requirements that have been laid down could be satisfied in a number of different ways. The customer not only

In English law, with certain exceptions, a contract does not have to be in writing. Clearly it is desirable that it should be.

needs to know a potential supplier's price but also the way in which they intend to satisfy the requirements – this will be particularly important where the contract is to build a new system from scratch.

In some relatively straightforward cases, it would be enough to have some post-tender clarification and negotiation to resolve issues in the supplier's proposal. With more complex projects a more elaborate approach may be needed. One way of getting the detail of the suppliers' proposals elaborated is to have a two-stage tendering process.

In the first stage, technical proposals are requested from potential suppliers who do not necessarily quote any prices. Some of these proposals can be dismissed out of hand as not being able to meet the mandatory requirements. The remaining ones could be discussed with representatives of the suppliers in order to clarify and validate the technical proposals. The suppliers might be asked to demonstrate certain aspects of their proposals. Where shortcomings in the proposal are detected, the supplier could be given the opportunity to remedy these.

The result of these discussions could be a *Memorandum of Agreement* (MoA) with each prospective supplier. This is an acceptance by the customer that the proposed solution (which might have been modified during discussions) offered by the supplier satisfactorily meets the customer's requirement.

In the second stage tenders are invited from all the suppliers who have signed individual Memoranda of Agreement. The tender would incorporate the MoA and would be concerned with the financial terms of a potential contract.

If a design has to be produced as part of the proposal made by a supplier in response to an invitation to tender then a difficulty would be that the supplier would have to do a considerable amount of detailed design work with only a limited prospect of being paid for it. One way of reducing this burden is for the customer to choose a small number of likely candidates who will be paid a fee to produce design proposals. These can then be compared and the final contract for construction awarded to the most attractive proposal.

The ISO 12207 has a rather different approach. Once a contract for software construction is signed, the supplier develops a design which then has to be agreed by the customer.

> This approach has been recommended for government ICT contracts in the United Kingdom.

Evaluation of proposals

This needs to be done in a methodical and planned manner. We have already mentioned the need to produce an evaluation plan describing how each proposal will be checked against the selection criteria. This reduces risks of requirements being missed and ensures that all proposals are treated consistently. It would be unfair to favour a proposal because of the presence of a feature that was not requested in the original requirement.

It will be recalled that an application could be either bespoke, off the shelf, or customized. In the case of off-the-shelf packages it would be the software itself that would be evaluated and it might be possible to combine some of the evaluation with acceptance testing. With bespoke development it would be a proposal that is evaluated, while COTS may involve elements of both. Thus different planned approaches would be needed in each case.

The process of evaluation may include:

- scrutiny of the proposal documents;
- interviewing suppliers' representatives;
- demonstrations;
- site visits;
- practical tests.

The proposal documents provided by the suppliers can be scrutinized to see if they contain features satisfying all the original requirements. Clarification might be sought over certain points. Any factual statements made by a supplier imply a legal commitment on their part if they influence the customer to offer the contract to that supplier. It is therefore important to get a written, agreed, record of these clarifications. The customer might take the initiative here by keeping notes of meetings and then writing afterwards to the suppliers to get them to confirm the accuracy of the notes. A supplier could, in the final contract document, attempt to exclude any commitment to any representations that may have been made in pre-contract negotiations – the terms of the contract need to be scrutinized in this respect.

Where the delivered product is to be based on an existing product there could be a demonstration. A danger is that demonstrations can be controlled by the supplier and as a passive observer it may be difficult to maintain full attention for more than, say, half-an-hour. Because of this, the customer organization should have their own schedule of what needs to be demonstrated, ensuring that all the important features are seen in operation.

With off-the-shelf software, the customer could actually try out the package. For example, a demonstration version could be made available which closes itself down after 30 days. Once again a test plan is needed to ensure that all the important features are evaluated in a complete and consistent manner. Once a particular package emerges as the most likely candidate, it needs to be carefully investigated to see if there are any previously unforeseen factors that might invalidate this choice.

A frequent problem is that while an existing application works well on one platform with a certain level of transactions, it does not work satisfactorily with the customer's ICT configuration or level of throughput. Demonstrations might not reveal this problem. Visits to operational sites already using the system could be more informative. In the last resort a special volume test could be conducted.

Exercise 10.6 How would you evaluate the following aspects of a proposal?

(i) The usability of an existing software application.

(ii) The usability of a software application which is yet to be designed and constructed.

(iii) The maintenance costs of hardware to be supplied.

(iv) The time taken to respond to requests for software support.

(v) Training.

Where substantial sums of money are involved, legal advice on the terms of the contract is essential.

Eventually a decision will be made to award the contract to one of the suppliers. One reason for using a structured and, as far as possible, objective approach to evaluation is to be able to demonstrate that the decision has been made impartially and on merit. In most large organizations, placing a contract involves the participation of a second party within the organization, such as a contracts department, who can check that the correct procedures have been carried out. Also, the final legal format of a contract will almost certainly require some legal expertise.

In any case, not only should the successful candidate be notified but the unsuccessful candidates should also be told of the decision. This might not be simply a matter of courtesy: under GATT or EU rules, there is a legal requirement to do this in certain circumstances. It makes dealing with unsuccessful bidders easier if they can be given clear and objective reasons why their proposals did not find favour.

10.6   Typical terms of a contract

In a textbook such as this, it is not possible to describe the all necessary content of contracts for ICT goods or services. It is possible, however, to outline some of the major areas of concern.

Definitions

The terminology used in the contract document may need to be defined, e.g. who is meant by the words 'client' and 'supplier'.

Form of agreement

For example, is it a contact of sale, a lease, or a licence? Also, can the subject of the contract, such as a licence to use a software package, be transferred to another party?

Goods and services to be supplied

Equipment and software to be supplied   This should include an actual list of the individual pieces of equipment to be delivered, complete with the specific model numbers.

Services to be provided   This would cover such things as:

● training;
● documentation;
● installation;
● conversion of existing files;
● maintenance agreements;
● transitional insurance arrangements.

Ownership of the software

Who has ownership of the software? There may be two key issues here: firstly, whether the customer can sell the software to others and, secondly, whether the supplier can sell the software to others. Where an off-the-shelf package is concerned, the supplier often simply grants a licence for you to use the software. Where the software is being written specially for a customer then that customer may wish to ensure that they have exclusive use of the software – they may object to software which they hoped would give them a competitive edge being sold to their rivals. They could do this by acquiring the copyright to the software outright or by specifying that they should have *exclusive use* of the software. This would need to be written into the contract. Where a core system has been customized by a supplier then there is less scope for the customer to insist on exclusive use.

Where software is written by an employee as part of their normal job, it is assumed that the copyright belongs to the employer. Where the customer organization have contracted an external supplier to write software for them, the contract needs to make clear who is going to retain the copyright – it cannot, in this case, be automatically assumed it is the customer. The customer may have decided to take over responsibility for maintenance and further development once the software is delivered and in this case will need access to the source code. In other cases, where the customer does not have an adequate in-house maintenance function, the supplier may retain the source code, and the customer may have to approach the supplier for any further changes. There are many potential dangers with this, not the least being that the supplier could go out of business. An *escrow* agreement can be included in the contract so that up-to-date copies of the source code are deposited with a third party. In the United Kingdom, the NCC Group provides an escrow service.

Any assignment of copyright would need to be in writing.

Environment

Where physical equipment is to be installed, the demarcation line between the supplier's and customer's responsibilities with regard to such matters as accommodation and electrical supply needs to be specified. Where software is being supplied, the compatibility of the software with the existing hardware and operating system platforms would need to be confirmed.

Customer commitments

Even when work is carried out by external contractors, a development project still needs the participation of the customer. The customer may have to provide accommodation for the suppliers and perhaps other facilities such as telephone lines.

Acceptance procedures

Some customers find that specially written or modified software is not thoroughly tested by the supplier before delivery. Some suppliers seem to think that it is cheaper to get the customer to do the testing for them!

Good practice would be to accept a delivered system only after it has undergone user acceptance tests. This part of the contract would specify such details as the time that the customer will have to conduct the tests, deliverables upon which the acceptance tests depend and the procedure for signing off the testing as completed.

Standards

This covers the standards with which the goods and services should comply. For example, a customer could require the supplier to conform to the ISO 12207 standard relating to the software life cycle and its documentation (or, more likely, a customized sub-set of the standard). Within the European Union, government customers with contracts for projects above a certain threshold value must, by law, ensure that the work conforms to certain standards.

Project and quality management

The arrangements for the management of the project must be agreed. Among these would be frequency and nature of progress meetings and the progress information to be supplied to the customer. The contract could require that appropriate ISO 9001 standards are followed. The ISO 12207 standard provides for the customer to have access to quality documentation generated internally by the supplier, so that the customer can ensure that there is adherence to standards.

Timetable

This provides a schedule of when the key parts of the project should be completed. This timetable will commit both the supplier and the customer. For example, the supplier may only be able to install the software on the agreed date if the customer makes the hardware platform available to them at that point.

Price and payment method

Obviously the price is very important. What also needs to be agreed is when the payments are to be made. The supplier's desire to be able to meet costs as they are incurred needs to be balanced by the customer's requirement to ensure that goods and services are satisfactory before parting with their money.

Miscellaneous legal requirements

This is the legal small print. A contract may have to have clauses which deal with such matters as the definition of terms used in the contract, the legal jurisdiction that will apply to the contract, what conditions would apply to the subcontracting of the work, liability for damage to third parties, and liquidated damages. *Liquidated damages* are estimates of the financial losses that the customer would suffer if the supplier were to fall short of their obligations. It is worth noting that under English law, the penalties laid down in penalty clauses must reflect the actual losses the customer would suffer and cannot be unrealistic and merely punitive. Even this limitation may not be enough in some cases as far as the supplier is concerned. As computer systems assume increasingly critical roles in many organizations and in safety-critical systems can even be life-threatening in the case of malfunction, the possible consequential damage could be astronomical. Suppliers will not unnaturally try to limit this kind of liability. The courts (in England and Wales) have tended to look critically at such attempts at limiting liability, so that suppliers will, in the case of major contracts, take out insurance to cover such liabilities.

If there is a dispute, resorting to litigation, while being lucrative to the lawyers involved, is likely to be time consuming and expensive. An alternative is to agree that disputes be settled by *arbitration*. This requires that any dispute is referred to an expert third party whose decision as to the facts of the case is binding. Even this procedure might not be quick and inexpensive and another option is *alternative dispute resolution* where a third party acts as a mediator who has only an advisory capacity and attempts to broker an agreement between the two sides.

10.7 Contract management

ISPL Euromethod offers guidance about how decision points may be planned.

We now need to consider the communications between the supplier and customer while the contracted work is being carried out. It would probably suit all concerned if the contractor could be left to get on with the work undisturbed. However, at certain *decision points*, the customer might wish to examine work already done and make decisions about the future direction of the project. The project could require representatives of the supplier and customer to interact at many points in the development cycle – for example, users may need to be available to provide information needed for the design of interfaces.

This interaction, or other external factors, could lead to changes being needed which effectively vary the terms of the contract and so a careful change control procedure is needed. Each of these topics will now be tackled in a little more detail.

Chapter 4 discusses incremental delivery.

When the contract is being negotiated, certain key points in the project may be identified where customer approval is needed before the project can proceed. For example, a project to develop a large system could be divided into increments. For each increment there could be an interface design phase, and the customer might need to approve the designs before the increment is built. There could also be decision points between increments.

For each decision point, the deliverables to be presented by the suppliers, the decisions to be made by the customer and their outputs all need to be defined. These decision points have added significance if payments to the supplier are based on them. Not only the supplier but also the customer has responsibilities with respect to these decision points – for example, the supplier should not be unnecessarily delayed while awaiting customer approval of interim deliverables.

Where work is contracted out there will be concern about the quality of that work. The ISO 12207 standard envisages the possibility of there being agents, independent of both the supplier or customer, who will carry out verification, validation and quality assurance. It also allows for joint reviews of project processes and products to be agreed when the contract is negotiated.

Major changes to requirements may emerge. These could vary the terms of the contract. Oral evidence is not normally admissible to contradict, add to, or vary the terms of a written contract, so that agreed changes need to be documented. An effective change control procedure is essential to record requests for changes, the supplier's agreement to them and any fees for the additional work.

It could happen that the supplier does not meet one or more of their legal obligations. This may be through no fault of theirs, if, for example, the customer has caused the delay by being tardy in giving the necessary approvals for intermediate products. If no action is taken when the default occurs, this might be taken to imply that the customer in fact condones the failure and could lead to the loss of a right to legal redress. The customer should protect their legal rights by officially notifying the supplier that the failure has been recognized. It will be recalled that under English law any claim for liquidated damages should be based on actual losses. From the point where the default occurs, the customer needs to keep an accurate record of the actual losses they have incurred as a result of the default.

10.8   Acceptance

When the work has been completed, the customer needs to take action to carry out acceptance testing. The contract may put a time limit on how long acceptance testing can take, so the customer must be organized to carry out this testing before the time limit for requesting corrections expires.

We have already noted that some software suppliers are rather cursory with their pre-acceptance testing. It seems that they would rather the users spent their time on testing than them. This imposition can be reduced by asking to approve the supplier's internal test plans. An associated pitfall is that once the main development work is completed, the supplier not unnaturally wants to reallocate their most productive staff to other projects. The customer could find that all their problem reports are being dealt with by relatively junior members of the supplier's staff, who may not be familiar with all aspects of the delivered system.

Part or all of the payment to the supplier should depend on this acceptance testing. Sometimes part of the final payment will be retained for a period of operational running and is eventually paid over if the levels of reliability are as contracted for. There may also be a period of warranty during which the supplier should fix any errors found for no charge. The supplier might suggest a very short warranty period of, say, 30 days. It may be in the customer's interests to negotiate a more realistic period of, say, at least 120 days.

10.9   Conclusion

Some of the key points in this chapter have been:

- the successful contracting out of work requires considerable amounts of management time;

- it is easier to gain concessions from a supplier before a contract is signed rather than afterwards;

- alternative proposals need to be evaluated as far as possible by comparing costs over the whole lifetime of the system rather than just the acquisition costs;

- a contract will place obligations on the customer as well as the supplier;

- contract negotiation should include reaching agreement on the management of the supplier–customer relationship during the execution of the project.

10.10   Further exercises

1. At IOE, the management are considering 'outsourcing' the maintenance accounting system, i.e. getting an outside specialist organization to take over the operation, maintenance, and support activities associated with the system. Write a short memorandum to management outlining the advantages and disadvantages of such a reorganization.

2. Exercise 4 at the end of Chapter 1 concerned a software house that needed a training course developed to introduce new users to an order processing application that they had developed. Assume that you are an independent training consultant

who has been approached by the software house to develop the training package. You have agreed in principle and now a contract is being negotiated for the work.

(a) List the points that you would want clarified and included in the contract.

(b) Having produced the list of points requiring clarification, examine it from the point of view of the software house. Are there any additional points that they would want clarified?

3. In each of the following cases, discuss whether the type of application package to be adopted would be most likely to be bespoke, off the shelf or COTS.

(a) A college requires a student fees application. It is suggested that the processes required in the application are similar to those of any billing system, with some requirements that are peculiar to the administration of higher education.

(b) A computer-based application is needed at IOE to hold personnel details of staff employed.

(c) A system is required by a national government that calculates, records and notifies individual taxpayers about income tax charges.

(d) A expert system for use in a hospital to diagnose the causes of eye complaints.

4. The schedule of charges per function point shown in Table 10.2 has higher rates for larger systems. Give arguments explaining why this might be justified and also arguments against.

5. Table 10.3 has a charge of 25% and 50% of the normal rate for deleting transactions from an application. This may seem to be rather high for simply removing code. What work would be involved in deleting functionality that could justify this cost?

6. Assume that IOE has decided on a COTS solution that will replace the whole of the existing maintenance accounting system rather than simply plugging in additional modules to deal with group accounts. Write a memorandum that Amanda could send to IOE's legal department outlining the important provisions that a contract to supply this system should have.

CHAPTER 11

Managing people and organizing teams

Objectives

When you have completed this chapter you will be able to:

- identify some of the factors that influence people's behaviour in a project environment;
- select and induct new staff into a project;
- increase staff motivation;
- improve group working;
- use the most appropriate leadership styles;
- evaluate the characteristics of the various team structures;
- take steps to reduce unnecessary stress and threats to health and safety.

11.1 Introduction

We are going to examine some of the problems that Amanda and Brigette could meet when dealing with members of their teams. Where possible, we will see if the writers on organizational behaviour (OB) can provide advice.

There will be three main concerns: staff selection, staff development and staff motivation.

We will look at how the project leader can encourage effective group working and decision making while giving purposeful leadership where needed. As part of the concern for the well-being of team members some attention will be paid to stress and other issues of health and safety.

The issues raised in this chapter have impacts at all stages of project planning and execution but in particular at the following points (see also Figure 11.1).

- Some objectives can address health and safety during the project (Step 1).
- Although project leaders might have little control over organizational structure, they need to be aware of its implications (Step 2).
- The scope and nature of activities can be set in a way that will enhance staff motivation (Step 4).

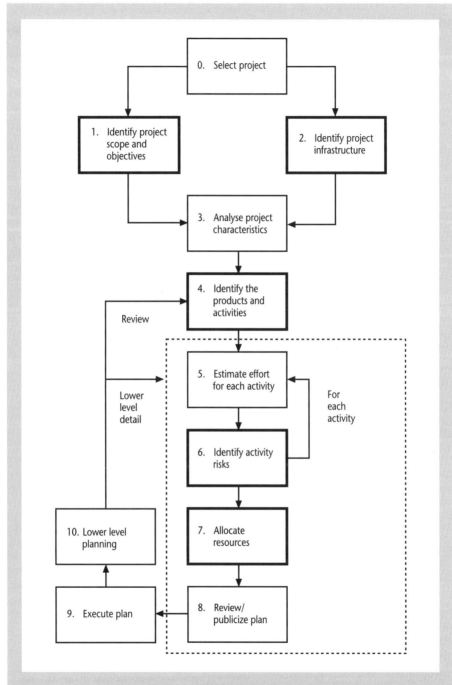

Figure 11.1 Some places in the Step Wise framework where staffing concerns are important

- Many risks to project success relate to staffing (Step 6).
- The qualities of individual members of staff should be taken into account when allocating staff to activities (Step 7).

11.2 Understanding behaviour

People with practical experience of projects invariably identify the handling of people as an important aspect of project management. People like Amanda and Brigette would want to know whether the effective and sensitive management of staff comes only from experience or whether expert advice can help.

The discipline of *organizational behaviour* has evolved theories that try to explain people's behaviour. These theories are often structured *'If A is the situation then B is likely to result'*. Attempts are made to observe behaviour where variables for A and B are measured and a statistical relationship between the two variables sought. Unlike physical science it is rarely, if ever, that it can be said that B *must* always follow A.

In the real world there will be a wide range of influences on a situation, many invisible to the observer. It is therefore difficult to decide which set of research findings is relevant. A danger is that we end up with a set of maxims which are little better than superstitions. However, by examining these issues people can at least become more sensitive and thoughtful about them.

Work Psychology by J. Arnold, C. L. Cooper and I. T. Robertson, 4th edition, FT Prentice Hall, 2004, is a good general text on these topics.

In what follows we will be making references to workers in the OB field such as Taylor, McGregor and Herzberg. Rather than overwhelming the reader with references, we recommend the reader who is interested in exploring this topic further to look at some of the books in the Further Reading section at the back of the book. Where we have given references these tend to be for works related specifically to an ICT environment.

11.3 Organizational behaviour: a background

The roots of studies in OB can be traced back to work done in the late 19th and early 20th centuries by Frederick Taylor. Taylor attempted to analyse the most productive way of doing manual tasks. The workers were then trained to do the work in this way.

Taylor had three basic objectives :

Frederick Winslow Taylor, 1856–1915, is regarded as the father of 'scientific management' of which OB is a part.

- to select the best people for the job;
- to instruct them in the best methods;
- to give incentives in the form of higher wages to the best workers.

'Taylorism' is often represented as crude and mechanistic. However, a concern for identifying best practice is valid. In the more mundane world of software development, the growth of structured methods is an example of an emphasis on best practice. Both Amanda and Brigette will be concerned that tasks are carried out in the proper way. More contentious is Taylor's emphasis on the exclusively financial basis of staff motivation, although Amanda and Brigette will find many colleagues who hold Taylor's view on the importance of 'performance-related pay'. Unfortunately, Amanda and Brigette are likely to have very little control over the financial rewards of their staff. However, they should be encouraged by find-ings that motivation rests not just on such rewards.

During the 1920s, OB researchers discovered, while carrying out a now famous set of tests on the conditions under which staff worked best, that not only did a group of workers for whom conditions were improved increase their work-rates, but also a control group for whom conditions were unchanged. Simply showing a concern for what workers did increased productivity. This illustrated how the state of mind of workers influenced their productivity.

The cash-oriented, or *instrumental*, view of work of some managers can thus be contrasted with a more rounded vision of people in their place of work. The two attitudes were labelled Theory X and Theory Y by Donald McGregor.

Theory X holds that:

- the average human has an innate dislike of work;
- there is a need therefore for coercion, direction and control;
- people tend to avoid responsibility.

Theory Y, on the other hand, holds that:

- work is as natural as rest or play;
- external control and coercion are not the only ways of bringing about effort directed towards an organization's ends;
- commitment to objectives is a function of the rewards associated with their achievement;
- the average human can learn to accept and further seek responsibility;
- the capacity to exercise imagination and other creative qualities is widely distributed.

One way of judging whether a manager espouses Theory X or Theory Y is to observe how staff react when the boss is absent: if there is no discernible change then this is a Theory Y environment; if everyone visibly relaxes, it is a Theory X environment. McGregor's distinction between the two theories also draws atten-tion to the way that expectations influence behaviour. If a manager (or teacher) assumes that you are going to work diligently and create products of good quality then you are likely to try to meet their expectations.

> The research that obtained these findings was done at the Hawthorne Works of Western Electric in Chicago, hence the 'Hawthorne Effect'.

> A 'reward' does not have to be a financial reward – it could be something like a sense of achievement.

11.4 Selecting the right person for the job

> B. W. Boehm considered the quality of staff the most important influence on productivity when constructing the COCOMO software cost model (Chapter 5).

Taylor stressed the need for the right person for the job. Many factors, such as the use of software tools and methodologies, affect programming productivity. However, one of the biggest differences in software development performance is between individuals. As early as 1968 a comparison of experienced professional programmers working on the same programming task found a ratio, in one case, of 1:25 between the shortest and longest time to code the program and, more sig-nificantly perhaps, of 1:28 for the time taken to debug it. Amanda and Brigette would therefore be rightly concerned to get the best possible people working for them.

What sort of characteristics should they be looking for? Is an experienced pro-grammer better than a new graduate with a first class mathematics degree? It is dangerous to generalize but, looking at behavioural characteristics, the American

P. M. Cheney, 'Effects of individual characteristics, organizational factors and task characteristics on computer programmer productivity and job satisfaction', in *Information and Management*, 7 (1984).

J. D. Couger and R. A. Zawacki, 'What motivates DP Professionals?', in *Datamation*, 24 (1978).

R. Meredith Belbin, *Team Roles at Work*, 2nd Edition, Butterworth-Heinemann, 1996.

researcher Cheney found that the most important influence on programmer productivity seemed to be experience. Mathematical aptitude had quite a weak influence in comparison.

Amanda and Brigette will want staff who can communicate well with each other and with users. Unfortunately, the American researchers Couger and Zawacki found that information systems (IS) professionals seemed to have much weaker 'social needs' than people in other professions. They quote Gerald Weinberg: *'If asked, most programmers probably say they prefer to work alone where they wouldn't be disturbed by other people.'* We see many who are attracted to writing software, and are good at it, but do not make good managers later in their careers.

Later surveys, however, have *not* found significant differences between IS and other staff. An explanation of this could be that IS has become broader and less purely technical in recent years.

The recruitment process

It must be stressed that often project leaders have little choice about the people who will make up their team – they have to make do with the 'materials that are to hand'. Recruitment is often an organizational responsibility: the person recruited might, over a period of time, work in many different parts of the organization.

Meredith Belbin usefully distinguishes between *eligible* and *suitable* candidates. *Eligible* candidates have a curriculum vitae (CV) which shows, for example, the 'right' number of years in some previous post and the 'right' paper qualifications. *Suitable* candidates can actually do the job well. A mistake is to select an eligible candidate who is not in fact suitable. Suitable candidates who are not officially eligible can, on the other hand, be ideal candidates as once in post they are more likely to remain loyal. Belbin suggests we should try to assess actual skills rather than past experience and provide training to make good minor gaps in expertise. It seems to us to show that policies that avoid discrimination on the grounds of race, gender, age or irrelevant disabilities can be not just socially responsible but also a shrewd recruitment policy.

A general approach might be the following.

- *Create a job specification*   Advice is often needed as there could be legal implications in an official document. However, formally or informally, the requirements of the job, including the types of task to be carried out, should be documented and agreed.

- *Create a job holder profile*   The job specification is used to construct a profile of the person needed to carry out the job. The qualities, qualifications, education and experience required would be listed.

- *Obtain applicants*   Typically, an advertisement would be placed, either within the organization or outside in the trade or local press. The job holder profile would be examined carefully to identify the medium most likely to reach the largest number of potential applicants at least cost. For example, if a specialist is needed it would make sense to advertise in the relevant specialist journal. The other principle is to give enough information in the advertisement to allow an element of self-elimination. By giving the salary, location, job scope and any essential qualifications, the applicants will be limited to the more realistic candidates.

A standard form which lists each selection criterion and the degree to which the candidate meets it should be used to ensure a consistent and fair approach.

- *Examine CVs*   These should be read carefully and compared to the job holder profile – nothing is more annoying for all concerned than when people have CVs which indicate clearly they are not eligible for the job and yet are called for interview.

- *Interviews etc.*   Selection techniques include aptitude tests, personality tests and the examination of samples of previous work. Any method must test specific qualities detailed in the job holder profile. Interviews are the most commonly used method. It is better if there is more than one interview session with an applicant and within each session there should not be more than two inter-viewers as a greater number reduces the possibility of follow-up questions and discussion. Some formal scoring system for the qualities being judged should be devised and interviewers should then decide scores individually which are then compared. An interview might be of a technical nature where the practical expertise of the candidate is assessed, or of a more general nature. In the latter case, a major part of the interview could be evaluating and confirming state-ments in the CV – for example, time gaps in the education and employment history would be investigated, and the precise nature of previous jobs would need to be explored.

- *Other procedures*   References will need to be taken up where necessary, and a medical examination might be needed.

Exercise 11.1   A new analyst/programmer is to be recruited to work in Amanda's team at IOE. The intention is to recruit someone who already has some experience. Make a list of the types of activities that the analyst/programmer should be capable of carrying out that can be used as the basis for a job specification.

11.5   Instruction in the best methods

Decisions will need to be made about whether a newcomer can more effectively pick up technical expertise on the job or on formal training courses.

This is the second concern that we have taken from Taylor. When new members of the team are recruited, the team leader will need to plan their induction into the team very carefully. Where a project is already well under way, this might not be easy. However, the effort should be made – it should pay off as the new recruit will become a fully effective member of the team more quickly.

The team leader should be aware of the need to assess continually the training needs of their team members. Just as you formulate a user requirement before considering a new system, and a job holder profile before recruiting a member of staff, so a training needs profile ought to be drawn up for each staff member when considering specific courses. Some training might be provided by commercial training companies. Where money is tight, alternative sources of training should be considered but training should not be abandoned. It could just be a team member finding out about a new software tool and then demonstrating it to col-leagues. Of course, the nice thing about external courses is talking to colleagues from other organizations – but attending meetings of your local branch of one of the computer-related professional associations, such as the IEE or the BCS, can serve the same purpose.

IEE is the Institution of Electrical Engineers and BCS is the British Computer Society.

The methods learnt need, of course, to be actually applied. Reviews and inspec-tions help to ensure this.

11.6 Motivation

The third of Taylor's concerns was that of motivating people to work. We are going to look at some models of motivation.

The Taylorist model

Piece-rates are where workers are paid a fixed sum for each item they produce. Day-rates refer to payment for time worked.

Taylor's viewpoint is reflected in the use of piece-rates in manufacturing industries and sales bonuses amongst sales forces. Piece-rates can cause difficulties if a new system will change work practices. If new technology improves productivity, adjusting piece-rates to reflect this will be a sensitive issue. Usually, radical changes in work practices have to be preceded by a move from piece-rates to day-rates. As will be seen later, the tendency towards dispersed or 'virtual projects' where staff work on their own premises at some distance from the sponsoring organization's site has seen a movement away from payment based on time worked.

Group norms are discussed further under group decision making.

Even where work practices are stable and output can be easily related to reward, people paid by the amount they produce will not automatically maximize their output in order to maximize their income. The amount of output will often by constrained by 'group norms', informal, even unspoken, agreements among colleagues about the amount to be produced.

Quoted by Wanda J. Orlikowski in *Groupware & Teamwork*, edited by Claudio U. Ciborra, Wiley and Sons, 1996.

Rewards based on piece-rates need to relate directly to work produced. Where a computer application is being developed, it is difficult to isolate and quantify work done by an individual, as system development and support is usually a team effort. As one member of staff in a study of software support work said: '*This support department does well because we're a team, not because we're all individuals. I think it's the only way the support team can work successfully.*'

In this kind of environment, a reward system that makes excessive distinctions between co-workers could damage morale and productivity. Organizations sometimes get around this problem by giving bonuses to project team members at the end of a successful project, especially if staff have 'volunteered' considerable unpaid overtime to get the project completed.

Exercise 11.2

A software development department want to improve productivity by encouraging the reuse of existing software components. It has been suggested that this could be encouraged through financial rewards. To what extent do you think this could be done?

Maslow's hierarchy of needs

The motivation of individuals varies. Money is a strong motivator when you are broke. However, as the basic need for cash is satisfied, other motivators are likely to emerge. Abraham Maslow, an American psychologist, suggested a hierarchy of needs. As a lower level of needs is satisfied then gradually a higher level of needs emerges. If these are then satisfied then yet another level will emerge. Basic needs include food, shelter and personal safety. The highest-level need, according to Maslow, is the need for 'self-actualization', the feeling that you are completely fulfilling your potential.

However, salary level can be important to staff approaching retirement because the amount of pension paid can depend on it.

In practice, people are likely to be motivated by different things at different stages of their life. For example, salary increases, while always welcome, probably have less impact on the more mature employee who is already relatively well paid, than on a lowly paid trainee. Older team-members might place more value on qualities of the job, such as being given autonomy, which show respect for their judgement and sense of responsibility.

Some individual differences in motivation relate simply to personality differences. Some staff have 'growth needs' – they are interested in their work and want to develop their work roles – while others simply see the job as a way of earning a living.

Exercise 11.3   Newspapers often report on the vast sums of money that are paid to the top executives of many companies. Does this mean that these people are at a low level in the Maslow hierarchy of motivation? Do they really need all this money to be motivated? What do you think the significance of these salaries really is?

Herzberg's two-factor theory

Some things about a job can make you dissatisfied. If the causes of this dissatisfaction are removed, this does not necessarily make the job more exciting. Research into job satisfaction by Herzberg and his associates found two sets of factors about a job:

● *hygiene or maintenance factors*, which can make you dissatisfied if they are not right, for example the level of pay or the working conditions;

● *motivators*, which make you feel that the job is worthwhile, like a sense of achievement or the challenge of the work itself.

Brigette, at Brightmouth College, might be in an environment where it is difficult to compete with the high level of maintenance factors that can be provided by a large organization like IOE, but the smaller organization with its closer contact with the users might be able to provide better motivators.

Exercise 11.4   Identify three incidents or times when you felt particularly pleased or happy about something to do with your work or study. Identify three occasions when you were particularly dissatisfied with your work or study. Compare your findings with those of your colleagues and try to identify any patterns.

The expectancy theory of motivation

Amanda and Brigette need to be aware of how the day-to-day ups and downs of system development affect motivation. A model of motivation developed by Vroom and his colleagues illustrates this. It identifies three influences on motivation:

● *expectancy*: the belief that working harder will lead to a better performance;

● *instrumentality*: the belief that better performance will be rewarded;

● *perceived value*: of the resulting reward.

Motivation will be high when all three factors are high. A zero level for any one of the factors can remove motivation.

Imagine trying to get a software package supplied by a third party to work. You realize that you will never get it to work because of a bug, and you give up. No matter how hard you work you will not be able to succeed (*zero expectancy*).

You are working on a package for a user and, although you think you can get it to work, you discover that the user has started employing an alternative package and no longer needs this one. You will probably feel you are wasting your time and give up (*zero instrumentality*).

Given that the users really do want the package, your reward might simply be the warm feeling of helping your colleagues and their gratitude. If in fact, when the users employ the package, all they do is complain and hold you responsible for shortcomings, then you might avoid getting involved if they later ask for help implementing a different package (*low perceived value of reward*).

11.7 The Oldham–Hackman job characteristics model

Managers should group together the elements of tasks to be carried out so that they form meaningful and satisfying assignments. Oldham and Hackman suggest that the satisfaction that a job gives is based on five factors. The first three factors make the job 'meaningful' to the person who is doing it:

● *skill variety*: the number of different skills that the job holder has the opportunity to exercise;

● *task identity*: the degree to which your work and its results are identifiable as belonging to you;

● *task significance*: the degree to which your job has an influence on others.

The other two factors are:

● *autonomy*: the discretion you have about the way that you do the job;

● *feedback*: the information you get back about the results of your work.

Oldham and Hackman also noted that both the job holders' personal growth needs and their working environment influenced their perception of the job. Some writers have pointed out that if people are happy with their work for other reasons, they are likely to rate it higher on the Oldham–Hackman dimensions anyway. Thus it might be that cause and effect are reversed.

In practical terms, activities should be designed so that, where possible, staff follow the progress of a particular product and feel personally associated with it.

Methods of improving motivation

To improve motivation the manager might therefore do the following.

● *Set specific goals*   These goals need to be demanding and yet acceptable to staff. Involving staff in the setting of goals helps to gain acceptance for them.

● *Provide feedback*   Not only do goals have to be set but staff have to have regular feedback about how they are progressing.

● *Consider job design*   Jobs can be altered to make them more interesting and give staff more feeling of responsibility.

Two measures are often used to enhance job design – job enlargement and job enrichment.

Job enlargement and job enrichment are based on the work of F. Herzberg.

● *Job enlargement*   The person doing the job carries out a wider variety of activities. It is the opposite of increasing specialization. For example, a software developer in a maintenance group might be given responsibility for specifying minor amendments as well as carrying out the actual code changes. Couger and Zawacki found that programmer/analysts had higher job satisfaction than programmers.

- *Job enrichment* The job holder carries out tasks that are normally done at a managerial or supervisory level. With programmers in a maintenance team, they might be given authority to accept requests for changes that involve less than five days' work without the need for their manager's approval.

11.8 Working in groups

A problem with major software projects is that they always involve working in groups, and many people attracted to software development find this difficult.

Formal groups can be either the departmental groupings seen on organization hierarchy diagrams reflecting the formal management structure, or *task groups* which carry out specific tasks. Task groups might call on people from different departments and would usually be disbanded once the task was completed.

11.9 Becoming a team

Simply throwing people together will not immediately enable them to work together as a team. Group feelings develop over time. It is suggested that teams go through five basic stages of development:

This classification is associated with B. W. Tuckman and M. A. Jensen.

- *Forming* The members of the group get to know each other and try to set up some ground rules about behaviour.
- *Storming* Conflicts arise as various members of the group try to exert leadership and the group's methods of operation are being established.
- *Norming* Conflicts are largely settled and a feeling of group identity emerges.
- *Performing* The emphasis is now on the tasks at hand.
- *Adjourning* The group disbands.

Sometimes specific team-building exercises can be undertaken. Some organizations, for example, send their management teams off on outdoor activities. Without going to these lengths, Amanda and Brigette might devise some training activities which promote team building.

Valuable research has examined the best mix of personalities in a project team. Belbin studied teams working together on management games. He initially tried putting the most able people into one group. Surprisingly, these élite teams tended to do very badly – they argued a lot and as a result important tasks were often neglected.

R. Meredith Belbin, *Management Teams: Why They Succeed or Fail*, 2nd edition, Elsevier, 2003, contains a self-assessment questionnaire which identifies the role a person is best suited to.

Belbin came to the conclusion that teams needed a balance of different types of people.

- *The chair*: not necessarily brilliant leaders but they must be good at running meetings, being calm, strong but tolerant.
- *The plant*: someone who is essentially very good at generating ideas and potential solutions to problems.

In *Team roles at work*, 1996, Belbin suggests that 'co-ordinator' and 'implementer' are better descriptions than 'chair' and 'team worker'. A new role is added: the 'specialist', the 'techie' who likes to acquire knowledge for its own sake.

- *The monitor-evaluator*: good at evaluating ideas and potential solutions and helping to select the best one.
- *The shaper*: rather a worrier, who helps to direct the team's attention to the important issues.
- *The team worker*: skilled at creating a good working environment, e.g. by 'jollying people along'.
- *The resource investigator*: adept at finding resources in terms of both physical resources and information.
- *The completer-finisher*: concerned with completing tasks.
- *The company worker*: a good team player who is willing to undertake less attractive tasks if they are needed for team success.

A person can have elements of more than one type. On the other hand, about 30% of the people examined by Belbin could not be classified at all.

To be a good team member you must be able to:

- time your interventions, e.g. not overwhelm the others in the team;
- be flexible;
- be restrained;
- keep the common goals of the team in mind all the time.

Group performance

The IBM manager was quoted by Angelo Failla in 'Technologies for co-ordination in a software factory' in *Groupware & Teamwork*, edited by C. U. Ciborra, Wiley & Sons, 1996.

Are groups more effective than individuals working alone? Given the preference of many people attracted to software development for working on their own, this is an important question. In many projects, judgements need to be made about which tasks are best carried out collectively and which are best delegated to individuals. As one manager at IBM said: '*Some work yields better results if carried out as a team while some things are slowed down if the work is compartmentalized on an individual basis.*' Part of the answer lies in the type of task being undertaken.

One way of categorizing group tasks is into:

- additive tasks;
- compensatory tasks;
- disjunctive tasks;
- conjunctive tasks.

Additive tasks mean the efforts of each participant are added to get the final result, e.g. a gang clearing snow. The people involved are interchangeable.

With *compensatory tasks* the judgements of individual group members are pooled so that the errors of some are compensated for by the inputs from others. For example, individual members of a group are asked to provide estimates of the effort needed to produce a piece of software and the results are then averaged. In these circumstances group work is generally more effective than the efforts of individuals.

With *disjunctive tasks* there is only one correct answer. The effectiveness of the group depends on:

Code reviews could be seen as an example of a compensatory task.

- someone coming up with the right answer;
- the others recognizing it as being correct.

Here the group can only be as good as its best member – and could be worse!

Conjunctive tasks are where progress is governed by the rate of the slowest performer. Software production where different staff are responsible for different modules is a good example of this. The overall task is not completed until all participants have completed their part of the work. In this case cooperative attitudes are productive: the team members who are ahead can help the meeting of group objectives by assisting those who are behind.

With all types of collective task, but particularly with additive ones, there is a danger of *social loafing*, where some individuals do not make their proper contribution. This can certainly occur with student group activities, but is not unknown in 'real' work environments. As one software developer has commented: '*[The contribution made to others] is not always recognized. Nor is the lack of any contributions ... nobody points out those who fail to make any contributions. Like when there's somebody with vital skills and you ask him for help, but he doesn't provide it.*'

The source of the quotation is the paper by Failla that is cited above.

Exercise 11.5 Social loafing is a problem that students often encounter when carrying out group assignments. What steps can participants in a group take to encourage team members to 'pull their weight' properly?

11.10 Decision making

Many of the techniques in Chapter 3 are attempts to make decision making more structured.

Before we can look more closely at the effectiveness with which groups can make decisions, we need to look in general terms at the decision-making process.

Decisions can be categorized as being:

- *structured*: generally relatively simple, routine decisions where rules can be applied in a fairly straightforward way, or

- *unstructured*: more complex and often requiring a degree of creativity.

Another way of categorizing decisions is by the amount of *risk* and *uncertainty* that is involved.

Some mental obstacles to good decision making

Many of the techniques in Chapter 3 on project selection are based on the rational-economic model.

So far we have rightly stressed a structured, rational, approach to decision making. Many management decisions in the real world, however, are made under pressure and based on incomplete information. We have to accept the role of intuition in such cases, but be aware of some mental obstacles to effective intuitive thinking, for example:

- *Faulty heuristics* Heuristics or 'rules of thumb' can be useful but there are dangers:

  - they are based only on information that is to hand, which might be misleading;

  - they are based on stereotypes, such as accepting a Welshman into a male voice choir without an audition because of the 'well-known' fact that the Welsh are a great singing nation.

- *Escalation of commitment* This refers to the way that once you have made a decision it is increasingly difficult to alter it even in the face of evidence that it is wrong.

- *Information overload*   It is possible to have too much information so that you 'cannot see the wood for the trees'.

Group decision making

There might be occasions where Amanda at IOE, for instance, might want to consult with her whole project team. With a project team different specialists and points of view can be brought together. Decisions made by the team as a whole are more likely to be accepted than those that are imposed.

Assuming that the meetings are genuinely collectively responsible and have been properly briefed, research would seem to show that groups are better at solving complex problems when the members of the group have complementary skills and expertise. The meeting allows them to communicate freely and to get ideas accepted.

Groups deal less effectively with poorly structured problems needing creative solutions. Brainstorming techniques can help groups in this situation but research shows that people often come up with more ideas individually than in a group. Where the aim is to get the involvement of end-users of a computer system, then prototyping and participatory approaches such as JAD might be adopted.

A different type of participatory decision-making might occur when end-users are consulted about the way a projected computer system is to operate.

Joint Application Development was discussed in Chapter 4.

Obstacles to good group decision making

Amanda could find that group decision making has disadvantages: it is time consuming; it can stir up conflicts within the group; and decisions can be unduly influenced by dominant personalities.

Conflict can, in fact, be less than might be expected. Experiments have shown that people will modify their personal judgements to conform to *group norms*, common attitudes developed by a group over time.

You might think that this would moderate the more extreme views that some in the group might hold. In fact, people in groups sometimes make decisions that carry more risk than where they make the decision on their own. This is known as the *risky shift*.

Once established group norms can survive many changes of membership in the group.

Measures to reduce the disadvantages of group decision making

One method of making group decision making more efficient and effective is by training members to follow a set procedure. The *Delphi technique* endeavours to collate the judgements of a number of experts without actually bringing them face to face. Given a problem, the following procedure is carried out:

- the cooperation of a number of experts is enlisted;
- the problem is presented to the experts;
- the experts record their recommendations;
- these recommendations are collated and reproduced;
- the collected responses are recirculated;
- the experts comment on the ideas of others and modify their recommendations if so moved;

- if the leader detects a consensus then the process is stopped, otherwise the comments are recirculated to the experts.

An advantage of this approach is that the experts could be geographically dispersed. However, this means that the process can be time consuming.

Exercise 11.6 What developments in information technology would be of particular assistance to use of the Delphi technique?

11.11 Leadership

When Amanda and Brigette first took on project management responsibilities, one of their private anxieties might well have been that staff would not take them seriously. Leadership is generally taken to mean the ability to influence others in a group to act in a particular way to achieve group goals. A leader is not necessarily a good manager or vice versa as managers have other roles such as organizing, planning and controlling.

Authorities on this subject have found it difficult to agree a list of the common characteristics of good leaders. It would, however, seem safe to say that they seem to have a greater need for power and achievement and have more self-control and more self-confidence than others.

Leadership is based on the idea of authority or power although leaders do not necessarily have much formal authority. Power may come either from the person's position (*position* power), from the person's individual qualities (*personal* power) or may be a mixture of the two. Position power has been further analysed into:

These ideas are associated with the work of J. R. P. French and B. H. Raven.

- *coercive* power, the ability to force someone to do something by threatening punishment;

- *connection* power, which is based on having access to those who have power;

- *legitimate* power, which is based on a person's title conferring a special status;

- *reward* power, where the holder can give rewards to those who carry out tasks to his or her satisfaction.

Personal power, on the other hand, can be further analysed into:

- *expert* power, which comes from being the person who is able to do a specialized task;

- *information* power, where the holder has exclusive access to information;

- *referent* power, which is based on the personal attractiveness of the leader.

Exercise 11.7 What kinds of power (as defined above) would the following people have?

(a) An internal auditor looking at the payroll system at Brightmouth College.

(b) A consultant who is called in to advise International Office Equipment about ways of improving software development productivity.

(c) The principal of Brightmouth College who has told staff that they must accept a new contract or face the sack.

(d) Brigette in respect to the users of the college payroll system.

(e) Amanda in respect of the people in the project team developing the group maintenance accounts application.

Leadership styles

Amanda and Brigette might be initially concerned about establishing their personal authority. Balanced against this is the need to involve the staff in decision making in order to make the best use of expertise and to gain commitment. Amanda and Brigette will need to judge when they must be authoritative and insist on things and when they must be more flexible and tolerant. Amanda, for example, may decide to be very democratic when formulating plans, but once the plans have been agreed, to insist on a very disciplined execution of the plan. Brigette, on the other hand, may find at Brightmouth College that she alone has the technical expertise to make some decisions, but, once she has briefed staff, they expect to be left alone to get on with the job as they see fit.

Attempts have been made to measure leadership styles on two axes: directive vs. permissive and autocratic vs. democratic:

This approach is associated with Rensis Likert.

- *directive autocrat*: makes decisions alone, close supervision of implementation;

- *permissive autocrat*: makes decision alone, subordinates have latitude in implementation;

- *directive democrat*: makes decisions participatively, close supervision of implementation;

- *permissive democrat*: makes decisions participatively, subordinates have latitude in implementation.

It should be emphasized that there is no one best style of management – it depends on the situation.

Another axis used to measure management styles has been on the degree to which a manager is *task-oriented*, that is, the extent to which the execution of the task at hand is paramount, and the degree to which the manager is concerned about the people around them (*people orientation*). It is perhaps not surprising that subordinates appear to perform best with managers who score highly in *both* respects.

Work environments vary with amount of control exerted over work. Some jobs are routine and predictable (e.g. dealing with batched computer output). Others are driven by outside factors (e.g. a help desk) or are situations where future direction is uncertain (e.g. at the early stages of a feasibility study). With a high degree of uncertainty subordinates will seek guidance from above and welcome a task-oriented management style. As uncertainty is reduced, the task-oriented manager is likely to relax, becoming more people-oriented, and this will have good results. People-oriented managers are better where staff can control the work they do, without referring matters to their line managers. It is then argued that if control becomes even easier the people-oriented manager will be tempted to get involved in more task-centred questions, with undesirable results.

Research also shows that where team members are relatively inexperienced, a task-oriented approach is most effective. As group members mature, consideration for their personal needs and aspirations becomes more valued. Where maturity is very high, there is no need for a strong emphasis on either of these approaches.

Exercise 11.8

What in your view would be the most appropriate management style when dealing with the following subordinates?

(a) At Brightmouth College, a former member of the local authority who has dealt with the college payroll for several years and who has been employed by the college to set up and manage the new payroll section.

(b) At IOE, a new trainee analyst/programmer who has just joined Amanda's group.

(c) At IOE, a very experienced analyst/programmer in their 40s, who was recruited into the software development department some time ago from the accounts department and who has been dealing with system support for the old maintenance accounts system that is now being revised.

11.12 Organizational structures

Formal versus informal structures

While organizational structures can have an enormous impact on the way a project is conducted, it is something that project leaders such as Amanda at IOE may find they can do little to change.

The *formal* structure is expressed in the staff hierarchy chart. It is basically concerned with *authority*, about who has which boss. It is backed by an *informal* structure of contacts and communication that grows up spontaneously between members of staff during the course of work. When the unexpected happens it is often this system that takes over. Over time the advantages and disadvantages of different organizational structures tend to even out – the informal organization gets built up and staff find unofficial ways of getting around the obstacles posed by the formal structure.

Hierarchical approach

The 'traditional' management structure is based on the concept of the *hierarchy* – each member of staff has only one manager, while a manager will have responsibility for several members of staff. Authority flows from the top down through the structure. A traditional concern has been with the *span of control* – the number of people that a manager can effectively control.

Staff versus line

Staff in organizations can often be divided into *line* workers who actually produce the end product and support *staff* who carry out supporting roles. In some organizations that produce software for the market or as a component of a larger product which is sold, the software specialists might be seen as part of the line. In a financial organization, on the other hand, the information systems department would probably be seen as part of the support staff.

Departmentalization

Differentiation concerns the departmentalization of organizations. This may be based on staff specialisms, product lines, categories of customer or geographical location, for example.

Software development is usually organized using either a *functional* or a *task-oriented* approach. With functional departmentalization, systems analysts may be put in a separate group to the programmers. The programmers would act as a pool from which resources are drawn for particular tasks. With a task-oriented approach the programmers and systems analysts are grouped together in project

As will be seen later, a functional division could facilitate outsourcing.

teams. The project team could be gathered to implement a specific long-term project or could exist on a permanent basis to service the needs of a particular set of users.

The functional approach can lead to a more effective use of staff. Programmers can be allocated to jobs on a need basis and be released for other work when the task is completed. For instance, in a project team there are bound to be periods of greater and lesser coding activity and software developers could experience times when they are under-utilized. The functional organization will also make it easier for the programmer to have a career which is technically oriented – there will probably be a career structure within the software development department which allows programmers to rise without changing their specialism. This type of organization should also encourage the interchange of new technical ideas between technical staff and the promulgation of company-wide standards.

However, having separate departments could lead to communication problems, especially if a developer is unfamiliar with an application area. There will also be problems with software maintenance – here it is helpful to have programmers who have built up a familiarity with particular parts of the application software. Users often prefer the established project team approach because they will have a group dedicated to their needs and will not find themselves in the position of always having to fight other departments for development resources. The project team structure tends to favour a pattern of career progression where software developers eventually become business analysts.

A third method of departmentalization is based on *life-cycle phase*. Here there are separate teams for development and maintenance. Some staff can concentrate on developing new systems with few interruptions while other teams, more oriented towards service and support, deal with maintenance.

Some organizations have attempted to get the best of all worlds by having a *matrix* structure. In this case the developer would have two managers: a project leader who would give them day-to-day direction about the work in hand and a programming manager who would be concerned about such things as career development.

Egoless programming

In the early days of computer development managers tended to think of the software developer as communing mysteriously with the machine. The tendency was for programmers to see programs as being an extension of themselves and to feel over-protective towards them. The effects of this on the maintainability of programs can be imagined. Gerald Weinberg made the then revolutionary suggestion that programmers and programming team leaders should read other people's programs. Programs would become in effect the common property of the programming group and programming would become 'egoless'. Peer code reviews are based on this idea. Weinberg's ideal programming team was a decentralized group freely communicating within itself.

Chief programmer teams

The larger the development group the slower it will get because of the increased communication. Thus large time-critical projects tend to have a more formalized, centralized structure. Brooks pointed out the need for design consistency when

Programme management can facilitate better sharing of staff between projects.

G. M. Weinberg, *The Psychology of Computer Programming*, Silver Anniversary Edition, Dorset House, 1998.

Brooks' *Mythical Man-Month* has already been referred to. He was in charge of the huge team that created the operating system for the IBM 360 range.

producing a large complex system and how this is difficult with a large number of people involved in producing a piece of software. He suggested reducing the number of people actually creating software but making these programmers as productive as possible by giving them as much support as possible.

The result was the *chief programmer* team. The chief programmer defines the specification, and designs, codes, tests and documents the software. He or she is assisted by a *co-pilot*, with whom the chief programmer can discuss problems and who writes some code. They are supported by an *editor* to write up the documentation drafted by the chief programmer, a *program clerk* to maintain the actual code, and a *tester*. The general idea is that this team is under the control of a single unifying intellect.

The chief programmer concept was used on the influential *New York Times* data bank project where many aspects of structured programming were tried out. In this case each chief programmer managed a senior-level programmer and a program librarian. Additional members could be added to the team on a temporary basis to deal with particular problems or tasks.

The problem with this kind of organization is getting hold of really outstanding programmers to carry out the chief programmer role. There is also the danger of information overload on the chief programmer. There is in addition the potential for staff dissatisfaction among those who are there simply to minister to the needs of the superstar chief programmers.

Extreme programming was discussed in Chapter 4

The new *extreme programming* concepts have inherited many of these ideas. Here software development by pairs of developers is advocated – this seems to be a new version of the chief programmer/co-pilot relationship.

11.13 Dispersed and virtual teams

At the beginning of Chapter 1, it was noted that a key feature of projects was that each project was to a greater or lesser extent a unique problem. They also usually required a team of people to carry them out, and the members of this team could each be a specialist in a particular field. Thus, the heart of many projects is *collaborative problem solving*. The Second World War underlined the importance of cooperation between individuals and groups to execute major global operations, and encouraged research after the conflict into effective team working. At that time, group working meant, almost by definition, that the team members worked in close physical proximity. However, in recent years the concept and practice of having *dispersed* or *'virtual teams'* have emerged.

See Tom DeMarco and Timothy Lister, *PeopleWare: Productive Projects and Teams*, 2e, Dorset House, 1999.

Project work, especially the development of large software products, needs coordination which in turn means that team members need to communicate. Being located in the same physical space clearly assists this. However, offices can be noisy places and while software development needs communication it also needs periods of solitary concentrated effort. DeMarco and Lister describe the condition of deep concentration needed for effective creative work as 'flow', and suggest that about 15 minutes of uninterrupted effort is needed to achieve this state. Every interruption destroys flow and requires another 15 minutes for its recovery.

It was noted earlier that project managers often have little control over who will be allocated to their team. They are even less likely to have control over the physical environment in which the team will work. Many years ago, research at IBM suggested that ideally each software developer should have:

- 100 square feet of dedicated space;
- 30 square feet of work surface;
- noise protection in the form of enclosed offices or high partitions at least six feet high.

For various reasons it is often difficult for software developers to be provided with this kind of accommodation, yet DeMarco and Lister found clear links between reported noise levels in the workplace and the number of defects found in the resulting software.

One answer is to send the software developers home. One recent (2004) survey found that 77% of businesses allowed at least some of their staff to work at home. Most of those working at home reported that they were more productive. The development of cheap internet-based communications, supported by broadband channels, has reduced the coordination problems that were the drawback of home working.

Modern communication technologies also mean that organizations can more easily form temporary teams to carry out specific projects from amongst their employees without having to relocate them. The nature of the work carried out in some projects means that the demand for certain specialist skills is intermittent. Ideally the project manager would like to have access to these skills for a short time but then be able to release them and thus avoid further costs. An example of this might be the passing need for a graphic designer to produce aesthetically pleasing designs for a web application project. This desire for flexible labour means that contract workers are often used. The internet allows these contractors to carry out well-defined tasks at their own premises without necessarily having to travel to their clients' site.

It is then only a short step to use 'off-shore' staff who live and work in a different part of the world. Hence we arrive at the dispersed or virtual team.

To recap the possible advantages of such an arrangement:

- A reduction in staff costs by using labour from developing countries where salaries are lower.
- A reduction in the overheads that arise from having your own employees on site, including costs of accommodation, social security payments, training.
- The flexible use of staff – they are not employed when they are not needed.
- Productivity might be higher.
- Use of specialist staff for specific jobs, rather than more general project workers, might improve quality.
- Advantage can be taken of people working in different time zones to reduce task durations – for example, software developers can deliver new versions of code to testers in a different time zone who can test it and deliver the results back at the start of the next working day.

Some of the challenges of dispersed working are:

- The requirements for work that is distributed to contractors have to be carefully specified.
- The procedures to be followed will need to be formally expressed, where previously practices might have been picked up through observation and imitation of co-workers on site.

The survey was carried out by the Economist Intelligence Unit and was reported on in 'Remote working boosts productivity' in *Computing*, 25th November, 2004, p. 6.

One estimate is that 24,000 IT and software development jobs will have been moved off-shore from the UK between 2003 and 2005, according to a British Computer Society working party report, *Offshoring – a challenge or opportunity for IT Professionals*, (British Computer Society 2004).

See Robert Johansen et al., *Leading Business Teams*, Addison-Wesley, 1991.

Table 11.1 Time/place constraints on some communication methods

	Same place	Different place
Same time	Meetings Interviews etc.	Telephone Instant messaging
Different times	Noticeboards Pigeon-holes	Email Voicemail Documents

- Coordination of dispersed workers can be difficult.
- Payment methods may need to be modified to make them fixed price or piece-rate.
- There may be a lack of trust of co-workers who are remote and never seen.
- Assessment of the quality of delivered products will need to be thorough.
- Different time zones can cause communication and coordination problems.

We will explore how some of these challenges can be met and how the advantages of dispersed teams can be exploited. To do this we must first look at characteristics of communication in such situations and then see how these characteristics can be employed in the execution of projects.

Modes of communication can be categorized as combinations of two opposites: same time/different time and same place/different place – see Table 11.1.

The nature of the information to be conveyed also needs to be considered.

- What is the extent and complexity of the information to be conveyed? A telephone conversation may be a very quick way of conveying simple messages – but has disadvantages as a medium for large amounts of information.

- Is it easy to understand? For example, is the context well known to both the sender and the recipient? If it is likely that the recipient will need clarification of aspects of the information, then a mode of communication that is two-way would be best.

- Where the communication is personally sensitive, then face-to-face contact is the most effective form of communication, even if it can be uncomfortable or inconvenient for those concerned.

Exercise 11.9

What would be the best mode of communication for the following?

(a) A developer needs clarification of what is meant by a particular term used in a specification.

(b) The users of a system have found what appears to be a fault in a software application that they use.

(c) A finance director needs to ensure that a software application is changed to conform with new legal requirements.

(d) A software developer can only complete her software component if another developer finishes his component first, but he has not. The first developer is under a lot of pressure from the client to complete the work.

At different stages of a project it is likely that different methods of communication are likely to be preferred.

Early stages of a project

Charles Handy, 'Trust and the virtual organization', *Harvard Business Review*, May/June, 1995, pp. 45–50.

At the start of the project, team members will need to build up their trust and confidence in their co-workers. For this same time/same place communication, actually meeting is probably best. It is argued that this is especially the case with dispersed projects: as Charles Handy has written: *'paradoxically, the more virtual an organization becomes, the more its people need to meet in person'*.

Julian Baggini, 'Touched by your absence', *The Guardian*, 6 January, 2005.

However, not everyone might agree with this. Julian Baggini, describing his experience of writing a textbook on philosophy with someone he had never met, argues: *'It is simply not necessary to know the whole person in order to have a good relationship with them. .... If you get to know and dislike the way that someone behaves outside the office, that can make you uncomfortable with them in it.'*

The early stages of a project are when at least some of the team will be involved in making decisions about the overall design of product to be delivered and the method by which it is to be created. In the preliminary stages at least same time/same place meetings are the most effective means of progressing.

Intermediate design stages of the project

Once the overall architecture of the product has been established, detailed design on different components could well be carried out in parallel in different locations. However, some points will need to be clarified and for this same time/different place communication could well be best, such as the use of teleconferencing.

Implementation stages of the project

Mazneski, M. L and Chudoba, K. M., 'Bridging space over time global virtual team dynamics and effectivness', *Organization Science*, Vol 11 No 5, 2000.

Once the design is clarified and everyone knows his or her role, work can progress. Where there is a need to exchange information at this point, different time/different place communication media such as e-mail are likely to be sufficient.

Even at this stage some recommend regular face-to-face meetings of at least some staff as this supplies a rhythm to the project which helps coordination of the project and maintains motivation. Martha Maznevski and Katherine Chudoba observed the workings of a dispersed project and have noted *'interaction between coordination meetings was mainly in response to the previous meeting or in anticipation of the next one. The coordination meeting served as a heartbeat, rhythmically pumping new life into the team's processes ...'.*

Communication plans

Communication is clearly a vital matter in the case of dispersed projects. Because of this, consideration of the way that project stakeholders will communicate ought to be a part of the project planning process. Some have gone as far as to suggest that a specific planning document ought to address communication issues affecting the project.

Figure 11.2 Hofstede's three levels of human mental programming

11.14 The influence of culture

One of the authors was waiting once in the office of a head of a university department, who happened to be a woman, early one morning for a meeting. When the head's secretary arrived at work, the head kissed her on the cheek. Readers from the United Kingdom will find this rather surprising. The explanation for the behaviour is simple: this happened in France and they do things differently there. It was a matter of *culture*.

When we describe the characteristics of a person, we can, at one level, talk about the universal characteristics that all humans share, such as the need for adequate sleep to prevent fatigue – these are *biological* (Figure 11.2). There are, on the other hand, characteristics that vary for each individual, such as a propensity to be cheerful or an ability to write software code. These characteristics could be inherited or they could be learnt. In between the individual and the universal, there are cultural characteristics that belong to groups of people. It must be emphasized that if we say that one group of people tend to have a characteristic while those in another do not, we are *not* saying that *all* in the group have that characteristic. We might suggest, for example, that systems analysts tend to have more communication with end-users than software developers. On average this might be true, but there are probably many cases where one given software developer has more user contact than a particular systems analyst. There is a risk that awareness of cultural differences can become stereotyping or even prejudice.

With increasing globalization and dispersed project working, cultural differences need to be increasingly considered. There can be cultural differences between organizations, but in this section the emphasis is on national differences.

In the late 1970s, Geert Hofstede conducted a survey for IBM of 100,000 of that organization's employees worldwide. Hofstede subsequently used the data collected for his own analysis of the differences between national groups.

He identified the following cultural differences between national groups.

- *Power distance*   Essentially this is the psychological distance between those who exercise authority and those who are subject to it, usually managers and staff. Where there is a large power distance, relations between managers and staff

G. Hofstede, *Culture's Consequences: International Differences in Work-related Values,* Sage, 1984.

would tend to be formal and managers' decisions would tend not to be questioned.

● *Uncertainty avoidance* Some people are more uncomfortable with ambiguity and uncertainty than others and want there to be clear rules and guidelines about how to proceed.

● *Individualism/collectivism* The primary concern of individualists is with their own interests, while collectivism reflects the way that some people relate primarily to a group such as a local community.

● *Masculine/feminine* Here we have to tread cautiously. Hofstede analysed his data to identify the dimensions upon which, globally, men tended to express different opinions and concerns from women. He found that men tended to put more emphasis on work-related goals such as earnings and promotion and on self-assertiveness, while women tended to value personal goals such as a friendly working atmosphere. Countries where these qualities tended to be found generally in the population as a whole were then identified as being more or less 'masculine'.

The 'masculinity' of a culture in Hostede terms seems to be a different concept from that of being 'macho'.

See Lisa Hoecklin *Managing Cultural Differences: Strategies for Competitive Advantage*, Addison-Wesley, 1995.

Some later research focused more specifically on the Far East. The researchers here could not distinguish cultures on the uncertainty avoidance dimension, but found another differentiating factor between national cultures – *long-term/short-term outlook*.

These cultural differences could clearly have an impact on the way projects are most effectively managed. For example, it could influence the degree to which decision making could be delegated, or the degree to which group as opposed to individual working should be encouraged. The experience of the authors is that caution is needed in interpreting the Hofstede ratings. One report described a situation where managers from the UK and Italy had to work together. The Italians perceived the British to be well-organized analytical thinkers, but to be very much preoccupied with rules and procedures. From this you might expect the Italians to have a lower uncertainty avoidance rating, yet the relevant scores – see Table 11.2 – were Italy 75 and the UK 35. In another instance, an American manager working with French staff found it difficult to get them to work together as a team, yet the individualism score for France was only 71, compared with the US score of 91.

Table 11.2 Hofstede scores and rankings for six example countries

Country	Power distance		Uncertainty avoidance		Individualism		Masculinity	
France	68	15=	86	10=	71	10=	43	35=
Greece	60	27=	112	1	35	30	57	18=
India	77	10=	40	45	48	21	56	20=
Italy	50	34	75	23	76	7	70	4=
United Kingdom	35	42=	35	47=	89	3	66	9=
USA	40	38	46	43	91	1	61	15
Singapore	74	13	8	53	20	39=	48	28

11.15   Stress

Quoted in *Death March* by Edward Yourdon, 2nd Edition, Prentice-Hall, 2003.

Projects are about overcoming obstacles and achieving objectives. Almost by definition both the project manager and team members will be under pressure. An American project manager is quoted as saying: *'Once a project gets rolling, you should expect members to be putting in at least 60 hours a week. . . . The project leader must expect to put in as many hours as possible . . . .'*

Some pressure is actually healthy. Boredom can make many jobs soul-destroying. Beyond a certain level of pressure, however, the quality of work decreases and health can be affected. There is good evidence that productivity and the quality of output goes down when more than about 40 hours a week are worked. As long ago as 1960 it was found in a US study that people under 45 years of age who worked more than 48 hours a week had twice the risk of death from coronary heart disease.

Many software developers are expected to work overtime on projects for no additional payment. In these cases, a fall in productivity is more than compensated for by the fact that the work is effectively free to the employer.

Clearly, it is sometimes necessary to put in extra effort to overcome some temporary obstacle or to deal with an emergency, but if overtime working becomes a way of life then there will be longer-term problems.

Good project management can reduce the reliance on overtime by the more realistic assessment of effort and elapsed time needed, based on careful recording and analysis of the performance of previous projects. Good planning and control will also help to reduce 'unexpected' problems generating unnecessary crises.

Stress can be caused by *role ambiguity* when staff do not have a clear idea of the objectives that their work is supposed to be fulfilling, what is expected of them by others and the precise scope of their responsibilities. The project manager could clearly be at fault in these instances.

Role conflict can also heighten stress. This is where the person is torn between the demands of two different roles. The parent of young children might be torn between the need to look after a sick child and the need to attend an important meeting to win new business.

Some managers claim to be successful through the use of essentially bullying tactics to push projects through. They need to create crises in order to justify the use of such tactics. This, however, is the antithesis of professional project management which aims at a rational, orderly and careful approach to the creation of complex products.

11.16   Health and safety

Health and safety issues are more prominent in construction and other heavy engineering projects than in ICT development. Sometimes, however, the implementation of office systems requires the creation of physical infrastructure which can have inherent physical dangers. ICT infrastructure could, for example, be installed in a building where construction work is still going on.

In this section we are not addressing general concerns relating to the safety of ICT equipment of which any organization using such equipment would need to be aware. Nor are we discussing the safety of products created by the software development process. We are focusing briefly on the health and safety issues that relate to the conduct of a project.

Various pieces of legislation govern safety policy and the details of these can be consulted in the appropriate literature. In the United Kingdom, legislation requires organizations employing more than five employees to have a written *safety policy* document. A project manager should be aware of the contents of the document that applies to the environment in which the project is to be undertaken.

Professional Issues in Software Engineering (3rd Edition) by M.F. Bott et al., Taylor and Francis, 2000, explores these issues in greater depth.

As far as the project manager is concerned, safety objectives, where appropriate, should be treated like any other project objectives, such as the level of reliability of the completed application or the overall cost of the project. The management of safety should therefore be embedded in the general management of the project.

Responsibility for safety must be clearly defined at all levels. Some points that will need to be considered include:

● top management must be committed to the safety policy;

● the delegation of responsibilities for safety must be clear;

● job descriptions should include definitions of duties related to safety;

● those to whom responsibilities are delegated must understand the responsibilities and agree to them;

● deployment of a safety officer and the support of experts in particular technical areas;

● consultation on safety;

● an adequate budgeting for safety costs.

Safety procedures must be brought to the attention of employees and appropriate training be given where needed.

This is a very cursory glimpse at some of the issues in this area. For a fuller treatment, the specialized literature should be consulted.

11.17   Conclusion

Some of the important points that have been made in this chapter are:

● people may be motivated by money, but they are motivated by other things as well;

● both staff selection and the identification of training needs should be done in an orderly, structured, way where requirements are clearly defined first;

● thoughtful job design can increase staff motivation;

● consideration should be given, when forming a new project team, to getting the right mix of people and to planning activities which will promote team building;

● group working is more effective with some types of activity than others;

● different styles of leadership are needed in different situations;

- the people who need to communicate most with each other should be grouped together organizationally;

- undue pressure on staff can have short-term gains, but is harmful to both productivity and personal health in the longer term;

- project objectives should include, where appropriate, those relating health and safety.

11.18 Further exercises

1. An organization has detected low job satisfaction in the following departments:
   - the system testing group;
   - the computer applications help desk;
   - computer batch input.
   How could these jobs be redesigned to give more job satisfaction?

2. In Exercise 11.1, a job specification was requested.
   (a) Write a job holder profile of the sort of person who would be able to fulfil the specification in terms of qualities, qualifications, previous education and experience.
   (b) For each element in the job holder profile that you have produced in (a) above, describe ways of finding out whether an applicant has met the requirement.

3. To what extent is the Belbin approach to balanced teams compatible with having chief programmer teams?

4. If you have been involved recently in a group activity or project, try to categorize each participant according to the Belbin classification. Were there any duplications or gaps in any of the roles? Did this seem to have any impact on progress?

5. Three different mental obstacles to good decision making were identified in the text: faulty heuristics, escalation of commitment and information overload. What steps do you think can be taken to reduce the danger of each of these?

6. In Exercise 11.8, the management style most appropriate for each of three different situations was asked for. Go back and consider how you as a manager would respond to each of these three situations in terms of practical things to do or avoid.

CHAPTER 12

Software quality

Objectives

When you have completed this chapter you will be able to:

- explain the importance of software quality to software users and developers;
- define the qualities of good software;
- design methods of measuring the required qualities of software;
- monitor the quality of the processes in a software project;
- use external quality standards to ensure the quality of software acquired from an outside supplier;
- develop systems using procedures that will increase their quality.

12.1 Introduction

While quality is generally agreed to be 'a good thing', in practice what people really mean by the 'quality' of a system can be vague. We therefore need to define precisely what qualities we require of a system. However, this is not enough – we need to judge objectively whether a system meets our quality requirements and this needs measurement. This would be of particular concern to someone like Brigette at Brightmouth College in the process of selecting a package.

For someone – like Amanda at IOE – who is developing software, waiting until the system exists before measuring it would be leaving things rather late. Amanda might want to assess the likely quality of the final system while it was still under development, and also to make sure that the development methods used were likely to produce that quality. This leads to a slightly different emphasis – rather than concentrating on the quality of the final system, a potential customer for software might try to check that the suppliers were using the best methods.

This chapter examines these issues.

12.2 The place of software quality in project planning

Quality will be of concern at all stages of project planning and execution, but will be of particular interest at the following points in the Step Wise framework (Figure 12.1).

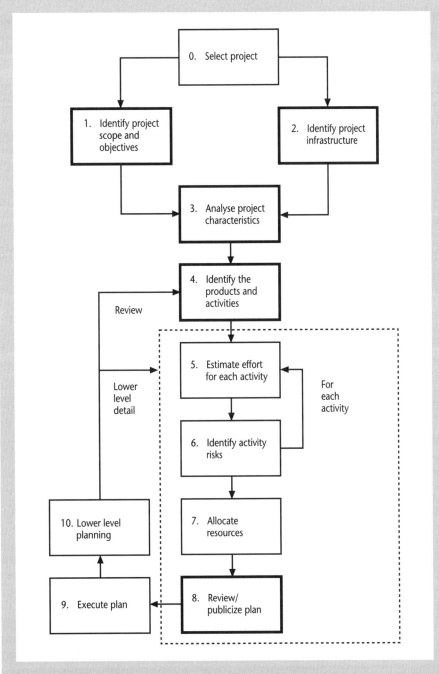

Figure 12.1 The place of software quality in Step Wise

- *Step 1: Identify project scope and objectives* Some objectives could relate to the qualities of the application to be delivered.

- *Step 2: Identify project infrastructure* Within this step, activity 2.2 identifies installation standards and procedures. Some of these will almost certainly be about quality.

- *Step 3: Analyse project characteristics* In activity 3.2 ('Analyse other project characteristics – including quality based ones') the application to be implemented will be examined to see if it has any special quality requirements. If, for example, it is extremely safety critical then a whole range of additional activities could be added such as *n*-version development where a number of teams develop versions of the same software which are then run in parallel with the outputs being cross-checked for discrepancies.

- *Step 4: Identify the products and activities of the project* It is at this point that the entry, exit and process requirements are identified for each activity. The nature of these requirements is described later in this chapter.

- *Step 8: Review and publicize plan* At this stage the overall quality aspects of the project plan are reviewed.

12.3 The importance of software quality

We would expect quality to be a concern of all producers of goods and services. However, the special characteristics of software, and in particular its intangibility and complexity, make special demands.

- *Increasing criticality of software* The final customer or user is naturally anxious about the general quality of software, especially its reliability. This is increasingly the case as organizations become more dependent on their computer systems and software is used more and more in areas which are safety critical, for example to control aircraft.

The intangibility of software presents particular problems – see Frederick P. Brooks, 'No Silver Bullet: Essence and Accidents of Software Engineering', *IEEE Computer*, April, 1987.

- *The intangibility of software* This makes it difficult to know that a particular task in a project has been completed satisfactorily. The results of these tasks can be made tangible by demanding that the developer produce 'deliverables' that can be examined for quality.

- *Accumulating errors during software development* As computer system development is made up of a number of steps where the output from one step is the input to the next, the errors in the earlier deliverables will be added to those in the later steps, leading to an accumulating detrimental effect. In general, the later in a project that an error is found the more expensive it will be to fix. In addition, because the number of errors in the system is unknown, the debugging phases of a project are particularly difficult to control.

For these reasons quality management is an essential part of effective overall project management.

12.4 Defining software quality

Quality is a rather vague term and we need to define carefully what we mean by it. For any software system, there should be three specifications:

See Jacobson, I., Booch, G., and Rumbaugh, J., *The Unified Software Development Process*, Addison-Wesley, 1999.

- a *functional specification* describing what the system is to do – this is the primary concern of methodologies such as the Unified Software Development Process;

- a *quality (or attribute) specification* concerned with how well the functions are to operate;

- a *resource specification* concerned with how much is to be spent on the system.

Exercise 12.1

At Brightmouth College, Brigette has to select the best off-the-shelf payroll package for the college. How should she go about this in a methodical manner?

One element of the approach could be the identification of criteria against which payroll packages are to be judged. What might these criteria be? How could you check the extent to which packages match these criteria?

Some qualities that can be defined for a software product reflect the external view of software that *users* would have, as in the case of usability. These *external qualities* have to be mapped to *internal factors* of which the *developers* would be aware. It could be argued, for example, that well-structured code is likely to have fewer errors and thus improve reliability.

Defining quality is not enough. If we are to judge whether a system meets our requirements we need to be able to measure its qualities. For each quality characteristic, one or more measures have to be invented which assess the degree to which the quality is present.

Measures may be:
- *relative quantity measures* where an attempt is made to quantify the presence of the quality, or
- *binary measures* where the quality is deemed either to be present or not present.

A good measure must be able to relate the number of units to the maximum possible in the circumstances. The maximum number of faults in a program, for example, is related to the size of the program so a measure of *faults per thousand lines of code* is more helpful than *total faults in a program* as a means of judging the quality of a program.

Trying to find measures for a particular quality helps to clarify what that quality really is. What is being asked is, in effect, 'how do we know when we have been successful?' Answering this allows the quality objectives to be communicated widely.

The measures may be *direct* where we can measure the quality directly or *indirect* where the thing being measured is not the quality itself but an indicator that the quality is present. For example, the number of enquiries by users received by a help desk about how one operates a particular software application might be an indirect measurement of its usability. By identifying measures management are setting targets for project team members so care has to be taken that an improvement in the measured quality is always meaningful. For example, the number of errors found in program inspections could be counted, on the grounds that the more thorough the inspection process, the more errors there will be discovered. This count could, of course, be improved by allowing more errors to go through to the inspection stage rather than eradicating them earlier – which is not quite the point!

When there is concern about the need for a specific quality characteristic in a software product then a quality specification with the following minimum details should be drafted:

- *definition/description*: definition of the quality characteristic;
- *scale*: the unit of measurement;
- *test*: the practical test of the extent to which the attribute quality exists;
- *minimally acceptable*: the worst value which might be acceptable if other characteristics compensated for it, and below which the product would have to be rejected out of hand;
- *target range*: the range of values within which it is planned the quality measurement value should lie;
- *now*: the value that applies currently.

There could be more than one measurement that is applicable to a quality characteristic. When drafting *quality specifications* a quality characteristic might be broken down into sub-characteristics. For example, a sub-characteristic of 'usability' might be 'communicativeness'. One aspect of this might be the ease of understanding of the menu structure, that is, how easy it is to find the command to carry out some function. Another aspect of communicativeness would be how informative the error messages were, while another would be the clarity of the 'help' pages.

Exercise 12.2   Suggest quality specifications for a word processing package. Give particular attention to the way that practical tests of these attributes could be conducted.

12.5   ISO 9126

Currently, in the UK, the main ISO 9126 standard is known as BS ISO/IEC 9126-1:2001. This is supplemented by some 'technical reports' (TRs), published in 2003, which are provisional standards. At the time of writing, a new standard in this area, ISO 25000, is being developed.

Over the years, various lists of software quality characteristics have been put forward, such as those of James McCall and of Barry Boehm. A difficulty has been the lack of agreed definitions of the qualities of good software. The term 'maintainability' has been used, for example, to refer to the ease with which an error can be located and corrected in a piece of software, and also in a wider sense to include the ease of making any changes. For some 'robustness' has meant the software's tolerance of incorrect input, while for others it has meant the ability to change program code without introducing errors. The ISO 9126 standard was first introduced in 1991 to tackle the question of the definition of software quality. The original 13-page document was designed as a foundation upon which further, more detailed, standards could be built. The ISO 9126 standards documents are now very lengthy. Partly this is because people with differing motivations might be interested in software quality, namely:

- *acquirers* who are obtaining software from external suppliers;
- *developers* who are building a software product;
- *independent evaluators* who are assessing the quality of a software product, not for themselves but for a community of users – for example, those who might use a particular type of software tool as part of their professional practice.

ISO 9126 has separate documents to cater for these three sets of needs. Despite the size of this set of documentation, it only relates to the definition of software quality attributes. A separate standard ISO 14598 describes the procedures that should be carried out when assessing the degree to which a software product conforms to the selected ISO 9126 quality characteristics. This might seem unnecessary, but it is argued that ISO 14598 could be used to carry out an assessment using a different set of quality characteristics to those in ISO 9126 if circumstances required it.

The difference between internal and external quality attributes has already been noted. ISO 9126 also introduces another type of quality – *quality in use* – for which the following elements have been identified:

- *effectiveness*: the ability to achieve user goals with accuracy and completeness;
- *productivity*: avoiding the excessive use of resources, such as staff effort, in achieving user goals;
- *safety*: within reasonable levels of risk of harm to people and other entities such as business, software, property and the environment;
- *satisfaction*: smiling users.

'Users' in this context includes not only the people who will actually operate the system in which the software will be embedded, but also those who will maintain and enhance the software. The idea of quality in use underlines how the required quality of the software is an attribute not just of the software but also of the context in which it will be used. Taking the IOE scenario as an example, suppose that the invoicing procedure varies considerably depending on the type of product being serviced. This could be because different inputs are needed in different situations in order to calculate the amount due from the client. Say that 95% of invoices currently belong to product type A and the remaining 5% to product B. If the software is written specially for this application, then despite good testing, some errors might still find their way into the operational system. As these are reported and corrected, the software would become more 'mature' as faults become rarer. If there were a rapid switch so that more product B invoices were being processed, there could be an increase in reported faults as coding bugs in the more obscure parts of the software code for product B invoices were flushed out by the increased number of product B transactions. Thus, changes to software use involve changes to software requirements: what is acceptable to one user might not be acceptable to others.

ISO 9126 identifies six major external software quality characteristics:

- *functionality*, which covers the functions that a software product provides to satisfy user needs;
- *reliability*, which relates to the capability of the software to maintain its level of performance;
- *usability*, which relates to the effort needed to use the software;
- *efficiency*, which relates to the physical resources used when the software is executed;
- *maintainability*, which relates to the effort needed to the make changes to the software;
- *portability*, which relates to the ability of the software to be transferred to a different environment.

ISO 9126 suggests sub-characteristics for each of the primary characteristics They are useful as they clarify what is meant by each of the main characteristics.

Characteristic	Sub-characteristics
Functionality	Suitability
	Accuracy
	Interoperability
	Functionality compliance
	Security

'Functionality compliance' refers to the degree to which the software adheres to application-related standards or legal requirements. Typically these could be auditing requirements. Since the original 1999 draft, a sub-characteristic called 'compliance' has been added to all six ISO external characteristics. In each case, this refers to any specific standards that might apply to the particular quality attribute.

'Interoperability' is a good illustration of the efforts of ISO 9126 to clarify terminology. 'Interoperability' refers to the ability of the software to interact with other systems. The framers of ISO 9126 have chosen this word rather than 'compatibility' because the latter causes confusion with the characteristic referred to by ISO 9126 as 'replaceability' (see below).

Characteristic	Sub-characteristics
Reliability	Maturity
	Fault tolerance
	Recoverability
	Reliability compliance

'Maturity' refers to the frequency of failure due to faults in a software product, the implication being that the more the software has been used, the more faults will have been uncovered and removed. It is also interesting to note that 'recoverability' has been clearly distinguished from 'security' which describes the control of access to a system.

Characteristic	Sub-characteristics
Usability	Understandability
	Learnability
	Operability
	Attractiveness
	Usability compliance

Note how 'learnability' is distinguished from 'operability'. A software tool could be easy to learn but time consuming to use because, say, it uses a large number of nested menus. This might be fine for a package used intermittently, but not where the system is used for many hours each day. In this case 'learnability' has been incorporated at the expense of 'operability'.

'Attractiveness' is a recent addition to the sub-characteristics of usability and is especially important where users are not compelled to use a particular software product, as in the case of games and other entertainment products.

Characteristic	Sub-characteristics
Efficiency	Time behaviour
	Resource utilization
	Efficiency compliance
Maintainability	Analysability
	Changeability
	Stability
	Testability
	Maintainability compliance

'Analysability' is the ease with which the cause of a failure can be determined. 'Changeability' is the quality that others have called 'flexibility': the latter name is perhaps a better one as 'changeability' has a slightly different connotation in plain English – it might imply that the suppliers of the software are always changing it!

'Stability', on the other hand, does not mean that the software never changes: it means that there is a low risk of a modification to the software having unexpected effects.

Characteristic	Sub-characteristics
Portability	Adaptability
	Installability
	Co-existence
	Replaceability
	Portability compliance

A new version of a word processing package might read the documents produced by previous versions and thus be able to replace them, but previous versions not be able to read all documents created by the new version.

'Portability compliance' relates to those standards that have a bearing on portability. The use of a standard programming language common to many software/hardware environments would be an example of this. 'Replaceability' refers to the factors that give 'upwards compatibility' between old software components and the new ones. 'Downwards' compatibility is not implied by the definition.

'Co-existence' refers to the ability of the software to share resources with other software components; unlike 'interoperability', no direct data passing is necessarily involved.

ISO 9126 provides guidelines for the use of the quality characteristics. Variation in the importance of different quality characteristics depending on the type of product is stressed. Once the requirements for the software product have been established, the following steps are suggested:

1. Judge the importance of each quality characteristic for the application   Thus reliability will be of particular concern with safety-critical systems while efficiency will be important for some real time systems.

2. Select the external quality measurements within the ISO 9126 framework relevant to the qualities prioritized above   Thus for reliability mean time between failures would be an important measurement, while for efficiency, and more specifically 'time behaviour', response time would be an obvious measurement.

3. Map measurements onto ratings that reflect user satisfaction   For response time, for example, the mappings might be as in Table 12.1.

Table 12.1 Mapping measurements to user satisfaction

Response time (seconds)	Rating
<2	Exceeds expectation
2–5	Within the target range
6–10	Minimally acceptable
>10	Unacceptable

4. Identify the relevant internal measurements and the intermediate products in which they appear This would only be important where software was being developed, rather than existing software being evaluated. For new software, the likely quality of the final product would need to be assessed during development. For example, where the external quality in question was time behaviour, at the software design stage an estimated execution time for a transaction could be produced by examining the software code and calculating the time for each instruction in a typical execution of the transaction. In our view the mappings between internal and external quality characteristics and measurements suggested in the ISO 9126 standard are the least convincing elements in the approach. The part of the standard that provides guidance at this point is a 'technical report' which is less authoritative than a full standard. It concedes that mapping external and internal measurements can be difficult and that validation to check that there is a meaningful correlation between the two in a specific environment needs to be done. This reflects a real problem in the practical world of software development of examining code structure and from that attempting to predict accurately external qualities such as reliability.

According to ISO 9126, measurements that might act as indicators of the final quality of the software can be taken at different stages of the development life cycle. For products at the early stages these indicators might be qualitative. They could, for example, be based on checklists where compliance with predefined criteria is assessed by expert judgement. As the product nears completion, objective, quantitative, measurements would increasingly be taken.

5. Overall assessment of product quality Is it possible to derive a value which conveys an overall judgement of the quality of a software product? This is a contentious issue. It can be seen that the qualities that we have been discussing can be very different from one another. In some cases it could be that the presence of one quality could be to the detriment of another. For example, the efficiency characteristics of time behaviour and resource utilization could be enhanced by exploiting the particular characteristics of the operating system and hardware environments within which the software will perform. This, however, would probably be at the expense of portability. Another factor which discourages attempts at combining the assessments of different quality characteristics is that they can, in practice, be very different and be measured in very different ways, which makes comparison and combination very problematic.

It was noted above that quality assessment could be carried out for a number of different reasons: to assist software development, acquisition or independent assessment.

During the development of a software product, the assessment would be driven by the need to focus the minds of the developers on key quality requirements. The aim would be to identify possible weaknesses early on and there would be no need in this case to produce an overall quality weighting.

In the situation where potential users are assessing a number of different software products in order to choose the best one for their purposes, the outcome will be along the lines that product A is more satisfactory than product B or C. Here some idea of relative satisfaction exists and it appears to us that there is justification in trying to model how this satisfaction might be formed. One approach recognizes some quality rating levels as mandatory. If a product fails to reach a mandatory rating level it must be rejected, regardless of how good it might other-

The problem here is to map an objective measurement onto an indicator of customer satisfaction which is subjective.

Table 12.2 Mapping response times onto user satisfaction

Response time (seconds)	Quality score
<2	5
2–3	4
4–5	3
6–7	2
8–9	1
>9	0

wise be. Other characteristics might be desirable but not essential. For these a user satisfaction rating could be allocated in the range, say, 0–5. This could be based on having an objective measurement of some function and then relating different measurement values to different levels of user satisfaction – see Table 12.2.

In addition to the rating for satisfaction, a rating in the range 1–5, say, could be assigned to reflect how important each quality characteristic was. The scores for the more or less important qualities could be given due weight by multiplying each one by its importance weighting. These weighted scores can then be summed to obtain an overall score for the product. The scores for various products can then be ordered to get a initial scale of preferences. For example, the quality of two products might be compared as to usability, efficiency and maintainability. The importance of each of these qualities might be rated as 3, 4 and 2 respectively, out of a possible maximum of 5. Quality tests might result in the situation shown in Table 12.3.

The final situation where a quality assessment might take place is where the assessor is working on behalf of a user community as a whole. For example, a professional body might be assessing software tools that support the working practices of its members. Unlike the selection by an individual user/purchaser, an attempt is being made to produce an objective assessment of the software, independently of a particular user environment. It is clear that the result of such an exercise would vary considerably depending on the weightings given to each software characteristic, and different users could have very different requirements in this respect. Extreme caution would be needed here.

Table 12.3 Weighted quality scores

Product quality	Importance rating (a)	Product A Quality score (b)	Product A Weighted score (a x b)	Product B Quality score (c)	Product B Weighted score (a x c)
Usability	3	1	3	3	9
Efficiency	4	2	8	2	8
Maintainability	2	3	6	1	2
Overall			17		19

12.6   Practical software quality measures

Below are some methods that might be used to measure particular qualities. It is emphasized that the measures are illustrations only and are certainly not definitive. Each project needs to devise its own measures to meet its specific needs. The measures described relate to the final software products of a project.

Reliability

This might be measured in terms of:

- *availability*: the percentage of a particular time interval that a system is usable;
- *mean time between failures*: the total service time divided by the number of failures;
- *failure on demand*: the probability that a system will not be available at the time required or the probability that a transaction will fail;
- *support activity*: the number of fault reports that are generated and processed.

Exercise 12.3

The IOE maintenance group accounts system has been installed, and is normally available to users from 8.00 a.m. until 6.00 p.m. from Monday to Friday. Over a four-week period the system was unavailable for one whole day because of problems with a disk drive and was not available on two other days until 10.00 in the morning because of problems with overnight batch processing runs.

What were the availability and the mean time between failures of the service?

Maintainability

Maintainability can be seen from two different perspectives. The user will be concerned with the *elapsed time* between a fault being detected and it being corrected, while the software development managers will be concerned about the *effort* involved.

A key component of this is *changeability*, which relates to the ease with which the software can be modified. However, before an amendment can be made, the fault has to be diagnosed. Maintainability can therefore be seen as changeability plus a new quality, *analysability*, which is the ease with which causes of failure can be identified.

Extendibility

When measuring changeability we could identify two aspects: one is the ease with which existing code can be changed while another could be the ease with which new functionality can be added. We might call the latter element of a sub-characteristic 'extendibility' and define it as the productivity needed to incorporate a new feature into an existing system expressed as a percentage of the normal productivity when developing the software from scratch.

CASE STUDY EXAMPLES

The original IOE maintenance billing system comprised 5000 SLOC (source lines of code) and took 400 workdays to implement. An amendment to the core system caused by the introduction of group accounts has led to 100 SLOC being added which took 20 workdays to implement, thus:

productivity for the original system
= 5000/400
= 12·5 SLOC/staff-day

productivity for the amendment
= 100/20
= 5 SLOC/staff-day

extendibility
= 5/12·5 × 100
= 40%

12.7 Product versus process quality management

The measurements described above relate to *products*. Where a product-based approach to the planning and control of a project is used – as is advocated by the PRINCE2 project management method – then this focus on products can be quite convenient. However, as we have seen, it is often easier to measure these product qualities once a computer application has been built rather than during its development. Although we can measure the attributes of intermediate products created at earlier stages of the development project and try to use this to predict the quality of the final application, this in practice is quite difficult. An alternative approach that will be explored in this section is to scrutinize the quality of the *processes* through which the software product is developed.

This model should already be very familiar from the discussion of precedence networks where the dependence of one or more activities on the completion of one or more preceding activities is taken into account.

The system development process is made up of a number of activities that are linked together so that the output from one activity is the input to the next (Figure 12.2). Thus program testing will depend on there being a program to test which will be the deliverable from the program coding stage. Errors can enter the process at any stage. They can either be introduced because of a defect in the way a process is carried out, as when software developers make mistakes in the logic of their software, or because information has not been passed clearly and unambiguously between development stages.

Errors that creep in at the early stages are more expensive to correct at later stages for the following reasons.

- The later the error is found, the more rework at more stages of development will be needed. An error in the specification found in testing will mean rework at all the stages between specification and testing.

- The general tendency is for each successive stage of development to be more detailed and less able to absorb change.

Figure 12.2 An example of the sequence of processes and deliverables

Errors should therefore be eradicated by careful examination of the deliverables of each stage before they are passed on to the next. To do this, the following *process requirements* should be specified for each activity.

These requirements may be laid out in installation standards, or a *Software Quality Plan* may be drawn up for the specific project if it is a major one.

● *Entry requirements*, which have to be in place before an activity can start. An example would be that a comprehensive set of test data and expected results be prepared and approved before program testing can commence.

● *Implementation requirements*, which define how the process is to be conducted. In the testing phase, for example, it could be laid down that whenever an error is found and corrected, all test runs must be repeated, even those that have previously been found to run correctly.

● *Exit requirements*, which have to be fulfilled before an activity is deemed to have been completed. For example, for the testing phase to be recognized as being completed, all tests will have to have been run successfully with no outstanding errors.

Exercise 12.4 In what cases might the entry conditions for one activity be different from the exit conditions for another activity that immediately precedes it?

Exercise 12.5   Amanda at IOE already has a quality manual that she can consult. Brigette at Brightmouth HE College has to specify her own entry and exit requirements. What might she specify as the entry and exit requirements for the process *code program* shown in Figure 12.2?

12.8   External standards

BS EN ISO 9001:2000

The British standard for Quality Management systems was previously called BS 5750. ISO 9001:2000 replaces a previous, 1994, standard.

At IOE, a decision might have been made to use an outside contractor to produce the maintenance group accounts subsystem rather than develop the software in-house. As a client using the services of an outside contractor they would be concerned that the contractor follows the best quality practices. It is now common to include in contracts terms covering the types of technique that a contractor will use. Various national and international standards bodies, including the British Standards Institution (BSI) in the United Kingdom, have inevitably got involved in the creation of standards for quality management systems. The British standard is now called BS EN ISO 9001:2000, which is identical to the international standard, ISO 9001:2000. Standards such as the ISO 9000 series try to ensure that a monitoring and control system to check quality is in place. They are concerned with the certification of the development process, not of the end-product as in the case of crash helmets and electrical appliances with their familiar CE marks. The standards in the ISO 9000 series govern quality systems in general terms and not just those in the software development environment.

ISO 9000 describes the fundamental features of a quality management system (QMS) and defines the terminology used. ISO 9001 describes how a QMS can be applied to the creation of products and the provision of services. ISO 9004 applies to process improvement.

There has been some controversy over the value of these standards. Stephen Halliday, writing in *The Observer*, had misgivings that these standards are taken by many customers to imply that the final product is of a certified standard although as Halliday says, '*It has nothing to do with the quality of the product going out of the gate. You set down your own specifications and just have to maintain them, however low they may be.*' It has also been suggested that obtaining certification can be an expensive and time-consuming process which can put smaller, but still well-run, businesses at a disadvantage. Finally, there has been a concern that a preoccupation with certification might distract attention from the real problems of producing quality products.

Putting aside these reservations, let us examine how the standard works. A primary task is to identify those things which are to be the subject of quality requirements. Having defined the requirements, a system must be put in place which checks that the requirements are being fulfilled and that corrective action is being taken where necessary.

Remember that these standards are designed for all kinds of production – not just software development.

An overview of BS EN ISO 9001:2000 QMS requirements

The standard is built on a foundation of the following principles:

● understanding by an organization of the needs of their customers so that they can meet, or even exceed, those requirements;

- leadership to provide the unity of purpose and direction needed to achieve quality objectives;
- involvement of staff at all levels;
- a focus on the individual processes which create intermediate or deliverable products and services;
- a focus on the systems of interrelated processes that create delivered products and services;
- continuous improvement of processes;
- decision making based on factual evidence;
- building mutually beneficial relationships with suppliers.

The way that these principles are applied is through cycles which involve the following activities:

1. determining the needs and expectations of the customer;
2. establishing a *quality policy*, that is, a framework which allows the organization's objectives in relation to quality to be defined;
3. design of the *processes* which will create the products (or deliver the services) which will have the qualities implied in the organization's quality objectives;
4. allocation of the responsibilities for meeting these requirements for each element of each process;
5. ensuring that adequate resources are available for the proper execution of these processes.
6. design of methods for measuring the effectiveness and efficiency of each process in contributing to the organization's quality objectives;
7. gathering of measurements;
8. identification of any discrepancies between the actual measurements and the target values;
9. analysis of the causes of discrepancies and action to eliminate these causes.

The procedures above should be designed and executed in such a way that there is continual improvement. They should, if carried out properly, lead to an effective QMS. More detailed ISO 9001 requirements include:

- *Documentation* of objectives, procedures (in the form of a *quality manual*), plans, and records relating to the actual operation of processes. The documentation must be subject to a change control system that ensures that it is current. Essentially one needs to be able to demonstrate to an outsider that the QMS exists and is actually adhered to.
- *Management responsibility* – the organization needs to show that the QMS and the processes that produce goods and services conforming to the quality objectives are actively and properly managed.
- *Resources* – an organization must ensure that adequate resources, including appropriately trained staff and appropriate infrastructure, are applied to the processes.
- *Production* should be characterized by:
  - planning;

- determination and review of customer requirements;

- effective communications between the customer and supplier;

- design and development being subject to planning, control and review;

- requirements and other information upon which the design is based being adequately and clearly recorded;

- design outcomes being verified, validated and documented in a way that provides sufficient information for those who have to use the designs; changes to the designs should be properly controlled;

- where components are purchased, there should be adequate measures to specify and evaluate their quality;

- production of goods and the provision of services should be under controlled conditions – these conditions include the adequate provision of information, work instruction, equipment, measurement devices, and post-delivery activities;

- measurement – to demonstrate products conform to standards, and the QMS is effective, and to improve the effectiveness of processes that create products or services.

Exercise 12.6 One of the processes involved in developing software is system testing and subsequent modification to the application in the light of errors found. If a software development organization were to attempt to conform to BS EN ISO 9001:2000, how might this affect system testing?

Exercise 12.7 Bearing in mind the criticisms of BS EN ISO 9001 that have been mentioned, what precautionary steps could a project manager take where some work for which quality is important is to be contracted out?

Capability process models

See H. S. Watts, *Managing the Software Process*, Addison-Wesley, New York, 1989.

Rather than just checking that a system is in place to detect faults, a customer might wish to check that a supplier is using software development methods and tools which are likely to produce good quality software. A customer might feel more confident, for instance, if they knew that the software supplier was using structured methods. In the United States, a number of influential *capability maturity models* (CMM) have been developed at the Software Engineering Institute (SEI), a part of the Carnegie-Mellon University, of which one, SW-CMM, relates specifically to software development. A relatively recent development is the creation of a new version of CMM, CMM Integration or CMMI, which attempts to bring the different models that have been produced for different environments into a single integrated framework. These models attempt to place organizations at one of five levels of process maturity which indicate the sophistication and quality of their production practices. These levels are defined as follows.

The SEI originally developed CMM for the US Department of Defense who wanted to be able to assess the capability of contractors from whom they procured software.

● *Level 1: Initial* The procedures followed tend to be haphazard. Some projects may be successful, but this tends to be because of the skills of particular individuals, including project managers. There is no level 0 and so any organization would be at this level by default.

For more detail, look at the SEI website, www.cmu.edu/sei

Table 12.4 CMMI Key process areas

Level	Key process areas
1. Initial	Not applicable
2. Managed	Requirements management, project planning and monitoring and control, supplier agreement management, measurement and analysis, process and product quality assurance, configuration management
3. Defined	Requirements development, technical solution, product integration, verification, validation, organizational process focus and definition, training, integrated project management, risk management, integrated teaming, integrated supplier management, decision analysis and resolution, organizational environment for integration
4. Quantitatively managed	Organizational process performance, quantitative project management
5. Optimizing	Organizational innovation and deployment, causal analysis and resolution

- *Level 2: Managed* Organizations at this level will have basic project management procedures in place. However, the way individual tasks are carried out will depend largely on the person doing it.

- *Level 3: Defined* The organization has defined the way that each task in the software development life cycle should be done.

- *Level 4: Quantitatively managed* The products and processes involved in software development are subject to measurement and control.

- *Level 5: Optimizing* Improvement in procedures can be designed and implemented using the data gathered from the measurement process.

For each of the levels, apart from the default level 1, *key process areas* (KPAs) have been identified as distinguishing the current level from the lower ones. These are listed in the Table 12.4.

The assessment is done by a team of assessors coming into the organization and interviewing key staff about their practices, using a standard questionnaire to capture the information. A key objective is not just to assess, but to recommend specific actions to bring the organization up to a higher level.

ISO 15504 Process assessment

The main reference in the UK for this standard is BS ISO/IEC 15504-1:2004.

ISO/IEC 15504 is a standard for process assessment that shares many concepts with CMMI. The two standards should be compatible. Like CMMI the standard is designed to provide guidance on the assessment of software development processes. To do this there must be some benchmark or *process reference model* against which a set of processes can be compared. The process reference model represents the ideal development life cycle against which the actual processes can be compared. Various process reference models could be used but the default model is the one described in ISO 12207 which has been briefly discussed in Chapters 1 and 10 and which describes the main processes – such as requirements analysis and architectural design – in the classic software development life cycle.

For a process to be judged to be at Level 3, for example, Levels 1 and 2 must also have been achieved.

Table 12.5 ISO 15504 framework for process capability

Level	Attribute	Comments
0. Incomplete		The process is not implemented or is unsuccessful
1. Performed process	1.1 Process performance	The process produces its defined outcomes
2. Managed process	2.1 Performance management	The process is properly planned and monitored
	2.2 Work product management	Work products are properly defined and reviewed to ensure they meet requirements
3. Established process	3.1 Process definition	The processes to be carried out are carefully defined
	3.2 Process deployment	The processes defined above are properly executed by properly trained staff
4. Predictable process	4.1 Process measurement	Quantitatively measurable targets are set for each sub-process and data collected to monitor performance
	4.2 Process control	On the basis of the data collected by 4.1 corrective action is taken if there is unacceptable variation from the targets
5. Optimizing	5.1 Process innovation	As a result of the data collected by 4.1, opportunities for improving processes are identified
	5.2 Process optimization	The opportunities for process improvement are properly evaluated and where appropriate are effectively implemented

Each of the processes that is to be assessed will be judged on the basis of nine process attributes – see Table 12.5.

When assessors are judging the degree to which a process attribute is being fulfilled they allocate one of the following scores:

Level	Interpretation
N – not achieved	0 to 15% achievement
P – partially achieved	>15% to 50% achievement
L – largely achieved	>50% to 85% achievement
F – fully achieved	>85% achievement

In order to assess the process attribute of a process as being at a certain level of achievement, indicators have to be found that provide evidence for the assessment. To see how this might work we will take the example of the process of *requirements analysis*. In Table 12.6, examples of what might be used as indicators are shown for each process attribute in relation to requirements analysis.

Table 12.6 Possible process attribute indicators for 'requirements analysis'

Process attribute	Example indicators
1.1 Process performance	A requirements analysis document exists.
2.1 Performance management	A plan of how the requirements analysis was to be carried out exists which has been kept up to date as tasks have been completed or modifications to the plan have been made.
2.2 Work product management	There is a standard template used for the requirements document and minutes of a meeting which reviewed the requirements document.
3.1 Process definition	A procedures manual exists which has a section on the conduct of requirements analysis.
3.2 Process deployment	A control document exists which has been signed off as each step of the requirements analysis process, including quality checks, has been completed.
4.1 Process measurement	Data about the performance of the requirements analysis process has been collected and can be examined.
4.2 Process control	Quantitative performance targets for requirements analysis have been identified and documented, for example the number of errors in the software product caused by incorrect requirements.
5.1 Process innovation	There exists a 'lessons learnt' report produced at the end of the project which identifies areas for process improvement.
5.2 Process optimization	There exist documents which assess the feasibility of proposed process improvements and which show consultation with appropriate stakeholders about implementation.

12.9   Techniques to help enhance software quality

So far in this chapter we have looked at the steps a customer might take to ensure the quality of software produced by an outside supplier. We now need to look at what techniques a project team might wish to employ to help them improve their own software development processes. Three main themes emerge.

Gerald Weinberg, *The Psychology of Computer Programming* Silver Anniversary Edition, Dorset House, 1998.

● *Increasing visibility*   A landmark in this movement towards making the software development process more visible was the advocacy by the American software guru, Gerald Weinberg, of 'egoless programming'. Weinberg encouraged the simple practice of programmers looking at each other's code.

● *Procedural structure*   At first, programmers were more or less left to get on with writing programs although there might be some general guidelines. Over the years there has been the growth of methodologies where every process in the software development cycle has carefully laid down steps.

The creation of an early working model of a system may still be useful, as the creation of prototypes shows.

● *Checking intermediate stages* It seems inherent in human nature to push forward quickly with the development of any engineered object until a 'working' model, however imperfect, has been produced which can then be 'debugged'. One of the elements of the move towards quality practices has been to put emphasis on checking the correctness of work at its earlier, conceptual, stages.

There has, in recent years, been a move away from checking the products of intermediate stages and towards building an application as far as possible as a number of relatively independent components which can be developed quickly and be tested at an early stage. This can avoid some of the problems, noted earlier, of attempting to predict the external quality of the software from early design documents.

We are now going to look at some specific techniques in more detail. The push towards more visibility has been dominated by the increasing use of walk-throughs, inspections and reviews. The movement towards more procedural structure inevitably leads to discussion of structured programming techniques and to its later manifestation in the ideas of 'clean-room' software development.

The interest in the dramatic improvements made by the Japanese in product quality has led to much discussion of the quality techniques they have adopted, such as the use of quality circles, and these will be looked at briefly. Some of these ideas are variations on the theme of inspection and clean-room development, but they are seen from a slightly different angle.

Inspections

The principle of inspection can be extended to any document produced at any stage of the development process. For instance, test cases need to be reviewed – their production is usually not a high profile task even though errors can get through to operational running because of their poor quality.

The main problem is maintaining the commitment of participants to a thorough examination of the work distributed to them after the novelty value of reviews has worn off a little.

Inspection means that when a piece of work is completed, copies of the work are distributed to co-workers who then examine the work noting defects. A meeting is then held to discuss the work and a list of defects requiring rework is produced. The work to be examined could be, for instance, a program listing that is free of compilation errors.

Our own experience of using this technique has been that:

● it is a very effective way of removing superficial errors;

● it motivates developers to produce better structured and self-explanatory software because they know that other people will be criticizing it;

● it helps spread good programming practices as the participants discuss the advantages and disadvantages of specific pieces of code;

● it can enhance team spirit.

This is sometimes called 'peer review', where 'peers' are people who are equals.

The item will usually be reviewed by colleagues who are involved in the same area of work, so that programmers, for example, will have their work reviewed by fellow programmers. However, to reduce the problems of incorrect communication between different stages there may be representatives from the stages that precede and follow the one which produced the work under review.

IBM put the review process on a more structured and formal basis, and produced statistics to show its effectiveness. A Fagan inspection (named after the IBM

See M. E. Fagan's article 'Design and code inspections to reduce errors in program development' in *IBM Systems Journal*, 15(3).

employee who pioneered the technique) is a much more formalized procedure which is led, not by the author of the work, but by a specially trained 'moderator'.

The general principles behind the Fagan method

- Inspections are carried out on all major deliverables.

- All types of defect are noted – not just logic or function errors.

- Inspections can be carried out by colleagues at all levels except the very top.

- Inspections are carried out using a predefined set of steps.

- Inspection meetings do not last for more than two hours.

- The inspection is lead by a *moderator* who has had specific training in the technique.

- The other participants have defined roles. For example, one person will act as a *recorder* and note all defects found and another will act as *reader* and take the other participants through the document under inspection.

- Checklists are used to assist the fault-finding process.

- Material is inspected at an optimal rate of about 100 lines an hour.

- Statistics are maintained so that the effectiveness of the inspection process can be monitored.

Exercise 12.8

Compare and contrast the peer review process described above with pair programming which is advocated as part of extreme programming (XP).

Exercise 12.9

This exercise needs to be done in groups. Select for review a small program that has been written by one of your colleagues.

Choose a moderator, a reader and a recorder for the group. Spend about 20 minutes examining listings of the program individually and then come together to review the code jointly.

Structured programming and clean-room software development

E. W. Dijkstra in 1968 wrote a letter to a learned computing journal which was entitled 'Go To Statement Considered Harmful'. This unfortunately led to the common idea that structured programming was simply about not using GO TOs.

One of the people most closely associated with the origins of structured programming is Dijkstra. In the late 1960s, software was seen to be getting more complex while the capacity of the human mind to hold detail remained limited. It was also realized that it was impossible to test any substantial piece of software completely – there were just too many possible combinations of inputs. Testing, at best, could prove the presence of errors, not their absence. It was suggested by Dijkstra and others that, because of this, the only way that we could reassure ourselves about the correctness of software was by actually looking at the code.

The way to deal with complex systems, it was contended, was to break them down into components which were of a size for the human mind to comprehend. For a large system there would be a hierarchy of components and sub-components. For this decomposition to work properly, each component would have to be self-contained, with only one entry and exit point.

The ideas of structured programming have been further developed into the ideas of clean-room software development by people such as the late Harlan Mills of IBM. With this type of development there are three separate teams:

Usage profiles reflect the need to assess *quality in use* as discussed earlier in relation to ISO 9126.

The incremental approach was discussed in Chapter 4.

- *a specification team*, which obtains the user requirements and also a *usage profile* estimating the volume of use for each feature in the system;
- *a development team*, which develops the code but which does no machine testing of the program code produced;
- *a certification team*, which carries out testing.

Any system is produced in increments, each of which should be capable of actual operation by the end-user. The development team does no debugging; instead, all software has to be verified by them using mathematical techniques. The argument is that software which is constructed by throwing up a crude program, which then has test data thrown at it and a series of hit-and-miss amendments made to it until it works, is bound to be unreliable.

The certification team carry out the testing which is continued until a statistical model shows that the failure intensity has been reduced to an acceptable level.

Formal methods

The section on clean-room development mentioned the use of mathematical verification techniques. These techniques use unambiguous, mathematically-based, specification languages of which Z and VDM are examples. They are used to define *pre-conditions* and *post-conditions* for each procedure. Pre-conditions define the allowable states, before processing, of the various items of data upon which a procedure is to work. The post-conditions define the state of those data items after the procedure has been executed. Because the mathematical notation is precise, a specification expressed in this way should be unambiguous. It should also be possible to prove mathematically (in much the same way that at school you learnt to prove Pythagoras' theorem) that a particular algorithm will work on the data defined by the pre-conditions in such a way as to produce the post-conditions. Clearly, in many cases this will be more easily said than done. In fact structured programming, and more latterly object-oriented development, can be seen as attempts to analyse a program structure into small, self-contained, procedures that will be amenable to this formal verification approach.

Software quality circles

Much interest has been shown in Japanese software quality practices. The aim of the 'Japanese' approach is to examine and modify the activities in the development process in order to reduce the number of errors that they have in their end-products. Testing and Fagan inspections can assist the removal of errors – but the same types of error could occur repeatedly in successive products created by a process. By uncovering the source of errors, this repetition can be eliminated.

Staff are involved in the identification of sources of errors through the formation of *quality circles*. These can be set up in all departments of an organization, including those producing software where they are known as software quality circles (SWQC).

A quality circle is a group of four to ten volunteers working in the same area who meet for, say, an hour a week to identify, analyse and solve their work-related problems. One of their number is the group leader and there could be an outsider, a *facilitator*, who can advise on procedural matters. In order to make the quality circle work effectively training needs to be given.

Together the quality group select a pressing problem that affects their work. They identify what they think are the causes of the problem and decide on a course of action to remove these causes. Often, because of resource or possible organizational constraints, they will have to present their ideas to management to obtain approval before implementing the process improvement.

Exercise 12.10	What are the important differences between a quality circle and a review group?

People may feel inhibited from contributing ideas to a group and brainstorming can help to reduce this inhibition.

Brainstorming is a technique particularly associated with quality circles. A subject or problem for which ideas are needed is nominated and the group then suggest as many ideas as possible. As ideas are suggested they are written down on a flip-chart. Other members of the group do not, at this stage, make any comments. At the end of the session the group go through the ideas listed and combine similar or overlapping ideas. Typically this technique would be used to generate the initial list of problems or a list of possible solutions to a particular problem.

Also associated with quality circles is the compilation of *most probable error lists.* For example, at IOE, Amanda might find that the maintenance group accounts project is being delayed because of errors in the requirements specifications. The project team could be assembled and spend some time producing a list of the most common types of error that occur in requirements specifications. This is then used to identify measures which can reduce the occurrence of each type of error. They might suggest, for instance, that test cases be produced at the same time as the requirements specification and that these test cases should be dry run at an inspection. Another result might be a checklist for use when conducting inspections of requirement specifications.

Exercise 12.11	This exercise has to be carried out as a group. Select a particular area of common experience where problems have arisen in the past. For example if you are a group of students you could use the course or module you are undertaking, or a recent assignment that you have just completed. By means of a brainstorming session, identify all the problems that the participants have had. At the end of the brainstorming session, group together similar problems and combine overlapping ones.

A further activity could be to select one of the problems and then brainstorm ideas for its solution.

The problems needing crisis management are often technical in nature. Quality circles can encourage problem solving activity at lower levels of the organization and prevent crises occurring as their causes are tackled.

The effectiveness of quality circles

For quality circles to work there must be full support for them at all levels of management. First-line management could feel threatened by them as they appear to undermine their authority. After all, problem solving is one of their main tasks. The proponents of quality circles see them as a way of giving management more time for planning and development. Any manager will have to devote time to 'fire-fighting', dealing with *ad hoc* crises, and this can detract from longer-term activities which will be able to improve the effectiveness of the organization.

12.10 Quality plans

Some organizations produce *quality plans* for each project. These, in essence, show how the standard quality procedures and standards that should be laid down in an organization's *quality manual* will actually be applied to a particular project. If an approach to planning such as Step Wise has been followed, quality-related activities and requirements should have been identified by the main planning process and a separate quality plan would not be required. However, where software is being produced for an external customer then their quality assurance staff might require the equivalent of a quality plan to make sure that the delivered products are likely to be of high quality. A quality plan might also be required as a kind of checklist that all quality issues have been dealt with by the planning process. In this case most of the content will be references to other documents.

A quality plan might have entries for:

This contents list is based on a draft IEEE standard for software quality assurance plans.

- purpose – scope of plan;
- list of references to other documents;
- management arrangements, including organization, tasks and responsibilities;
- documentation to be produced;
- standards, practices and conventions;
- reviews and audits;
- testing;
- problem reporting and corrective action;
- tools, techniques and methodologies;
- code, media and supplier control;
- records collection, maintenance and retention;
- training;
- risk management – the methods of risk management that are to be used.

12.11 Conclusion

Important points to remember about software quality include the following.

- Quality by itself is a vague concept and practical quality requirements have to be carefully defined.

- There have to be practical ways of testing for the relative presence or absence of quality.

- Most of the qualities that are apparent to the users of software can only be tested for when the system is completed.

- Therefore ways are needed of checking during development what the quality of the final system is likely to be.

- Some quality-enhancing techniques concentrate on testing the products of the development process while others try to evaluate the quality of the development processes used.

12.12 Further exercises

1. An organization is contemplating the purchase of a project planning software tool, such as MS Project, and has decided to draw up quality specifications for the package.

   The features that they are particularly concerned with are:

   - setting up details of new projects;
   - allocating resources to project tasks, taking account of the need for resource smoothing;
   - updating the project details with information about actual tasks completed;
   - the effective presentation of plans.

   Draw up quality specifications in respect of the qualities of:

   - usability
   - reliability
   - recoverability.

2. The following is an excerpt from a report generated from a help-desk logging system.

Module	Date fault reported	Fault corrected	Effort (hours)
AA247	1.4.2004	2.4.2004	5
AA247	10.4.2004	5.5.2004	4
AA247	12.4.2004	5.5.2004	3
AA247	6.5.2004	7.5.2004	2

   Assess the maintainability of module AA247 from the point of view of:

   - the user management;
   - the developer management.

3. Discuss how meaningful the following measurements are.
   (a) The number of error messages produced on the first compilation of a program.
   (b) The average effort to implement changes requested by users to a system.
   (c) The percentage of lines in program listings that are comments.
   (d) The number of pages in a requirements document.

4. How might you measure the effectiveness of a user manual for a software package? Consider both the measurements that might be applicable and the procedures by which the measurements might be taken.

5. What might the entry, implementation and exit requirements be for the process *design program structure*?

6. In Table 12.6, possible indicators were suggested which might show that the requirements analysis process within an organization was satisfactory at various process attribute levels. Show how similar indicators could be identified for the process of acceptance testing.

7. Identify a task that you do as part of your everyday work. For that task identify entry, process and exit requirements.

8. What BS EN ISO 9001 requirements have a bearing on the need for an effective configuration management system?

CHAPTER 13

Small projects

Objectives

When you have completed this chapter you will be able to:

- avoid some of the pitfalls that occur with students' projects;
- product an initial planning document for a small, ICT-related project.

13.1 Introduction

Many of the readers of this book are students who will have to plan their own projects that they will have to carry out as part of their course of studies. In some cases, these will be undertaken for an external client. In other cases, a piece of software, perhaps of an experimental nature, is to be produced where there is no identifiable client, apart from a project tutor. Although the projects that are carried out for 'real' clients are more convincing tests of the student, they are in many ways more risky than the purely academic ones.

One of the problems that students face when planning projects is applying techniques that they have learnt on software project planning courses and that were designed for much larger scale projects than their own. In this chapter we present an outline of how students should set out their plans. It is based on a structure that we have recommended to our own students over the years. It contrasts with the material in Appendix A on PRINCE2, which is designed to support the management of large projects. The overall Step Wise approach is still applicable to the planning of your project – but the techniques used at the different steps of the planning process will need to be carefully chosen as appropriate to the scaled-down application.

13.2 Some problems with student projects

There are some problems or risks that seem particularly to affect student projects.

Note that here we are discussing a practical application of the risk identification and avoidance policies.

Use of unfamiliar tools

Very often students will be using a new software tool (for example, an application builder in a Windows environment) that they have not used before. Clearly, time

283

will need to be allocated in the project plan to learning the package. When trying to formulate plans, because of their ignorance of the software tool, students might have difficulties estimating how long tasks will take. There will also be risks that unexpected technical problems will halt or delay the project's process. Students often have other things on their minds, such as examinations, in the period leading up to the start of the project, but the risks of technical problems will be reduced if they are able to try out the software tools at this point.

If you are really keen to learn about and use a new tool, you might consider framing the objectives of the project to include an evaluation of the tool. Technical difficulties then become transformed from being obstacles to being interesting data.

Uncertain design requirements

Many project assignments require students to demonstrate a careful analysis and design process and then to build at least part of the application. Until the analysis has been done, it can be difficult to plan exactly how design and software building is to be executed.

Two points are worth making here. The first is that the structure of the project is going to be dictated to a large extent by the amount of time available.

Say that you have ten weeks in which to carry out a project that involves analysing user requirements, designing a new system and building it. It is not a bad idea to start planning on the basis of doing the project in nine weeks in order to allow for slippage. Working backwards from the end, of those nine weeks, it might be decided that the last two should be reserved for testing and evaluation. This might seem an excessive amount of time to some students, but with most assessment schemes your project is likely to gain really good marks if you can demonstrate that it is of good quality and that you have evaluated it carefully. You might decide to allocate proportions of the remaining first seven weeks to analysis, design and system building so that you get the following skeleton schedule:

- *weeks 1–2*: analysis;
- *week 3*: design;
- *weeks 4–7*: system building;
- *weeks 8–9*: testing and evaluation;
- *week 10*: contingency.

The actual breakdown will vary, depending on the circumstances of your particular project. A very well-structured problem area means that you can spend less time on analysis, while, on the other hand, if you know the software building tools that you are going to use, you might decide to reduce the time for analysis in favour of devoting more effort to a more sophisticated operator interface.

The second point, a one that we have already emphasized, is that you should be prepared to delay planning a particular phase of a project in detail until more information becomes available. When you have completed your analysis phase at the end of the second week in the above plan, you should be in a much better position to plan the design and system building phases in more detail – you will know, for example, what the main transactions are going to be in an information systems application. You should also be in a position to cut down the scope of the application to fit the time available to build it!

In Chapter 8 we discussed the practice of design to cost, that is, designing the system to fit the resources available to build it.

In Chapter 4 we discussed the incremental approach which is relevant here.

Incomplete systems

Sometimes students simply run out of time and so do not have a working system to demonstrate. In the case of student projects, it is a good idea to try to arrange things so that you have something, even if it is not much, to demonstrate from a relatively early stage of the project. In the skeleton plan described above, it would not be a bad idea to have certain features of the application up and running after the first week or so of system building. Having these 'in the bag' so to speak, you can go on and add new functions or features, secure in the knowledge that at any point you will have at least something to demonstrate. You might find that you can even break the work down into increments to give you something similar to the following:

- *weeks 1–2*: analysis;
- *week 3*: design increment 1;
- *week 4*: build/test increment 1;
- *week 5*: design increment 2;
- *week 6*: build/test increment 2;
- *week 7*: design increment 3;
- *week 8*: build/test increment 3;
- *week 9*: evaluate complete system;
- *week 10*: writing up/contingency.

If something went wrong so that increment 3 could not be completed on time, you would still have increments 1 and 2 to demonstrate and in your project evaluation report you could describe your proposed design for increment 3.

In the skeleton plan above, we have allowed week 10 for writing up. As a general rule, it is best to try and write up as much of your project as you can as you go along. It will not save you any time if you leave it and you will be able to write more clearly and fully about your analysis process, for example, while it is still clear in your mind. Pausing to do this writing should also help you to reflect on what you are doing and help you consider coolly what needs to be done next.

Lack of commitment from clients

In most cases, where a project is for an external client, the student will not be being paid. The advantage of this is that the outside organization might be attracted to the chance of having a free resource and take on a project for a student about whose capabilities they know little or nothing. The danger is that because the resource is free, there will be little commitment from the client to the project. If they had to pay for the work, they would think more carefully about whether they really needed the work before agreeing to the project and they would pay attention to getting value for money.

There is no such thing as a completely free project, even when the student's efforts are free. The student might need access to hardware and software facilities to be provided by the client and even where this is not the case, the client needs to be prepared to give up some spare time to discuss requirements and to evaluate intermediate results. It has to be said that sometimes clients can let students down as far as this is concerned. Our advice to students would be to try to get to know your client thoroughly before the project starts. Try, for instance, to meet all the people in the organization who will be affected by your work before you actually get going on the project. Show a copy of your initial project plan to the clients and get them to comment on it. Arrange beforehand to have regular meetings with them to discuss progress.

13.3 Content of a project plan

We discuss below what should be in your project planning document. It is suggested that the plans for small projects being done for outside clients should follow this format. Specific course requirements (for example, learning objectives) are not covered.

1 Introduction

In the introduction to any document, it is always a good idea to explain briefly what the document is and why it has been produced. The introduction to the project plan should also include:

- identity of client – that is, the organization or department for whom the work is to be done;
- short description of project – not more than two or three brief lines;
- identity of the project authority – the person or persons within the client organization who will have authority over the project's direction. It is essential that such an authority be identified.

2 Background

This includes:

- relevant information about the client's business;
- descriptions of the existing software/hardware environment;
- circumstances or problems leading to the current project;
- work already carried out in the area of the project;
- stakeholders in the projects, in other words, all those who will be affected by the project or who have some other interest in it.

3 Objectives of the project

These might already have been defined in a terms of reference (TOR) document. If so, then it can be attached as an appendix to the plan.

The objectives must define what is to be achieved and the method of measuring the extent of that achievement. One problem with small projects conducted by students is that the project's success is evaluated in course terms soon after its completion, whereas the project's true value to the users will take much longer to emerge (if ever!). As this document is in part for the benefit of the client, the objectives from the client's viewpoint should have the emphasis here.

Students sometimes have problems distinguishing between their personal objectives and those of the project. The project objectives are those that are held

Objectives and goals were discussed in Chapter 1.

in common between the client and the developer in relation to the project. For example, a university student could be producing a timetabling system for a local school. The creation of this timetabling system would be a project objective shared by the developer (the student) and the client (the school). The student will also have a personal objective of getting a good grade that is not shared by the school (although they will usually be sympathetic to it). From the viewpoint of the student's personal objectives the creation of the timetabling system is seen as a sub-objective, or goal, a step on the way to achieving the overarching objective of getting the good grade.

Where there are several objectives, an order of priority should be given to them if this is possible.

4   Constraints

It is convenient to merge this into the project objectives, above. Constraints include:

- externally imposed time scales;
- legal requirements;
- specific standards;
- limitations on the people who can be approached for information.

5   Methods/technology to be used

These might have already have been laid down for you, or it might be that part of the project will involve the selection of the most appropriate technologies and methods. In other cases, you need to specify the general approach you will take – for instance that you are going to use a structured systems analysis and design method (like SSADM), or a soft system methodology (like SSM) approach. In a small project it is unlikely that you will have time for a full structured analysis/design approach and you might decide to use a subset of the techniques – this should be specified.

The methods selected will, of course, govern much of what will go into Section 6 below on project products and Section 7 on activities. When discussing prototypes, we emphasized that a prototype should always be a tool for learning or clarifying something (for instance, the best interface for the user). If you claim you are producing a prototype, you must be prepared to define learning objectives for the prototype, a method of evaluation and an analysis of what has been learnt.

If you are developing software, the choice of software tools should be stated in this section.

Some justification of the decisions made here should be given, as they can be crucial to the success of the project.

The training and other resource requirements (perhaps the need to purchase a particular package) that result from the decisions should be noted.

6   Project products

This is a list of all the products or deliverables that the project will produce, such as software modules, documentation, user guides and reports.

Intermediate products, such as design documents, should be included.

7   Activities

The drawing up of a Product Flow Diagram helps to bridge between the product list and the activity plan – see Chapter 2.

This is a list of the main activities that the project will involve. There must be activities to produce all the products listed in Section 6. Also, in general, each activity should result in some deliverable: avoid tasks like 'familiarization with department procedures' in favour of 'documentation of departmental procedures'. In identifying activities, new interim products will often be discovered.

For each activity, define:

- *pre-requisites*: what has to be done before this activity can start;
- *dependent activities*: activities that need this one to be completed first;
- *estimated time/effort*: this may be a range of values;
- *quality checks*: details of how you are going to verify and validate the product of the activity.

PERT or Gantt charts may be used, but are often not needed.

8   Resources

This includes staff time, accommodation and hardware/software requirements.

9   Risk analysis

Identify the main things that can be seen as possibly going wrong. Typically this might include:

- unavailability of resources (as with a delay in getting a software package);
- unavailability of key client personnel;
- technical problems (such as software bugs).

Roughly a probability rating of 2 means 2 chances out of 10 of it occurring

A priority can be given to each risk by allocating a *probability rating* (1–10) and a seriousness of *impact rating* (1–10). Multiplying the two together gives an overall score for priority purposes.

For the most serious risks (those with the highest scores), *preventive* measures to reduce or remove the risk should be specified. For example, in order to prevent problems with the unavailability of key client personnel, meetings must be arranged with them at the planning stage and holiday plans could be ascertained. In some cases *contingency* measures that can be undertaken once the risk has actually materialized are more appropriate.

13.4   Conclusion

In this chapter, we have tried to show how some of the broader issues of project planning that have been covered elsewhere in the book can be related to the kind of task a student might be asked to undertake as a project. On the other hand, a student undertaking a substantial industrial placement might be involved in a project team undertaking a large project and using a method such as PRINCE2, described in Appendix A, to control the project.

Important points to remember include:

- take care when using techniques or tools that are completely new to you in a project:

- you will have to adjust the scope of your project to fit the time available;

- take steps to maintain the commitment of the client to your 'free' project;

- recognize the distinction between the project objectives and your personal objectives;

- avoid planning activities for which there is no tangible result – such as 'familiarization'.

PRINCE2 – an overview

A.1 Introduction to PRINCE2

The OGC is the Office of Government Commerce, which has replaced the CCTA, the Central Computer and Telecommunications Agency.

PRINCE stands for 'PRojects IN Controlled Environments'.

Large organizations can have a number of software and other projects being executed at the same time. Some of these might use external suppliers of products and services. In such an environment it would be helpful if the procedures by which each project were run were standardized rather than having to be continually reinvented. However, each project will make different demands on management: some, for example, might be more technically challenging, might affect particularly critical areas of the business or might involve larger numbers of different types of users. Because the adoption of a management method is not cost-free, the degree of control that will be cost-effective will vary from project to project. Hence any standard approach should incorporate mechanisms to tailor management procedures and structures to suit localized needs. In the UK, the government has sponsored, through the OGC, a set of such procedures, called PRINCE, which has, after several years, been revised as PRINCE2.

The precursor to PRINCE was a project management method called PROMPT, which suffered from the defect that it was not flexible enough to deal adequately with all types of project. This was followed by the first version of PRINCE, which was designed primarily for an ICT development environment so that, for example, it was made to have a good fit with SSADM. It soon became apparent, however, that the method was applicable to projects outside the strictly ICT domain and PRINCE2 makes no specific references to ICT development.

It is now possible to take examinations in PRINCE2 and to be thus recognized as a PRINCE practitioner.

A.2 The components of PRINCE2

The method does not claim to cover all aspects of project management. It has the following components:

- organization;
- planning;
- controls;

- stages;
- management of risk;
- quality;
- configuration management;
- change control.

The following list provides a convenient structure that we will use to explain PRINCE2:

- techniques;
- organization;
- documentation;
- procedures.

This appendix will not explore the supplementary techniques where the PRINCE2 manual lays down some basic requirements. We do not describe these areas in detail since there is sufficient material elsewhere in this book. They include:

- risk management;
- quality management;
- configuration management;
- change control.

Below, we will outline the general approach to planning that PRINCE2 advocates. It will be noted that PRINCE2, compared, for example, to SSADM, is rather light in its description of techniques. It is stronger in its rules for the project management structures that should be adopted. In our view, its main focus is on the project as an information system. Project management information is identified and the procedures by which the various elements of this information are created, processed and used are described at some length. This project information is mainly associated with the delivery of *products*, in a controlled environment, resulting in benefits to the business.

A.3 PRINCE planning technique

The Step Wise approach was outlined in Chapter 2, while risk was discussed in Chapter 7.

Figure A.1 shows the stages in the planning process that are suggested by PRINCE2. The first of these – *Design a plan* – is essentially deciding what kind of information is to go into the plan, particularly at what level of detail the plan is to be drawn. The remaining steps are very similar to the Step Wise approach to planning that was outlined in Chapter 2, except that in the Step Wise approach the risk analysis was carried out immediately after the estimation of effort for each activity. This was because in our view risk identification follows on naturally from estimation: you work out how long you think it will take to do an activity and then you consider what factors could work to make that estimate incorrect. Also, the identification of risks can lead to new activities being introduced to avoid the risks occurring and this is conveniently done before the schedule is put together by allocating resources. However, the Step Wise approach is not necessarily at odds with PRINCE2 as PRINCE2 does emphasize the iterative nature of risk analysis.

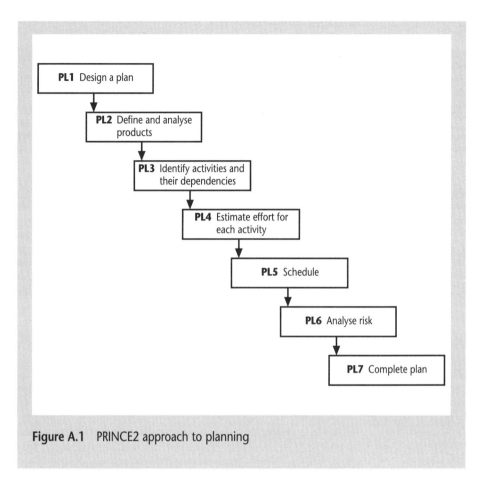

Figure A.1   PRINCE2 approach to planning

Like Step Wise, PRINCE2 is very product-based. In the second planning phase, PL2 in figure A.1, all the business products, plus the management and quality documents needed to control their delivery, are identified.

This sequence of steps can be used in several places in the PRINCE2 procedural framework to produce a variety of different types of plan.

A.4   PRINCE2 project organization

PRINCE identifies roles rather than jobs. Depending on the circumstances, a role could, in fact, be carried out by more than one person, or a single person could assume more than one role.

PRINCE2 is based on the perception that the project will involve *users* of the products of the project, on the one hand, and *suppliers* of goods and services needed by the project on the other. While the users and suppliers could in fact belong to the same organization, for management and control purposes the two sides need to be carefully distinguished. Furthermore, on the customer side, two management roles exist. Any development project is carried out, not for its own sake, but to do something useful for the customer organization. The *Executive* role has the responsibility of ensuring that the project continues to meet these business requirements. A danger, for example, is that development costs might grow in such a way that they exceed any benefits of the completed project. The customer side will also, of course, contain the community who will actually use the completed system on a day-to-day basis. Although we have talked about the supplier and customer sides, it could also be argued that the suppliers who will provide the system and the users who will operate it need to cooperate together to ensure that the operational system provides the benefits sought after by their customer, the 'Executive'.

PRINCE2 specifies that the three roles of *Executive*, *Supplier* and *User* are represented on a *Project Board* which has overall accountability for the success of the project and responsibility for the commitment of resources.

Note that we have followed the convention of indicating specific PRINCE2 terms by initial capital letters, Project Board, for example. All these terms are as in the PRINCE2 manual, which has Crown copyright.

The senior staff carrying out the respective roles will be responsible officers within their respective organizations and the oversight of the project will probably by only one of many responsibilities. Hence, the task of managing the project on a day-to-day basis will be delegated by the Project Board to a *Project Manager*. On a large project it could be necessary for the Project Manager to delegate the managing of certain aspects of the project to specialist *Team Managers*.

Conscientious and motivated staff will inevitably focus on meeting user requirements and give a lower priority to dealing with what they might see as project management 'red tape'. It could even be that the Project Manager with the daily burden of pushing the project forward might not be immune to this. However, this 'red tape' is needed to ensure that the project remains under control and that it continues to meet its business justification. Thus, some assurance is needed, independent of project management, that project management procedures are being properly followed. The ultimate responsibility for this assurance resides with the Project Board, but in practice detailed project assurance could be carried out by staff, independent of the team executing the project, who report to the Project Board members. Different types of project assurance specialists might be employed to ensure the business justification of the project is maintained, that the users' needs are being met and that the necessary technical requirements are being adhered to by the suppliers.

Project support

The Project Board, Project Manager, Team Leaders and project assurance and support staff are known collectively in PRINCE2 as the Project Management Team.

The Project Manager can require day-to-day support with the administration of the project. This might involve such tasks as processing time sheets or updating a computer-based project management tool such as Microsoft Project. It could be convenient for one group within an organization to supply this support to a number of projects. A key member of the project support team will be the Configuration Librarian, who will keep track of the latest versions of the products and documents generated by the project.

A.5 Project Stages

It is sensible to divide large projects into more manageable segments. PRINCE2 caters for this through the idea of *Stages*. These are subsets of the project activities and are managed as a sequence of individual units. Normally, the Project Manager will, at any one time, be authorized by the Project Board to execute only the current Stage. The Project Manager will be able to start the next Stage only when the Project Board has met to give its approval for the plans for that Stage. The end of a Stage signals a decision point when the Project Board will review the progress to date and reassure itself that the project is still viable from a business point of view – in particular, that the expected benefits are still likely to justify the projected costs.

The typical system development life cycle contains a number of phases, where each phase makes use of different specialist techniques. These technical phases might be the typical steps outlined in Chapter 1: requirements analysis and specification, logical design, physical design, build, testing and installation. It is convenient in many cases for the management Stages specified by PRINCE2 to be mapped onto these technical phases, but the PRINCE2 standards are at pains to stress that it is not always convenient to do this – for instance the project might be more manageable if more than one technical phase were combined to create a Stage.

As will be explained in more detail in Section A.8 on 'Starting a project', at the beginning of a project a *Project Plan* will be created which will give the envisaged Stages. Only the first of these Stages will need to have a detailed *Stage Plan* immediately available. For the later stages, it is better to complete the detailed Stage Plan just a little while before the Stage is due to start. In that way, the Stage Plan can take account of a more complete picture of the project: at the beginning of the project, for example, it would be impossible to plan the system building stage in detail when the system requirement has not yet been clearly defined.

Once the Stage has been authorized and its execution has been embarked upon, the Project Board should not need to meet as long as any deviations from planned time and cost are only minor and are within laid-down project tolerances. It should be sufficient for members of the Project Board to receive regular reports from the Project Manager. If these tolerances are likely to be exceeded, then the Project Manager has a responsibility to produce an Exception Report for the Project Board. If the problems are serious enough to undermine the Stage Plan, then the Project Manager might then be required to produce a modified Stage Plan, or more properly an Exception Plan, which the Project Board will need to approve formally. In extreme circumstances the Project Board might at this point decide to terminate the project prematurely.

A.6   Project procedures

Table A.1 lists the main project management processes for which PRINCE2 lays down procedures to deal with the various events that the Project Management Team might encounter.

The levels of staff who are involved with each of the groups of project management processes in Table A.1 are indicated in Figure A.2. The general planning process PL is not shown as this can take place at various times and places for different reasons. For example, it could take place during the 'Initiating a project' (IP) process to create the Project Plan, or during 'Managing stage boundaries' (SB) when a Stage Plan for the next Stage is constructed or when an Exception Plan needs to be produced.

Table A.1 Major PRINCE2 processes

PRINCE ID	Major processes
SU	Starting up a project
IP	Initiating a project
DP	Directing a project
CS	controlling a stage
MP	Managing product delivery
SB	Managing stage boundaries
CP	Closing a project
PL	Planning

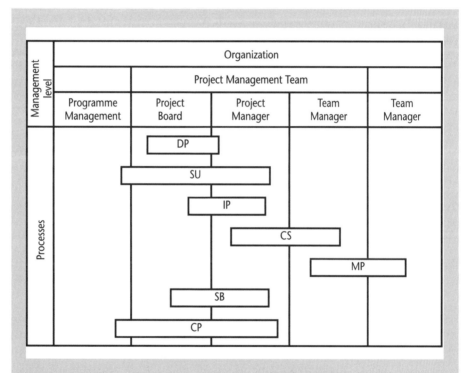

Figure A.2 Project management roles (see Table A.1 for key)

A.7 Directing a project

The main points where the Project Board have to be active are covered by the DP processes – *Directing a project*. These points are:

● authorizing initiation – agreeing to the start of detailed planning of a project;
● authorizing a project – agreeing, after the planning has been completed, that the project can go ahead;

- authorizing a Stage or Exception Plan;
- giving *ad hoc* direction;
- closing a project.

A.8   Starting up a project

With the first version of PRINCE there were sometimes difficulties knowing at which point the project had really started. The separate processes of Start Up and Initiation could avoid this.

As we noted in Chapter 3, the decision to undertake a project does not spring out of thin air. Where a customer organization has a coherent strategy, it is likely that there will be a layer of *programme management* where the 'programme' is a group of projects that are coordinated to meet an integrated set of business requirements. The current project could therefore be triggered by the programme managers. In any case, PRINCE2 envisages that the project cycle will be sparked by some kind of *Project Mandate,* which will identify the customer and the general subject of the project. The PRINCE2 Start Up process is essentially concerned with getting into a position where detailed planning of the proposed project can begin. As a starting point, this will need the recruitment of people to the various roles in the Project Management Team. The Project Mandate, which could be a rather insubstantial or imprecise document, might need to be refined and expanded into a *Project Brief,* which defines the objectives of the project. Based on this, the general technical approach to be adopted to meet these objectives needs to be decided upon and documented in the *Project Approach*. The kinds of issue raised in Chapter 4 will need to be considered at this point. This could involve decisions about whether an off-the-shelf package can be bought or whether a bespoke package is required, and, if so, whether its development is to be carried out 'in-house' or by external contractors. All these activities lead to the formulation of a general plan of how the detailed planning is to be carried out.

A.9   Initiating the project

Having completed the Start Up Process, the Project Board can now decide that there are sufficient grounds to go on to more detailed planning. This begins with the consideration of a *Project Quality Plan*. Despite what some books suggest, quality levels do have cost implications. Different projects will have different quality requirements – faults in a college timetabling system are annoying but do not have the same consequences as the failure of a system controlling the flight of a passenger aeroplane. These quality requirements will have an effect on the activities that will have to be scheduled and the resources that will have to be found. This Project Quality Plan, plus the information in the Project Brief and Project Approach documents, now allow a *Project Plan* to be drafted. This will contain:

- the major products to be created;
- the main activities to be undertaken;
- project risks and their counter-measures;
- effort requirements;
- timescales;
- key decision points.

We now have a much clearer idea of the overall cost of the project than we did at the time of the original Project Mandate. The business case can now be reviewed to see whether the proposed project is still viable. The reliability of the business case will depend on the validity of the assumptions upon which it is based. The possibility that particular assumptions are incorrect is assessed and documented in a *Risk Log*. The final parts of project initiation are specifying how the project is to be controlled in terms of reporting and decision-making responsibilities and the setting up of project files.

The culmination of Initiating a Project is the putting together of a *Project Initiation Document*, which brings together the documentation generated by the Start Up and Initiation processes. If the Project Board can approve this document then the first proper Stage of the project can start.

A.10 Controlling a Stage

Once a Stage has been initiated, the Project Manager should be able to get on with the direction of the Stage without having to organize regular formal meetings with the Project Board.

Table A.2 shows the actions that the Project Manager might have to carry out while the Stage is being executed and for which the originators of PRINCE2 have laid down procedural guidelines.

The Project Manager will have to authorize *Work Packages* (CS1), tasks that have to be carried out to create the products that should be the desired outcome of the project, such as software modules. On a substantial project, these authorizations will be passed not directly to the people who will do the work but to Team Managers.

Once the work has been authorized, the Project Manager will then need to find out how that work is progressing (CS2). This involves the kinds of task touched on in Chapter 9 on project control. For instance, progress information will have to be gathered to see if tasks are likely to be completed on time; feedback on recent quality-checking activities will also be needed to ensure that apparent progress is not being made by releasing products before they are really ready. Eventually, for each Work Package the Project Manager will be informed that the work can be signed-off as completed (CS9). This progress data will be used to add actual

Table A.2 PRINCE2 processes when controlling a Stage

PRINCE ID	Controlling Stages (CS) processes
CS1	Authorize Work Package
CS2	Assess progress
CS3	Capture Project Issues
CS4	Examine Project Issues
CS5	Review Stage status
CS6	Report highlights
CS7	Take corrective action
CS8	Escalate project issue
CS9	Receive completed Work Package

completion dates to the details of planned activities that have been recorded in the Stage Plan.

A major part of a Project Manager's job during the execution of a Stage is bound to be 'fire-fighting' – dealing with the unexpected problems that are certain to occur. PRINCE2 lays down a procedure (CS3 *Capturing Project Issues*) to ensure that these 'issues' are properly recorded. The 'issues' could be changes to requirements, changes to the environment such as new legal obligations, and other problems that might or might not have been foreseen by the risk analysis for the project. All these issues should be logged. Another PRINCE2 procedure (CS4) is designed to ensure that all these issues are dealt with in an effective way. Outcomes can include a *Request for Change* to modify the user requirement or an *Off-Specification*, which records known and accepted errors and omissions in the product to be delivered.

The process of assessing progress (CS2) requires the Project Manager to look at the individual strands of work going on in his or her area of responsibility. PRINCE2 envisages a separate but related activity where having gathered this progress information and also any outstanding Project Issues, the Project Manager checks the health of the Stage as a whole (CS5). In particular, the Project Manager will want to be reassured that the project as a whole is still progressing within its *tolerances*, the boundaries within which the Project Manager is allowed to manoeuvre without having to obtain clearance from the Project Board. One outcome of CS5 could be the carrying out of corrective action (CS7) that might include authorizing new Work Packages to deal with specific problems. Where work is progressing so that Project Issues are being kept under control and the Stage is within tolerances, then it will be enough to communicate progress to the Project Board by means of *Highlight reports* (CS6). In some cases the Project Manager might feel unable to progress with a matter without guidance from higher management and will request advice. Where activities have taken longer than planned or have taken up more resources than were budgeted so that the Project Manager is in danger of having to act outside the tolerances laid down in the Stage Plan, the Project Manager might have to 'escalate' a particular issue (CS8) by drafting an *Exception Report* to be considered by the Project Board. This should not only explain why the Stage has gone adrift from its original plan, but also detail possible options for recovering the situation and make a specific recommendation to the Project Board.

A.11 Managing product delivery

The processes described in 'Controlling a Stage' all assume that the work needed to complete a Stage is under the direct control of the Project Manager. Of course, it could be the case that, as described in Chapter 10 on contract management, some of the work is to be carried out by third party suppliers, that is, by an external organization that is not the primary supplier in direct contact with the customer, but a sub-contractor who carries out work on behalf of the supplier. These sub-contractors might not be using PRINCE2. Hence the situation could need careful handling and PRINCE2 provides some guidelines to help this – see Table A.3.

Once the Project Manager has authorized a Work Package (CS1), as described in the 'Controlling a Stage' section, the person who is to be responsible for the execution of the Work Package needs to check the requirements of the Work

Table A.3 PRINCE2 processes when managing product delivery

PRINCE ID	Managing product delivery (MP) processes
MP1	Accept Work Package
MP2	Execute Work Package
MP3	Deliver Work Package

Table A.4 PRINCE2 processes when managing stage boundaries

PRINCE ID	Managing stage boundaries
SB1	Planning a Stage
SB2	Updating the Project Plan
SB3	Updating the project business case
SB4	Updating the Risk Log
SB5	Reporting a Stage End
SB6	Producing an Exception Report

Package to ensure that there is common understanding on what exactly is to be delivered, the constraints that might apply to the work and the requirements of any interfaces with other work (MP1). The Team Manager who is accepting the work must be confident that the targets can be realistically achieved. This could involve working out a *Team Plan* detailing how the work is to be done.

Once the work has been accepted, work can start on executing the Work Package (MP2). As this could be done by a sub-contractor who does not use PRINCE2, PRINCE2 lays down the general requirement that the responsible Team Manager should have the information ready to hand to report back to the Project Manager on progress as laid down in the authorized Work Package document. Finally, the need to define and agree the process by which completed Work Packages are handed over to the Project Manager is identified (MP3).

A.12 Managing Stage boundaries

The transition from one Stage to another will involve the processes shown in Table A.4.

A key PRINCE2 principle is to avoid too detailed planning at too early a stage. At the beginning of the project, for instance, the overall Project Plan is produced, but the more detailed Stage Plan is only produced for the first Stage. Towards the end of a Stage, the detailed plan for the next Stage can be mapped out as a clearer idea of the project requirements emerges (SB1). The creation of the Stage Plan for the next Stage could show up inadequacies in the overall Project Plan, which might need to be updated. For example, the design Stage of a project might reveal that the functionality of the system is greater than was foreseen when the first Project Plan was produced. More time might therefore be needed at the build Stage and this needs to be reflected in the Project Plan (SB2).

More time needed at build Stage will almost certainly mean that the date by which the project will be finally completed will be put back. This will lead to increasing development costs and the deferment of any income from the implemented system. At this point we need a process that checks that the project is still viable, that is, that the benefits of the delivered system will still outweigh the costs (SB3).

The situation with regard to risks might also have changed and this too needs to be reviewed (SB4). For example, as the project moves from design to build, some risks will disappear – if users were heavily involved in a design phase based around prototyping, a risk such as the non-availability of users for prototype evaluation will no longer be applicable and can be struck out. Other risks might, however, have materialized – a new version of the software building tool to be used could have been imposed by the organization and there is the possibility that developers might have technical difficulties adapting to the new product.

When all these things have been done, the new Stage will still need to wait for the successful completion of the last Stage. When this happens, the Project Manager can report the completion of the Stage (SB5) and the approval of the Project Board for the new Stage Plan can be requested.

A.13 Closing the project

PRINCE2 divides the closing of a project into three separate processes:

- decommissioning a project (CP1);
- identifying follow-on actions (CP2);
- evaluating the project (CP3).

One follow-on action will be to plan for the Post Project Review which evaluates the effectiveness of the installed system after a set period of operation.

Decommissioning is mainly ensuring that all the loose ends are tied up. All Project Issues should either have been resolved or have been recorded as requiring *Follow-on Actions*. All the planned project products should have been accepted by the client and the requested operational and maintenance arrangements should be in place. Project files will have to be stored away into an archive and all parties involved should be notified that the project is now closed. PRINCE2 does not specify that team members and key users should have a celebratory drink, but now might be the time to consider this. Decommissioning might have been caused by an *ad hoc* direction (DP4) to terminate a project prematurely as it is no longer required and in this case a wake could be more appropriate.

In organizations where development resources are scarce, there might appear to be little time available to reflect on practice and to dwell on past mistakes. However, if this is not done, time will be wasted in dealing with recurrent problems. PRINCE2 recognizes this by specifying that at this point a *Project End Report* should be produced, documenting the extent to which the project has met the objectives set out in the Project Initiation Document, and also a *Lessons Learnt Report*, which should make suggestions about how problems could be avoided in future projects.

APPENDIX B

BS 6079:1996 – an overview

B.1 Introduction

Both as individuals and as organizations, we are continually exchanging goods and services – this is very much the basis of the commercial world we know today. This free exchange would be impeded unless on the whole there were a basic trust and common expectations about the nature and quality of the products involved and the processes by which those products had been created. To this end, business communities and governments have worked to produce standards. An important part of this has been the definition of agreed terminology so that we have a clear idea of what is meant by particular terms.

We would hope that standards are reasonably precise and unambiguous while being flexible enough to deal with the vagaries of the real world. It would also be hoped that standards would reflect accepted current best practice. A desirable feature of such standards would be some kind of accreditation of qualified practitioners so that customers for a product or service could know that they were dealing with someone competent in the particular area of expertise.

The British Standards Institution has had a leading role in the United Kingdom in this field and in 1996 published BS 6079 'Guide to project management'. While this 49-page document may have some claim to approach being a 'standard' because it reflects what the compilers of the document feel is current best practice, it is really, as its name suggests, a set of guidelines that are often couched in general terms of broad advice. In many ways it is like a general essay on project management.

Adrian Dooley, 'BS 6079 A base for the future?', *Project Manager Today*, 9(4), pp. 12–13, April 1997.

The advantage of its being in the form of a British Standard, as Adrian Dooley has pointed out, is that this can give these broad, but important, project management principles more credibility in some quarters of the business community. A disadvantage of this format, in our view, is that apart from other BSI standards, the project manager reading this text is given no information about where further guidance on the techniques described can be obtained.

Pippa Newman, 'PRINCE2 The method for the next millennium', pp. 14–15 of the same issue of *Project Manager Today* as above.

A key question is how this standard fits in with the other UK standard PRINCE2 or even why two separate standards are necessary. It is emphasize by the promoters of these two standards that they are not meant to be competitors. Pippa Newman, a CCTA Associate involved with promoting PRINCE2 has written of PRINCE2 that *'one of its major roles is to provide a means by which the British Standard can be implemented'*. As will be seen, this could imply a degree of coordination between the developers of the two approaches that is not evident when the two documents are closely studied. One of the reasons for the differences in the two approaches might be their different origins – although PRINCE2 is now meant for a rather wider context, its origins are in ICT development, while BS 6079 has more of a hard engineering background. However, once again, as Adrian Dooley commented:

With a bit of work an organisation could be consistent with both. The biggest problem is the need to harmonise the differing terminologies used by the two approaches. As someone who is keen to see project management develop as a mature discipline, I feel terribly frustrated by the lack of consistency in the profession. Why is it that the two bodies developing tools to promote better project management, both funded by the government, producing their respective documents at about the same time, cannot work closely together to agree consistent terminology at even the simplest level?

Some of the differences between PRINCE2 and BS 6079 are summarized in Table B.1.

Table B.1 Comparison of PRINCE2 and BS 6079

Topic	PRINCE2	BS 6079
Main focus	Procedures	Techniques
Definition of project	Temporary organization to deliver a business product	Covers the *whole* system life cycle
Project organization	Supplier vs. Customer focus	Functional departments vs. project team
Project authority	Project Board	Sponsor
Stage organization	Detailed planning done by Stage	Concept of phases/milestones matches Stages – but no focus on incremental planning at phase level
Planning method	Product-driven (product Breakdown Structures)	Task-driven (Work Breakdown Structures)
Work definitions	Product descriptions in the plan – turned into Work Packages by Project Manager	Statements of Work (SOW) in the plan
Techniques	Only minimal reference to techniques (such as to Activity Networks)	Detailed descriptions of techniques like Earned Value Analysis
Supporting techniques	Configuration, quality and risk management	Those for PRINCE2, plus financial control and procurement
Financial control	Cost control not dealt with in detail	Financial control dealt with more fully

The main elements of project management dealt with by BS 6079 are:

- the project life cycle;
- project organization;
- the planning process;
- project control;
- supporting techniques.

We will now look at each of these in turn.

The project life cycle

BS 6079 sees a 'project' in terms different from those of PRINCE2. It uses the word to refer to the whole of the system life cycle from the initial idea right through the system's operation to final decommissioning. The BS 6079 definition of project is similar to the view of a 'project' used in Chapter 3, when the cash projections for alternative 'projects' were calculated. When developing information systems, however, the development project is more usually seen as starting after the feasibility study has established that the project appears to be worthwhile and finishing when the system is handed over for operation. In fact, it is possible to treat individual phases within that project as projects in their own right. As it happens, despite the BS 6079 definition of project, most of the BS 6079 guidelines for planning and control are compatible with the information systems development view of the project being completed at system hand-over.

Figure B.1 illustrates the main project phases as seen by BS 6079. Note that 'implementation' in this context means 'implementation of the project plan'. Information systems developers often use the term 'implementation' to refer merely to the installation of the system once it has been developed. A further interesting point is that while the standard recommends the equivalent of the PRINCE2 Project End and Lessons Learnt Reports, no mention is made of the Post Implementation Review, or Post Project Review as it is now called.

Project organization

BS 6079 does not have PRINCE2's emphasis on the Supplier–Customer relationship. Neither is the concept of a Project Board or steering committee presented. The focus of attention is on the project as a set of activities that cut across the normal functional structures of most organizations. A heavy emphasis is put on the desirability of a matrix management structure, where staff belong to a particular functional group in the longer term but may be allocated from time to time to multi-disciplinary teams that have been given the responsibility for achieving the objectives of a particular project.

It can be argued that the need to create an environment for successful projects, which can take time, is an important message for the perceived readership of BS 6079.

One usually expects standards to be applicable fairly immediately, but the writers of BS 6079 warn that it might take an organization three to five years to move from a totally functional to a matrix organization. Rather surprisingly for a document that is supposed to be focused on project management, there is a section on the broader topic of how to bring about organizational change. This is an

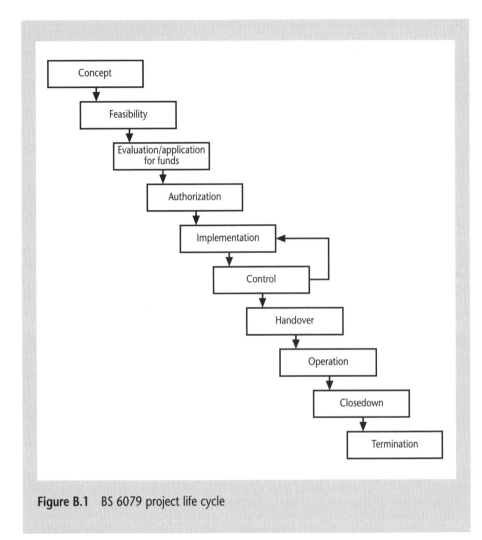

Figure B.1   BS 6079 project life cycle

example of where a reference to a fuller treatment in another text would have been useful.

The other management role that BS 6079 emphasizes is that of *task owners*. Each task that is identified as needing doing in a project requires an owner, someone who will be accountable for its successful completion. Figure B.2 shows the relationships among the different project roles as envisaged in BS 6079.

B.2   The planning process

According to BS 6079, a plan should have five main elements:

● introduction;

● commitment acceptance;

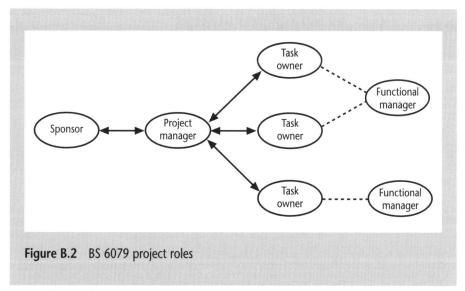

Figure B.2 BS 6079 project roles

- work breakdown structure;
- schedule;
- statements of work.

The terms 'Work Breakdown Structure' and 'Statement of Work' (SOW) will be explained later in this section.

One of the major differences between BS 6079 and PRINCE2 is that, while PRINCE2 advocates a product-driven approach to planning, where the products the project has to create are initially identified, BS 6079 uses an activity-based approach, featuring a *Work Breakdown Structure* (WBS), right from the beginning.

The standard does not put the same heavy emphasis on a Stage structure for projects as PRINCE2. Passing references are, however, made to having project phases with milestones between the phases where there would be critical reviews of the progress that has been made and where decisions would be made about the continuing viability of the project. However, basing planning cycles on these phases, as PRINCE2 does, is not suggested.

Apart from the WBS, the other important element in project documentation, according to this standard, is the *Statement of Work* (SOW), which combines elements of PRINCE2's Product Description and Work Package. A SOW is created for each element in the WBS. These documents contain sections that cover such details as:

- summary of requirements;
- task ownership;
- key deliverables and their delivery dates;
- task dependencies;
- cost breakdown;
- risk assessment;
- performance criteria;
- progress reporting arrangements.

BS 6079 does mention a 'product-based WBS' which equates to a PRINCE2 'Product Breakdown Structure', but does not use Product Flow Diagrams.

B.3 BS 6079 planning steps

The major BS 6079 planning steps are summarized below:

Obtain project authorization

Establish project organization

Develop WBS   It is suggested that it is useful to produce a cross-reference table showing which activities are the responsibility of which parts of the organization.

Analyse project tasks   This includes the identification of the task owner, of the way that the performance of the task is to be measured, its criticality to the project, its cost elements and any risks.

Assign task owner   The importance of having people who have responsibility and accountability for the successful completion of each project task is very strongly stressed in BS 6079.

Develop the statements of work

Monte Carlo simulation was discussed briefly in Chapter 7.

Balance time, cost, integrity of specification and risk   This is where the planner tries out different options for allocating effort and timescale targets to activities to see what the likely consequences would be. Although Monte Carlo simulation is not mentioned by name, its possible use is implied.

Obtain commitments to do project tasks   Task owners are asked to agree formally and commit themselves to the relevant tasks. Before the task owners can do this, they will need to quantify the resources that will be needed and to match this requirement against available resources, reserving the selected resources for use in the project.

Finalize agreements

B.4 Project control

Project control in BS 6079 is considered under the three distinct headings of change control, financial control and progress monitoring.

Change control   BS 6079 recognizes that it is essential to have a formal mechanism to control changes, but while the requirements of such an administrative system are outlined, it does not specify any detailed steps. A major change can call for the planning cycle to be re-executed.

Financial control   BS 6079 makes more specific references to financial control than PRINCE2. The need is recognized for a process whereby the expenditure by the sponsoring organization on the project can be allocated to annual budgets. As time passes and progress is made, arrangements must be in place for the required funding to be released. Even with the best regulated projects, circumstances can require additional expenditure for unforeseen contingencies and a management reserve ought to be available for this.

Monitoring progress   The BS 6079 emphasis on financial control is seen once again in the requirement that the project manager has a prime responsibility to report actual costs compared to planned costs. Task owners are required to pass on to the project manager revised estimates of the overall cost and projected completion dates for each task for which they have responsibility.

The compilers of BS 6079 clearly had a very strong preference for earned value analysis and the method is given considerable space in the standards document.

Not only does the project manager receive reports of progress from task owners, but he or she should warn the task owners of any external threats to their areas of activity. A report of a delay by one task owner can require the owners of tasks dependent upon the delayed task to be warned.

The need for risks to be continually assessed is stressed. Risk assessment techniques based on statistical probability are recommended.

The need for project managers to motivate and, if needs be, negotiate with, task owners is recognized by the document. Thus having good communications is stressed, and readers are warned that specifying additions to requirements is easier before a contract is signed than afterwards!

> Earned value analysis has been described in Section 9.6.

> The kind of risk management techniques that BS 6079 recommends have been discussed in Chapter 7.

B.5   Supporting techniques

It will be recalled that PRINCE2 described the basic requirements for some supporting techniques, in particular, change and configuration management, quality management and risk management. BS 6079 adopts a similar approach but adds procurement and financial control.

With regard to procurement, the different organizational arrangements for making purchases for a project are outlined. For example, the buyers might belong to a centralized group or might be dedicated to the specific projects. The key role of purchase order documents as a control mechanism is highlighted. The need to have some way of identifying trustworthy and qualified vendors, perhaps by maintaining a list of preferred vendors who have a satisfactory track record, is described in the BS 6079 document. The document also warns of the need to have in place procedures to expedite external work and to ensure the satisfactory standard of delivered work through inspections.

The section on financial control illustrates quite nicely the differences in approach between BS 6079 and PRINCE2. In the BS 6079 document, two very specific quantitative techniques are described in some detail, namely the calculation of the net present value of a potential project and the analysis of the earned value of a project currently being executed. PRINCE2 tends to avoid describing detailed technical data manipulation, with some notable exceptions to do with core planning methods, and concentrates on the necessary administrative procedures that need to be in place.

Answer pointers

Chapter 1

1.1 Examples of projects

The order you put these projects in is, of course, to a large degree subjective. Here is one example of a possible ordering.

1. **Putting a robot vehicle on Mars to search for signs of life**   Almost everybody puts this one first. The huge scale of the task, the relative novelty of the project, all the different specialisms involved and the international nature of the project make it special. Note that the successful achievement of the project from the engineering point of view is the safe landing of the robot, not the discovery of signs of life.

2. **Writing an operating system**   This is a prime example of a software development project.

3. **Amending a financial system to deal with a common European currency**   This project is modifying an existing system rather than creating a new one from scratch. Many software projects have this characteristic and it does not make them any less a software project.

4. **Installing a new version of a word processing package in an organization**   Although no software is being produced or modified, many of the stages that are associated with software projects will be involved and the techniques of software project management would be appropriate.

5. **Investigation into the reasons why a user has a problem with a computer system**   This will have many of the stages common to software projects, although the precise nature of the end result is uncertain at the outset. It could be that the user needs some simple remedial training. On the other hand, it could turn out to be quite a considerable software modification task.

6. **Getting married**   There should be lots of arguments about this one! Some will be reluctant to give a high rating to this because of its personal nature. The degree to which this is 'project-like' will depend very much upon the cultural milieu in which it takes place. Very often it requires a high degree of planning, involves lots of different people and, for most people, is a non-routine operation.

7. **A research project into what makes a good human–computer interface**   Compared to some of the projects above, the objectives of the research project are more open-ended and the idea of a specific client for the end-product may

be less well defined. Research projects are in some ways special cases and the approach to their planning needs a rather different approach, which is outside the scope of this book.

8. **Producing an edition of a newspaper**   In some ways this has all the characteristics of a project. There are lots of different people with lots of different specialisms whose work needs to be coordinated in order to produce an end-product under very tight time constraints. What argues against this as a typical project is that it is repeated. After a while, everyone knows what he or she needs to do and most of the problems that arise are familiar and the procedures to deal with them are well defined.

9. **A second-year programming assignment for a computing student**   This is not being done for a customer, although it could be argued that the tutor responsible for setting and assessing the assignment is, in effect, a surrogate client. Not all the stages of a normal project will be gone through.

1.2   Brightmouth College payroll: Stages of a project

1. **Project evaluation**   All the costs that would be incurred by the college if it were to carry out its own payroll processing would need to be carefully examined to ensure it would be more cost effective than letting the local authority carry on providing the service.

2. **Planning**   The way that the transfer to local processing is to be carried out needs to be carefully planned with the participation of all those concerned. Some detailed planning would need to be deferred until more information was available, for example which payroll package was to be used.

3. **Requirements elicitation and analysis**   This is finding out what the users need from the system. To a large extent it will often consist of finding out what the current system does, as it may be assumed that in general the new system is to provide the same functions as the old. The users might have additional requirements, however, or there might even be facilities that are no longer needed.

4. **Specification**   This involves documenting what the new system is to be able to do.

5. **Design/coding**   As an 'off-the-shelf' package is envisaged, these stages will be replaced by a package evaluation and selection activity.

6. **Verification and validation**   Tests will need to be carried out to ensure that the selected package will actually do what is required. This task might well involve parallel running of the old and new systems and a comparison of the output from them both to check for any inconsistencies.

7. **Implementation**   This would involve such things as installing the software, setting system parameters such as the salary scales, and setting up details of employees.

8. **Maintenance/support**   This will include dealing with users' queries, liaising with the package supplier and taking account of new payroll requirements.

1.3 Estimation of the height of the building you are in

We will not spoil the fun by suggesting a particular method.

1.4 The nature of an operating system

Many large organizations that are committed to computer-based information systems have specialists responsible for the maintenance of operating systems. However, as an operating system is primarily concerned with driving the hardware, it is argued that it has more in common with what we have described as embedded systems.

1.5 Brightmouth College payroll: objectives-driven vs. product-driven

This project is really driven by objectives. If in-house payroll processing turns out not to be cost effective, then the project should not try to implement such a solution. Other ways of meeting the objectives set could be considered: for example, it might be possible to contract out the processing to some organization other than the local authority at a lower cost.

1.6 A day in the life of a project manager

Planning:

- staffing requirements for the next year.

Representing the section:

- at the group meeting;
- when communicating with the human resources manager about replacement staff;
- when explaining about the delay to users.

Controlling, innovating, directing:

- deciding what needs to be done to make good the progress that will be lost through temporarily losing a member of staff.

Staffing:

- deciding which member of staff is to do what;
- discussion with human resources about the requirement for temporary staff;
- planning staffing for the next year.

Note: the same activity can involve many different roles.

1.7   Defining objectives

Among the comments and queries that could be made in each case are:

(i)   Has the actual time and the amount of the budget been specified somewhere? Deadline and budget constraints normally have to be set against the scope and the quality of the functions to be delivered. For example, if the deadline were not achieved, would the customer rather have the full set of function-ality at a later date, or an essential sub-set of the function on the deadline date?

(ii)   'The fewest possible software errors' is not precise. Removing errors requires effort and hence money. Can developers spend as much money and time as they like if this reduces errors?

(iii)   What does 'user-friendly' really mean? How is it measured? Normally 'ease of use' is measured by the time it takes for a beginner to become proficient in carrying out standard operations.

(iv)   What does 'full documentation' mean? A list of the types of document to be produced, perhaps with an indication of the content layout, would be more useful.

1.8   Brightmouth college payroll: objectives, goals and measures of effectiveness

The original objective might have been formulated as: '*To carry out payroll processing at less cost while maintaining the current scope and quality of services*'.

In order to achieve this, sub-objectives or goals will usually have been ident-ified, for example:

● to transfer payroll processing to the college by 1st April;

● to implement in the new system those facilities that exist in the current system less those identified in the initial report as not being required;

● to carry out the implementation of the payroll processing capability within the financial constraints identified in the initial report.

It should be noted that the objectives listed above do not explicitly mention such things as putting into place ongoing arrangements to deal with hardware and software maintenance, security arrangements and so on. By discussing and trying to agree objectives with the various people involved, the true requirements of the project can be clarified.

Measures of effectiveness for the sub-objectives listed above might include the following:

● *Date of implementation*   Was the new system being used operationally by the agreed date?

● *Facilities*   In parallel runs, were all the outputs produced by the old system still required and also produced by the new system?

● *Costs*   How did the actual costs incurred compare with the budgeted costs?

1.9   Brightmouth college payroll: stakeholders

Major stakeholders would include:

- the finance department;
- the human resources department, who would need to supply most of the employee details needed;
- heads of departments, who would need to submit details of hours worked for part-time staff;
- staff, who would naturally be concerned that they are paid correctly;
- site management: the new arrangements may mean that the office layout has to be rearranged physically;
- software and hardware vendors.

One group of stakeholders that might not be readily identified at first is the local government authority and its staff. It might seem strange to list the people who used to do the job, but who are no longer required. The project manager's job will be made a lot easier if their cooperation and help can be obtained. The project manager would do well to sound out tactfully how the local authority staff feel about losing this work. It could be that they are pleased to be shot of the workload and hassle involved! Arrangements that take into account existing local authority staff might be possible. For example, if the college needs to recruit new staff to deal with payroll, it might smooth things to give the job to a member of the local authority staff who already deals with this area.

1.10 Collecting control data

The project seems to have two major components: training and document transfer. If trainers were expected to tour offices giving training then one would expect there to be a schedule indicating when each office was to receive training. The following information about the progress of the information might therefore be collected:

- the number of offices that had received training – this could be compared with the schedule;
- the number of staff who had received training – to ensure that all staff were attending;
- feedback from staff on the perceived quality of training – for example, by post-training evaluation forms.

For the document transfer aspect, the following might be usefully collected for each office on a regular basis during the transfer process:

- number of documents transferred;
- estimated number of documents still needing to be transferred;
- number of staff-hours spent on transferring documents – to monitor the budget and transfer productivity;
- number of staff involved in the transfer.

When all documents have been transferred, performance tests to check response times might be required.

Chapter 2

2.1 External stakeholders in IOE accounts system

The main stakeholders who need to be considered are the IOE customers. It will be worth consulting some representative customers about the layout of the new monthly statement, for example.

2.2 Creating an invitation to tender (ITT) – product flow diagram

Figure C.1 illustrates a product flow diagram for the products needed to create an invitation to tender for Brightmouth College payroll.

Figure C.1 Product flow diagram for the creation of an 'invitation to tender'

2.3 Invitation to tender activity network

Figure C.2 illustrates the activity network, showing the activities needed to create an invitation to tender for the Brightmouth College payroll.

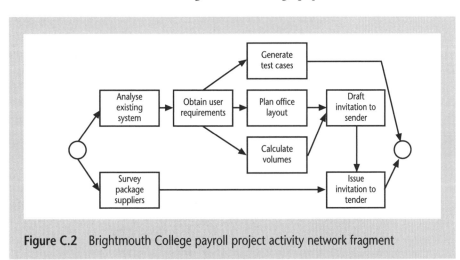

Figure C.2 Brightmouth College payroll project activity network fragment

2.4 Including a checkpoint

Figure C.3 illustrates the inclusion of a checkpoint in Amanda's activity network.

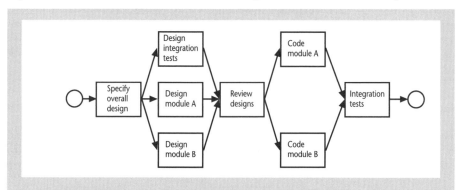

Figure C.3 An activity network for a software development task, modified to include a checkpoint

2.5 Quality checks on user requirements

The users will need at least to read and approve the system specification. This might be rather late to make major changes, so user approval of earlier documents such as interview notes would be helpful.

2.6 Cross-reference of a planning document to Step Wise activities

Table C.1 suggests the Step Wise activities needed to create the different sections of a plan.

Table C.1 Sections of a plan cross-referenced to Step Wise activities

Section of plan	Step Wise activities
Introduction	
Background	1.3 Identify stakeholders
	2.1 Establish relationship between project and strategic planning
Project objectives	1.1 Identify objectives and measures of effectiveness
	1.4 Modify objectives in the light of stakeholder analysis
Constraints	1.1 Identify objectives and measures of effectiveness
	2.2 Identify installation standards and procedures
Methods	3. Analyse project characteristics
	4.2 Document generic product flows (this could help establish a methodology)
Project products	4.1 Identify and describe project products
Activities to be carried out	4.4 Produce ideal activity network
	4.5 Modify ideal activity network
Resources to be used	3.6 Review overall resource estimates
	5.1 Carry out bottom-up estimates
	7. Allocate resources
Risks to the project	3.3 Identify high-level project risks
	6. Identify activity risks
Management of the project	1.2 Establish project authority
	1.5 Establish methods of communication with all parties
	2.3 Identify project team organization

Table C.2 Costs and benefits for the Brightmouth College payroll system

Category	Cost/benefit
Development costs	Software purchase – software cost plus selection and purchasing cost Project team employment costs
Setup costs	Training include costs of trainers and operational staff time lost while training Staff recruitment Computer hardware and other equipment which might have a residual value at end of projected life Accommodation – any new/refurbished accommodation and furniture required to house new system Initial systems supplies – purchase of stationery, disks and other consumables
Operational costs	Operations staff – full employment costs Stationery – purchase and storage Maintenance and standby – contract or estimation of occurrence costs Accommodation including heating, power, insurance etc.[1]
Quantified and valued	Saving on local authority fees Later payment – increase interest income through paying salaries later in the month
Quantified but not valued	Improved accuracy – the number of errors needing to be corrected each month
Identified but not easily valued	Improved management information – this should lead to improved decision making but it is very difficult to quantify the potential benefits

---

[1] These items, and some other elements, might show corresponding savings or costs through no longer being required. For example, although new office furniture might be required for the new system, the existing furniture might be redeployed or sold.

Chapter 3

3.1 Costs and benefits for the Brightmouth College payroll system

Table C.2 lists costs and benefits for the proposed Brightmouth HE College payroll system. It is not comprehensive but illustrates some of the types of items that you should have listed.

3.2 Ranking project cash flows

Obviously you will have your own views about which have the best and worst cash flows. You should, however, have considered the following points: project 2 requires a very large investment compared to its gain – in fact we could obtain £100,000 by undertaking both projects 1 and 3 for a lower cost than project 2. Both projects 1 and 4 produce the bulk of their incomes relatively late in their lives compared with project 3, which produces a steady income over its life.

3.3 Calculating payback periods

The payback periods for each of the projects will occur during the year indicated: project 1 year 5, project 2 year 5, project 3 year 4 and project 4 at the end of year 4.

We would therefore favour project 3 or 4 over the other two. Note that, in reality, with relatively short-term projects such as these we would produce a monthly (or at least quarterly) cash flow forecast and it is therefore likely that project 3 would be seen more clearly to have a shorter payback period than project 4.

3.4 Calculating the return on investment

The return on investments for each of the projects is: project 1: 10%, project 2: 2%, project 3: 10% and project 4: 12.5%. Project 4 therefore stands out as being the most beneficial as it earns the highest return.

3.5 Calculating the net present value

The net present value for each of the projects is calculated as in Table C.3. On the basis of net present value, project 4 clearly provides the greatest return and project 2 is clearly not worth considering.

Table C.3 Calculating the net present value of projects 2, 3 and 4

Year	Discount factor	Discounted cash flow (£)		
		Project 2	Project 3	Project 4
0	1.00	−1,000,000	−100,000	−120,000
1	0.90	181,820	27,273	27,273
2	0.82	165,280	24,792	24,792
3	0.75	150,260	22,539	22,539
4	0.68	136,600	20,490	20,490
5	0.62	186,270	18,627	46,568
NPV		−179,770	13,721	21,662

3.6 Calculating the effect of discount rates on NPV

Table C.4 illustrates the effect of varying discount rates on the NPV. In each case the 'best' project is indicated in bold. In this somewhat artificial example, which project is best is very sensitive to the chosen discount rate. In such a case we must either have a very strong reason to use a particular discount rate or take other criteria into account when choosing among the projects.

Table C.4 The effect on net present value of varying the discount rate

Year	Cash flow values (£)		
	Project A	Project B	Project C
0	−8,000	−8,000	−10,000
1	4,000	1,000	2,000
2	4,000	2,000	2,000
3	2,000	4,000	6,000
4	1,000	3,000	2,000
5	500	9,000	2,000
6	500	−6,000	2,000
Net Profit	£4,000	£5,000	£6,000
NPV @ 8%	£2,111	£2,365	**£2,421**
NPV @ 10%	£1,720	**£1,818**	£1,716
NPV @ 12%	**£1,356**	£1,308	£1,070

3.7   Project evaluation using cost–benefit analysis

Expected sales of £500,000 per year over four years would generate an expected net income of £1.2m (after allowing for annual costs of £200,000), which, by almost any criteria, would provide a good return on an investment of £750,000. However, if sales are low, and there is a 30% chance of this happening, the company will lose money – it is unlikely that any company would wish to take such a risk knowingly.

This example illustrates one of the basic objections to using this approach for one-off decisions. Were we to repeat the project a large number of times we would expect, *on average*, an income of £500,000 per annum. However, the company is developing this package only once – they can't keep trying in the hope of, on the average, generating a respectable income. Indeed, a severe loss on this project could mean it is the last project they are able to undertake.

Chapter 4

4.1   Classification of systems

(a) A payroll system is a data-oriented or information system that is application specific.

(b) The bottling plant system is a process control or industrial system which contains embedded software.

(c) This looks like an information system that will may make use of computer graphics. The plant itself might use control software which might be safety critical but this is not the subject of the project under consideration.

(d) Project management software tools are often categorized as general packages. There would be a considerable information systems element to them.

(e) This could use an information retrieval package that is a general software package. It is also a strong candidate for a knowledge-based system.

4.2   Identification of risks

The user staff could, arguably, be regarded as a project resource. The writers' view is that it is useful to add a fourth category of risks – those belonging to the *environment* in which the system is to be implemented.

Among the risks that might be identified at Brightmouth College are:

● conflict of views between the finance and personnel departments;

● lack of staff acceptance for the system, especially among personnel staff;

● lack of cooperation by the local authority that used to carry out payroll work;

● lack of experience with running payroll at the college leading to errors and delays in processing;

● lack of administrative computing expertise at the college;

● possible inadequacy of the chosen hardware;

● changes to the payroll requirements.

4.3   Selection of project approaches

(a) This would appear to be a knowledge-based system that is also safety critical. Techniques associated with knowledge-based systems could be used for constructing the system. Testing would need to be very carefully conducted. A lengthy parallel run where the system is used to shadow the human decisions made in real cases and the results compared could be considered. Another approach would be to develop two or more systems in parallel so that the advice offered could be cross-checked.

(b) This is an information system that will be on a relatively large scale. A structured approach designed for information systems applications, like SSADM, would be justified. When student loans were first introduced there was no existing system and so there might have been some scope for a prototype.

(c) This is an embedded system that is safety critical. Measures that might ensure the reliability of the system include:

- use of mathematics-based specification languages to avoid ambiguity;
- developing parallel versions of the same software so that they can be cross-checked;
- statistical control of software testing to allow for the estimation of the reliability of the software.

4.4   Feedback between project review and feasibility study

The review might find that the benefits forecast in the original feasibility study report have not been achieved. 'Corrections' to the existing system could allow those benefits and others to be realized. This could lead to a proposal for a new project to modify the installed option.

4.5   Stages of a project where a prototype can be appropriate

(a) A prototype could be useful as part of the feasibility study. A mock-up of an executive information system loaded with current management information could be set up manually and then be tried out by the managers to see how easy and useful they found it.

(b) A prototype could be used to assist in the design of the user dialogues. SSADM allows for prototypes for this purpose as part of its requirement specification module.

(c) A prototype of the most response-critical transactions could be made at the physical design stage to see whether Microsoft Access could produce software that gave a satisfactory performance.

Chapter 5

5.1 Calculating productivity rates and using productivity rates to project effort

Tables C.5 and C.6 illustrate productivity rates and estimated project effort.

Table C.5 Productivity rates

Project	Work-months	SLOC	Productivity (SLOC/month)
a	16.7	6,050	362
b	22.6	8,363	370
c	32.2	13,334	414
d	3.9	5,942	1524
e	17.3	3,315	192
f	67.7	38,988	576
g	10.1	38,614	3823
h	19.3	12,762	661
i	59.5	26,500	445
Overall	249.3	153,868	617

Table C.6 Estimated effort

Project	Estimated work-months	Actual	Difference
a	6050/617 = 9.80	16.7	6.90
d	5942/617 = 9.63	3.9	−5.73

There would be an under-estimate of 6.9 work-months for project *a* and an over-estimate of 5.7 for project *d*.

5.2 Course staff costs program – activities required

A list of activities might include:

- obtaining user requirements;
- analysis of the structure of the data already held;
- design of the report layout;
- writing user proposal;
- planning test cases;
- technical specification;
- design of the software structure;
- software coding;
- testing software;
- writing the operating instruction;
- acceptance testing.

The most difficult tasks to estimate are often those that are most sensitive to the size and the complexity of the software to be produced, in this case the design, writing and testing of the software. Writing the technical specification can also be difficult because of this, but estimating problems tend to be concealed here as deadlines can be met by omitting detail that can be added later when deficiencies are found.

The duration of activities that are to be carried out by users may also present problems, as this might depend upon their sense of priorities.

5.3 Effort drivers for a student assignment

The most obvious effort driver would seem to be the number of words required. Difficulty factors might include:

- *availability of material*, for example, in the library;
- *familiarity* of the student with the topic;
- *breadth/depth* required, that is, a broad survey of a wide field or an in-depth study of a narrow area;
- *technical difficulty* – some topics are easier to explain than others.

It could be argued that time available is the constraint. The student just does what can be done in the time available (see 'design to cost').

5.4 Calculating Euclidean distance

The Euclidean distance between project B and the target case is the square root of $((7 - 5)^2 + (15 - 10)^2)$, that is 5.39. Project A is therefore a closer analogy.

5.5 Albrecht function points

External input types	none
External output types	the report, that is 1
Logical internal file types	none
External interface file types	payroll file, staff file (timetabling,) courses file (timetabling), that is 3
External inquiry types	none

The function point counts are as follows:

External enquiry types	none
External output types	$1 \times 7 = 7$
Logical internal file types	none
External interface types	$3 \times 7 = 21$
External inquiry types	none
Total	28

Calculation of SLOC from Albrecht function points

The estimated lines of Cobol $= 28 \times 91 = 2548$. With a productivity rate of 50 SLOC per day, this gives an estimated effort of 2548/50, that is approximately 51 days.

5.7   Mark II function points

The function types are:

Input data types	6
Entities accessed	1
Output data types	1

Unadjusted function points = $(0.58 \times 6) + (1.66 \times 1) + (0.26 \times 1) = 5.4$.

5.8   Data movements

Data movement	Type
Incoming vehicle sensed	E
Access vehicle count	R
Signal barrier to be lifted	X
Increment vehicle count	W
Outgoing vehicle sensed	E
Decrement vehicle count	W
New maximum input	E
Set new maximum	W
Adjust current vehicle count	E
Record adjusted vehicle count	W

Note that different interpretations of the requirements could lead to different counts. The description in the exercise does not, for example, specify that the system should output a message that the car park is full or has spaces, although this might be expected.

5.9   SLOC estimate for customer insertion program

Figure C.4 gives an outline program structure using a Jackson structured diagram. The numbers in circles are our estimates of the lines of 'generic' code needed to implement each sub-process in the program. They should add up to 95 SLOC.

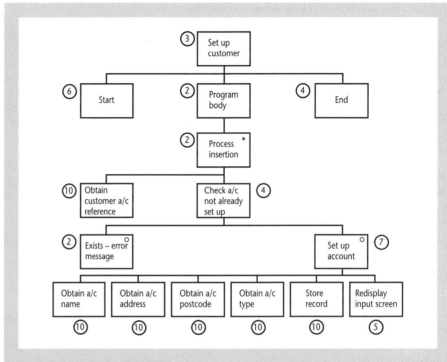

Figure C.4 Outline program structure for 'set up customer' transaction

5.10 COCOMO estimates

Table C.7 shows a comparison of the actual work-months from Table 5.1 and the COCOMO estimates. It illustrates the need for the calibration of COCOMO to suit local conditions.

Table C.7 Comparison of COCOMO estimates and actual effort

SLOC	Actual (work-months)	COCOMO estimates	Difference (work months)	Difference (%)
6,050	16.7	15.9	−0.8	−4.9
8,363	22.6	22.3	−0.3	−1.2
13,334	32.2	36.4	4.2	13.1
5,942	3.9	15.6	11.7	299.7
3,315	17.3	8.4	−8.9	−51.2
38,988	67.7	112.4	44.7	66.0
38,614	10.1	111.2	101.1	1001.5
12,762	19.3	34.8	15.5	80.2
26,500	59.5	74.9	15.4	25.9

5.11 COCOMO – calculating the development multiplier

Table C.8 shows development effort multipliers (*dem*) for the IOE project.

Table C.8 Calculating the development multiplier

Factor	Rating	Multiplier
ACAP	very high	0.71
AEXP	low	1.13
PCAP	high	0.86
VEXP	high	0.90
LEXP	low	1.07

$dem = 0.71 \times 1.13 \times 0.86 \times 0.90 \times 1.07 = 0.62$
final estimate = 4 person-months $\times$ 0.62 = 2.66 staff months

5.12 COCOMO II Maximum size of sf

The maximum possible value for *sf* is:

$$1.01 + 0.01 \times 5 + 5 + 5 + 5 + 5 = 1.26$$

5.13 COCOMO II calculating a scale factor

Table C.9 Exponent drivers and ratings for the project

Exponent driver	Rating
Precedentedness	3
Development flexibility	0
Architecture/risk resolution	4
Team cohesion	1
Process maturity	4
Total	12

Table C.9 illustrates the exponent drivers and ratings for this project.
Therefore, $sf = 1.01 + 0.01 \times (3 + 0 + 4 + 1 + 4) = 1.13$.

Chapter 6

6.1 Drawing a CPM network

A solution is given in Figure 6.14. If your solution is not exactly the same as this, do not worry. Just check that it is *logically* the same and that it follows the precedence network conventions of layout and labelling etc.

6.2 The precedence network

Figure C.5 illustrates a precedence network for Amanda's project, showing an earliest completion date of day 104.

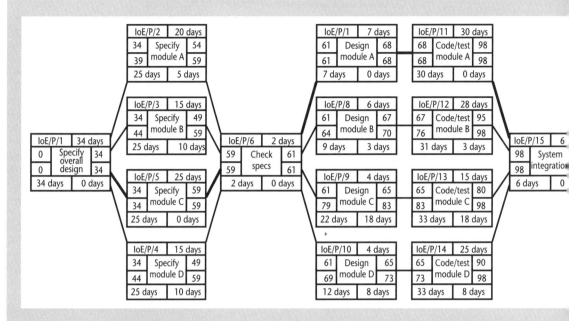

Figure C.5 Amanda's precedence network

6.3 Calculating activity floats

Free float and interfering float for each of the activities are shown in Table C.10. Note that activity A has no free float since any delay in its completion will delay the start of activity C. Float must be regularly monitored as a project progresses since a delay in any activity beyond its free float allowance will eat into the float of subsequent activities.

Table C.10 Activity floats

Activity	Total float	Free float	Interfering float
A	2	0	2
B	3	0	3
C	2	0	2
D	3	1	2
E	3	3	0
F	0	0	0
G	0	0	0
H	2	2	0

6.4 Shortening a project duration

Shortening activity F to 8 weeks will bring the project completion date forward to week 11 – that is, it will save 2 weeks on the duration of the project. However, there are now two critical paths, start–F–G–finish and start–A–C–H–finish, so that reducing the duration of activity F any further will not shorten the project duration any further. If we wish to complete the project earlier than week 11 we must save time on both of these critical paths.

6.5 Errors drawing activity networks

(a) Activity D dangles, giving the project two 'end events'. This network should be drawn as below. To aid comparison with the original, the nodes have not been renumbered, although we would normally do so.

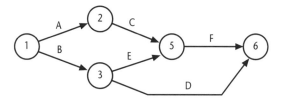

(b) Once again, this network has two end nodes, but in this case the solution is slightly different since we should introduce a dummy activity if we are to follow the standard CPM conventions.

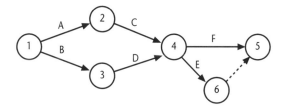

(c) Either this one has a dangle (although, because of the way it is drawn, it is less obvious) or activity E has its arrow pointing in the wrong direction. We need a bit more information before we can redraw this one correctly.

(d) Strictly speaking, there is nothing wrong with this one – it is just badly drawn and the nodes are not numbered according to the standard conventions. It should be redrawn as in the following example.

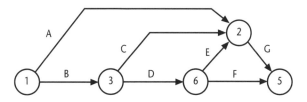

In this diagram the nodes have retained their original numbers (to aid identification) although they should of course be renumbered sequentially from left to right.

(e) This one contains a loop – F cannot start before G has finished, G cannot start before E has finished and E cannot start before G has finished. One of the arrows is wrong! It is probably activity F that is wrong but we cannot be sure without further information.

6.6 Drawing Brigette's activity network as a CPM network

Brigette's payroll CPM network should look like the diagram shown in Figure C.6. If your diagram is not exactly the same as this, check that it is logically the same.

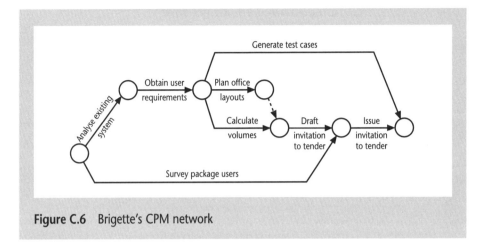

Figure C.6   Brigette's CPM network

Chapter 7

7.1   Matching causes and effects

There is no one correct answer to this. An example of a possible answer is provided below.

(a) i and ii. Staff inexperience leads to code that has many errors in it and which therefore needs additional testing time. Inexperienced staff will take longer to carry out development in any case.

(b) iv. If top management do not have a strong commitment to the project they will not act with a sense of urgency.

(c) ii. New technology takes time to get used to.

(d) iii. If users are uncertain of their requirements then they are likely to identify new requirements as the project progresses.

Exercise 7.2   Identifying risks

Once again the answer below can only be indicative – there is no one correct answer.

Domain	IOE	Brightmouth payroll
Actors	Possible user resistance – see Section 2.5	Lack of experience running payroll – see answer to Exercise 4.2
Structure	Not all stakeholders are represented on the Project Board – see Section 2.3	Lack of co-operation between the local authority and the college
Tasks	Uncertainty about time needed to change existing software – see Section 2.8	Evaluation of packages – software may be difficult to access to carry out evaluation testing
Technology	Existing hardware is not adequate to deal with new application	Existing hardware is not adequate to deal with new application

Exercise 7.3   Why the proposed measures might not be successful

Among the points that might be considered are that while the increase in staff salaries might decrease staff turnover in the short term, management pressures will still exist. Management pressure might even increase as salary costs could contribute to a decline in profits. Higher salaries might not be enough to compensate for this in the longer term. The use of a requirements prototype would not address the underlying problem that the external environment forces changes in requirements.

Exercise 7.4   Conditions needed for successful pooling arrangement

Among the conditions would be the following.

● The chance of flooding is precisely 1 in 100. As this is only an estimate of an average, this could not be guaranteed. If flooding happened at a second location, the pool would already have been exhausted. Having a larger number of contributors and a larger pool would reduce, but not eliminate, this risk.

● The sites would have to be at completely different locations so that a flood at one site does not affect the others.

● Each site has the same chance of flooding. If the people at a site were aware that the chance of flooding was a lot less in their location, they might object to having to effectively subsidize other sites.

● The amount of damage caused is always the same.

Exercise 7.5   Pre-conditions to facilitate contingency actions

Staff illness is just one of several reasons why you might need to transfer staff between job roles in the middle of an activity. Such transfers would be made easier if:

● there was a standard methodology for the way that the work was carried out;

● intermediate steps were well documented;

● other staff were involved in reviewing products at regular intervals;

● job descriptions were flexible.

It is interesting to note that in an extreme programming environment, the recommended approach of pair programming should provide an alternative way of dealing with this problem.

The factors to be taken account of could include costs and human factors. The structured approach to development that the bullet points above imply would involve costs in selecting the right methodology, training and other aspects of implementation and management of the process to ensure that staff adhere to the requirements of the methodology. Very flexible staffing arrangements where staff could be switched between jobs at short notice could have implications for morale (which might be positive as well as negative).

7.6 Calculating expected activity durations

Table C.11 shows the activity duration estimates from Table 7.8 along with the calculated expected durations, t_e.

Table C.11 Calculating expected activity durations

| | Activity durations (weeks) | | | |
Activity	Optimistic (a)	Most likely (m)	Pessimistic (b)	Expected (t_e)
A	5	6	8	6.17
B	3	4	5	4.00
C	2	3	3	2.83
D	3.5	4	5	4.08
E	1	3	4	2.83
F	8	10	15	10.50
G	2	3	4	3.00
H	2	2	2.5	2.08

7.7 The forward pass to calculate expected completion date

The expected duration and the expected dates for the other project events are shown in Figure 7.8. An expected duration of 13.5 weeks means that we expect the project to be completed halfway through week 14, although since this is only an expected value it could finish earlier or later.

7.8 Calculating standard deviations

The correct values are shown in Figure 7.5. Brief calculations for events 4 and 6 are given here.

Event 4: Path A + C has a standard deviation of $\sqrt{(0.50^2 + 0.17^2)} = 0.53$
Path B + D has a standard deviation of $\sqrt{(0.33^2 + 0.25^2)} = 0.41$
Node 4 therefore has a standard deviation of 0.53.

Event 6: Path 4 + H has a standard deviation of $\sqrt{(0.53^2 + 0.08^2)} = 0.54$
Path 5 + G has a standard deviation of $\sqrt{(1.17^2 + 0.33^2)} = 1.22$
Node 6 therefore has a standard deviation of 1.22.

7.9 Calculating z values

The z value for event 5 is $\dfrac{10 - 10.5}{1.17} = -0.43$, for event 6 it is $\dfrac{15 - 13.5}{1.22} = 1.23$.

7.10 Obtaining probabilities

Event 4: The z value is 1.89 which equates to a probability of approximately 3%. There is therefore only a 3% chance that we will not achieve this event by the target date of the end of week 10.

Event 5: The z value is −0.43 which equates to a probability of approximately 67%. There is therefore a 67% chance that we will not achieve this event by the target date of the end of week 10.

To calculate the probability of completing the project by week 14 we need to calculate a new z value for event 6 using a target date of 14. This new z value is

$$z = \frac{14 - 13.5}{1.22} = 0.41$$

This equates to a probability of approximately 35%. This is the probability of not meeting the target date. The probability of meeting the target date is therefore 65% (100% − 35%).

Chapter 8

8.1 Smoothing resource demand

Smoothing analyst/designer demand for stage 4 is reasonably easy. The design of module D could be scheduled after the design of module C. Stage 2 is more problematic as scheduling the specification of module D to start after the completion of B would delay the project. Amanda might consider doing this if whoever is specifying module A could also be allocated to module D for the last six days – although she may well decide that drafting an extra person into a specification activity is unsatisfactory.

8.2 Drawing a revised resource histogram

If the activities are scheduled at the earliest dates, then the plan still calls for four analyst/designers as shown in Figure C.7. By delaying the start of some activities, however, Amanda is able to ensure that using three analyst/designers is sufficient except for a single day. This is shown in Figure C.8.

When activities are scheduled at their earliest start dates, the shaded area of each bar represents the activity's total float. Once an activity is scheduled to start later than its earliest date, part of its total float will be 'used up' by that delay.
The amount of total float that has been consumed in this way is indicated by the left-hand portion of an activity's shaded bar.

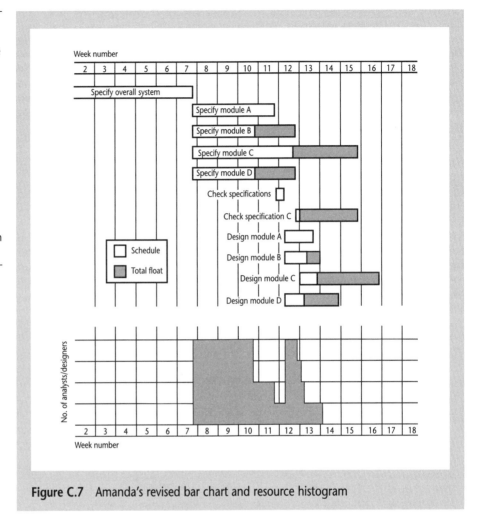

Figure C.7 Amanda's revised bar chart and resource histogram

Note that if the specification of module C were to be delayed for a further day, the project could be completed with only three analyst/designers, although its completion day would, of course, be delayed.

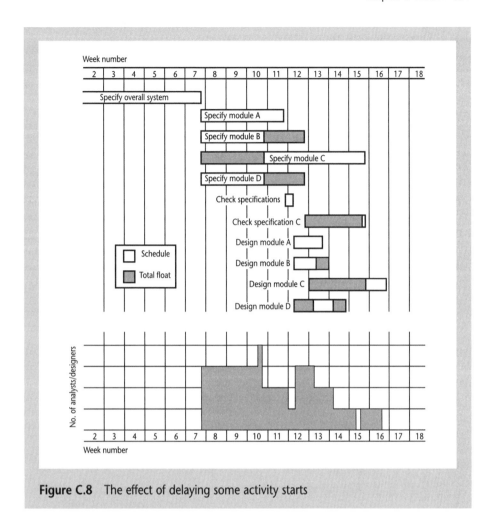

Figure C.8   The effect of delaying some activity starts

8.3   Identifying critical activities

The critical path is now as shown in Figure C.9. Note the lag of 15 days against activity IoE/P/4, ensuring that its start is delayed until an analyst/designer is expected to be available.

However, the availability of an analyst/designer for IoE/P/4 is dependent upon IoE/P/3 or IoE/P/5 being completed on time – these two activities are therefore also now critical in the sense that a delay in both of them would delay IoE/P/4, which is on the normal critical path. These two activities, although not on the critical path, are, in that sense, critical.

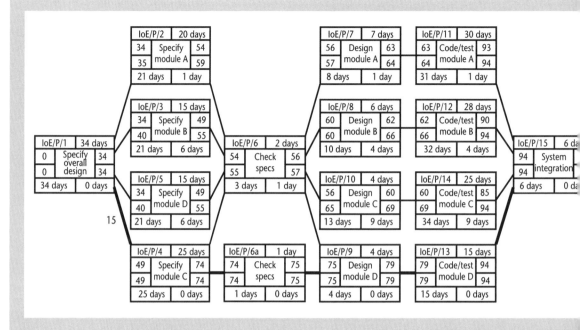

Figure C.9 The critical activities after delaying the start of module C

8.4 Assigning staff to activities

Belinda must specify module B as she will then be available in time to start the specification of module C. This leaves Daisy for the specification and design of module A. Belinda cannot do the design of module B as she will still be working on the module C specification when this needs to be done (6 days between days 56 and 66). This will have to be left to Tom, as he should be free on day 60.

Can you think of any other way in which she might have allocated the three team members to these activities?

8.5 Calculating project costs

The easiest way to calculate the total cost is to set up a table similar to Table C.12.

Table C.12 Calculating the cost of Amanda's project

Analyst	Daily cost (£)	Days Required	Cost (£)
Amanda	300	110[2]	33,000
Belinda	250	50	12,500
Tom	175	25	4,375
Daisy	225	27	6,075
Gavin	150	30	4,500
Purdy	150	28	4,200
Justin	150	15	2,250
Spencer	150	25	3,750
Daily oncost	200	100	20,000
Total			90,650

[2] This includes 10 days for pre-project planning and post-project review.

Calculating the distribution of costs over the life of the project is best done as a per week or per month figure rather than as daily costs. The expenditure per week for Amanda's project is shown as a chart in Figure 8.9.

Chapter 9

9.1 Lines of code as a partial task completion indicator

There are many reasons why the proportion of lines coded is not a good indicator of completeness. In particular, you should have considered the following:

- the estimated total number of lines of code might be inaccurate;
- the lines of code so far might have been easier, or harder, than those to follow – for example, reuse of existing components might speed up development;
- a program is not generally considered complete until it has been tested – even when all the code has been written, a program will still be incomplete until tested.

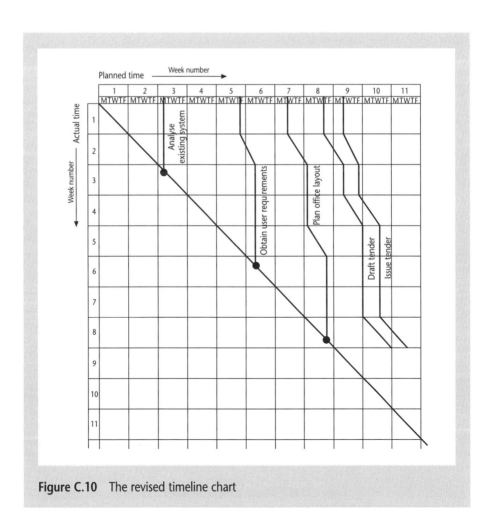

Figure C.10 The revised timeline chart

With more knowledge of what has been done and what is left to complete it might be possible to make a reasonable estimate of completeness. Breaking the development task into smaller sub-tasks such as software design, coding and unit testing might be of some assistance here.

9.2 Revising the timeline chart

At the end of week 8, the scheduled completion dates for drafting and issuing the tender need to be revised – note both need to be changed since they are both on the critical path (Figure C.10).

Subsequently, Brigette needs to show only the completion of each of these two remaining activities on the timeline chart – the project being completed by the Thursday of week 11 (Figure C.11).

9.3 Amanda's earned value analysis

It should be apparent from Figure 9.12 that the initial activity, 'specify overall system', has slipped by one day. It may not be quite so obvious from Figure 9.12 alone what else has happened to her project – inspection of Figure 9.12 and Table 9.2 should, however, make it possible to see that 'specify module D' has taken 2

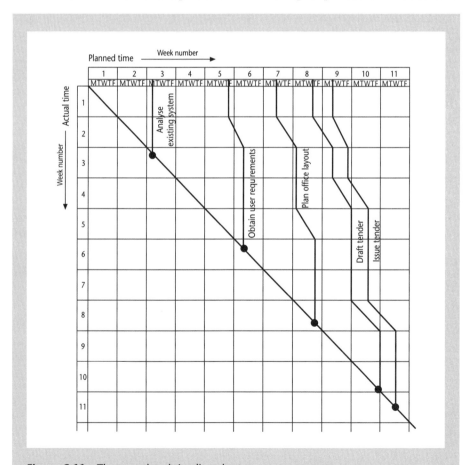

Figure C.11 The completed timeline chart

days longer than forecast and 'specify module B' has taken 5 days longer. Thus, the project has earned 34 workdays by day 35, 49 workdays by day 52 and 64 workdays by day 55.

From Figure 9.12 it is not possible to deduce the underlying causes of the slippage or to forecast the consequences for the project. The use of earned value analysis for forecasting is described later in Section 9.6.

9.4 The effects of specification changes

Among the items most likely to be affected by the change are test data, expected results and the user handbooks.

9.5 Control procedures for development systems

Stages 1 to 6 will be basically the same except that an estimate on the effect of the project's timescale will need to be included in steps 3 and 4. Step 7 might not be required as system acceptance might not have taken place yet and acceptance testing of the changes will be included in that.

The release of software in step 8 will not be needed if the system is not yet operational, although master copies of products will need to be updated.

9.6 Reasons for scope creep

There can be several different system designs that meet the users' requirements and one may be selected which is more elaborate and involves more processing.

Essential housekeeping and security-driven requirements might become apparent – for example, additional validation of the input to ensure that the database remains consistent.

Chapter 10

10.1 Choice of type of package at IOE

The problem for Amanda at IOE would be that the new maintenance group accounts subsystem would essentially be an extension to and enhancement of the existing maintenance accounting system, so that the interfacing of an off-the-shelf package might involve quite a few difficulties. This seems to indicate that bespoke development is needed. An alternative approach might be to consider replacing the whole of the maintenance accounting system with a new off-the-shelf application.

10.2 Calculation of charges for a project

For the first 2000 FPs	$967 × 2,000	=	$1,934,000
For the next 500 FPs	$1,019 × 500	=	$509,500
For the next 500 FPs	$1,058 × 500	=	$529,000
For the last 200 FPs	$1,094 × 200	=	$218,800
for all 3,200 FPs			$3,191,300

10.3 Calculating the cost of additional functionality

For changed FPs $500 \times 600 \times (150/100)$ $=$ \$450,000

For additional FPs 200×600 $=$ \$120,000

Total charge   \$570,000

10.4 Advantage to customer of variable cost charges

The supplier will need to quote a price that will include a margin to cater for possible increases in equipment prices. It might turn out that actual prices do not increase as much as was estimated – in the case of ICT equipment some prices are likely to go down – but the customer would still have to pay the additional margin. If the contract specifies a fixed charge plus the actual cost of materials and equipment, then the customer in this case would be better off.

10.5 Calculating value for money

System X savings would be £20 × 20 hours × 4 years = £1,600, for the automatic scale point adjustment facility, and £20 × 12 hours × 2 times a year × 4 years = £1,920, for the bar-chart production facility. In total the saving for system X would be £3,520.

For system Y, the saving would be £300 × 0.5 (to take account of the probability of change). That is, £150.

Even though system X costs £500 more, it will still give better value for money. Note that discounted cash flow calculations could be applied to these figures.

10.6 Evaluation methods

i. The usability of an existing system could be evaluated by such means as the examination of user handbooks, the observation of demonstrations and practical user trails.

ii. This is clearly tricky. One would have to evaluate the methods that the developers intend to use to see whether they adhere to good interface design practice. One might also examine any interface standards that are in use by the supplier.

iii. Note that the question focuses on the costs of maintenance, rather than that of reliability. The cost of unexpected maintenance could be reduced, at least for a short time, by passing this risk to the supplier if there is a comprehensive warranty. The warranties provided by suppliers would therefore need to be scrutinized. Discussion with reference sites might also be helpful.

iv. Once again guarantees could be put in place by suppliers concerning this. The nature of these guarantees could be examined. Discussion with reference sites could once again be helpful

v. Training materials could be examined. The training staff could be interviewed and their CVs examined. Reference sites who have already used the supplier's training services could be approached for their views.

Chapter 11

11.1 Tasks and responsibilities of an analyst/ programmer

Analyst/programmers are expected to be able to carry out both analysis and programming tasks. It is likely, however, that the kinds of analysis tasks undertaken will be restricted. They may, for example, do the analysis work for enhancements to existing systems but not of completely new applications. Making this broad assumption, a list of tasks and responsibilities might be as follows:

- carry out detailed investigations of new requirements for existing computer applications;
- analyse the results of investigations and review the solutions to problems experienced, including the estimation of relevant costs;
- prepare systems specifications in accordance with organizational standards;
- conduct appropriate systems testing;
- prepare functional module specifications;
- produce and modify module structure diagrams;
- code and amend software modules;
- carry out appropriate unit testing;
- produce and amend user documentation;
- liaise with users, carrying out appropriate training in the use of computer applications where required.

11.2 Rewarding reuse

A problem here is that the software developers who make most use of reused components will, as a consequence, be producing less code themselves. You also want to encourage programmers to produce software components that other people can use: this might help the productivity of the organization but not that of the current project that they are working on!

You need to have a method, like function point analysis, which measures the functions and features actually delivered to the user. You also need to have some way of measuring the code used in the application that has been taken from elsewhere. Percentage targets of the amount of reused code to new code could be set and staff rewarded if the targets are met. As an alternative, the savings made by reuse could be measured and a profit-sharing scheme could be operated.

Programmers could be encouraged to produce and publish reusable components by a system of royalties for each time a software component is reused.

11.3 Financial incentives for top executives

This exercise was designed to be thought-provoking. Some thoughts that have come out of discussion on this topic are given below.

- To some extent, material wants and, therefore, the motivation to obtain more money to satisfy these wants can be generated through the marketing and advertising of new types of goods and services – but how likely is this to be at the very top?

- Large salaries are associated with status, esteem and success. It could be that these are the real reward.
- Historically, wealth has been associated with power, such as the ownership of land.

The essential point is that for many people money is not just a means of satisfying material wants.

11.4 High and low motivational incidents

This will obviously depend on individual experiences.

11.5 Social loafing

Among other ideas, the effects of social loafing can be reduced by:

- making the work of each performer individually identifiable;
- involving and interesting group members in the outcome of group efforts;
- rewarding individuals for their contributions to the group effort (rather like sports teams who pick out a 'club player of the year').

11.6 Effect of ICT on the Delphi technique

Developments in ICT that assist cooperative working, especially the advent of electronic mail and groupware such as Lotus Notes, will cut quite considerably the communication delays involved in the Delphi technique.

11.7 Classification of types of power

More than one type of power can be involved in each case.

i. Some *expert* power is involved here, but for those who are subject to the audit, the main type of power is *connection* power as the auditor will produce a report that will go to higher management. External auditors often have *coercive* power.

ii. Here, power will mainly be *expert-* and *information-based*, but as the consultant will report to higher management, *connection* power also exists.

iii. This sounds pretty *coercive*.

iv. Brigette has some *connection* power. The technical expertise that is involved in her job means she has some *expert* power. She has little or no *coercive* power as she is not the manager of the staff involved. She might be able to exert some *reward* power on the basis of an informal 'I'll do you a favour if you'll do me a favour' arrangement!

v. Amanda is unlikely to have direct *coercive* powers although she might be able to institute disciplinary procedures. Through the system of annual reviews common to many organizations, she might have some *reward* power. *Connection* power, through her access to higher management, is also present. Her access to users means she has *information* power. If she brings specific expertise to the project (such as analysis skills) she might have some *expert* power. By acting as a role model that other project team members might want to emulate she may even be displaying *referent* power!

11.8 Appropriate management styles

i. The clerk will know much more than anyone else about the practical details of the work. Heavy *task-oriented* supervision would therefore not be appropriate. As the clerk is working in a new environment and forging new relationships, a considerable amount of people-oriented supervision/support might be needed initially.

ii. Both task-oriented and people-oriented management would be needed with the trainee.

iii The experienced maintenance programmer has probably had considerable autonomy in the past. The extensions to the systems could have a considerable, detailed, impact on this person's work. A very carefully judged increase in task-oriented management will be required for a short time.

11.9 Modes of communication

Once again, there is no one correct set of answers. Discussion points might be:

(a) The developer might not be familiar with the context of the application domain – for example the terminology employed by the users. Ideally, clarification should be via same time/same place or same time/different place (e.g. telephone), as the business analyst and developer could go through a cycle of questions and answers quickly, and follow-up questions could be posed where answers were not completely clear.

(b) To start with, same time/different place (e.g. a call to a help desk) might be most appropriate as the problem might be a simple misunderstanding. If a fault in the software was actually found then a different time/different place mode of communication would be needed to record the fault report so that it could be dealt with by the software maintenance team.

(c) The requirement could be very complex and need considerable analysis, so initially different time/different place communication involving studying and writing documents might be best. Different options might need to be considered by the business and for this a same time/same place meeting might be expedient.

(d) There might be good reasons why the second developer is late. For example, he might have been on sick leave. It might also be that he is unaware of the urgency of the task. Informal communication, ideally face to face, might be appropriate, at least initially.

Chapter 12

12.1 Selection of payroll package for college

(a) Carry out an investigation to find out what the users' requirements really are. This might uncover that there are different sets of requirements for different groups of users.

(b) Organize the requirements into groups relating to individual qualities and attributes. These might be, for example, functionality (the range of features that the software has), price, usability, capacity, efficiency, flexibility and reliability.

(c) Some of these requirements will be of an absolute nature. For example, an application will have to hold records for up to a certain maximum number of employees. If it cannot, it will have to be immediately eliminated from further consideration.

(d) In other cases the requirement is relative. Some of the relative requirements are more important than others. A low price is desirable but more expensive software cannot be ruled out straightaway. This can be reflected by giving each of the requirements a rating, a score out of 10, say, for importance.

(e) A range of possible candidate packages needs to be identified. If there are lots of possibilities, an initial screening, for instance, by price, can be applied to reduce the contenders to a manageable shortlist.

(f) Practical ways of measuring the desired qualities in the software have to be devised. In some cases, for example with price and capacity, sales literature or a technical specification can be consulted. In other cases, efficiency for instance, practical trials could be conducted, while in yet other cases a survey of existing users might provide the information required.

(g) It is likely that some software is going to be deficient in some ways, but that this will be compensated by other qualities. A simple way of combining the findings on different qualities is to give a mark out of 10 for the relative presence/absence of the quality. Each of these scores can be multiplied by a score out of 10 for the importance of the quality (see (d)) and the results of all these multiplications can be summed to give an overall score for the software.

12.2 Possible quality specifications for word processing software

There are many that could be defined and just two examples are given below. One point that may emerge is that the software might be best broken down into a number of different functional areas, each of which can be evaluated separately, such as document preparation, presentation, mail merging and so on. For example:

- *quality*: ease of learning;
- *definition*: the time taken, by a novice, to learn how to operate the package to produce a standard document;
- *scale*: hours;
- *test*: interview novices to ascertain their previous experience of word processing. Supply them with a machine, the software, a training manual and a standard document to set up. Time how long it takes them to learn how to set the document up.
- *minimally acceptable*: > 2.5 to 4 hours;
- *target range*: 1 to 2.5 hours;
- *now*: 3 hours;

  or

- *quality*: ease of use;
- *definition*: the time taken for an experienced user to produce a standard document;

- *scale*: minutes;
- *test*: time user who has experience of package to produce the standard document;
- *minimally acceptable*: 40 to 45 minutes;
- *target range*: 30 to 40 minutes;
- *current*: 45 minutes.

This topic of evaluation is an extensive one and the pointers above leave all sorts of unanswered questions in the air. Readers who wish to explore this area should read one of the more specialist books on the topic.

12.3 Availability and mean time between failures

Each day the system should be available from 8 a.m. to 6 p.m., that is 10 hours.
Over four weeks that should be 10 × 5 × 4 hours = 200 hours.
It was unavailable for one day, i.e. 10 hours.
It was unavailable until 10.00 on two other days, = 4 hours.
The hours available were therefore 200 − 10 − 4 = 186 hours.
Availability would therefore be 186/200 × 100 = 93%

Assuming that three failures are counted, *mean time between failures* would be 186/3 = 62 hours.

12.4 Entry requirements for an activity different from the exit requirements for another activity that immediately precedes it

It is possible for one activity to start before the immediately preceding activity has been completely finished. In this case, the entry requirement for the following activity has been satisfied, even though the exit requirement of the preceding activity has not. For example, software modules could be used for performance testing of the hardware platform even though there are some residual defects concerning screen layouts.

Another situation where the entry requirements could vary from the preceding exit requirements is where a particular resource needs to be available in order for the new activity to start.

12.5 Entry and exit requirements

- *Entry requirements* A program design must have been produced that has been reviewed and any rework required by the review must have been carried out and been inspected by the chair of the review group.
- *Exit requirements* A program must have been produced that has been compiled and is free of compilation errors; the code must have been reviewed and any rework required by the review must have been carried out and been inspected by the chair of the review group.

It should be noted that the review group could use checklists for each type of product reviewed and these could be regarded as further entry/exit requirements.

12.6 Application of BS EN ISO 9001 standards to system testing

There would be a need for a documented procedure that governs system testing.

The quality objective for system testing might be defined as ensuring that the software conforms to the requirements laid down in the user specification.

Processes to ensure this could include documented cross-references from test cases to sections of the specification.

The results of executing test cases would need to be recorded and the subsequent remedying of any discrepancies would also need to be recorded.

12.7 Precautionary steps when work is contracted out

The project manager could check who actually carried out the certification. They could also discover the scope of the BS EN ISO 9001 certification that was awarded. For example, it could be that certification only applied to the processes that created some products and not others.

Perhaps the most important point is that the project manager will need to be reassured that the *specification* to which the contractors will be working is an adequate reflection of the requirements of the client organization.

12.8 Comparison of peer review and pair programming

Here are some ways in which they might be contrasted:

Pair programming	Peer review
Work on principle that two heads are better than one	Peer review groups could be made up of more people.
Driver and navigator are jointly responsible for producing the software product	Developer solely responsible for the initial creation of the product which is then reviewed.
Discussion of the rationale for the design as it is being produced	Reviewers see the final product only, not the reasoning behind it unless design documentation provides the rationale.
Real-time interaction between participants	Batch orientation with focus on the documents.
Development effort doubled	The time of several members of staff needed to study documents and then attend the review meeting.

There could be further discussion of the respective advantages and disadvantages of each approach.

12.10 The important differences between a quality circle and a review group

The quality circle would be looking at the process in general while the review group would look at a particular instance of a product. The use of review groups alone could be inefficient because they could be removing the same type of defect again and again rather than addressing, as the quality circle does, the task of stopping the defects at their source.

Further reading

General books on project management – not IS specific

Field, Mike and Laurie Keller, *Project Management*, London, International Thomson Business Press, 1998.

Haynes, Marion E., *Project Management: Practical tools for success*, Mento Park, CA, Crisp Publications, 2002.

Haynes, Marion E., *Project Management: From idea to implementation*, London, Kogan Page, 1996.

Lock, Dennis, *Project Management* (8th edition), Aldershot, Gower, 2003.

Lockyer, Keith and James Gordon, *Project Management and Project Planning*, London, Financial Times Prentice Hall, 2005.

Nickson, David and Suzy Siddons, *Managing Projects*, Made Simple Books, Oxford, Butterworth-Heinemann, 1997.

General books on software and IS management

Bennatan, E. M., *On Time Within Budget: Software project management practices and techniques*, Chichester, Wiley, 2000.

Cadle, James and Donald Yeates, *Project Management for Information Systems* 4th edition, London, FT Prentice Hall, 2004.

Hughes, Bob (editor) *Project Management for IT-related Projects*, London, The British Computer Society, 2004.

Scwalbe, Kathy, *IT Project Management*, London, Thomson Course Technology, 2005.

Other books worth looking at

Frederick Brooks, *The Mythical Man-Month : Essays on Software Engineering*, Anniversary Edition, Reading, MA, Addison-Wesley, 1995. A slightly dated but classic exposition of the central issues of software project management from the man who was in charge of the IBM 360 Operating System development project. You should try to look at it at some time.

Chris Kemerer (ed) *Software Project Management – Readings and Cases*, Chicago, Irwin, McGraw-Hill, 1997. A collection of classic papers on topics such as estimation, risk management, life cycles, reuse and process improvement. Strongly recommended.

Strategic planning and programme management

CCTA, *An Introduction to Programme Management*, London, The Stationery Office, 1993.

Gilb, Tom and Susannah Finzi, *Principles of Software Engineering Management*, Wokingham, Addison-Wesley, 1988.

Office of Government Commerce, *Managing Successful Programmes*, London, The Stationery Office, 2003.

Ould, Martyn, *Managing Software Quality and Business Risk*, Chichester, Wiley, 1999.

Reiss, G., *Programme Management Demystified*, London, Spon Press, 1996.

Project process models

Stapleton, Jennifer, *DSDM: A Framework for business-centred development*, Harlow, Addison-Wesley, 2002.

Beck, Kent with Cynthia Andreas, *Extreme Programming Explained: Embrace change*, 2nd edition, Harlow, Addison-Wesley, 2004.

Booch, Grady, *Object Solutions: Managing the object oriented project*, Reading, MA, Addison-Wesley, 1996.

Wood, Jane and Denise Silver, *Joint Application Development*, New York, Wiley, 1995.

PRINCE2

Bentley, Colin, *Practical PRINCE2*, London, The Stationery Office, 2002.

CCTA, *Managing Successful Projects with PRINCE2*, London, The Stationery Office, 2002.

Office of Government Commerce, *People Issues and PRINCE2*, London, The Stationery Office, 2002.

Estimation

Boehm, Barry W. et al., *Software Estimation with COCOMO II*, Upper Saddle River, NJ, Prentice Hall, 2002.

Boehm, Barry W., *Software Engineering Economics*, Prentice Hall, 1981. Along with Brooks' *Mythical man-month*, one of the most frequently cited books on software project management.

Common Software Measurement International Consortium (COSMIC), *COSMIC-FFP Measurement Manual* (www.1rgl.uqam.ca/cosmic-ffp/manual.html)

DeMarco, Tom, *Controlling Software Projects: Management, measurement and estimation*, Englewood Cliffs, NJ, Yourdon Press, 1982.

Hughes, Bob, *Practical Software Measurement*, London, McGraw-Hill, 2002. Clearly we have an interest here! Could be seen as a companion book to this one.

Symons, Charles R., *Software Sizing and Estimating Mk II FPA (Function Point Analysis)*, Chichester, Wiley, 1991. A book by the inventor of Mark II function points

Control, risk and quality

Boehm, Barry W., *Software Risk Management*, IEEE Computer Society Press, 1989.

Down, Alex, Michael Coleman and Peter Absolon, *Risk Management for Software Projects*, Maidenhead, McGraw-Hill, 1994.

Grey, Stephen *Practical Risk Assessment for Project Management*, Chichester, Wiley, 1995.

Humphrey, Watts S., *Managing the Software Process*, Reading, MA, Addison-Wesley, 1990.

Leach, L. P., *Critical Chain Project Management*, Norwood, MA, Artech House, 2000.

Manns, Tom and Michael Coleman, *Software Quality Assurance* 2nd Edition, Basingstoke, Macmillan, 1996.

Youll, David P. *Making Software Development Visible: Effective project control*, Chichester, Wiley, 1990.

People management

Arnold, John, Cary Cooper and Ivan Robertson, *Work Psychology: Understanding human behaviour in the workplace* 4th Edition, London, FT Prentice-Hall, 2004.

Belbin, R. Meredith, *Management Teams: Why they succeed or fail*, 2nd edition, Oxford, Elsevier, 2003.

Belbin, R. Meredith, *Team Roles at Work*, Oxford, Butterworth-Heinemann, 1996.

DeMarco, Tom and Timothy R. Lister, *Peopleware: Productive projects and teams* 2nd Edition, New York, Dorset House, 1999.

Handy, Charles B., *Understanding Organizations* 4th Edition, London, Penguin, 1993.

Healy, Patrick L., *Project Management: Getting the job done on time and in budget*, Oxford, Butterworth-Heinemann, 1997.

Weinberg, G. M., *The Psychology of Computer Programming*, Silver Anniversary Edition, New York, Dorset House, 1998.

Yourdon, Edward, *Death March* 2nd edition, Englewood Cliffs, NJ, Yourdon Press, 2003. We have reservations about some aspects of this book, but certainly worth looking at.

Ethical and legal issues

Bainbridge, David, *Introduction to Computer Law* 5th edition, Harlow, Longman, 2004.

Bott, Frank, *Professional Issues in Software Engineering*, 3rd edition, London, Taylor and Francis, 2000.

Newtown, Jeremy and Jeremy Holt, *A Manager's Guide to IT Law*, London, The British Computer Society, 2004.

Burnett, Rachel, *IT Legal Risk Management*, London, Institute for the Management of Information Systems, 2003.

Project management and other standards

British Standards Institution, *BS 6079 Guide to Project Management*, London, BSI, 1996.

Project Management Institute and PMI Standards Committee, *A Guide to the Project Management Body of Knowledge*, Upper Derby, PA, PMI, 1996 (http://www.pmi.org).

ISO/IEC 12207:1995 Information technology: software lifecycle processes (amended 2002 and 2004).

IS0/IEC 15504-1:2004 Information technology: process assessment Part 1 Concepts and vocabulary.

IS0/IEC 15504-2:2004 Information technology: process assessment Part 2 Performing and assessment.

IS0/IEC 15504-3:2004 Information technology: process assessment Part 3 Guidance on performing an assessment.

IS0/IEC 15504-4:2004 Information technology: process assessment Part 4 Guidance on use for process improvement and process capability determination.

ISO/IEC 14598-1:1999 Information technology: software product evaluation Part 1 General overview.

ISO/IEC 14598-2:2000 Information technology: software product evaluation Part 2 Planning and management.

ISO/IEC 9126-1:2001 Information technology: software product quality Part 1 Quality model.

ISO/IEC TR 9126-2:2003 Software engineering: product quality Part 2 External metrics.

ISO/IEC TR 9126-3:2003 Software engineering: product quality Part 3 Internal metrics.

Index

Page numbers for figures have suffix **f,** those for tables have suffix **t**